1998

ALSO BY LEWIS HYDE

The Gift: Imagination and the Erotic Life of Property

This Error Is the Sign of Love (Poems)

TRICKSTER MAKES THIS WORLD

TRICKSTER

MAKES
THIS
WORLD

Mischief,
Myth,
and Art

LEWIS HYDE

Farrar, Straus and Giroux / New York

Farrar, Straus and Giroux
19 Union Square West, New York 10003

LIBRARY OF CONGRESS CATALOGING-IN-PUBLICATION DATA
Hyde. Lewis, 1945–
    Trickster makes this world : mischief, myth, and art / Lewis Hyde.
—1st ed.
      p.   cm.
    Includes bibliographical references and index.
    ISBN 0-374-27928-4 (alk. paper)
    1. Trickster.   2. Mythology.   3. Arts.   I. Title.
GR524.H93   1998
398.2—dc21   97-18032

And at his mother's home, Hermes . . .
slipped sideways through the keyhole,
like fog on an autumn breeze.

CONTENTS

LIST OF ILLUSTRATIONS

TRICKSTER MAKES THIS WORLD

INTRODUCTION

Every generation occupies itself with interpreting Trickster anew. . . .
—*Paul Radin*

We interpret always as transients.
—*Frank Kermode*

The first story I have to tell is not exactly true, but it isn't exactly false, either.

Once during the winter after I got out of college I was hitchhiking north of Winslow, Arizona. Just after sundown three Navajo men in an old green Chevy picked me up. The driver I remember distinctly as his hair was as long as mine, and he had lost the top of his right ear. He and his friends had been working a construction site near the New Mexico border and were headed home to Tuba City for the weekend. Two or three times in the fading light we came upon coyotes crossing the road or slinking along in the nearby brush, and there began a somewhat reverent and somewhat joking discussion of coyotes and their ability to see in the dark, which led in turn to my hearing what I only later understood to be a very old story.

Long ago, the driver said, Coyote was going along and as he came over the brow of a hill he saw a man taking his eyes out of his head and throwing them up into a cottonwood tree. There they would hang until he cried out, "Eyes come back!" Then his eyes would return to his head. Coyote wanted very much to learn this trick and begged and begged until the man taught it to him. "But be careful, Coyote," the man said. "Don't do this more than four times in one day." "Of course not. Why would I do that?" said Coyote. (The others in the car laughed at this, but not the driver.)

When the man left, Coyote took his eyes out and threw them into the cottonwood tree. He could see for miles then, see over the low hills, see where the stream went, see the shape of things. When he had done this four times, he thought, "That man's rule is made for his country. I don't think it applies here. This is my country." For a fifth time he threw his eyes into the tree and for a fifth time he cried "Eyes come back!" But they didn't come back. Poor Coyote stumbled about the grove, bumping into trees and crying. He couldn't think what to do, and lay down to sleep. Before too long, some mice came by and, thinking Coyote was dead, began to clip his hair to make a nest. Feeling the mice at work, Coyote let his mouth hang open until he caught one by the tail.

"Look up in that tree, Brother Mouse," said Coyote, talking from the side of his mouth. "Do you see my eyes up there?" "Yes," said the mouse. "They are all swollen from the sun. They're oozing a little. Flies have gathered on them." The mouse offered to retrieve the eyes, but Coyote didn't trust him. "Give me one of your eyes," he said. The mouse did so, and Coyote put the little black ball into the back of his eye socket. He could see a little now, but had to hold his head at an odd angle to keep the eye in place. He stumbled from the cottonwood grove and came upon Buffalo Bull. "What's the matter, Coyote?" asked the Bull. The Buffalo took pity on him when he heard the story, and offered one of his own eyes. Coyote took it and squeezed it into his left eye socket. Part of it hung out. It bent him down to one side. Thus he went on his way.

The driver eventually dropped me off at a cheap motel ("Heat in Rooms!") outside Tuba City. The parting was too brief; I had wanted to offer a story of my own, or chip in on gas, though in fact I was tongue-tied and short of cash. I couldn't make head or tail of the Coyote story, and wondered nervously if it hadn't been directed at me in some way. It was weird and dream-like. It was not like anything I'd read in college. No one exchanges body parts in the transcendentalist classics I'd been reading my senior year, for example. True, in *Walden*, Thoreau likes to get himself above it all, but he never has any trouble with his eyes; there is that "transparent eyeball" thing in Emerson, but it's a peak moment of American individualism, not a problem to be solved by helpful animals. Years later I began to get some sense of how Coyote works, but at the time I only felt that a hidden world had been briefly revealed and that its revelation belonged somehow to the situation of the story's telling—the car moving quickly through the winter dusk, the brief intimacy of strangers on the road, and coyotes barely visible beyond the headlights of the car.

I can never recall the scene without getting a little rush of pleasure, a rising sense of possibility, of horizons that melt away as the ankle joint pumps the gas. I get that feeling whenever I start on a journey. Once or twice a year for decades now I have ridden the train between Boston and New York, and invariably as all that iron and baggage picks up rolling speed my imagination stirs. So much seems possible at the beginning of a trip, so many things seem brimmed with meaning. The small towns slipping by, the unspent time ahead, herons meditating in marsh grass, a pigeon mummified beneath a bridge, the back seats of cars waiting at the clanging gate ("crossing / crossing"), the little decoration some nineteenth-century mason worked into the high peak of a factory wall, now abandoned, now disappearing over the horizon. Each thing seems all the more declarative for its swift arrival and swift departure. From a moving train I don't see the opaque weave of the real, I see the more expansive view the shuttle gets as again and again the warp threads briefly rise. I always take out my pen and begin to write, as if the landscape itself were in a manic and voluble mood and I its lucky and appointed scribe. I become convinced that just before me is the perfect statement of how things are.

That is a traveler's delusion. The writing I do on trains never turns into much. Maybe Jack Kerouac sniffing Benzedrine could do first and final drafts at one crack, but I can't. In the last book Italo Calvino wrote, he meditates on Hermes and Mercury, Europe's old quick-witted gods (the ones with wings on their shoes, the ones whose statues still adorn the train depots), and Calvino confesses that he always looked to their speed with the jealous longing of a more methodical craftsman. "I am a Saturn who dreams of being a Mercury, and everything I write reflects these two impulses," he says. Saturn is the slow worker, the one who can build a coin collection and label all the envelopes in a neat script, the one who will rewrite a paragraph eleven times to get the rhythm right.

Saturn can finish a four-hundred-page book. But he tends to get de-pressed if that is all he does; he needs regular Mercurial insight to give him something delicious to work on.

Not much of this book was written on a train, then, but it is full of "Saturn dreaming of Mercury." It is, among other things, a description and invocation of the kind of imagination that stirs to life at the beginning of a journey. It is about trickster figures—Coyote, Hermes, Mercury, and more—and all tricksters are "on the road." They are the lords of in-between. A trickster does not live near the hearth; he does not live in the halls of justice, the soldier's tent, the shaman's hut, the monastery. He passes through each of these when there is a moment of silence, and he enlivens each with mischief, but he is not their guiding spirit. He is the spirit of the doorway leading out, and of the crossroad at the edge of town (the one where a little market springs up). He is the spirit of the road at dusk, the one that runs from one town to another and belongs to neither. There are strangers on that road, and thieves, and in the underbrush a sly beast whose stomach has not heard about your letters of safe passage. Travelers used to mark such roads with cairns, each adding a stone to the pile in passing. The name Hermes once meant "he of the stone heap," which tells us that the cairn is more than a trail marker—it is an altar to the forces that govern these spaces of heightened uncertainty, and to the intelligence needed to negotiate them. Hitchhikers who make it safely home have somewhere paid homage to Hermes.

The road that trickster travels is a spirit road as well as a road in fact. He is the adept who can move between heaven and earth, and be-tween the living and the dead. As such, he is sometimes the messenger of the gods and sometimes the guide of souls, carrying the dead into the underworld or opening the tomb to release them when they must walk among us. Sometimes it happens that the road between heaven and earth is not open, whereupon trickster travels not as a messenger but as a thief, the one who steals from the gods the good things that humans need if they are to survive in this world. Tricky Prometheus stealing fire is the famous Western example, but the motif of freeing some needed good from heaven is found all over the world. Along the North Pacific coast, for example, the trickster Raven is a thief of water and daylight; on the island of Japan, it was a trickster who released the arts of agriculture from their heavenly enclosure. (It is at well-guarded barriers that these figures are especially *tricksters*, for here they must be masters of deceit if they are to proceed.)*

In short, trickster is a boundary-crosser. Every group has its edge, its sense of in and out, and trickster is always there, at the gates of the city and the gates of life, making sure there is commerce. He also attends the internal boundaries by which groups articulate their social life. We constantly distinguish—right and wrong, sacred and profane, clean and dirty, male and female, young and old, living and dead—and in every case trickster will cross the line and confuse the distinction. Trickster is the creative idiot, therefore, the wise fool, the gray-haired baby, the cross-dresser, the speaker of sacred profanities. Where someone's sense of honorable behavior has left him unable to act, trickster will appear to suggest an amoral action, something right/wrong that will get life going again. Trickster is the mythic embodiment of ambiguity and ambivalence, doubleness and duplicity, contradiction and paradox.

That trickster is a boundary-crosser is the standard line, but in the course of writing this book I realized that it needs to be modified in one important way, for there are also cases in which trickster *creates* a boundary, or brings to the surface a distinction previously hidden from sight. In several mythologies, for example, the gods lived on earth until something trickster did caused them to rise into heaven. Trickster is thus the author of the great distance between heaven and earth; when he becomes the messenger of the gods it's as if he has been enlisted to solve a problem he himself created. In a case like that, boundary creation and boundary crossing are related to one another, and the best way to describe trickster is to say simply that the boundary is where he will be found—sometimes

---

* Many, myself included, find the connotations of "trickster" too limited for the scope of activities ascribed to this character. Some have tried to change the name (one writer uses Trickster-Transformer-Culture Hero, which is apt but a touch unwieldy). Others stick to local names, complaining that the general term "trickster" is an invention of nineteenth-century anthropology and not well fitted to its indigenous objects.

This is partly true; indigenous terms doubtless allow a fuller feeling for trickster's sacred complexity. But his trickiness was hardly invented by ethnographers. Hermes is called *mechaniôta* in Homeric Greek, which translates well as "trickster." The West African trickster Legba is also called *Aflakete*, which means "I have tricked you." The Winnebago Indian figure is called *Wakdjunkaga*, which means "the tricky one." Trickery appeared long before anthropology.

drawing the line, sometimes crossing it, sometimes erasing or moving it, but always there, the god of the threshold in all its forms.

I have been speaking of trickster as "he" because all the regularly discussed figures are male. There is no shortage of tricky women in this world, of course, or of women in myth fabled for acts of deception, but few of these have the elaborated career of deceit that tricksters have. There are several reasons why this might be. Most obvious, all the canonical tricksters operate in patriarchal mythologies, and it would seem that patriarchy's prime actors, even at the margins, are male. That being the case, one wonders if we won't find female tricksters by looking to situations in which women have a substantial share of power. Such a search bears fruit, but not a lot. One of the only developed female tricksters in Native American lore, a female Coyote, can be found among two Pueblo Indian groups (the Hopi and the Tewa), both of which are matrilineal and matrilocal. This female Coyote, however, operates alongside a more traditional male Coyote, and the bulk of the tales belong to him. Moreover, there are plenty of other matrilineal and matrilocal tribes in North America, and in all of them the trickster is male.

Another line of inquiry might begin by noting the odd fact that tricksters are ridden by lust, but their hyperactive sexuality almost never results in any offspring, the implication being that the stories are about non-procreative creativity and so get assigned to the sex that does not give birth. In this same line, the consequences of trickster's on-the-road and opportunistic sexuality are clearly more serious for women than for men (and in fact lust is *not* one of the female Coyote's characteristics).*

In the chapters that follow, much more will be added to this initial description of trickster figures—about how their appetites drive their wanderings, for example; about their shamelessness and their great attraction to dirt. But these themes by themselves do not interest me as much as their conjunction with the final thing that must be said to round out an initial portrait: in spite of all their disruptive behavior, tricksters are regularly honored as the creators of culture. They are imagined not only to have stolen certain essential goods from heaven and given them to the race but to have gone on and helped shape this world so as to make it a hospitable place for human life. In one Native American creation story, the Great Spirit speaks to Coyote about the coming of human be-

---

* I elaborate these brief remarks in an appendix on gender at the end of the book.

ings: "The New People will not know anything when they come, not how to dress, how to sing, how to shoot an arrow. You will show them how to do all these things. And put the buffalo out for them and show them how to catch salmon." In the Greek tradition, Hermes doesn't simply acquire fire, he invents and spreads a method, a *techne*, for making fire, and when he steals cattle from the gods he is simultaneously presenting the human race with the domestic beasts whose meat that fire will cook. A whole complex of cultural institutions around killing and eating cattle are derived from the liar and thief, Hermes.

The arts of hunting, the arts of cooking meat—such things belong to the beginnings of time, when trickster was first involved in shaping this world. But he has not left the scene. Trickster the culture hero is always present; his seemingly asocial actions continue to keep our world lively and give it the flexibility to endure. The specifics of what this means will emerge in the chapters to come; I raise the point here to widen the sense of what this book is about. I not only want to describe the imagination figured in the trickster myth, I want to argue a paradox that the myth asserts: that the origins, liveliness, and durability of cultures require that there be space for figures whose function is to uncover and disrupt the very things that cultures are based on. I hope to give some sense of how this can be, how social life can depend on treating antisocial characters as part of the sacred.

A ny discussion of this old mythology soon raises the question of where tricksters appear in the modern world.* A first answer is that they appear where they always have—in Native American winter story-telling, in Chinese street theater, in the Hindu festivals celebrating Krishna the Butter Thief, in West African divination ceremonies. African tricksters traveled west in the slave trade and can still be found in African-American storytelling, in the blues, in Haitian voodoo, and so on. I have been to a Yoruba diviner in Oakland, California, and seen the seventeenth palm nut set aside for the trickster Eshu.

A second answer reverses the first. Outside such traditional contexts there are no modern tricksters because trickster only comes to life in the

---

* As for the pre-modern or traditional tricksters, the notes to this introduction contain a list of those who will come forward in this book.

complex terrain of polytheism. If the spiritual world is dominated by a single high god opposed by a single embodiment of evil, then the ancient trickster disappears. Here it is worth pausing to explain that the Devil and the trickster are not the same thing, though they have regularly been confused.* Those who confuse the two do so because they have failed to perceive trickster's great ambivalence. The Devil is an agent of evil, but trickster is *a*moral, not *im*moral. He embodies and enacts that large portion of our experience where good and evil are hopelessly intertwined. He represents the paradoxical category of sacred amorality. One doesn't usually hear said of the Christian Devil what the anthropologist Paul Radin says of the Native American trickster:

> Trickster is at one and the same time creator and destroyer, giver and negator, he who dupes others and who is always duped himself. . . . He knows neither good nor evil yet he is responsible for both. He possesses no values, moral or social . . . yet through his actions all values come into being.

It might be argued that the passing of such a seemingly confused figure marks an advance in the spiritual consciousness of the race, a finer tuning of moral judgment; but the opposite could be argued as well—that the erasure of trickster figures, or the unthinking confusion of them with the Devil, only serves to push the ambiguities of life into the background. We may well hope our actions carry no moral ambiguity, but pretending that is the case when it isn't does not lead to greater clarity about right

---

* In Nigeria in the late 1920s, ethnographers found their informant telling tales of the Yoruba trickster Eshu as being about "the Devil," for this is what the missionaries had taught him to do. (Translations of the Bible into Yoruba use "Eshu" for "Devil.") The same thing happened in neighboring Dahomey, where Christians were sure they'd found Satan disguised as the trickster Legba, and recast the story of Adam and Eve with Legba hired locally to play the serpent.

In America, when Paul Radin worked among the Winnebago (circa 1908–18), he found members of "the new semi-Christian Peyote cult" convinced that the Winnebago trickster Wakdjunkaga was the Devil. Commenting on a story in which trickster has fooled a flock of birds, an informant told Radin, "We, the Winnebago, are the birds and Wakdjunkaga is Satan." In the thirteenth century, a similar confusion arose around the Norse trickster Loki.

and wrong; it more likely leads to unconscious cruelty masked by inflated righteousness.

But to come back to the question of where tricksters might be found in the modern world, I've offered two answers so far: they're found where they always were; they aren't found at all, if by "modern" we mean a world in which polytheism has disappeared. Both of these are somewhat narrow answers, however. "What is a god?" asks Ezra Pound, and then replies, "A god is an eternal state of mind." If trickster stirs to life on the open road, if he embodies ambiguity, if he "steals fire" to invent new technologies, if he plays with all boundaries both inner and outer, and so on—then he must still be among us, for none of these has disappeared from the world. His functions, like the bones of Osiris, may have been scattered, but they have not been destroyed. The problem is to find where his gathered body might come back to life, or where it might already have done so.

In America, one likely candidate for the protagonist of a reborn trickster myth is the confidence man, especially as he appears in literature and film (most actual confidence men don't have the range of the imaginary ones, and come to sadder ends). Some have even argued that the confidence man is a covert American hero. We enjoy it when he comes to town, even if a few people get their bank accounts drained, because he embodies things that are actually true about America but cannot be openly declared (as, for example, the degree to which capitalism lets us steal from our neighbors, or the degree to which institutions like the stock market require the same kind of confidence that criminal con men need).

If the confidence man is one of America's unacknowledged founding fathers, then instead of saying that there are no modern tricksters one could argue the opposite: trickster is everywhere. To travel from place to place in the ancient world was not only unusual, it was often taken to be a sign of mental derangement (if a story began "So and so was wandering around aimlessly," listeners knew immediately that trouble was at hand), but now everyone travels. If by "America" we mean the land of rootless wanderers and the free market, the land not of natives but of immigrants, the shameless land where anyone can say anything at any time, the land of opportunity and therefore of opportunists, the land where individuals are allowed and even encouraged to act without regard to community, then trickster has not disappeared. "America" is his apotheosis; he's pandemic.

Such in fact was the diagnosis of many Native Americans when white Europeans first appeared on the scene. Here was a race and a way of life that took as central many things which aboriginally belonged at the periphery. Surely trickster was at hand. In pre-contact Cheyenne, the word for "trickster" also meant "white man" (I think because trickster is sometimes "old man" and the old are white-haired), a linguistic coincidence that seemed to be no accident at all after the Europeans arrived. In fact, as I was researching this book I found a Cheyenne Coyote tale recorded in 1899 that begins "White man was going along . . ." and then goes on to tell the eye-juggler story, the one I heard all those years ago in the Arizona dusk, substituting "white man" for "Coyote" throughout. Suddenly I was more convinced than ever that the story had been directed at me; it was I, after all, who was hitchhiking aimlessly around the countryside, playing by my own rules, burning up other men's gasoline. I was being offered a little advice.

The Navajo have a number of motives for telling Coyote tales. At the simplest level, the stories are entertaining; they make people laugh; they pass the time. Beyond that, they teach people how to behave. Coyote ought not to do things more than four times; he ought to have proper humility; he ought to have proper respect for his body. Part of the entertainment derives from his self-indulgent refusal of such commands, of course, for there is vicarious pleasure in watching him break the rules, and a potentially fruitful fantasizing, too, for listeners are invited, if only in imagination, to scout the territory that lies beyond the local constraints (what does Coyote see from that high tree?).

According to the folklorist Barre Toelken, who lived among the Navajo for many years, several other levels of motive lie beneath these. Most important, Navajo Coyote stories are used in healing rituals. They are a kind of medicine. "Eye-juggler" is not just a critique of Coyote's egotism; its telling also plays a role in any healing ritual intended to cure diseases of the eye. (Did I have some "eye disease" after four years of college? Maybe it was time for a break from book learning?) As entertainment, the story stirs up a fantasy of amusing disorder; as medicine, it knits things together again after disorder has left a wound. In fact, to tell the story without such moral or medicinal motives does a kind of violence to it, and to the community (so that the teller would be suspected of engaging in witchcraft).

All this makes it clear that there are limits to the idea that trickster is everywhere in the modern world. It is true that such has occasionally been the aboriginal diagnosis of whites who take such pride in having created a mobile, individualistic, acquisitive civilization. But once one has a sense of the complex uses of Coyote tales one can see that most modern thieves and wanderers lack an important element of trickster's world, his sacred context. If the ritual setting is missing, trickster is missing. If his companions—all the other spiritual forces within whose fixed domains he carries on his mischief—are no longer with us, then he is no longer with us. Hermes cannot be rightly imagined without the more serious Apollo whose cattle he steals, or the grieving Demeter whose daughter he retrieves from the underworld. The god of the roads needs the more settled territories before his traveling means very much. If *everyone* travels, the result is not the apotheosis of trickster but another form of his demise. Here we have come back in a roundabout way to the earlier point: trickster belongs to polytheism or, lacking that, he needs at least a relationship to other powers, to people and institutions and traditions that can manage the odd double attitude of both insisting that their boundaries be respected and recognizing that in the long run their liveliness depends on having those boundaries regularly disturbed.

Most of the travelers, liars, thieves, and shameless personalities of the twentieth century are not tricksters at all, then. Their disruptions are not subtle enough, or pitched at a high enough level. Trickster isn't a run-of-the-mill liar and thief.* When he lies and steals, it isn't so much to get away with something or get rich as to disturb the established categories of truth and property and, by so doing, open the road to possible new worlds. When Pablo Picasso says that "art is a lie that tells the truth," we are closer to the old trickster spirit. Picasso was out to reshape and revive the world he had been born into. He took this world seriously; then he disrupted it; then he gave it a new form.

In this book, in any event, it is mostly to the practices of art that I turn in hopes of finding where this disruptive imagination survives among us. A handful of artists play central roles in my narrative—Picasso is

---

* People have regularly suggested to me that tricky politicians are modern tricksters, but I'm skeptical. It isn't just that their ends are usually too mundane and petty, but that the trickster belongs to the periphery, not to the center. If trickster were ever to get into power, he would stop being trickster. The deceitful politician is a crook, not a culture hero.

one, but also Marcel Duchamp, John Cage, Allen Ginsberg, Maxine Hong Kingston, and several others. (I also devote a chapter to the American slave Frederick Douglass, whose art was oratory and whose field of action politics.) My argument is not, however, that any of these figures is a trickster. "Trickster" is abstraction enough, already distanced from particular embodiments like Hermes and Coyote. Actual individuals are always more complicated than the archetype, and more complicated than its local version, too. Ralph Ellison once wrote a peeved response to a friend's attempt to fit *Invisible Man* into the pattern suggested by West African tricksters and their American progeny such as Brer Rabbit. "Archetypes, like taxes," Ellison wrote, "seem doomed to be with us always, and so with literature, one hopes; but between the two there must needs be the living human being in a specific texture of time, place and circumstance. . . . Archetypes are timeless, novels are time-haunted." Such is the voice of the specific (the ectype) complaining about the general, the mottled evidence talking back to the refined theory. "Don't dip my novel in that vat of archetype acid."

My own position, in any event, is not that the artists I write about are tricksters but that there are moments when the practice of art and this myth coincide. I work by juxtaposition, holding the trickster stories up against specific cases of the imagination in action, hoping that each might illuminate the other. If the method works, it is not because I have uncovered the true story behind a particular work of art but more simply that the coincidences are fruitful, making us think and see again. Such goals are in keeping with trickster's spirit, for he is the archetype who attacks all archetypes. He is the character in myth who threatens to take the myth apart. He is an "eternal state of mind" that is suspicious of all eternals, dragging them from their heavenly preserves to see how they fare down here in this time-haunted world.

PART ONE

TRAP OF NATURE

I

·······················

SLIPPING THE TRAP OF APPETITE

The whitebait
Opens its black eyes
In the net of the Law.
—Basho

THE BAIT THIEF

The trickster myth derives creative intelligence from appetite. It begins with a being whose main concern is getting fed and it ends with the same being grown mentally swift, adept at creating and unmasking deceit, proficient at hiding his tracks and at seeing through the devices used by others to hide theirs. Trickster starts out hungry, but before long he is master of the kind of creative deception that, according to a long tradition, is a prerequisite of art. Aristotle wrote that Homer first "taught the rest of us the art of framing lies the right way." Homer makes lies seem so real that they enter the world and walk among us. Odysseus walks among us to this day, and he would seem to be Homer's own self-portrait, for Odysseus, too, is a master of the art of lying, an art he got from his grandfather, Autolycus, who got it in turn from *his* father, Hermes. And Hermes, in an old story we shall soon consider, invented lying when he was a hungry child with a hankering for meat.

But I'm making a straight line out of a narrative that twists and turns, and I'm getting ahead of myself. We must begin at the beginning, with trickster learning how to keep his stomach full.

Trickster stories, even when they clearly have much more complicated cultural meanings, preserve a set of images from the days when what mattered above all else was hunting. At one point in the old Norse tales, the mischief-maker Loki has made the other gods so angry that he has to flee and go into hiding. In the mountains, he builds himself a house with doors on all sides so he can watch the four horizons. To amuse himself by day, he changes into a salmon, swimming the mountain streams, leaping the waterfalls. Sitting by the fire one morning, trying to imagine how the others might possibly capture him, he takes linen string and twists it into a mesh in the way that fishnets have been made ever since. Just at that moment, the others approach. Loki throws the net into the fire, changes into a salmon, and swims away. But the gods find the ashes of his net and from their pattern deduce the shape of the device they need to make. In this way, Loki is finally captured.

It makes a nice emblem of trickster's ambiguous talents, Loki imagining that first fishnet and then getting caught in it. Moreover, the device in question is a central trickster invention. In Native American creation stories, when Coyote teaches humans how to catch salmon, he makes the first fish weir out of logs and branches. On the North Pacific coast, the trickster Raven made the first fishhook; he taught the spider how to make her web and human beings how to make nets. The history of trickery in Greece goes back to similar origins. "Trick" is *dólos* in Homeric Greek, and the oldest known use of the term refers to a quite specific trick: baiting a hook to catch a fish.

East and west, north and south, this is the oldest trick in the book. No trickster has ever been credited with inventing a potato peeler, a gas meter, a catechism, or a tuning fork, but trickster invents the fish trap.

Coyote was going along by a big river when he got very hungry. He built a trap of poplar poles and willow branches and set it in the water. "Salmon!" he called out. "Come into this trap." Soon a big salmon came along and swam into the chute of the trap and then flopped himself out on the bank where Coyote clubbed him

to death. "I will find a nice place in the shade and broil this up,"
thought Coyote.

Trickster commonly relies on his prey to help him spring the traps
he makes. In this fragment of a Nez Percé story from northeastern Idaho,
Coyote's salmon weir takes advantage of forces the salmon themselves
provide. Salmon in a river are swimming upstream to spawn; sexual appetite or instinct gives them a particular trajectory and Coyote works with
it. Even with a baited hook, the victim's hunger is the *moving* part. The
worm just sits there; the fish catches himself. Likewise, in a Crow story
from the Western Plains, Coyote traps two buffalo by stampeding them
into the sun so they cannot see where they are going, then leading them
over a cliff. The fleetness of large herbivores is part of their natural
defense against predators; Coyote (or the Native Americans who slaughtered buffalo in this way) takes advantage of that instinctual defense by
directing the beasts into the sun and toward a cliff, so that fleetness itself
backfires. In the invention of traps, trickster is a technician of appetite
and a technician of instinct.

And yet, as the Loki story indicates, trickster can also get snared in
his own devices. Trickster is at once culture hero and fool, clever predator
and stupid prey. Hungry, trickster sometimes devises stratagems to catch
his meal; hungry, he sometimes loses his wits altogether. An Apache
story from Texas, in which Rabbit has played a series of tricks on Coyote,
ends as follows:

> Rabbit came to a field of watermelons. In the middle of the
> field there was a stick figure made of gum. Rabbit hit it with his
> foot and got stuck. He got his other foot stuck, then one hand and
> then his other hand and finally his head. This is how Coyote found
> him.
>
> "What are you doing like this?" asked Coyote.
>
> "The farmer who owns this melon patch was mad because I
> would not eat melons with him. He stuck me on here and said
> that in a while he would make me eat chicken with him. I told
> him I wouldn't do it."
>
> "You are foolish. I will take your place."
>
> Coyote pulled Rabbit free and stuck himself up in the gum

trap. When the farmer who owned the melons came out and saw Coyote he shot him full of holes.

Coyote doesn't just get stuck in gum traps, either; in other stories, a range of animals—usually sly cousins such as Fox or Rabbit or Spider—make a fool of him and steal his meat.

So trickster is cunning about traps but not so cunning as to avoid them himself. To my mind, then, the myth contains a story about the incremental creation of an intelligence about hunting. Coyote can imagine the fish trap precisely because he's been a fish himself, as it were. Nothing counters cunning but more cunning. Coyote's wits are sharp precisely because he has met other wits, just as the country bumpkin may eventually become a cosmopolitan if enough confidence men appear to school him.

Some recent ideas in evolutionary theory echo these assertions. In *Evolution of the Brain and Intelligence*, Harry Jerison presents a striking chart showing the relative intelligence of meat-eaters and the herbivores they prey on. Taking the ratio of brain to body size as a crude index, Jerison finds that if we compare herbivores and carnivores at any particular moment in history the predators are always slightly brainier than the prey. But the relationship is never stable; there is a slow step-by-step increase in intelligence on both sides. If we chart the brain-body ratio on a scale of 1 to 10, in the archaic age herbivores get a 2 and carnivores a 4; thirty million years later the herbivores are up to 4 but the carnivores have gone up to 6; another thirty million years and the herbivores are up to 6 but the carnivores are up to 8; finally, when the herbivores get up to 9, the carnivores are up to 10. The hunter is always slightly smarter, but the prey is always wising up. In evolutionary theory, the tension between predator and prey is one of the great engines that has driven the creation of intelligence itself, each side successively and ceaselessly responding to the other.

If this myth contains a story about incrementally increasing intelligence, where does it lead? What happens after the carnivore gets up to 10?

There is a great deal of folklore about coyotes in the American West. One story has it that in the old days sheep farmers tried to get rid of wolves and coyotes by putting out animal carcasses laced with strychnine. The wolves, they say, were killed in great numbers, but the coyotes wised up and avoided these traps. Another story has it that when trappers set metal leg traps they will catch muskrat and mink and fox and skunk, but coyote only rarely. Coyotes develop their own relationship to the trap; as one naturalist has written, "it is difficult to escape the conclusion that coyotes . . . have a sense of humor. How else to explain, for instance, the well-known propensity of experienced coyotes to dig up traps, turn them over, and urinate or defecate on them?"

With this image we move into a third relationship between tricksters and traps. When a coyote defecates on a trap he is neither predator nor prey but some third thing. A fragment of a native Tlingit story from Alaska will help us name that thing:

> [Raven] came to a place where many people were encamped fishing. . . . He entered a house and asked what they used for bait. They said, "Fat." Then he said, "Let me see you put enough on your hooks for bait," and he noticed carefully how they baited and handled their hooks. The next time they went out, he walked off behind a point and went underwater to get this bait. Now they got bites and pulled up quickly, but there was nothing on their hooks.

Raven eventually gets in trouble for this little trick (the fishermen steal his beak and he has to pull an elaborate return-ruse to get it back), but for now the point is simply that in the relationship between fish and fishermen this trickster stands to the side and takes on a third role.

A similar motif appears in Africa with the Zulu trickster known as Thlókunyana. Thlókunyana is imagined to be a small man, "the size of a weasel," and in fact one of his other names also refers to a red weasel with a black-tipped tail. A Zulu storyteller describes this animal as

> cleverer than all others, for its cunning is great. If a trap is set for a wild cat, [the weasel] comes immediately to the trap, and takes away the mouse which is placed there for the cat: it takes it out first; and when the cat comes the mouse has been already eaten by the weasel.

If a hunter does manage to trap this tricky weasel, he will have bad luck. A kind of jinx or magical influence remains in the trap that has caught a weasel and that influence forever after "stands in the way" of the trap's power; it will no longer catch game.

Coyote in fact and folklore, Raven and Thlókunyana in mythology—in each of these cases, trickster gets wise to the bait and is therefore all the harder to catch. The coyote who avoids a strychnined carcass is perhaps the simplest case; he does not get poisoned but he also gets nothing to eat. Raven and Thlókunyana are more cunning in this regard; they are bait-thief tricksters who separate the trap from the meat and eat the meat. Each of these tales has a predator-prey relationship in it—the fish and the fishermen, for example—but the bait thief doesn't enter directly into that oppositional eating game. A parasite or epizoon, he feeds his belly while standing just outside the conflict between hunter and hunted. From that position the bait thief becomes a kind of critic of the usual rules of the eating game and as such subverts them, so that traps he has visited lose their influence. What trapper's pride could remain unshaken once he's read Coyote's commentary?

In all these stories, trickster must do more than feed his belly; he must do so without himself getting eaten. Trickster's intelligence springs from appetite in two ways; it simultaneously seeks to satiate hunger and to subvert all hunger not its own. This last is an important theme. In the Okanagon creation story, the Great Spirit, having told Coyote that he must show the New People how to catch salmon, goes on to say: "I have important work for you to do . . . There are many bad creatures on earth. You will have to kill them, otherwise they will eat the New People. When you do this, the New People will honor you . . . They will honor you for killing the People-devouring monsters and for teaching . . . all the ways of living." In North America, trickster stepped in to defeat the monsters who used to feed on humans.

The myth says, then, that there are large, devouring forces in this world, and that trickster's intelligence arose not just to feed himself but to outwit these other eaters. Typically, this meeting is oppositional—the prey outwitting the predator. The bait thief suggests a different, non-oppositional strategy. Here trickster feeds himself where predator and prey meet, but rather than entering the game on their terms he plays with its rules. Perhaps, then, another force behind trickster's cunning is the desire to remove himself from the eating game altogether, or at least see how far out he can get and still feed his belly (for if he were to stop eating entirely he would no longer be trickster).

EATING THE ORGANS OF APPETITE

What god requires a sacrifice of every man,
woman, and child three times a day?
—*Yoruba riddle*

Not many stories purport to explain the origins of appetite, but one may be found at the beginning of the Tsimshian Raven cycle from the North Pacific coast. A desire to escape the trap of appetite, and some limit to that desire, organizes "Raven Becomes Voracious."

It seems that the whole world was once covered with darkness. On the Queen Charlotte Islands there was a town in which the animals lived. An animal chief and his wife lived there with their only child, a boy whom they loved very much. The father tried to keep his son from all danger. He built the boy a bed above his own in the rear of his large house. He washed him regularly, and the boy grew to be a young man.

When he was quite large, this youth became ill, and before long, he died. His parents wept and wept. The animal chief invited the tribe to his house. When they had assembled, he ordered the youth's body to be laid out. "Take out his intestines," he said. His attendants laid out the youth's body, removed the intestines, burned them at the rear of the house, and placed the body on the bed which the father had built for his son. Under the corpse of their dead son, the chief and the chieftainess wailed every morning, and the tribe wailed with them.

One morning before daylight, when the chieftainess went to mourn, she looked up and saw a young man, bright as fire, lying where the body of her son had lain. She called to her husband, who climbed the ladder and said, "Is it you, my beloved son? Is it you?" "Yes, it is I," said the shining youth, and his parents' hearts were filled with gladness.

When the tribe came to console their chief and chieftainess, they were surprised to see the shining youth. He spoke to them. "Heaven was much annoyed by your constant wailing, so He sent me down to comfort your minds." Everyone was very glad the prince lived among them again; his parents loved him more than ever.

The chief had two great slaves—a miserable man and his wife. The great slaves were called Mouth at Each End. Every morning they brought all kinds of food into the house. Every time they came back from hunting, they brought a large cut of whale meat with them, threw it on the fire, and ate it.

The shining youth ate very little. Days went by. He chewed a little fat, but he didn't eat it. The chieftainess tried to get him to eat, but he declined everything and lived without food. The chieftainess was very anxious about this; she was afraid her son would die again. One day when the shining youth was out for a walk, the chief went up the ladder to where his son had his bed. There was the corpse of his own son! Nevertheless, he loved his new child.

Sometime later, when the chief and chieftainess were out, the two great slaves called Mouth at Each End came in, carrying a large cut of whale meat. They threw the whale fat into the fire and ate it. The shining youth came up to them and asked, "What makes you so hungry?" The great slaves replied, "We are hungry because we have eaten scabs from our shinbones." "Do you like what you eat?" asked the shining youth. "Oh yes, my dear," said the slave man.

"Then I will taste the scabs you speak about," replied the prince. "No, my dear! Do not wish to be as we are!" cried the slave woman. "I will just taste it and spit it out again," said the prince. The slave man cut a bit of whale meat and put a small scab in it. The slave woman scolded him, "O bad man! What are you doing to the poor prince?"

The shining prince took the piece of meat with the scab in it, tasted it, and spat it out again. Then he went back to bed.

When the chief and his wife returned, the prince said to his mother, "Mother, I am very hungry." "Oh dear, is it true, is it true?" She ordered the slaves to feed rich food to her beloved son. The youth ate it all. As soon as he finished, he became ravenous again. The slaves gave him more and more to eat, and he ate everything. He ate for days. Soon all the provisions in his father's house were gone. The prince then went from house to house in the village and devoured all the stores of food, for he had tasted the scabs of Mouth at Each End.

Soon the entire tribe's stores of food were almost exhausted. The great chief felt sad and ashamed on account of his son. He assembled the tribe and spoke: "I will send my child away before he eats all our food." The tribe agreed with this decision; the chief summoned his son and, sitting him in the rear of the house, said to him: "My dear son, I shall send you over the ocean to the mainland." He gave his son a small round stone, a raven blanket, and a dried sea-lion bladder filled with all kinds of berries. "When you put on this raven blanket you will become Raven, and fly," the chief told him. "When you feel weary flying, drop this round stone on the sea, and you shall find rest. When you reach the mainland, scatter the various kinds of fruit over the land; and scatter the salmon roe in all the rivers and brooks, and also the trout roe, so that you may not lack food as long as you live in the world." The son put on the raven blanket and flew toward the east.

Such is the story of the origin of Raven and his hunger. In the parts of the cycle that follow, Raven creates the world as we know it: he places the fish in the rivers and scatters the fruit over the land. When he arrives in this world he finds it has no light but, remembering that there was light in the heaven from which he came, he returns and steals it so that this world will not be in darkness.

To reflect on the story of Raven's hunger, note first that the shining prince in this tale is not exactly the chief's son (the corpse, after all, remains); he is some sort of emissary from heaven, come in the youth's stead as an antidote to grief. The island on which the boy's parents live lies between heaven and earth; Raven travels from heaven to the world of the animal tribe, and then he travels from that world to this one, where appetite has no end and where the berries and fish have no end. In short, as in many trickster tales, the Tsimshian Raven is a go-between, a mediator. There are three spheres of being in the story, and Raven moves among them.

From the point of view of Raven's final home—this world of hunger and food—the father who loves his son is bound to fail in his attempt to keep the boy from all harm. In this world, people die; animals die. To desire the contrary is to desire a changeless perfection, a heaven, an ideal. Seeing that, perhaps we can now link three enigmas in the story: Why does the father have his son's intestines burnt? Why are the slaves called Mouth at Each End? What are those shin scabs?

To begin with, eating and death are part of the world of change (just as their suppression would be part of changeless perfection), so let us say that the intestines are a sign of our mutable world, and that their name is Mouth at Both Ends. The slaves are therefore the alimentary canal, that servant of the body who brings all kinds of food into our home every day. The story is built around the question whether or not the intestines will own the boy. The father hopes they won't, and so he has his attendants remove and burn them when the boy dies, a nice image for getting rid of appetite. If he could live, a boy without intestines might be freed from hunger, freed from attachments, freed from sickness and death. In any event, the parents' grief and sacrifice summon up a weird "ideal" being who shines like fire and does not eat, as if he had been gutted.

The shin scabs seem the most mysterious image here. In the far north, Raven is sometimes called "the trickster with the scaly legs"; perhaps to native eyes when a raven rubs its beak against its legs it appears to be self-eating, the Hungry One tasting its own scabs. To read the image more figuratively, let's first remember how scabs come to be, and what their function is. Scabs bespeak some kind of rough contact with the world. They follow wounds, and are the healing of wounds. As we heal, we slough them off; as such, they are a kind of bodily excrement. They are also a kind of fruiting, flesh producing flesh out of itself, a strange fruit to be sure, but one that is actually eaten in this case.

If we begin with the idea of "rough contact," perhaps the shin scabs in the story, like calluses on the hands, represent work, the labor by which humankind must get its keep (these are food-getting slaves, after all, whose shins are scabbed). It is a widespread motif in this mythology that once upon a time we humans did not have to work for our food (every morning there was a bowl of hot acorn mush outside the lodge), but then trickster came along, did something foolish, and now we must labor. So perhaps "to eat shin scabs" is to enter the world of scarcity and work.

Because scabs are linked with wounds, they may also indicate that Raven is born of woundedness. But what wound is there in this tale? Remember that the father here hopes to keep his son from all harm, and that his hopes are twice defeated, once when the boy dies and once again when the scabs turn his spirit into a shamefully hungry creature. I suspect the second defeat arises from the father's response to the first. He had his people cut out the boy's intestines, and then the slaves—who are in some way like intestines—appear, wounded and scabbing. Raven is not the father's hoped-for ideal youth who has escaped this world; he is, rather, a restless, hungry beast who is in this world precisely because his father's idealism wounded him, and he has tasted the fruit of that wound.

Finally, if scabs are a kind of excrement, perhaps the story means that Raven comes to life where the body sheds its wastes. (Ravens, in fact, will eat excrement, and the mythology is full of scatological episodes.) But "excrement" may be too precise a word here, for in this case what the body sheds becomes food. Perhaps Raven comes to life where waste turns into fruit, or better, where one's *own* waste becomes one's food (it is their own scabs that the slaves eat). There is a circularity to eating here which suggests that, at some level, eating is self-eating, or that all who eat in this world must eventually themselves be eaten. In this world, everything that feeds will someday be food for other mouths; that is the law of appetite, or—as we'd now say—of ecological interdependence. If I'm right to imagine that the removed intestines reappear as the slaves, then in this story, at the "beginning of things," we find Raven tasting the fruit of his own wounded guts and by that self-eating setting in motion this world of endless hunger.

Here it should be noted that there is some natural history woven into this story. When hunters kill an animal in the woods they typically gut it on the spot, then carry the carcass home; later, ravens will come to eat the guts (and coyotes and wolves will follow, drawn by the ravens). Raven is said to have told the Athabascan Indians that they would be able to catch deer if they would leave the guts for him to feed on each time the game is killed; elsewhere, the entrails of the kill are left as a gift to Coyote. Each case presents an image of appetite eating the organs of appetite.

One thing draws together these various readings: in each, Raven comes down to this world. "Raven Becomes Voracious" is a story of descent. In heaven there are beings who do not eat; in this lower world of stomachs and fish there are mortals who eat constantly. The trickster Raven is a mixture, the shining boy plus appetite, a being of considerable power who is unable to satiate his hunger. Trickster makes the world, gives it sunlight, fish, and berries, but he makes it "as it is," a world of constant need, work, limitation, and death.

· · ·

A s I said at the outset, there are not many stories like this one in which we learn something about the genesis of appetite, but trickster tales in most traditions are filled with examples of trickster's hunger and its consequences. To take a case in point, in a Native American (Colville) story Coyote has made a new pair of horns for Old Buffalo Bull and in gratitude Buffalo gives Coyote a magic cow and a little advice:

> "Never kill this cow, Coyote. When you are hungry, cut off a little of her fat with your flint knife. Rub ashes on the wound. The cut will heal. This way, you will have meat forever."
>
> Coyote promised this is what he would do. He took the buffalo cow with him back over the mountains. Whenever he was hungry he would cut away a little fat and then heal the wound with ashes as Buffalo Bull had said. But after a while he got tired of the fat. He wanted to taste the bone marrow and some fresh liver. By this time he had crossed the plains and was back in his own country.
>
> "What Buffalo Bull said is only good over in his country," Coyote said to himself. "I am chief here. Buffalo Bull's words mean nothing. He will never know."
>
> Coyote took the young cow down to the edge of the creek. "You look a little sore-footed," he told her. "Stay here and rest and feed for a while."
>
> Coyote killed her suddenly while she was feeding. When he pulled off her hide crows and magpies came. When Coyote tried to chase them off, more came. Even more came, until they had eaten all the meat. . . .

Coyote ends up empty-handed and of course his magic cow is dead and there's nothing he can do about it. The plot is typical: the trickster is given something valuable with a condition set on its use, time passes, and before too long trickster's hunger leads him to violate the condition. As a consequence, the plenitude of things is inexorably diminished. Hunger devours the ideal, and trickster suffers. There seem to be only two options: limited food or limited appetite. Coyote, unable to choose the latter, has the former forced upon him. Such is one common plot in the mythology of tricksters.

But this mythology always seems to go in two directions at once, and so at times we find the opposite plot as well, one in which trickster has limits to appetite forced upon him. I am thinking in particular of the trickster cycle told by the Winnebago Indians in Wisconsin, several episodes of which amount to a sort of "Raven Becomes Voracious" in reverse.* At the beginning of the Winnebago cycle, trickster is pictured as having a long penis coiled in a box on his back, and his intestines wrapped around his body, an apt image of someone ridden by appetite. In the course of the story, however, these bizarre organs are reduced and rearranged until trickster looks more or less like a human being.

In the episode concerning his intestines, trickster has caught some ducks and set them roasting. He plans to nap while they cook, but before settling down he addresses his anus: "Now, you, my younger brother, must keep watch for me while I go to sleep. If you notice any people, drive them off." As soon as trickster falls asleep, some small foxes, having scented the meat, come to steal it; the anus farts at them, but they pay it no mind and eat their fill. When trickster awakes he discovers the meat is gone and cries out:

> "Alas! Alas! They have caused my appetite to be disap-
> pointed, those covetous fellows! And you, too [he says to his anus],
> you despicable object, what about your behavior? Did I not tell
> you to watch this fire? You shall remember this! As a punishment
> for your remissness, I will burn your mouth so that you will not
> be able to use it!"
>
> Thereupon he took a burning piece of wood and burnt the
> mouth of his anus. He was, of course, burning himself and, as he
> applied the fire, he exclaimed, "Ouch! Ouch! This is too much! I
> have made my skin smart. Is it not for such things that they call
> me Trickster? . . ."
>
> Then he went away. As he walked along the road he felt cer-
> tain that someone must have passed along it before, for he was

---

* This cycle of tales was first printed in the key early work on trickster figures, Paul Radin's *The Trickster: A Study in American Indian Mythology* (1956). Radin was an anthropologist with a 1910 doctorate from Columbia University. He lived and worked with the Winnebago in Wisconsin for many years, and his commentary places their trickster cycle in its cultural context with great finesse.

on what appeared to be a trail. Indeed, suddenly, he came upon a piece of fat that must have come from someone's body. "Someone has been packing an animal he had killed," he thought to himself. Then he picked up a piece of fat and ate it. It had a delicious taste. "My, my, how delicious it is to eat this!"

As he proceeded however, much to his surprise, he discovered that it was part of himself, part of his own intestines, that he was eating. After burning his anus, his intestines had contracted and fallen off, piece by piece, and these pieces were the things he was picking up. "My, my! Correctly, indeed, am I named Foolish One, Trickster! . . ." Then he tied his intestines together. A large part, however, had been lost.

In this way, trickster's intestines become normal.* As for his penis, it is also a little oversized at the beginning of the story. He has trouble with it lifting his blanket up like a tent pole, and he can send it like a snake under the water to copulate with a chief's daughter bathing in the river. But late in the cycle he hears a voice teasing him about how strange his penis looks. He becomes self-conscious about the weird shape of his body, and begins to rearrange himself, placing his penis and testicles where they belong on the human body. At the same time, he is angered by the teasing voice, which turns out to come from a chipmunk. When the chipmunk runs into a hollow tree, trickster sends his penis in after it.

So he took out his penis and probed the hollow tree with it. He could not, however, reach the end of the hole. So he took some more of his penis and probed again, but again he was unable to reach the end of the hole. So he unwound more and more of his penis and probed still deeper, yet all to no avail. Finally he took what still remained, emptying the entire box, and probed and probed but still he could not reach the end of the hole. At last he sat up on a log and probed as far as he could, but still he was unable to reach the end. "Ho!" said he impatiently, and suddenly withdrew his penis. Much to his horror, only a small piece of it

---

* Trickster eats his own intestines. He does not do this intentionally, but nonetheless it is a kind of self-sacrifice. When Carl Jung said that the trickster "is a forerunner of the savior," he had in mind this motif of unconscious agony.

was left. "My, what a great injury he has done me! You contemptible thing I will repay you for this!"

Then he kicked the log to pieces. There he found the chipmunk and flattened him out, and there, too, to his horror he discovered his penis all gnawed up. "Oh, my, of what a wonderful
organ he has deprived me! But why do I speak thus? I will make
objects out of the pieces for human beings to use."*

Trickster transforms the pieces of his penis into edible plants—po-
tatoes, artichokes, rice, ground beans, and so on. In many tales when
trickster loses his intestines they, too, become plants that humans can
eat. That is, when trickster's organs of appetite are diminished they are
turned into foodstuffs, the objects of human appetite. Such foods are a
mixed blessing, giving rise to hunger even as they satisfy it. To end our
craving we must eat the organs of craving, and craving then returns. If
the foods that nourish us are trickster's gifts, to eat them is to become
like trickster, like that Raven who can never be satisfied and who would
devour all the provisions of his native village were he not banished to
this world.

The general point here is that a trickster will be less ridden by lust
and hunger if his organs of appetite have been whittled away. In this
case, trickster simply suffers the loss; it happens to him. He may benefit
from it, but the benefit is accidental, not a fruit of his own cunning or
design. But perhaps the accident leads to the cunning. That is to say,
just as trickster may acquire his trapping wits as a consequence of having
been trapped, so the suffering that trickster endures from his unrestrained
appetites may lead to some consciousness in regard to those appetites. I
say this because, however one might imagine the connection, there are
trickster tales in which a limit to appetite is intended rather than accidental. In fact, we have already seen such a moment: when the father in

---

* This could be read as a strange version of the vagina-dentata motif (which does occasionally appear in trickster stories). If so, rather than understanding the toothed vagina
as an image of horrific castration, we could take it as an image for the conversion of
crippling desire into appropriate desire. These teeth don't devour the sexual organ, they
shape it.

the Raven story has his son's intestines burned, he consciously attempts to effect the change that the Winnebago trickster suffers witlessly.

If we turn to the Homeric Greek tradition, we will find a similar pattern, though somewhat differently elaborated. The *Homeric Hymn to Hermes* tells about the days immediately following Hermes' birth.* He is the illegitimate child of Zeus and a nymph named Maia. At the beginning of the story, the newborn babe wanders from his mother's cave, stumbles upon a turtle, and, from its shell, makes the first lyre. After singing a song about himself on this instrument, Hermes lays it aside. "His mind wandered to other matters. For Hermes longed to eat meat." He sets off to steal cattle from the herd of his half brother, Apollo.

In many a Coyote story the phrase "he longed to eat meat" would lead willy-nilly to some sort of disaster. And the frank declaration of carnivorous desire in the *Homeric Hymn* makes it clear that this Greek trickster is a cousin to Coyote, as does a later remark that Apollo makes when he finally catches his thieving brother: "You're going to be a great nuisance to lonely herdsmen in the mountain woods when you get to hankering after meat and come upon their cows or fleecy sheep."

So the *Hymn* itself lets us know that Hermes is a meat thief like Coyote, and given his transgressive nature, we will not be surprised if he breaks the rules and eats the cow he steals. But the plot of this particular story differs in one significant detail. The crucial scene occurs after Hermes has led the stolen cattle to a barn near the river Alpheus. Having kindled a fire in a trench, Hermes drags two of the cows from the barn and butchers them.

> He cut up the richly marbled flesh and skewered it on wooden spits; he roasted all of it—the muscle and the prized sirloin and the dark-blooded belly—and laid the spits out on the ground. . . .
>
> Next he gladly drew the dripping chunks of meat from the spits, spread them on a stone, and divided them into twelve portions distributed by lot, making each one exactly right.†

---

* The *Homeric Hymns* are a group of poems, each to a specific god (Demeter, Dionysus, Apollo, etc.), written in the style of the *Iliad* and the *Odyssey*. The *Hymn to Hermes* was probably written down around 420 B.C., though the material it contains is of great antiquity. My own translation of this hymn appears in the first appendix at the end of the book.
† There is a bit of a joke here. There are twelve Olympian gods and Hermes is one of

And glorious Hermes longed to eat that sacrificial meat. The sweet smell weakened him, god though he was; and yet, much as his mouth watered, his proud heart would not let him eat. Later he took the fat and all the flesh and stored them in that ample barn, setting them high up as a token of his youthful theft. That done, he gathered dry sticks and let the fire devour, absolutely, the hooves of the cattle, and their heads.

And when the god had finished, he threw his sandals into the deep pooling Alpheus. He quenched the embers and spread sand over the black ashes. And so the night went by under the bright light of the moon.

Here, then, is a meat-thief trickster who does not eat (at an ordinary Greek sacrifice, by the way, those who conducted the rite *would* eat; Hermes is doing something unusual). I shall later speak more fully of why "his proud heart" prevails, but suffice it to say for now that Hermes restrains one desire in favor of another. It seems that Hermes' status is not clear at the beginning of the *Hymn*: is he an Olympian god or is he a half-breed from a single-parent cave? As he himself says to his mother after returning from his night of crime:

> "I'm ready to do whatever I must so that you and I will never go hungry. You're wrong to insist we live in a place like this. Why should we be the only gods who never eat the fruits of sacrifice and prayer? Better always to live in the company of other death-less ones—rich, glamorous, enjoying heaps of grain—than for-ever to sit by ourselves in a gloomy cave."

If the trickster in the Raven cycle comes down from heaven to the world of fish and work, here we find a cousin trickster hoping to travel in the opposite direction on the same road. In deciding not to eat meat, Hermes is preparing himself to be an Olympian. To eat meat is to be confined to the mortal realm, and Hermes has higher goals. He doesn't want to be a cave boy, he'd rather be a shining prince. He is hungry for

---

them, or rather he'd like to be. Here he includes himself in the sacrifice so as to stake his claim. He's like a politician nominating himself for high office, seconding the nomi-nation, and counting the votes—all in secret.

the food of the gods, "the fruits of sacrifice and prayer," not the meat itself. By *not* eating, it's as if he's sacrificing his own intestines along with the meat, or, in the imagery of the *Hymn*, denying his salivary glands in favor of his heart's pride. Against the rules he stole a cow and killed it, as Coyote did, but having violated that limit he imposes another in its stead. Or rather, what I've translated as his "heart" imposes another. The Greek word in question is *thymos*, usually translated as "heart," "soul," or "breath"; it can also mean "mind," because the Homeric Greeks located intelligence in the chest and the speaking voice, not in the silent brain. In this story, then, we see a meat-thief intelligence setting a limit to appetite and by so doing avoiding death, the hook hidden in that meat.

MEAT SACRIFICE

It is often said that when Hermes slaughters the cattle he is inventing the art of sacrifice.* I'm not sure the *Hymn* itself offers enough evidence for that claim. It does say clearly that Hermes invents the lyre and the shepherd's pipes; it says he "is responsible for fire-sticks and fire"; but it is silent as to who invented sacrifice. Nonetheless, if we set the *Hymn* in the context of other trickster tales the claim becomes more plausible. In West Africa, as we shall see in Chapter 5, the Yoruba trickster Eshu is "the father of sacrifice," having gotten human beings to offer meat to the gods in return for insight into the will of heaven. Another example, the one that will help us see Hermes in context, appears in the story of that other Greek trickster, Prometheus. Both Prometheus and Hermes dream up clever tricks to change their relationship to meat, but Hermes turns out to be the more cunning of the two, for Prometheus is a little slow to figure out where the dangers of appetite really lie.

As the ancients tell the tale, Prometheus and Zeus got into a fight toward the end of the Golden Age. Prometheus had created people out of clay; from the events that follow, it seems likely that he wished to increase

---

* Jean-Pierre Vernant in *The Cuisine of Sacrifice*: "He establishes the first sacrifice." T. W. Allen in *The Homeric Hymns*: Hermes "ordained the ritual of sacrifice." Walter Otto in *The Homeric Gods*: "He is . . . regarded as the prototype for offering sacrifice." Walter Burkert in *Greek Religion*: "He invents fire, fire-sticks, and sacrifice." (And see Burkert's essay "Sacrificio-sacrilegio: il trickster fondatore.") For two who disagree, see the first chapter of Kahn's *Hermès Passe* and the chapter on Hermes in Clay's *The Politics of Olympus*.

their portion in the world. In the Golden Age, humankind neither grew old quickly nor died in pain, but they were nonetheless mortal and perhaps Prometheus wished them immortality. In any event, he and Zeus got into a dispute that focused on which parts of a slaughtered ox the gods would eat and which would be food for human mouths. Prometheus divided the ox into two portions, and because Zeus was to have first choice, he disguised them: the better part (the edible meat) he made unappealing by covering it with the ox's stomach (Greeks did not eat the belly, the tripe); the lesser part (the inedible bones) he covered with fat to make it look like rich meat.

Zeus was not deceived, however; he could see beneath the surfaces of the Promethean shell game. And yet he didn't choose the "better" portion, he chose the bones. Hesiod writes: "Zeus, whose wisdom is everlasting, saw . . . the trick, and in his heart he thought mischief against mortal men. . . . With both hands he took up the white fat. . . ." Then Hesiod adds the point that is of interest here: "And because of this the tribes of men upon earth burn white bones to the deathless gods upon fragrant altars." Promethean trickery thus leads to the first sacrifice.

It leads to much more, as well, which should be mentioned briefly. The "mischief" that Zeus "thought against mortals" took several forms: he hid fire from them and, after Prometheus stole that fire back, he sent Pandora as a sort of poisonous gift. For Hesiod, that earliest of misogynists, it is Pandora who really brought an end to the all-male Golden Age club, for with her came sexual reproduction, sickness, insanity, vice, and toil. After Prometheus, humans have fire and meat; they also age quickly and die in pain.

If we now look closely at the way in which Prometheus apportions the slaughtered ox, we will see that he is in fact a witless trickster here, abandoned by his fabled foresight. Not unlike Coyote, who gets too caught up in hunger to escape from it, Prometheus fails to perceive the true meaning of the portions he so carefully arranges. To see that meaning, to see what Zeus apparently sees, it helps to know that for the Greeks the bones stand for immortality. They are the undying essence, what does not decay (they are, for example, what was preserved when the Greeks cremated a body). Conversely, in all ancient Greek literature the belly stands for needy, shameless, inexorable, overriding appetite. In this tradition, the belly is always called "odious," "evil-doing," "contemptible," "deadly," and so on. At one point in the *Odyssey*, Odysseus exclaims: "Is there nothing more doglike [or shameless] than this hateful belly? It always arouses us, obliges us not to forget it, even at the height of our troubles and anguish."

The symbolism suggests, then, that those who eat the belly-wrapped meat must take the same thing as their portion in the world. When Zeus leaves for mortals that Promethean "better" share, mortals perforce become the very thing that they have eaten; they become meat sacks, bellies that must be filled over and over with meat simply to delay an inexorable death. Prometheus tries to be a cunning encoder of images, but Zeus is a more cunning reader, and the meat trick backfires.

The story of Promethean sacrifice, then, is not one in which a hungry trickster sacrifices appetite or intestines but one in which, as a result of a foolish trick, human beings get stuck with endless hunger as their portion. Like the tale of Raven eating the shin scabs, it is a story of the origin of appetite, and of descent. After Prometheus, humans are snared in their own hunger, a trap in which they quickly age and die. Prometheus does not suffer that human fate himself, nor does he become an insatiable eater like Raven, but Zeus binds him to a rock where an eagle eternally devours his liver—each night the liver grows back, each day the eagle eats it again. In his own way, then, Prometheus suffers from unremitting hunger, as do humans—and Raven.

With this Promethean trick in mind, let's now return to the question of whether or not trickster invents sacrifice. To answer, it helps to know that, in the culture from which Prometheus and Hermes come, *sacrifice is ritual apportionment*. That is to say, the distributed portions of a Greek sacrifice represented the more abstract "portions" of the parties involved, their political and spiritual functions. The bones, for example, are the gods' concrete portion but also stand for their spiritual portion, their immortality. Or—another example—priests cooked and ate the viscera of a sacrificed animal; it was at once their portion in fact and a symbol of their place in the community. The way the Greeks divided an animal made a map of the way their community was divided. If you saw someone eating the thigh of an ox, you could assume he was a high magistrate of the city.

In such a system, when people imagine the first sacrifice they will also be imagining an original apportioning. And if the beginnings amount to a *change* in apportionment,* as seems to be the case with both Hermes and Prometheus, then sacrifice will probably be invented by way of some trick or deceit, for such a change usually has the less powerful taking a share away from the more powerful (in this case, for example, Prometheus hopes to take power away from the gods). Whatever trickster pulls this trick does not initially invent sacrifice, therefore; *first* he invents the trick of reapportionment, some sleight of hand by which the thigh of an ox ends up on the plate of a slave. In the case of Prometheus, the trick backfires (humans get the meat and their lot in life becomes more grim); in the case of Hermes, the trick works (he refuses the meat and his lot improves). In both cases, though, there is a change of apportionment and a form of sacrifice emerges that memorializes both the trick and its consequences, the new order of things.

We can now give a general shape to this material on the sacrifice of appetite, and link it to the earlier discussion of traps. A trickster is often imagined as a sort of "hungry god." The image can be read from two sides: tricksters are either gods who have become voracious eaters, smothered in intestines; or they are beings full of appetite who become a little more god-like through some trimming of the organs of appetite. The stories we've seen have a hierarchy: at the lower levels, trickster is bound by appetite (Coyote must eat his entire cow); at the higher levels, he is either freed from appetite (that anorexic shining prince) or given an appetite for more ethereal foods (the smoke of sacrifice). Moreover, trickster walks the path between high and low (descending into hunger at the end of the Raven and Prometheus stories; ascending and restraining hunger in the *Hymn to Hermes* and the opening of the Raven story). On this path between high and low we also find sacrifice. At its simplest, it seems unintended (the devoured penis, the lost intestines of many Coyote stories); at other times, there is conscious action (the burned intestines in the Raven story, Hermes' restraining pride).

Now let us return to the idea that trickster intelligence arises from the tension between predators and prey. Behind trickster's tricks lies the desire to eat and not be eaten, to satisfy appetite without being its object.

---

* I realize that there can't be a change if we're talking of beginnings, but we are in mythic time here, and in mythic time first things needn't come first.

If trickster is initially ridden by his appetites, and if such compulsion leads him into traps, then we might read intentional sacrifice as an attempt to alter appetite—to eat without the compulsion or its consequences. In the Greek case, the foods identified with heaven satisfy an appetite shed of its usual, odious baggage: old age, sickness, and death. These stories imagine a final escape from the eating game in which, beyond the edge of predator-prey relationships, immortal eaters feast on heavenly foods and never themselves become a meal for worms or for time.

As I have been suggesting, in these tales of sacrifice a hook is hidden in the meat portion: mortality itself. Prometheus doesn't see it, and the Golden Age ends with humans hooked on meat, and mortal. Hermes avoids it. He changes the eating game by inventing a sacrificial rite in which he forgoes the meat and, more important, his own *desire* for meat. Figuratively, to slip the trap of appetite he sacrifices the organ of that appetite, his odious belly. So, although the *Hymn* contains no direct declaration in this regard, I think it is correct to say that Hermes invents the art of sacrifice and that he does so out of a struggle over appetite.

Moreover, when he refrains from eating he is not only sacrificing appetite, he has also gotten "wise to the bait." Coyotes who avoid poisoned carcasses restrain their hunger and do not get killed. Hermes does the same thing, if eating the meat means becoming mortal. But for those with actual bellies, such restraint is only a partial solution. No one imagines that coyotes avoiding strychnine give up eating, and even Hermes makes it clear that he doesn't eat the cattle because he hopes *later* to enjoy the fruits of sacrifice and prayer. (Those are more ethereal foods, but they are foods nonetheless; when Hermes imagines heaven he doesn't imagine an absence of hunger, he imagines gods who eat.) Let us say, then, that wise-to-the-bait Hermes is a bait thief as well. Raven, remember, figures out how to eat the fat and avoid the hook. Hermes steals the cattle and, dedicating the smoke of sacrifice to himself, consumes only the portion that will not harm him. To say that Hermes will enjoy "the fruit of sacrifice and prayer" is an elevated way of saying we've met another trickster who eats the fat and leaves an empty hook behind.

2

....

"THAT'S MY WAY, COYOTE, NOT YOUR WAY"

THE BUNGLING HOST

To say simply that trickster lives on the road doesn't give the full nuance of the case, for the impression one often gets is that trickster travels around *aimlessly*, and roads lead from one place to another. Here's how the Chinese Monkey King is described at one point: "Today he toured the east; and tomorrow he wandered west. . . . He had no definite itinerary." Moments of transition in Native American stories typically read: "As he continued his aimless wandering. . . ." Maybe the point of saying that trickster is on the road is to say that he has "the context of no context," in George W.S. Trow's wonderful phrase. To be in a particular town or city is to be situated; to be on the road is to be between situations and not, therefore, oriented in the ways that situations orient us.

In any event, trickster sometimes loses his bearings completely, and that is where we see most clearly the aimless portion of his traveling. In a story known widely in North America, Coyote has put his head into the empty skull of an elk and can't get it out.

Coyote began to cry because he didn't know what to do. He couldn't see where he was going. He yelled . . . and tried to pull the skull off but it was no use. Finally he wandered off.

Coyote bumped into something with his foot. "Who are you?" he asked.

"I am a cherry tree."

"Good. I must be near the river."

Coyote went on slowly like that, feeling ahead with his feet. If he could find the river he would know which way to go.

He bumped into something again. "Who are you?"

"I am a cottonwood," the tree said to him.

"I must be very near the river now."

Again he felt something with his foot. "Who are you?"

"I am a willow."

"Indeed! I must be right at the river."

Coyote was stepping very carefully now but still he was falling over things. Finally he tripped and fell in the river and the current took him away.

The motif of wandering blindly is repeated in the Winnebago trickster cycle. Here trickster has committed a series of wildly antisocial acts, ending in the accidental killing of a group of children during a fit of hunger. The father of these children chases trickster all over; he finally escapes only by running to "the place where the sun rises, the end of the world," and leaping into the ocean. "As he did not . . . know where to find the shore, he swam along aimlessly." Soon he bumps into some fish. Several species are named, the last of which—the white fish—is able to orient him and he finds the shore. Then, "again he wandered aimlessly about the world."

Before long, he comes upon a plant that says to him: "He who chews me will shit!" Trickster does not believe it, eats the plant, and ends up producing such a pile of feces that he has to climb a tree. Then he falls from the tree and is blinded by his own filth.

He started to run. He could not see anything. As he ran he knocked against a tree. [He] cried out in pain. He reached out and felt the tree and sang:

"Tree, what kind of a tree are you? Tell me something about yourself!"

And the tree answered, "What kind of a tree do you think I am? I am an oak tree. I am the forked oak tree that used to stand in the middle of the valley."

As in the earlier story, trickster bumps into one tree after another until he is led to water where he is able to wash himself.

The trees and fish in these stories have what I'd like to call "species knowledge." They are the opposite of the aimless wanderer. They are placed in space the way a species is placed by its needs. Some species of fish swim near the shore, others don't; there are trees like the willow that grow only at the water's edge and trees that can grow at greater and greater distances from water. These stories, then, seem deliberately to set trickster's aimless wandering against beings that are anything but aimless, beings that are situated in space by their nature.

Now let us set these tales alongside one of the most famous Native American stories, "The Bungling Host," in which trickster, hungry as ever, drops in on some animal friend—bear or kingfisher or muskrat or snipe—who catches and prepares food in his own special way. Here is an episode from the Okanagon version (in which, by the way, Mole is Coyote's wife):

One time there was no food at Coyote's lodge. He . . . went to visit his brother Kingfisher.

"Kingfisher, what have you got to eat," asked Coyote. "I am very hungry."

Kingfisher did not like this rude way of talking, but he sent for his son and told him to go get three willow sticks.

Boy Kingfisher went out and got the sticks and came back. Kingfisher heated them over the fire until they were strong. Then he took them out, twisted them up and tied them to his belt.

He flew up onto the top of his lodge and from there he flew to the river and down through a hole in the ice. When he came up there was a fish hanging on each willow stick.

Coyote ate until his belly was round, but he saved some fish for his wife and his children at home.

"You must come over to see me tomorrow," said Coyote.

"I don't think I will come over," said Kingfisher.

"Oh, you must come over. We will have a nice meal, you will like it. You come over tomorrow."

Kingfisher didn't want to go, but said he would.

The next day when Kingfisher came over Coyote told his son to go get three willow sticks. When Boy Coyote came back Coyote stuck the sticks in the fire until they were hard. Then he bent them up and stuck them on his belt. Then Coyote crawled up to the top of his lodge.

"What are you doing up there?" asked his wife.

"Why, you know I've done this before. I am getting food for our brother, Kingfisher."

Coyote jumped off the top of the lodge down to the river but he missed the hole and broke his neck and was killed.

Kingfisher had been watching all the time. He walked over to where Coyote lay and took the three sticks from his belt and jumped into the hole in the ice. Soon he came up with many fish. Then he stepped over Coyote four times and Coyote came back to life.

"This is my way, not your way," said Kingfisher. "I do not imitate others like you do."

Coyote took the fish up to his lodge and showed them to Mole and to his children.

"Look at these big fish. I caught them the way Kingfisher did. Kingfisher is afraid of my power. He told me not to do this again. He knows my medicine is strong."

Mole cooked the fish.

Two things—the stories just cited about "species knowledge" and the fact that one of trickster's names is "imitator"—lead me to read "The Bungling Host" as a tale of an animal that does not have, as Kingfisher says, "a way." Kingfisher, Snipe, Polecat, Bear, Muskrat—each of these animals has a way of being in the world; each has his nature. Specifically, each of them has his own way of hunting and, in these stories at least, he is never hungry, because he has that way. Coyote, on the other hand, seems to have no way, no nature, no knowledge. He has the ability to copy the others, but no ability of his own.

This lack has several consequences. For one thing it means, as Carl Jung put it, that trickster is "stupider than the animals." Animals at least have inborn knowledge, a way of being, and trickster doesn't. The animals know not to eat that plant that causes them to defecate mountains; the animals know which way the river is; the animals know how to hunt for their particular foods. Trickster knows none of this, and so ends up hungry, stumbling around covered in his own mess.*

It seems a dangerous position for an animal to be in, stripped of instinct. What possible use could there be in having lost the mother wit to be in the world? What conceivable advantage might lie in a way of being that has no way?

A first answer might be that whoever has no way but is a successful imitator will have, in the end, a repertoire of ways. If we can imitate the spider and make a net, imitate the beaver and make a lake, imitate the heron's beak and make a spear, imitate the armadillo and wear armor, imitate the leopard and wear camouflage, imitate poison ivy and produce chemical weapons, imitate the fox and hunt downwind, then we become more versatile hunters, greater hunters. And although in "The Bungling Host" trickster fails as an imitator, elsewhere imitation is part of his power.

Perhaps having no way also means that a creature can adapt itself to a changing world. Species well situated in a natural habitat are always at risk if that habitat changes. One reason native observers may have chosen coyote the animal to be Coyote the Trickster is that the former in fact does exhibit a great plasticity of behavior and is, therefore, a consummate survivor in a shifting world. For one thing, coyote young, like human young, remain dependent on their parents for a long time. One naturalist writes that such neoteny, as it is called, "is a characteristic of all species that have not inherited a fixed repertory of behavior, but must *learn* how to survive. . . . The neotenal coyote . . . meets change by learning new responses and is therefore capable of developing a whole new lifestyle." As if by way of illustration, another naturalist, François Leydet, tells us that, in the early days of the American West, coyotes were much more social animals; they hunted in packs the way wolves do. But now

---

* And, it should be said, terribly dependent on others, though "dependent" might not be the right word: trickster can be a bungling host because he's such an agile parasite.

big gatherings of coyotes are seldom seen. . . . Persecution forced the coyote to adopt more solitary ways, and since he subsists largely on small game that he can catch unassisted, he has been able to do so. This has allowed him to survive in regions where the big gray wolf has been exterminated: a hunter of large game, *Canis lupus* would not or could not abandon the pack organization which made him highly vulnerable to man.

Watching coyotes hunt in packs, the eighteenth-century wolf might well have said to them, "This is my way, not your way." But two hundred years later the wolf, trapped in his "way," is endangered, while coyotes are eating purebred poodles in Beverly Hills.

So this is one advantage a being, especially a predator, might have if it is not constrained to one way but has instead the ability to copy many ways. We can turn the conceit around, too, and find situations in which a being that is hunted might benefit from having no way, no instinctual knowledge. To set up this line of thought, let me begin with a question: Do animals lie?

The answer is both yes and no. Animals of course communicate with one another. Birds call from the trees, whales sing in the oceans, the deer gives its hoarse warning cry, or—to take the famous example—the honeybee dances to tell the hive how far away the flowers are, and in what direction. Moreover, in most cases these animals are telling the "truth" when they communicate with one another. Honeybees do not lie. Their "language" is constrained by instinct; no bee ever comes into the hive and says "The flowers are due west" when in fact they are northeast. The deer does not cry wolf when there is no wolf at hand.

Having granted all that, however, it is not hard to think of complications and exceptions. Surely there are deceptive animals. There are insects evolved to look as if they are twigs or dead leaves; there are flowers that eat insects by luring them with false advertising. In the Louisiana swamps, one finds the remarkable alligator snapping turtle, one of whose features is a "lure tongue," a stubby white appendage which it sticks out until an unsuspecting fish checks to see if it's edible. The frightened possum pretends to be dead, as does the pangolin. In the classic case, when the fox threatens the mother grouse, she pretends to have a broken wing so as to lead the fox away from her nest. Small birds feeding at ground level in the rain forests give a warning cry when danger is near, but one species can give a false warning cry, so as to have the ground to itself for a while.

So animals sometimes lie. But there is an important way in which these lying animals are just like animals that do not lie: both are constrained by instinct. The lying animal cannot lie creatively; it cannot vary its repertoire. The mother grouse never plays possum and the possum never plays grouse.

Such constraint makes lying animals vulnerable to any predator that gets wise to the ruse. Here we return to the first part of the chapter, for any animal bound by instinct is vulnerable to what I call "technicians of instinct." As there are traps of appetite, so there are traps of instinct, traps that exploit an animal's inborn methods, including the methods by which it otherwise eludes its enemies (as when Coyote turns the Buffalo's fleetness against it). In short, an animal with one instinctual deception in its repertoire has some advantage over an animal with none, but that advantage is lost when it meets a predator who knows how to decipher the deception. Then it is stuck, trapped in its own defense.

So we have a second reason why it might be useful to have no way, no nature, no fixed instinctual responses. Having no way, trickster can have many ways. Having no way, he is dependent on others whose manner he exploits, but he is not confined to their manner and therefore in another sense he is more independent. Having no way, he is free of the trap of instinct, both "stupider than the animals" and more versatile than any. He stumbles around covered in his own filth, but by the same token he feeds in the house of the Kingfisher, and the house of Bear, the house of Muskrat, the house of Bee. Moreover, if someone tries to trap him to bring him home for dinner, trickster can counter with a series of deceptions and slip from the trap. Bee and Bear, who cannot tell a lie, are easier to trap than Grouse, who has her single famous fib. But Grouse is easier to trap than trickster, whose fabulations never end.

In fact, we must now add creative lying to our list of trickster's inventions. Trickster discovers creative fabulation, feigning, and fibbing, the playful construction of fictive worlds. It is trickster who invents the gratuitous untruth. In Northern California, the Maidu creation myth has several creators who collaborate to make the world, including a beneficent Earth-Initiate and a bungling Coyote. At one point Coyote laughs just when Earth-Initiate has warned him not to. Called to account, Coyote says, "Oh no, that wasn't me who laughed." This was the first lie.

HALLMARKS OF TRICKSTER'S MIND

The fish swims through its expansive, watery world and suddenly trickster blocks its passage, makes its world less expansive, less fluid. If the fish itself is tricky, if it has the wit to slip the trap, it will do so by finding a breach in the wickerwork, a rip in the net, an escape hatch its enemy has not noticed. Either way, we have a first mark of trickster's cunning: it closes off a passage to capture its prey, or it finds a hole to elude its foe. It can seize an opportunity or block an opportunity.

I say "opportunity" because there is an old link between that word and the open passage a fish trap blocks. In *The Origins of European Thought*, Richard Onians explains that "opportunity" comes from the Latin *porta*, which is an "entrance" or "passage through." The word is associated with doors and entranceways (portal, porch, portico), and an *opportunus*, then, is what offers an opening, or what stands before an opening, ready to go through. For the Romans, a *porta fenestella* was a special opening that allowed Fortune to enter. The Greek root is *poros*, which is a passageway for ships but also any passageway, including one through the skin, that is, a pore. *Poroi* are all the passages that allow fluids to flow in and out of the body. A pore, a portal, a doorway, a nick in time, a gap in the screen, a looseness in the weave—these are all opportunities in the ancient sense. Each being in the world must find the set of opportunities fitted to its nature. The giant's pathway is often blocked, but bacterial landscapes are almost pure *poroi*. The briar patch is a wide-open field for Brer Rabbit. Darkness is opportunity to the owl and bat, water is opportunity to the fish—until some fish trap blocks the way.

But let us leave these etymological haunts and return to trickster's opportunistic craft. A good example immediately follows "Raven Becomes Voracious" in the Tsimshian Raven cycle. Remember that before Raven acquires his appetite the world is covered in darkness, and that when he arrives in this world to distribute the fish and edible berries, he finds the people distressed by this endless night. He's distressed, too—after all, how will he feed himself if it's always dark? Remembering that there was light in the heaven from which he has come, Raven resolves to return and steal it.

Putting on his raven skin, he flies upward until he finds the hole in the sky. Entering it, he takes off his raven skin and goes to sit by a spring near the house of the chief of heaven. There he waits until the chief's daughter comes to fetch water, whereupon Raven changes himself into a leaf from a cedar tree; the girl swallows him when she drinks the water. She becomes pregnant and bears a child. Her family is delighted; they wash the boy regularly and soon he has grown enough to crawl around the lodge. But all the time he cries. As he crawls he cries out, "Hama, hama!" and the great chief becomes troubled. He summons his wise men to help him quiet the child. One of them understands that the child wants the box that hangs on the wall of the chief's lodge, the box where daylight is kept. They put it on the floor by the fire and the child stops crying. He rolls the Daylight-Box around the house for several days, occasionally carrying it to the door. One day, when the people have more or less forgotten about him, he shoulders the box and makes a dash for the hole in the sky. The family gives chase but before they can catch him he slips on his raven skin and flies down to the earth. There he breaks the box and now, thanks to Raven the thief, we have daylight in this world.

Perhaps all theft is opportunity theft in the sense that where something is protected a thief needs a break or pore in the guard through which to enter and carry off the goods. The hole in the sky that frames this part of the Tsimshian Raven cycle is only one of several such pores Raven finds or creates. For one thing, he slips into the family by finding, as it were, a porous woman and a way to enter her. As a crying baby he then subverts the group's defenses (as con artists sometimes use their children to soften up the mark). All good people are vulnerable to the helpless, unhappy child. If Raven had approached the lodge armed with weapons and demanding the Daylight-Box in a loud voice, he would have had a fight on his hands. But as a helpless babe he is not only welcomed and washed, he is actually given the prize. Trickster, then, is a pore-seeker. He keeps a sharp eye out for naturally occurring opportunities and creates them ad hoc when they do not occur by themselves.

Now let's reverse the picture and come back to trickster as trapper. As opportunism is a part of this cunning, so, too, is the blocking of opportunity, and to block opportunity one needs to create the impenetrable or non-porous, the net so fine there is no way to slip through. Natural history provides many examples of such pore-blocking wit at work. One of my favorites is the method that humpback whales use to trap the tiny fish they feed on. When the humpback whale comes upon a school of herring, it dives deep and then swims in a slow circle, exhaling all the while, so that a cone of bubbles rises through the water. The herring in the school misperceive this "bubble net" as a barrier through which they cannot swim. Having confined the school, the whale then rises through the center of the bubble net, its mouth open and filling with fish.

The octopus has a similar trick, only this one is used defensively. When threatened by a predator, the octopus darkens the water with a jet of ink, turning transparency into a murky, impenetrable, non-porous medium. In both cases, of course, the impenetrability is an illusion. The darkness around the octopus is only an artificial night; the herring are trapped not by bubbles but by their own defenses and perceptive limitations. Still, in each case the artifice suffices.

Trickster himself plays with the porous and non-porous in any number of tales that focus on tunnels and burrowing animals. Remember that the Zulu trickster Thlókunyana is a small being associated with the weasel. In one story, he has moved into the leopard's household, tricked the mother leopard, and eaten her children. Knowing he will eventually be discovered, Thlókunyana makes himself an escape route, a long tunnel with a distant, hidden outlet. When the leopard finally realizes what has happened to her children, Thlókunyana disappears into his hole. The leopard follows, thinking the burrow has a single entrance and Thlóku-nyana will easily be trapped. But before the leopard knows what's happening, wily Thlókunyana has come out his secret exit, doubled back, and set spears around both entrances; when the baffled leopard emerges she is killed. In a common North American version of this "tunnel trick," Coyote lures his enemy into a tunnel, then builds fires at each end—trapping his victim and roasting his dinner at the same time.

The initial trick in all such tales is to have made a burrow in the first place. The rabbit with a hole has a pore in the earth, a self-made opportunity to escape the fox. But the animal with a single-entrance burrow is also in danger of being trapped in its own hole, so the second trick is to dig a second entrance, or a third, or fourth. The Greeks thought the fox the epitome of animal cunning and imagined her dwelling to have seven entrances. But no matter how many entrances, we're still in the land of opportunism, of ever increasing porosity. The third trick, then, is to block the entrances when need be, turning pores into barriers. Just as the Greek *poros* is a passageway, a hole in the skin, so *aporos* is an impassable place, something that cannot be seen through. What Thlókunyana or

Coyote do is to turn an escape route into a trap, a hole into a snare, a *poros* into an *aporos*, a clear medium into an aporia.

In rhetoric and logic, "aporia"—the English word derived from *aporos*—means a contradiction or irreconcilable paradox. To experience aporia is to be caught in a tunnel with a fire at either end, to be bewildered by clouds of ink or encircled by a net of bubbles. No matter how many times you reverse yourself, you're still caught. Aporia is the trap of bafflement, invented by a being whose hunger has made him or her more cunning than those who only think to travel forward through a transparent world.

One mark of trickster's mind, then, is that it exploits and frustrates opportunity. To move to a related but distinct feature—trickster's cunning in regard to doubling back or reversing himself—let us take a somewhat more complicated example of the trap of bafflement. When the baby Hermes steals fifty of his brother Apollo's cattle, he resorts to several clever ruses to hide his theft. First of all, he makes the cattle walk backward so that their footprints give the impression they were walking *toward* the meadow from which they were stolen. Second, Hermes makes himself a pair of tricky sandals, binding to his feet bunches of myrtle twigs and tamarisk, leaves and all. His own tracks are thus hard to read; they seem to point in all directions; they have no orientation. Hermes also zigzags as he walks and perhaps, being Hermes, flies a little between steps so that his apparent stride is strange. Later, Hermes throws his sandals into a river and spreads sand over the ashes of his sacrificial fire. (This is what travelers do to hide their camps; they bury each night's campfire so as to move invisibly on their journey.)

In short, Hermes makes all the signs of his theft hard to find and harder to read. He covers his tracks, obviously, and those he doesn't cover he confuses with what I'd like to call "confounded polarity." Hermes' sandals have no "heel and toe," and therefore seem to go both ways at once, just as the cattle do when they move forward backward. Folklore about foxes has it that a fox, pursued by the hounds, will sometimes run a distance and then double back on its own tracks; when the hounds come to the place where the fox turned they are flummoxed and wander around barking at one another.

With both the cattle tracks and his sandals Hermes similarly confuses or erases polarity. It is as if, lost in the woods, you took out a compass and the needle spun aimlessly instead of pointing north. You could not then get oriented or find a path; you could not proceed. In this way, confounded polarity makes the world unpassable and is a kind of aporia. It blocks all passage by destroying the orientation that passage requires. When Apollo comes upon the tracks that Hermes and the cattle leave, he is stopped in his own tracks, unable to move:

> And when the Great Archer made out the footprints, he cried out:
> "Well, well! This is remarkable, what I'm seeing. Clearly these
> are longhorned cattle tracks, but they all point backwards, toward
> the fields of daffodils! And these others, they are not the tracks
> of a man or a woman, nor of a gray wolf or a bear or lion. And I
> don't think the shaggy-maned Centaur leaves such prints. What
> swift feet took these long strides? The tracks on this side of the
> path are weird, but those on the other side are weirder still!"

Such is the voice of the baffled man caught in a set of cunning reversals.

A scene such as this, with one character tracking another, points back to the earlier discussion of cunning that arises from the tension between predators and their prey. The animal able to read tracks has an invaluable tool in its hunting repertoire, as the animal able to disguise its tracks has a tool for its defense. Moreover, to read a track is an ancient and elemental interpretive act. From a broken twig, the depth of a footprint, a whiff of urine, a bit of fur snagged on a thorn, the hunter infers the presence of a particular animal, infers its direction, speed, size, habits. From potentially cryptic signs, the hunter speculates toward larger meanings. Stories about tricksters and tracking are therefore stories about reading and writing. The tale of Hermes and Apollo, in particular, pits a skilled encoder against a skilled decoder, a wary writer against a cunning reader. The writer makes his tracks lie in hopes of misleading the reader; the reader tries to get at a second or third level of signification so he can figure out what really happened.

Some humor is built into this scene, for normally Apollo is the god who can read a sign. Whenever a bird drops from the clouds, Apollo is the one who notices it and announces the meaning hidden from all less gifted readers. Apollo knows the mind of Zeus; he has prophetic powers; he has his own oracle at Delphi that brings him a handsome little income. In any other tale he would surely be able to read a set of tricky footprints, but this hymn belongs to Hermes, and he seems to be inventing something his older sibling hasn't seen before. The tracks he leaves have multiple meanings, disguised meanings, contextual meanings, ambiguity, a first hint of something that will come forward in the next chapter, the idea that the *Hymn to Hermes* is a creation myth for the mind that is a master of signs.

Seizing and blocking opportunity, confusing polarity, disguising tracks—these are some of the marks of trickster's intelligence. The last of them leads to the final item on this initial list: if trickster can disguise his tracks, surely he can disguise himself. He can encrypt his own image, distort it, cover it up. In particular, tricksters are known for changing their skin. I mean this in two ways: sometimes tricksters alter the appearance of their skin; sometimes they actually replace one skin with another.

The latter may be harder to imagine, so let's begin with an example from natural history. Because the mythology suggests it, I have been deriving each of trickster's tricks from predator-prey relationships; to illustrate skin-changing, let's take a case in which the prey is humankind and the predator is a microbe, *Trypanosoma brucei*, the protozoan that causes African sleeping sickness. This worm-like creature kills thousands of people each year in Africa. It enters the bloodstream through the bite of the tsetse fly and then begins to multiply. Once the invader is detected, the victim's immune system fights back with the single weapon at its command: it produces antibodies specific to the shape of the intruder's skin, or outer protein coat. But this trypanosome can change its skin into as many as a thousand shapes, and the immune system never catches up. Each time it produces an antibody specific to any one skin, *brucei* drops that skin and produces another from its enormous wardrobe. *Brucei* is like a con man at a masquerade; it is not attached to any particular mask or face or persona, but fluidly alters each as the situation demands.

There are many such shifty-skinned or versipellis animals. The flounder, like the chameleon, eludes its enemies by mimicking the sea floor: when it swims in pebbled seas it sports a pebbled back; when it swims in sandy seas it sports a sandy back. In the Greek tradition the creature most renowned for its wily skin is the octopus, which takes both the shape and the color of the rock to which it clings, then reaches out from that mineral disguise to snare and eat its prey.

For the Greeks, skin-shifting versatility was a virtue. The elegiac poet Theognis praises the octopus for its flexibility. It is better to shift one's ground than to stand inflexibly and fight, Theognis says.

> Present a different aspect of yourself to each of your friends. . . .
> Follow the example of the octopus with its many coils which as-
> sumes the appearance of the stone to which it is going to cling.
> Attach yourself to one on one day and, another day, change color.
> Cleverness is more valuable than inflexibility.

Theognis' word for "inflexibility" is *atropia*, or as we might Anglicize it, a kind of non-tropic-ness. "Tropic" means "turning" (the phototropic plant turns to follow light); thus the non-tropic being is unturning, inflexible, fixed in its skin and quite unlike the octopus.

I introduce these lines from Theognis because they offer a neat link between skin-shifting and another way that trickster's shiftiness has been figured. Trickster is polytropic, which in its simplest sense means "turning many ways" (though the Greek *polutropos* is also translated "wily," "versatile," and "much-traveled"). There are three and only three characters in Greek literature who are said to be polytropic: Hermes, Odysseus, and that deceitful Athenian general and Socratic pretty-boy, Alcibiades. Odysseus is named a polytropic man in the first line of the *Odyssey*; Hermes is the polytropic child in the *Homeric Hymn.** As for Alcibiades, Plutarch's *Lives* tells of the time when the Spartans sent orders that he be put to death. Alcibiades discovered the plot and escaped:

> Resorting to Tissaphernes . . . for safety, he was soon first and
> foremost in that grandee's favour. For his versatility [*polutropon*]
> and surpassing cleverness were the admiration of the Barbarian,

---

* Hermes becomes Mercurius or Mercury in Rome and in the Middle Ages. Carl Jung points out that in alchemical texts "Mercurius, following the tradition of Hermes, is many-sided, changeable, and deceitful. Dorn speaks of 'that inconstant Mercurius,' and another calls him *versipellis* (changing his skin, shifty)."

who was no straightforward man himself, but malicious and fond of evil company. And indeed no disposition could resist and no nature escape Alcibiades, so full of grace was his daily life and conversation. Even those who feared and hated him felt a rare and winning charm in his society and presence.

Thus is trickster and thus is the polytropic man, shifty as an octopus, coloring himself to fit his surroundings, putting on a fresh face for each man or woman he meets, charming, disarming, and not to be trusted. (He makes a good politician, especially in a democracy, where many voters call for many faces.)

For the ancients, the ability to change one's skin was not merely a matter of disguise, because the skin was often imagined to reveal the inner being. In some traditions, when a person wished to make it clear that he stood behind his deeds, when he wished to say "my true self did that," he would say, "My skin did that." To be able to *change* the skin therefore raises serious puzzles about identity, the kind of puzzle the immune system faces when trying to identify a trypanosome. If Odysseus can play so many roles, if he can play a part, as Athena once says, "as if it were [his] own tough skin," then who is the real Odysseus? If the Norse trickster, Loki, can appear as a bird, a flea, a horse, and a fire, then who is the real Loki? If Raven can shed his raven cloak and become a cedar leaf, who is the real Raven? It is our habit to imagine a true self behind the shifting images, but it is sometimes difficult to know if that self is really there, or just the product of our imaginings.

Take the hero of Herman Melville's novel *The Confidence-Man*, for example. In the course of that complicated book, a confidence man appears in a series of masks and roles, never as himself. That being the case, can we rightly say he has a self? And if he does, how can we describe that self with any, well, confidence? Melville's hero wears so many seamless masks that many readers find him a little devilish, and consequently read the novel as an allegory: the Confidence-Man is the Devil. I suspect that Melville himself leaned toward that reading at times, but his novel doesn't finally allow it. One can almost as easily make the counter case—that the Confidence-Man is a savior who only seems dark because he must work in a fallen world—and once that's been done, if he might be the Devil or he might be Christ, we must probably admit that his "true self" is hopelessly hidden, or doesn't exist.

Some classicists have argued that a similar problem faces the reader hoping to find the true Odysseus. Pietro Pucci contends that because Odysseus is always manipulating reality, disguising his body and telling lies about his past, he "removes himself from his 'real' self and falls into shadowy and intermediary postures in which he will at once be himself and not himself, true to his temper and disloyal to it." If we presume to identify a real Odysseus behind his fabulations we should at least be aware that the presumption is ours, Pucci argues, concluding that "the disguising scenes [themselves] are what create the illusion of his 'real self.' "

These are difficult cases; identifying the "self" of an animal predator such as *Trypanosoma brucei* may be a little easier because all its disguises serve a single end: they help it feed upon its host. The real self is in the feeding. The real octopus has a constant belly below its shifting skin. But not all shape-shifters have such unitary and identifiable ends. If we find a trickster who has managed to distance himself from appetite, how can we be sure what really moves his reversals? As soon as we begin to think that Melville's Confidence-Man is governed by greed alone, we find him giving away gold pieces. With some polytropic characters it is possible that there is no real self behind the shifting masks, or that the real self lies exactly there, in the moving surfaces and not beneath. It's possible there are beings with no way of their own, only the many ways of their shifting skins and changing contexts.

3

....

THE FIRST LIE

A SIGN OF YOUTHFUL THEFT

As I write these pages a mother cardinal nesting near the house is driving herself nuts pecking at her own reflection in my study window. She is convinced there is another bird there, an interloper, a threat to her nest, her eggs, her territory. If I pull the shade, or even prop a book up against the glass, the reflection disappears and the bird calms down. But some days I forget to perform this small, interspecies favor and now the glass is covered with the greasy smudges of her wing tips, like a script with only two brush strokes, a cryptic testament to the stubborn persistence of her limited brain.

A story we'll call "The Reflected Plums" was once told all over the North American continent. Here is the version in the Winnebago trickster cycle:

Trickster happened to look in the water and much to his surprise he saw many plums there. He surveyed them very carefully and then he dived down into the water to get some. But only small stones did he bring back in his hands. Again he dived into the water. But this time he knocked himself unconscious against a rock at the bottom. After a while he floated up and gradually came to. He was lying on the water, flat on his back, when he came to and, as he opened his eyes, there on the top of the bank he saw many plums. What he had seen in the water was only a reflection. Then he realized what he had done. "Oh, my, what a stupid fellow I must be! I should have recognized this. Here I have caused myself a great deal of pain."

In the Winnebago cycle, immediately following this event trickster fools some mother raccoons into leaving their children alone so that he might eat them. To get the raccoons to leave their young, trickster tells them where the plums are: "You cannot possibly miss the place . . . for there are so many plums there. . . . If, toward evening, as the sun sets, you see the sky red, you will know that the plums are causing it. Do not turn back for you will surely find it." As Paul Radin points out, the joke here is that for the Winnebago "a red sky is the stereotype symbol for death. This is what it should have meant to the foolish women for their children are about to be killed." Trickster is toying with them, offering them a figurative hint as to what is about to happen; they take his language literally, however, and suffer the consequences, just as trickster himself took the reflected plums literally and consequently suffered. As is often the case, we see trickster being simultaneously stupid and clever—one minute taking an image for the real thing, the next teasing others too dumb to hear an image for its layered senses.

Whether or not it is right to say that this story's sequence of events describes trickster learning something, it is right, I think, to say that the story portrays a character living on the cusp of reflective consciousness. Trickster embodies reflection coming into being; in him we see both the need for reflective consciousness (without it he suffers) and the rewards of that consciousness (with it he exploits the world). In addition, we have a narrative in which mental experience (trickster playing with an image) replaces physical experience (trickster actually jumping in the water, hitting his head). We see trickster waking to symbolic life or becoming aware of his own imagination and its powers.

How, in the history of an individual consciousness, does such an awakening come about? More perplexing, how, in the history of the race, did imagination itself emerge? How did mind first acquire the ability to make images and how then did it come to *reflect* on its images? In trickster's case, how did mental fakery come to replace incarnate fakery? What happened between the witless straight man who takes reflected plums literally and the double-talker who says "red sky" to mean "I'm about to eat your kids"?

We cannot take on such questions without pausing to differentiate some things that I have been mixing up. In describing the marks of trickster's cunning, I have been conflating natural history with mental and cultural phenomena. It is one thing for trypanosomes to change their skins; another for Raven to become a leaf floating in spring water; another still for storytellers to have imagined Raven in the first place, or for one of us to reimagine him. Before picking these strands apart, however, we should remember that the mythology itself asks us to confuse them. Coyote stories point to coyotes to teach about the mind; the stories themselves look to predator-prey relationships for the birth of cunning. These myths suggest that blending natural history and mental phenomena is not an unthinking conflation but, on the contrary, an accurate description of the way things are. To learn about intelligence from the meat-thief Coyote is to know that we are embodied thinkers. If the brain has cunning, it has it as a consequence of appetite; the blood that lights the mind gets its sugars from the gut.

Nevertheless, the cunning of animals is not the cunning of Alcibiades. The octopus, the flounder, the trypanosome—each of these creatures has its tricks, but none reflects upon its own devices. The alligator snapping turtle has that clever tongue, but it's a one-trick turtle, never able to fashion new lures for new suckers. As we've seen, even when these creatures lie, their deceptions lack the plasticity of human deceit. The octopus has no choice in the matter; if for some strange reason it would be useful to turn scarlet on a gray rock, it couldn't do it. It is bound to its own reflexes in which gray rocks evoke gray skins. And the feedback system that produced those reflexes is not located in the octopus's mind but in evolution's slow, dimwitted carnage.

That said, let us ask again how, in the history of cunning, the lure tongue gives way to the mind that imagines lures.

As with inquiries into the origin of language, there may be no good way to answer such questions. In earlier drafts of this chapter, I rehearsed some of the ways that evolutionary biologists have tried to respond, but

I always had the feeling that mysteries were being shunted from one area to another, rather than resolved. The strangeness and wonder of reflective imagination seems still to elude the grasp of biological narrative. I suspect it still eludes all narrative. And yet, with humility beforehand, it's hard to resist speculation.

Several places in the trickster mythology itself seem to me to suggest a creation story for the imagination. "The Reflected Plums," as we've seen, implies that the pain of trickster's witlessness moves him toward reflection. To this, let's add a thought-provoking sequence of events from the *Hymn to Hermes*. Remember what happens as Hermes finishes his sacrifice:

> Then glorious Hermes longed to eat the sacrificial meat. The sweet odor weakened him, immortal though he was; and yet, much as his mouth watered, his proud heart would not let him eat. Later he stowed the meat and fat away in the high-roofed barn, setting them high up as a token [*sêma*] of his youthful theft.

Hermes, that is, takes some of the sacrificial flesh and hangs it up in the barn to show what he's done. The *Hymn* calls this meat a *sêma*, which in Homeric Greek means a marker, sign, or token. To reflect a little on what's going on in this scene, we might first decide who is meant to see this sign. For what audience has Hermes posted it? One likely answer is Apollo. After all, later Hermes seems to provoke a confrontation with Apollo, and perhaps, now that his theft has been carried out, he's beginning to advertise.

This makes some sense, but in fact Apollo never does notice the token, and when Hermes leaves it in the barn he is still wrapping himself in secrecy (in the same scene he dumps his trick shoes in the river and hides the traces of his fire). It seems more likely, then, that Hermes is presenting this *sêma* to himself. This is the child, after all, who makes a sacrifice in complete solitude so as to direct a crucial part of it to himself. There is a strong self-reflective strain in this *Hymn*; the god is making a world for himself. Like the writing we do in our journals, some tokens are addressed first and foremost to their maker. Hermes in this case may be creating an image for his own reflection. I'll come back to this point in a moment, but to give it its full weight let's turn to the question of what the token stands for.

The *Hymn* itself tells us the first way to understand it: it's a sign of Hermes' "youthful theft." It has something to do with childhood and with cunning appropriation. Moreover, if this scene describes the invention of sacrifice, if sacrifice is ritual apportionment, and if Hermes' invention is rightly read as a *change* in apportionment, a change in the rules—then the meat in the barn betokens all of that as well. It is a sign of a shift in the order of things, a new wrinkle in the code by which the portions are to be distributed.

Finally, let's not forget that the immediate context of this *sêma* is the pivotal moment in which Hermes desires but does not eat the sacrificial meat. This seems crucial: there could be no meat from which to make a token if Hermes *had* eaten; therefore, the token must carry with it the meaning "meat-not-eaten" and with that the memory of appetite re-strained, the belly denied in favor of something else. In this line it is useful to know that in Homeric Greek the word *sêma* belongs to a group of related words, a semantic cluster that includes the word for "mind" (*nóos*) and verbs that have to do with noticing, recognizing, interpreting, encoding, and decoding. *Nóos* and *sêma* go together; you don't get the one without the other. You don't get a sign without the mental faculty to encode and decode its meanings.

My suggestion, then, is that this "*sêma* of his youthful theft" marks the move from incarnate life (meat one actually eats) to symbolic or men-tal life (meat made to stand for something else). It marks that transition and stands for that transition. Furthermore, marking the move from belly-meat to mental-meat, it marks as well the awakening of the *nóos*, the mind that creates and reflects upon signs. This *nóos* is no flounder-brain with its hard-wired reflexes, but the mind of a mammal without a "way"— one that can step back from the objects of its desire and imagine them. The scene is a little *nóos* creation story in which Hermes, getting wise to the bait, imagines but does not eat the mortal portion.

This trickster tale also tells us several things about how that encoding (imagining, signifying) mind comes into being. First, it implies that *nóos* awakes with restraint of appetite. We do not get a *sêma* until we have the "not" of meat-not-eaten. It should be pointed out that this restraining "not" comes from Hermes himself, rather than any external authority. This is not the psychoanalytic narrative in which a child's acquisition of language coincides with his or her growing sense of parental constraint. Here we get the link between mastery of symbols and a prohibitory "no," but when Hermes' heart says that "no" to his salivating mouth, the constraint is self-made and the mood is one of bright-eyed duplicity rather than loss and guilt.

Such bright-eyed duplicity, in fact, is the second thing the *Hymn* marks about the encoding mind. After all, stolen from Apollo and then used in a sort of Hermetic shell game to change the character of ritual sacrifice, this meat-not-eaten appears as the consequence of a series of cunning subterfuges. In this story, only a thief could have effected the shifts in question; it is by virtue of that thief's duplicity that the meat takes its double or, rather, multiple meanings. In *A Theory of Semiotics*, Umberto Eco has this to say about what makes something a "sign":

> Semiotics is concerned with everything that can be taken as a sign. A sign is everything which can be taken as significantly substituting for something else. . . . Thus semiotics is in principle the discipline studying everything *which can be used in order to lie*. If something cannot be used to tell a lie, conversely it cannot be used to tell the truth: it cannot in fact be used "to tell" at all.

The baited hook, that "first trick" we looked at early on, might make a good example of a sign in this sense. A worm with no hook in it, a worm the fish can eat in safety, has, by Eco's way of thinking, no significance, but the worm that says "I'm harmless" when in fact it hides a hook tells a lie and by that lie worms begin to signify (and fish, if they are smart, will begin to read before they eat). Only when there's a possible Lying Worm can we begin to speak of a True Worm, and only then does Worm become a sign.

We shall return to questions of lying, but first I want to link Eco's definition of a "sign" to the substitutions involved in thieving, and to the duplicity that produces the meat-not-eaten. To begin, I need to say a bit about what Apollo's cattle mean and how they come to have that meaning. The classicist Jean-Pierre Vernant tells us that the cattle of the unmown meadow are somewhat unusual before Hermes steals them: they are neither wild nor domestic; they do not reproduce sexually (and thus have a fixed number); they are peaceful, beautiful, and immortal. Hermes, Vernant says, "takes these cows from the divine world . . . to the world of men, where they acquire domestic status" and where they become part of "the world as it is"; henceforth they live in stables, reproduce sexually, and are slaughtered to be eaten by humankind.

Eco is arguing, it seems to me, that what Vernant has as the cattle's initial meaning—their immortality, and so on—exists only retroactively. If meaning cannot exist without the possibility of substitution, then so long as the cattle cannot be moved from their unmown meadow they cannot mean anything. Conversely, the moment at which they may be butchered and eaten is the moment at which their earlier state acquires its significance. Their meat means one thing on the hoof, another in the fire, and yet another hung in the barn. Hermes-the-Thief moves the meat from one situation to another and by such substitutions it comes to have its significance; it becomes a sign that can "tell" something. Especially in a case like this, where there is a rule against moving the cattle, there can be no signification without trickster's duplicity, and the mind of a thief is the mind most fully able to encode and decode.

That given, let me come back to the idea that *nóos* is also born of restraint. We usually think of restraint as a virtue and when the *Hymn* mentions Hermes' "proud heart" it's hard to get away from the notion that something good is happening—this youngster is maturing, getting control of his impulses, and so forth. That is obviously the case in one regard, but we must not forget that duplicity surrounds the whole endeavor. No one imagines Hermes is about to shape up and become an Apollonian banker. This young god is restraining appetite now in favor of appetite later. Remember again what he says to his mother:

"Why should we be the only gods who never eat the fruits of sacrifice and prayer? Better always to live in the company of other deathless ones—rich, glamorous, enjoying heaps of grain—than forever to sit by ourselves in a gloomy cavern."

In short, we are seeing appetite deferred or displaced rather than any full restraint or denial. As I argued earlier, Hermes has not given up eating; dedicating the smoke of sacrifice to himself, he forgoes the mortal portion so as to feast on a portion that will do him no harm.

• • •

It may be helpful at this point to summarize the ground we have covered and formulate a few conclusions. I ended the last chapter by presenting several ways in which trickster's cunning has been imagined. He knows how to slip through pores, and how to block them; he confuses polarity by doubling back and reversing himself; he covers his tracks and twists their meanings; and he is polytropic, changing his skin or shifting his shape as the situation requires. Natural history offers wonderful examples of each of these. We see this cunning in the humpback whale casting its bubble net, in the fox doubling back to baffle the hounds, in the octopus blending with its chosen rock.

And yet these images fail to catch the full flavor of what we mean by cunning. We are speaking here of a kind of mind, and mind has a plasticity not usually found in the animal world. Odysseus and the octopus are both polytropic, but Odysseus is more so. Like an octopus, Odysseus could put on a rock-colored cloak if he needed to, but the octopus can never, like Odysseus, dress as a beggar against regal surroundings. The octopus does not consider its coloration. Odysseus and those who imagine him, on the other hand, have *nóos*, the mind that can form an image or representation of some sort and "float" it, detached, to be considered and shaped or changed before it is either discarded or acted upon. The story of Hermes hanging his meat-sign up in the barn suggests one answer to how such a mind came to be. Duplicity and deferral of appetite are key to its emergence, the implication being that signification evolved to help this animal slip the trap of appetite or at least better manage its constraints.

However the shift from unconsidered to considered trickery took place, once it has appeared we must reread the stories out of natural history as "just so" stories about cognition and culture. Now, in addition to the fox with its seven-holed lair, we have all forms of mental and social opportunism, from the mind that can sense loopholes in an argument to the pickpockets who hang out around railway depots. Now, in addition to the octopus squirting ink, we have the mind that can hide its assumptions in clouds of rhetoric or spin out opaque mythologies to preserve the barriers of caste and class. Beyond the fox that turns on its own scent to baffle the hounds, we now have the logician's paradoxes and ideologies that conceal their own contradictions. In addition to animals that disguise their tracks and predators that see through the disguise, we now have the encoding and decoding mind, and all the arts of reading. In addition to nature's polytropic beasts, we now have the imagination itself—the mastermind of tropes—and the world of art and artifice, from the bard who weaves a captivating tale to the disinformation officer who floats a cover story to lead an enemy astray.

In short, trickster's cunning now takes on its mental, social, cultural, and even spiritual forms. But it does so with one particular limitation. Earlier, I suggested that if trickster were free of all appetite he would no longer be trickster. In a sense, this is a matter of definition; the mythology we're looking at is constantly gustatory, sexual, and scatological. It seems to require, then, that we connect trickster's inventive cunning to the body's needs. With that in mind, I want to return to a topic we have several times approached, the idea that trickster invents the art of lying, for in this mythology that invention arises precisely where artifice and hunger are knit to one another.

"MERE BELLIES"

The woman next to me leaned back and closed her eyes
and then so did all the others as I sang to them
in what was surely an ancient and holy tongue.
—Tobias Wolff, "The Liar"

Hermes is a day old when he steals Apollo's cattle, and this first theft he follows smartly with his first lie. First theft, first lie: isn't the same sequence of events a part of each of our childhoods? When I was five or six years old, living in England, I stole a five-pound note from my parents' *au pair*. I hid this treasure in a tiny hole in the trunk of a fir tree down by the fish pond. The five-pound note in England in the early 1950s was as big as a handkerchief and must have been printed with richly colored inks, for now as I conjure my wadded hoard to rise from the pool of memory it appears with emerald and ruby highlights. (If they don't want children to steal money, why do they make it so attractive?) There was consternation in the household when this theft was discovered and suspicion naturally fell on my brother and me. As with the time I lit a fire in my wastebasket, I denied everything. I held out as long as I could, but my mother must have brought me around because I remember leading her to the hiding hole. I think I resolved the tension by making up a story about *another* boy, a recent houseguest, whose clever crime I had had the luck to witness. My mother let the improbability pass, and I guided her, with a touch of pride, to the secret depository. The hole into which I had put the note I took to be the home of some small bird; memory's narrative of my theft ends with gem colors lifting from the duff and fibers of that nest.

Such stories border on the mythology of the trickster; perhaps all of childhood does. Who among us in early youth did not sometime steal food or money and then lie about the theft? When we did, what did it mean? Reading mythologically, how should we understand our first transgressions?

For one thing, these crimes play with the possibility of separation from one's elders. At least briefly, there are two worlds, the real one of the theft and the imaginary one of the lie. For an actual child, if memory serves me, this doubling comes with some anxiety. There is the threat of punishment and anger, of course, but beyond that a separation from our parents is a risk because theirs is our only world and we depend upon it. With or without that anxiety, the first lie is a particularly weighted act of imagination. It is a motivated fiction, and a probe into the craft thereof. We may not actually doubt the reality of our parents' world, but still, a lie is a bit of an experiment with its solidity, an artificial world sent out to see if it can blend in and survive. If it can, the authority of the "real" may be shaken slightly and the first lie bring an early awareness of artifice.

Here let me refine an earlier point about lying. I began with Umberto Eco's idea that a sign is something that can be taken as substituting for something else, and I used Apollo's cattle as an example: Hermes switches them from place to place and by these substitutions they begin to signify, first one thing and then another. The idea was that trickster's duplicity is a precondition of signification, a point I qualified by noting that in this case there is a rule against moving the cattle. Without the qualification, we get the general case, which is simpler: "substitution" is the precondition of signification, whether or not thieving is involved. An example will clarify the point and, by contrast, help show why, in this mythology, we get the special case in which thieving and lying are in fact a necessary part of the creation of meaning.

At one point in the *Odyssey*, Odysseus is given a task: he must take an oar and travel inland until someone mistakes it for a winnowing fan. A winnowing fan is a sort of shovel used to toss grain into the air so that wind will carry away the chaff; it looks exactly like an oar. There is a complicated point to this task in the *Odyssey*, having to do with making reparations for an insult to the god of the sea, but what is of interest here is the simpler matter of mistaking one thing for another or, better, the idea that a single thing can have two meanings in two places. The same object is "oar" at the seaside and "winnowing fan" up in some hill town. With that, we see how Traveler-Odysseus is connected to Cunning-Speaker-Odysseus, for only the person who has traveled (in fact or in mind) can realize that the meaning of an object (or a word) is connected to its location or context. Men and women who have never left the village might not know that. Only the polytropic, "much-traveled" mind can know that.

The oar begins to signify as soon as it substitutes for the winnowing fan, a substitution possible because Odysseus can carry the oar from one place to another. It's as if nothing is significant until it's portable; we must be able to move it, in fact or in mind, from one context to another. That motion needs no theft or lie in the case of Odysseus' oar, but Apollo's cattle are another matter. As I argued earlier, the meaning the cattle have in their unmown meadow—their immortality, their asexuality, and so on—exists only retroactively. They can't mean anything until they can be moved from the meadow. The moment at which they show up in another context, butchered, is the moment at which their earlier state takes on its significance. So again we come to the point that *in this mythology* theft is the beginning of meaning. To put it another way, a prohibition on theft is an attempt to constrain meaning, to stop its multiplication, to preserve an "essence," the "natural," the "real." There is no prohibition on carrying an oar inland, so any traveler may multiply its meanings. There is a prohibition on moving the cattle of Apollo; only a thief can make them signify.

Both lying and thieving multiply meanings against the grain, as it were. A lie is a kind of mental imitation of a theft (when Hermes lies about the cattle, he does with words what he did with the cows themselves). A child's first theft and first lie are pivotal in the history of the intellect, then, for with them the child is not just in the world of signification, fantasy, fabulation, and fiction; she is in that world as an independent creator, setting out to make meaning on her own terms, not subject to the prohibitions that preceded her, just as, with his theft and his lies, Hermes sets out to make a cosmos on his own terms. Such is the mythological weight of the first lie. I myself was a failure as a mythic thief and liar, of course; I never leveraged those five pounds into a world of my own design; with my confession I scurried back to a childhood authored by my parents. Though, come to think of it, I never fully confessed. There, too, I told a lie, a secondary fib featuring a second little boy. I see him still, standing near the pine tree with a wooden sword the gardener helped me make.

I am seeking out the mythological meaning of the first lie that trickster tells. If we come at the question from another angle—trickster's relationship to truth-telling—we will be able to link his lies to our initial topic, appetite. At the beginning of Hesiod's *Theogony*, the Muses come down from Mount Helicon and speak to the poet. He's with friends tending flocks of sheep, and the Muses address them with scorn—"Shepherds living in the fields, base objects of reproach, mere bellies!"—and go on to point out how different are those who live on the high mountain: "We know how to say many falsehoods that look like genuine things, but we can also, whenever we are willing, proclaim true things."

The Muses believe that human beings are unlikely to tell the truth because they are "mere bellies," ridden by their appetites. This is an old conceit, well illustrated by several scenes in the *Odyssey*. Visiting the Phaeacian court, for example, Odysseus says that his belly makes him forget his story, and asks to be fed. He doesn't say directly that he will *lie* if he isn't fed, he says he will "forget," but it amounts to the same thing, for the root of "forget" is *leth-*, and to tell the truth is to be *a-lethes*. "If you want me to speak the truth," Odysseus is saying, "you had better tend to my shameless belly."

Similarly, when Hesiod's Muses say they are "willing" to speak truth, the line probably echoes Eumaios, the swineherd in the *Odyssey*, who says that hungry wanderers are "unwilling" to tell true things. The remark comes late in the epic when Odysseus has returned to Ithaca disguised as a beggar. The first man he runs into is this swineherd who tells him that travelers often show up in Ithaca pretending to have news of the lost king, Odysseus. As the swineherd explains it, "Wandering men tell lies for a night's lodging, for fresh clothing; truth doesn't interest them."

Of course Odysseus is in fact the returned king, and he keeps dropping hints to that effect. He even says at one point, "Your lord is now at hand," but the swineherd won't believe him. He asks Odysseus to get serious and tell his "true" story, and Odysseus obliges with a lie. "My native land is the wide seaboard of Crete," he says, and spins a tale full of the concrete, specific detail that liars use to make falsehoods seem like the truth. He ends by saying that he has heard Odysseus will soon return, to which Eumaios replies, "Why must you lie . . . ? You needn't lie to be a guest here." The swineherd rejects as a fabrication the single part of the story that is true. (The recurrent lies Odysseus tells at the end of the *Odyssey* are called "Cretan lies" because he typically begins them saying "My native land . . . is Crete." Cretans were understood to be "lazy bellies" and liars by nature, so Odysseus is hanging a lantern on his own fibs, though—as we shall see—only one of his auditors sees the light.)

The general point here is that, in the Homeric world, travelers and itinerant oral poets were presumed to adjust their tales to fit the tastes and beliefs of a local audience. Sometimes in the *Odyssey* people say a wanderer will always lie because he has a belly; other times they say he will lie until he's fed. Either way, we have again the link the Muses claim between lying and being a mortal who must eat. Conversely (as we saw when speaking of sacrifice), an immortal being is by definition one who is free of the odious stomach; the Muses have it that immortal truths cannot be uttered except by those who are similarly free.

The classicist Gregory Nagy suggests that the Muses' claim to belly-free truth can be better understood if it is set in the history of archaic Greece. Before the eighth century B.C., Greek cities were quite separate from one another; after the eighth century, less so. Before the eighth century, each city would have its own gods and its own poetic traditions, often radically distinct from one another. After the eighth century, Greece was marked by a growing pan-Hellenism—a "surge of intercommunication among the cities"—and with it a muting of differences in tradition and belief.

These two periods bring with them two kinds of poets. On the one hand, when localities differ radically from one another, it is understood that a traveling poet will vary his repertoire as he moves around. If the true and the false shift as the poet wanders, then the poet will be shifty, too. On the other hand, the pan-Hellenic bard hoped to recite, says Nagy, "to Hellenes at large—to listeners from various city-states who congregate at events like pan-Hellenic festivals—and what he recites *remains unchanged as he travels* from city to city."

Odysseus fits the earlier model, the poet who adjusts his song to his setting. When Odysseus is not sure of his position, he tells people what they want to hear. He even lies to his wife when he first finds her among the suitors, "making many falsehoods . . . seem like the truth," until the tears flow down her face. By contrast, we can take Hesiod himself as a model of the later poet; his poems are addressed to pan-Hellenic audiences and attempt to embody values common to all Greeks.

Thus Nagy argues that the opening lines of the *Theogony* "can be taken as a manifesto of pan-Hellenic poetry, in that the poet Hesiod is to be freed from being a mere 'belly'—one who owes his survival to his local audience with its local traditions: all such local traditions are *pseúdea* 'falsehoods' in face of the *alethéa* 'true things' that the Muses impart specially to Hesiod." In this *Theogony*, "the many local theogonies of the various city-states are to be superseded by one grand Olympian scheme."

The tension around which this history is built—variant local truths versus invariant global truths—is not unique to ancient Greece, of course. The story has surely been repeated all over the world whenever travel and contact forced contests of belief upon people who once felt secure in their isolation. To illustrate with a tension from the project at hand, a tricky character in Native American mythology is called Raven on the North Pacific coast, Mink or Blue Jay farther south; on the Plains, the Plateau, and in California he is Coyote; in the Southeast he is Rabbit; in the Central Woodlands he is Manabozho or Wiskajak; the Iroquois call him Flint and Sapling; Glooscap is his name among the Northeast Algonquins. Moreover, he is not the same in each place. Coyote never steals whale fat from any fisherman's hook. Raven makes his parents-in-law young again in an Eyak story from the Copper River delta in Alaska; that story isn't told anywhere else on the continent. In an Ingalik tale from the lower Yukon, Raven becomes the *lord* of the land of the dead, a detail that appears nowhere else on the continent.

Any theorist who comes along and says that a figure called "trickster" unites all these is a bit like Hesiod, making a pan-American tale out of many local stories. Nor is it just modern scholars who work selectively with the tales, highlighting parts that fit the pattern and passing over those that don't. Oral cultures always have. Homer did. Native Americans did for centuries (groups in the upper Yukon reshaped coastal Raven

stories to their own purposes, to take but one example). Wherever travelers carry stories from place to place there will be reimaginings, translations, appropriations, and impurities. Only the new versions won't be
described with those words; artfully told, they will be known as "the
truth."

In this line, Nagy notes that the firming up of a pan-Hellenic theogony
must have entailed the extinction of many local theogonies, and it will
be useful for a moment to imagine the status of the Muses' claim to "truth"
from the point of view of one of those contested or suppressed "local
truths." If you thought that Demeter was the Queen of the Gods, how
does it look to have her subsumed under Zeus' shield (especially by the
misogynist Hesiod)? If Raven was your culture hero, how does it feel to
have him subordinated to some character called Smart-Beaver? From the
local position, the assertion that mountain Muses speak the "truth" may
seem the ultimate falsehood, and the claim that they are free from the
belly just a clever disguise, a rhetorical trick by which lies are made to
look like genuine things. From this point of view, Hesiod's assertion that
his picture of the world comes from beings who do not suffer hunger is
a poet's clever way of masking his own falsehoods.

Moreover, from the point of view of a contested "local truth," what
does it mean to be free of the belly? It could be that those who claim
such freedom are just well fed. The belly is less demanding when there
is plenty to eat, after all, and one is not buffeted by hunger if one is not
regularly hungry. I'm simply saying that it's easier to control one's appetites if one controls the food supply. An old canard has it that self-
restraint is inborn in the ruling classes; it's more likely the case that
aristocrats can appear to govern their neediness because they aren't in
fact needy at all.

In short, the counterclaim to the Muses' scorn of hungry shepherds
would have it that the satiated are the ones who bend the truth to their
own ends. The well fed take the artifice of their situation and pass it off
as an eternal verity. They claim their poets create a bridge to the gods
"that bypasses the Promethean sacrifice, one that does not go through
the belly" (as one scholar says of Hesiod). In the mythology of the trickster, when such claims are made, some "mere" but hungry belly will see
through the artifice and speak, if not the truth, then at least a falsehood
sufficiently cunning to change the way the food is distributed. Or he will
perpetrate thefts and tell lies that not only feed the belly (that's the easy

part) but upset the boundary markers by which the true and the false are differentiated.

"BEAUTIFUL UNTRUE THINGS"

The truest poetry is the most feigning.
    —*Shakespeare*

The mind-boggling falsity that calls the truth itself into question is what interests me here, not the simple counterfactual statement ("I didn't," when in fact I did). Anyone whose lies merely contradict the truth is still part of a game whose rules have preceded him; he or she merely inverts the case, offering not-A in place of A. The problem is to make a "lie" that cancels the opposition and so holds the possibility of new worlds. Let's go back to the *Hymn to Hermes* for an example, a case of lying that muddies the line between the true and the false.

Remember that Hermes' crime spree starts because "he was hungry to eat meat." At the outset, that is, he is a mere belly, an agent of hunger's cunning, and though he doesn't eat he nonetheless later lies in the way that bellies will. For the first of his falsehoods we find him back in his mother's cave, snuggled down in his cradle as if he hadn't been out all night stealing. Here Apollo, who has been searching high and low for his missing kine, discovers the thief and threatens to throw him into the underworld unless he confesses his crime. Hermes, cooing in his blankets, denies all guilt:

> "Why are you yelling like a bully, Apollo? You've come here looking for cows from your pasture? I haven't seen them. I haven't heard a word about them. No one's told me a thing. I can't give you any information, nor could I claim the reward for information.
>
> "Do I look like a cattle driver? A big strong guy? That is not my kind of work. I am interested in other things: I care for sleep above all, and the milk of my mother's breasts, and a blanket over my shoulders, and warm baths.
>
> "I'd advise you not to talk like this in public; the deathless gods would think it odd indeed, a day-old child bringing field animals into the courtyard. You're talking wildly. I was born yesterday; my feet are tender and the ground is rough beneath them.

"Still, if you insist, I am willing to swear a great oath by my father's head, and vow that I didn't steal your cows and that I haven't seen anyone else steal your cows—whatever 'cows' may be, for, to tell you the truth, I only know of them by hearsay."

The straight-shooting god of sunlight and order is momentarily charmed out of his anger: "Far-working Apollo laughed softly then, and said to Hermes: 'My dear boy, what a tricky-hearted cheat you are!'" This is the first of two Olympian chuckles in the *Hymn*, each of which offers Hermes an opportunity to change the world into which he has been born. In this case, Apollo's laugh marks the moment at which he first loosens his grip on the cattle; his laughter melts his righteous anger and a touch of detachment enters.

With such humor, trickster's first lie differs from the way I earlier imagined a child lying about a theft. Trickster feels no anxiety when he deceives. He is often dependent on others, to be sure, but that dependence rarely constrains him. He does not fear separation from his elders and so can tell his lies with creative abandon, charm, playfulness, and by that affirm the pleasures of fabulation. Krishna or Hermes, Coyote or Raven—when one of these speaks his first lie he is the *eternal* child who cannot be significantly damaged and so may cleave to the pure and playful delight of floating fiction in the face of stern reality.

But to come back to the idea that trickster's lies somehow call the truth into question, let me juxtapose Hermes' fibs to those that Krishna tells in a similar situation. In the typical tale of Krishna as a child, his mother Yasoda has to leave the house and tells her boy not to steal the household butter while she's gone. As soon as she leaves, Krishna goes to the larder, breaks open the pots full of butter, and eats it hand to mouth. When Yasoda returns she finds her child on the floor, his dark face besmeared with creamy white. To her reprimands Krishna has many clever replies. He says, for example, "I wasn't stealing butter; there were ants in the butter jars and I was simply trying to keep them out." Or he says that his apparent naughtiness is actually *her* fault: "These little bracelets you gave me chafed my wrists; I tried to soothe the sores by smearing butter on them." For our purposes, however, the most telling reply is this: "I didn't steal the butter, Ma. How could I steal it? Doesn't everything in the house belong to us?" At this point Yasoda, like Apollo, laughs, charmed by her cunning and shameless child.

Our ideas about property and theft depend on a set of assumptions about how the world is divided up. Trickster's lies and thefts challenge those premises and in so doing reveal their artifice and suggest alternatives. One of the West African tricksters, Legba, has been well described in this regard as "a mediator" who works "by means of a lie that is really a truth, a deception that is in fact a revelation." That's how Krishna works, too. When he is the thief of hearts, for example, he disturbs all those who have been foolish enough to think their hearts are their own property, not the property of god. As the thief of butter Krishna upsets the categories that his mother has established to separate him from that food of foods. It is in this sense that his lies subvert what seemed so clear a truth just moments ago. Suddenly the old verities are up for grabs. Who gave Apollo those cattle in the first place, anyway? Who exactly decides how the sacrifice should be apportioned? Who was the original owner of the butter that Yasoda guards so carefully? Who gave all of Pennsylvania to William Penn?

For trickster's lies to provoke doubt in this way, he must draw his adversaries into his own uncanny territory. It is a space ruled by the disarming charm of the very young child. It is a traveler's space where everything is on the road, cut loose from any clear locale. Here the citizens walk their livestock backward and speak a weird reversing language. Krishna's lie belongs to a class of statements that double back to subvert their own contexts. His is cunning or crooked speech because it undercuts the situation from which it takes its meaning. In Greek philosophy it was Parmenides who declared that "Cretans are always liars," but the joke is that Parmenides himself was a Cretan, so the sentence plus its speaker make a befuddlement, an aporia, an inky sea.

The same joke is built into the Cretan lies that Odysseus tells, though, as I said earlier, only one of his auditors gets it. After Odysseus is set on the shores of Ithaca, Athena appears to him, disguised as a shepherd. She asks who he is and wary Odysseus pretends to another identity, inventing a tale to explain why he might be left alone on this shore: he killed an evil man, but had to flee; his shipmates abandoned him, and so forth. The tale begins with the words, "Far away in Crete . . ." and Athena is amused. Her smile is the facial gesture of those who knowingly occupy the space of trickster's lies, for mind itself is amused by these reversals.

Athena's smile, then (like Apollo's and Yasoda's), must also indicate that we are in the presence of that consciousness called *nóos*. The sequence of Cretan lies points to this conclusion. Not long after his conversation with Athena, Odysseus deals with the oafish suitor whom he must defeat to regain his kingdom. He lies to this man, too, but the fellow hasn't a clue what's going on, a point that Homer underscores with the man's name: Antínoös. This man is wholly unable to hear the complexity of Odysseus' words and pays for his deafness with his life. Only *nóos* gives the mental poise needed to navigate in deep ambiguity. Antínoös is little more than fish bait in those seas.

The thieving and lying that initiate the trip into this inky territory give trickster the chance to remake the truth on his own terms. Another look at the *Hymn to Hermes* will illustrate how this might work. As I read the story, Hermes, born in a cave of a secret liaison, is out to change his station in life. To that end, he not only steals the cattle and lies to everyone; once he has gotten their attention, he makes a kind of peace with Apollo. At the appropriate moment he turns on the charm. Taking out his lyre and playing a beautiful melody, he begins "to soften that stern, far-shooting archer," and before long, "bright Apollo laugh[s] for joy as the sweet throb of that marvelous instrument stole into his heart, and a gentle longing seized his listening soul." Hermes sings Apollo a theogony, "the story of the gods . . . how each came to be . . . and how each came to have what now is theirs." I suspect we are meant to imagine this as a theogony of Hermes' own design, a reshaping of old stories, as Hesiod must have reshaped old stories. In addition, I suspect that this new Hermetic theogony includes both Hermes and Apollo in its cast and as such amounts to simultaneous self-promotion and flattery. At the end Apollo is helplessly enchanted, whereupon Hermes gives him the lyre. In return, Apollo "placed his shining whip in Hermes' hand, ordaining him Keeper of the Herds." From now on, this newcomer will "tend . . . the ranging, twisted-horned cattle."

By the end of the *Hymn*, then, Hermes has been made the Keeper of the Herds and, in scenes I haven't cited, much more: he is admitted to the Pantheon, he is an acknowledged son of Zeus, he has been given a share of prophetic powers, he has become the messenger of the gods, the guide to Hades, and so on. None of this would have happened had he confessed guilt when Apollo first approached him. On the contrary, a true confession would have been an accession to the status quo and would have locked him in it forever. Spoken at the boundary of what is and is not the case, however, his lies unsettled and moved that boundary. Thieving and lying were not his only tools, to be sure (he is a charmer and enchanter as well), but the theft and the lie are the crucial first steps.

Moreover, once he has been ordained the Keeper of the Herds, Hermes' profession of innocence seems less like a lie, for when the keeper of a thing takes possession of it he is not rightly called a thief. Hermes might take a leaf from Krishna's book and say, "I didn't steal the cattle; aren't I their Keeper? Don't I carry the herder's whip?" Such is the fruit of that journey into paradox and befuddlement that the first lie initiates. It upsets the polarity between truth and falsity to emerge later with a new polarity, perhaps ("Hermes is truly the Keeper of the Herds"), but one set up with different boundary markers (the herder's whip has been shifted from one hand to another).

I want to back off a little here in order to widen this point and connect it to questions of appetite. All cultures have particular vocabularies that are deployed in paradigmatic patterns, in locally understood webs of signification. We enter such a web when we hear "Raven Becomes Voracious." The Tsimshian have all these terms and characters—intestines, salmon roe, the animal chief, sunlight, the Queen Charlotte Islands, slaves, sea-lion bladders, and on and on—which hang together in a locally felt manner. There is no story about burning the brain of a dead boy, only the intestines; the ancient Raven doesn't fly toward the Islands, only away from them. The terms are knit together in certain ways, not in others. American capitalist democracy has its webs too, of course. Weight loss, natural foods, Valley Forge, atomic power, the family, free trade, white bread: any citizen can spin a narrative of these things that will make sense to any other citizen. The story is always that George Washington didn't tell a lie; the cigarette always has a natural flavor.

Typically, such webs of signification are built around sets of opposites: fat and thin, slave and free, for example, or—more categorically— true and false, natural and unnatural, real and illusory, clean and dirty. What tricksters sometimes do is to disturb these pairs and thus disturb the web itself.

Earlier I showed how any animal that is prey for a baited trap does well to develop the wit to see past the bait. The stories themselves suggest a kind of incrementally growing cunning that ends with a creature smart enough to defer hunger and steal the bait. Now, we see similar cunning in terms of the polarities that organize webs of signification. At the start of the *Homeric Hymn*, for example, Hermes is at one pole of such a set of opposites: he is not-Olympian, not-legitimate, not-the-object-of-sacrifice. He could have settled for that position or he could have settled for simple contrariety (stealing food for the rest of eternity). He does neither. He leaves what Theodore Roethke called "the weary dance of opposites" and finds a third thing. Just as the bait thief turns the predator-prey relationship itself into his feeding ground, so the master liar (thief, deceiver) takes the web of signification itself as the site of his operations. When he does so, that web loses its charm, its magic. After Thlókunyana has stolen the bait from a trap, that trap no longer catches game. After Hermes has told the lie that makes Apollo laugh and played his charming lyre, Apollo's righteousness no longer serves. Yasoda's sense of mine and thine is subverted when Krishna makes her smile.

Once the web has lost its charm, its terms lose theirs; suddenly they seem contingent and open to revision. For those epi-predators who work with the signifiers themselves rather than the things they supposedly signify, language is not a medium that helps us see the true, the real, the natural. Language is a tool assembled by creatures with "no way" trying to make a world that will satisfy their needs; it is a tool those same creatures can disassemble if it fails them.

It is in this line that I understand a remark in Plato to the effect that Hermes invented language. In the *Cratylus* Plato discusses the origins of certain words, especially the names of the gods. At one point he says, "I should imagine that the name Hermes has to do with speech, and signifies that he is the interpreter [*hermeneus*], or messenger, or thief, or liar, or bargainer; all that sort of thing has a great deal to do with language. . . ." He goes on to propose that two Greek words meaning "to tell" and "to contrive" were combined to form "the name of the God who invented language and speech," because Hermes is "the contriver of tales or speeches."

The idea that Hermes invented language seems in accord with the earlier suggestion that duplicity is the precondition of signification. When discussing the token that Hermes makes to honor his youthful crime, I underscored the combination of theft, appetite, and restraint that went into its creation, and I took that stolen "meat-not-eaten" to mark the simultaneous appearance of signs and of the double-dealing mind that creates them. Plato works from a similar intuition: without the wit to deceive, he assumes, one would not have the wit to come up with language in the first place.

The notion that trickster invents language appears more than once in this mythology, though with considerable variation. Sometimes he creates multiple languages to replace a single primal tongue; sometimes he invents the "inner writing" of memory or the "inner language" of self-knowledge; sometimes he invents picture writing or hieroglyphics; and sometimes, as in Plato, he is the author of language itself. A trickster from the Canadian north woods, for example, is said to have been around before human speech and, in ancient times, to have "brought words over" from the animals to human beings. A somewhat more modest claim is the most common of all: what tricksters quite regularly do is create lively talk where there has been silence, or where speech has been prohibited. Trickster speaks freshly where language has been blocked, gone dead, or lost its charm. Here again Plato's intuition—that deceit and inventive speech are linked—holds, for usually language goes dead because cultural practice has hedged it in, and some shameless double-dealer is needed to get outside the rules and set tongues wagging again.

But here I want to pause; a full discussion of speech and speechlessness belongs in a later chapter. I have organized this first part of the book around questions of appetite, and now that I have come to language itself and its webs of signification we are at an outer limit of that hunger narrative. There is a quantum leap between "traps of appetite" and the "traps of culture" that people weave with language; an inquiry into the latter belongs to the sections that follow.

That said, however, let us not forget that appetite brought us this far. We have traveled from the invention of the fish trap to the invention of language, from the alligator snapping turtle luring suckers with its pale tongue to silver-throated Hermes baiting Apollo with charming lies. The point throughout has been to show that the mythology of trickster figures is, by one reading, the story of intelligence arising from appetite. To recall much of the argument so far, remember the image of Raven diving into the ocean to steal fat from fishermen's baited hooks. Set in the tension of predator-prey relationships, tricksters seem by turns wise and witless: Smart-Trickster invents that baited hook, Witless-Trickster would swallow it, and in the give-and-take between those poles other levels of intelligence slowly appear until we get to Even-Smarter-Trickster, the one who has the wit to steal the bait. Raven is that epi-predator who continues to satisfy his needs while managing enough distance from them that he responds to the smell of meat with reflection rather than reflex.

Part of this mythology links that distancing from need to the invention of sacrifice, as if trickster, ensnared in his own intestines, burns a part of them, consciously restraining his hunger in hopes of its later and more durable satisfaction. In some of the stories, trickster seems to have stepped back from instinct as well as need. Wandering aimlessly, stupider than the animals, he is at once the bungling host and the agile parasite; he has no way of his own but he is the Great Imitator who adopts the many ways of those around him. Unconstrained by instinct, he is the author of endlessly creative and novel deceptions, from hidden hooks to tracks that are impossible to read.

This genealogy of trickery brought us finally to questions of lying and truth-telling, to the sort of contingent claims that make up those webs of signification we call mythologies, cultures, ideologies—claims such as "The cattle belong to Apollo," or "There are seven major impulse disorders"; claims like "A modest woman covers her face," "American policy supports emerging democracies," "Hispanics can be of any race," "All men are created equal."

Long ago, Friedrich Nietzsche offered a wonderful way to think of such assertions. The truth, he said in a famous passage, is

a mobile army of metaphors, metonyms, anthropomorphisms, in short, a sum of human relations which were poetically and rhetorically heightened, transferred, and adorned, and after long use seem solid, canonical, and binding to a nation. Truths are illusions about which it has been forgotten that they *are* illusions.

The stories we've been looking at suggest adding a few lines about hunger to Nietzsche's formulation. Trickster lies because he has a belly, the stories say; expect truth only from those whose belly is full or those who have escaped the belly altogether. Not that adding stomachs to Nietzsche's idea changes it significantly, but it may shed some light on the matter of *forgetfulness* that he introduces at the end. To be forgetful of illusion is to be unconscious of it and in these stories it is hunger, I think, that threatens to disturb any such unconsciousness. Hunger prompts "mere bellies" to reveal the fictive nature of illusory truths, as if stomach acid, when it has nothing else to work on, will strip illusion of its protective amnesia. Hunger is the agent of a kind of anamnesis or *un*forgetting that Plato didn't imagine, one that recovers the memory of artifice rather than the memory of eternals. (This is what happens in the *Homeric Hymn*: Hermes is hungry, and he disrupts the supposed eternal order of things.)

But such revelation is only half of trickster's power in regard to "truth." Just as he can slip a trap, then turn around and make his own, so he can debunk an illusion, then turn around and conjure up another (as Hermes does when he sings to Apollo). Where, after all, does Nietzsche's "army of metaphors" come from in the first place, if not from some enchanting mastermind of tropes? And how did it fall into the unconscious? Perhaps that army carries with it some drug or soporific to induce forgetting in the provinces it conquers. In a variant version of the Hermes story, there are dogs set out to guard Apollo's cattle, and Hermes puts them into a stupor. The Greek for "stupor" is *lethargon*, a combination of *lethe* (forgetfulness) and *argon* (lazy or slow). It's the *forgetful* part I wish to mark. When Hermes is ordering the world on his own terms, he takes the watchdogs of the mind—acute, open-eyed, up all night—and numbs them with forgetfulness. Under his enchantment, illusion sinks below the threshold of consciousness and appears to be the truth.

I say all this partly to review the territory we have covered, but also to indicate how that territory opens onto issues that will concern me in the chapters that follow. My project here is not just to derive intelligence from appetite but to think more broadly about the kind of inventiveness that is figured in this mythology, the kind of art, in particular, that might spring from trickster's spirit. In this line there is a long tradition that locates art in that trickster shadowland where truth and falsity are not well differentiated. The idea probably goes back to Aristotle, who thought the epic poets to be Cretan liars of a sort. "Homer more than any other," he wrote, "has taught the rest of us the art of framing lies the right way."

It is an old notion, then, that art and lying share a common ground, one that has had a hardy efflorescence in the modern world. The authors of modern novels have been known to describe themselves with that same language, from Defoe (who was said to "lie like the truth") to Balzac (who said that "fiction is a dignified form of lies") to Dostoevsky (who described *Don Quixote* as a novel in which truth is saved by a lie), down to Mario Vargas Llosa (who once declared: "When we write novels, what we do is create a profoundly distorted manifestation of reality, which we impose on readers, on society. Real literature has never told the truth. It has imposed lies as truths"). Virginia Woolf stirs the same muddy water in her introduction to *A Room of One's Own*: "Fiction here is likely to contain more truth than fact. . . . Lies will flow from my lips, but perhaps there is some truth mixed up with them." Ralph Ellison has said that *Invisible Man* "take[s] advantage of the novel's capacity for telling the truth while actually telling a 'lie,' which is the Afro-American folk term for an improvised story." Even that highly ethical modern poet, Czeslaw Milosz, can be found defending "the right of the poet to invent—that is, to lie."

In the visual arts, Pablo Picasso was the great confounder of the presumed distinction between truth and lies: "Art is a lie that makes us realize truth, at least the truth that is given us to understand. The artist must know the manner whereby to convince others of the truthfulness of his lies." Perhaps the most extended exposition on this theme is found in Oscar Wilde's 1891 essay "The Decay of Lying," an aesthete's defense of art against the service crowd who are always out to impress it into their own private army of metaphors. "The telling of beautiful untrue things is the proper aim of Art," says Wilde, thinking of all those great creations (Milton's Satan, Hamlet, Jane Eyre) who are more real and durable than the perishable women and men we know in fact. Thus Wilde honors Balzac, saying his characters "dominate us, and defy skepticism. One of the greatest tragedies of my life is the death of Lucien de Rubempré. It is a grief from which I have never been able completely to rid myself. It haunts me in my moments of pleasure. I remember it when I laugh. But Balzac is no more a realist than Holbein was. He created life, he did not copy it." Thus might we hope to have great liars at our dinner table rather than trivial pursuers of fact. "The aim of the liar," Wilde writes, "is simply to charm, to delight, to give pleasure. He is the very basis of civilized society. . . ."

Such assertions contain their own puzzles (What does Wilde mean by "*beautiful* untrue things"? How does Picasso "*convince* others"?), but for now I want merely to note where these artists place their work. Many of these statements are hard to understand if we cleave to any simple sense of what is meant by "truth" and "lies." They are easier to understand if such opposites collapse, whereupon we are dropped back into trickster's limbo, where boundary markers shift at night, shoes have no heel and toe, inky clouds attack transparency, and every resting place suddenly turns into a crossroads. These artists, that is to say, claim a part of trickster's territory for their own, knowing it to be one of the breeding grounds of art and artifice.

Be that as it may, in what follows I hope to widen my reading of this mythology by turning more fully to that world of art and artifice. Not that we haven't been there all along. In these pages I, too, have been slowly marshaling an army of metaphors, one I hope to deploy when I need it in pages to come. But I have tried, also, to organize this section around a single and somewhat literal-minded reading of the material. The trickster stories themselves suggest we look to appetite and the natural world for the roots of trickster's cunning, and I have tried to do that. But to the degree that I've succeeded I have sometimes turned myself into Witless Coyote, thinking there are some plums to eat in "The Reflected Plums," or thinking the marbled meat of Apollo's cattle could really make Hermes' mouth water.

It's not that questions of appetite don't lead to an interesting reading, it's just that now that we have seen that Homer is a liar, now that we have come to travelers who multiply meanings as they move, we should be wary of getting too comfortable with any single line of analysis. These stories have as many senses as the contexts of their telling. Their tracks point every which way. Odysseus' oar may also be a winnowing fan, but that hardly exhausts its meanings. Burying the handle of a winnowing fan in a heap of grain is a sign that the harvest is done. Burying a sailor's oar in a heap of earth is the sign that marks that sailor's grave. Maybe when an oar stands over a grave it does come to the end of its meanings, for then the traveler's journey is done. But who would want such closure? "Rabbit jumped over Coyote four times. He came back to life and went on his way."

INTERLUDE

THE LAND OF THE DEAD

In the winter of 1929–30, Archie Phinney went to the Fort Lapwai Indian reservation in northeastern Idaho to record stories told by his sixty-year-old mother, Wayílatpu, a Nez Percé who spoke only her native tongue, no English. In 1934, Columbia University Press brought out Phinney's book, *Nez Percé Texts*, which records about forty of these tales with the native Shahaptian interlined by a literal translation and followed by a free translation.

Phinney includes two versions of a story in which Coyote travels to the Land of the Dead. In the first, Coyote's daughter has been killed and Coyote follows her to the spirit world; he is allowed to try to carry her back to the world of the living, provided that he not look behind him on the way. The second version of the tale, in Phinney's translation, follows.

Coyote and the Shadow People

Coyote and his wife were dwelling there. His wife became ill. She died. Then Coyote became very, very lonely. He did nothing but weep for his wife.

There the death spirit came to him and said, "Coyote, do you pine for your wife?" —"Yes, friend, I long for her . . ." replied Coyote. "I could take you to the place where your wife has gone but, I tell you, you must do everything just exactly as I say; not once are you to disregard my commands and do something else." —"Yes," replied Coyote, "yes, friend, and what could I do? I will do everything you say." There the ghost told him, "Yes. Now let us go." Coyote added, "Yes, let it be so that we are going."

They went. There he said to Coyote again, "You must do whatever I say. Do not disobey." —"Yes, yes, friend. I have been pining so deeply, and why should I not heed you?" Coyote could not see the spirit clearly. He appeared to be only a shadow. They started and went along over a plain. "Oh, there are many horses; it looks like a roundup," exclaimed the ghost. "Yes," replied Coyote, though he really saw none, "yes, there are many horses." They had arrived now near the place of the dead. The ghost knew that Coyote could see nothing but he said, "Oh look, such quantities of serviceberries! Let us pick some to eat. Now when you see me reach up you too will reach up and when I bend the limb down you too will pull your hands down." —"Yes," Coyote said to him, "so be it that thus I will do." The ghost reached up and bent the branch down and Coyote did the same. Although he could see no berries he imitated the ghost in putting his hand to and from his mouth in the manner of eating. Thus they picked and ate berries. Coyote watched him carefully and imitated every action. When the ghost would put his hand into his mouth Coyote did the same. "Such good serviceberries these are," commented the ghost. "Yes, friend, it is good that we have found them," agreed Coyote. "Now let us go." And they went on.

"We are about to arrive," the ghost told him. "There is a long, very, very long lodge. Your wife is there somewhere. Just wait and let me ask someone." In a little while the ghost returned and said to Coyote, "Yes, they have told me where your wife is. We are coming to a door through which we will enter. You will do in every way exactly what you see me do. I will take hold of the door flap, raise it up, and, bending low, will enter. Then you too will take hold of the door flap and do the same." They proceeded in this manner now to enter.

It happened that Coyote's wife was sitting right near the entrance. The ghost said to Coyote, "Sit here beside your wife." They both sat. The ghost added, "Your wife is now going to prepare food for us." Coyote could see nothing, except that he was sitting there on an open prairie where nothing was in sight; yet he could feel the presence of the shadow. "Now she has prepared our food. Let us eat." The ghost reached down and then brought his hand to his mouth. Coyote could see nothing but the prairie dust. They ate. Coyote imitated all the movements of his companion. When they had finished and the woman had apparently put the food away the ghost said to Coyote, "You stay here. I must go around to see some people."

He went out but he returned soon. "Here we have conditions different from those you have in the land of the living. When it gets dark here it has dawned in your land and when it dawns for us it is growing dark for you." And now it began to grow dark and Coyote seemed to hear people whispering, talking in faint tones, all around him. Then darkness set in. Oh, Coyote saw many fires in a long-house. He saw that he was in a very, very large lodge and there were many fires burning. He saw the various people. They seemed to have shadow-like forms but he was able to recognize different persons. He saw his wife sitting by his side.

He was overjoyed, and he joyfully greeted all his old friends who had died long ago. How happy he was! He would march down the aisles between the fires, going here and there, and talk with the people. He did this throughout the night. Now he could see the doorway through which his friend and he had entered. At last it began to dawn and his friend came to him and said, "Coyote, our night is falling and in a little while you will not see us. But you must stay right here. Do not go anywhere at all. Stay right here and then in the evening you will see all these people again." —"Yes, friend. Where could I possibly go? I will spend the day here."

The dawn came and Coyote found himself alone sitting there in the middle of a prairie. He spent the day there, just dying from the heat, parching from the heat, thirsting from the heat. Coyote stayed there several days. He would suffer through the day but always at night he would make merry in the great lodge.

One day his ghost friend came to him and said, "Tomorrow you will go home. You will take your wife with you." —"Yes, friend, but I like it here so much. I am having a good time and I should like to remain here." —"Yes," the ghost replied; "nevertheless you will go tomorrow, and you must guard against your inclination to do foolish things. Do not yield to any queer notions. I will advise you now what you are to do. There are five mountains. You will travel for five days. Your wife will be with you but you must never, never touch her. Do not let any strange impulses possess you. You may talk to her but never touch her. Only after you have crossed and descended from the fifth mountain may you do whatever you like." —"Yes, friend," replied Coyote.

When dawn came again Coyote and his wife started. At first it seemed to him as if he were going alone yet he was dimly aware of his wife's presence as she walked along behind. They crossed one mountain and now Coyote could feel more definitely the presence of his wife; like a shadow she seemed. They went on and crossed the second mountain. They camped at night at the foot of each mountain. They had a little conical lodge which they would set up each time. Coyote's wife would sit on one side of the fire and he on the other. Her form appeared clearer and clearer.

The death spirit, who had sent them, now began to count the days and to figure the distance Coyote and his wife had covered. "I hope that he will do everything right and take his wife through to the world beyond," he kept saying to himself.

Here Coyote and his wife were spending their last night, their fourth camping, and on the morrow she would again assume fully the character of a living person. They were camping for the last time and Coyote could see her very clearly, as if she were a real person who sat opposite him. He could see her face and body very clearly, but only looked and dared not touch her.

But suddenly a joyous impulse seized him; the joy of having his wife again overwhelmed him. He jumped to his feet and rushed over to embrace her. His wife cried out, "Stop! Stop! Coyote! Do not touch me. Stop!" Her warning had no effect. Coyote rushed over to his wife and just as he touched her body she vanished. She disappeared—returned to the shadowland.

When the death spirit learned of Coyote's folly he became deeply angry. "You inveterate doer of this kind of thing! I told you not to do anything foolish. You, Coyote, were about to establish the practice of returning from death. Only a short time away the human race is coming, but you have spoiled everything and established for them death as it is."

Here Coyote wept and wept. He decided, "Tomorrow I shall return to see them again." He started back the following morning and as he went along he began to recognize the places where he and his spirit friend had passed before. He found the place where the ghost had seen the herd of horses, and now he began to do the same things they had done on their way to the shadowland. "Oh, look at the horses; it looks like a roundup." He went on until he came to the place where the ghost had found the serviceberries. "Oh, such choice serviceberries! Let us pick and eat some." He went through the motions of picking and eating berries.

He went on and finally came to the place where the long lodge had stood. He said to himself, "Now when I take hold of the door flap and raise it up you must do the same." Coyote remembered all the little things his friend had done. He saw the spot where he had sat before. He went there, sat down, and said, "Now, your wife has brought us food. Let us eat." He went through the motions of eating again. Darkness fell, and now Coyote listened for the voices, and he looked all around, he looked here and there, but nothing appeared. Coyote sat there in the middle of the prairie. He sat there all night but the lodge didn't appear again nor did the ghost ever return to him.

AN OLD STORY

Some years after I began to think about tricksters, I sat down to write a short description of what I hoped would be the central themes and shape of this book. At the time I had been browsing in Homeric hymns other than the one to Hermes and when I finished the proposal I appended as an epigraph a line spoken by Apollo in the hymn that tells his story:

> *"The Muses sing of the sufferings of men . . .*
> *How they live witless and helpless and cannot*
> *Find healing for death or defense against old age."*

It was late winter at the time. My wife and I were living in a rented house near the Cape Cod light in North Truro, Massachusetts, and when I finished typing I walked out into the constant wind and stood at the edge of the high scarp over the Atlantic, relieved for having written out the shape of the book at last, but feeling some sadness or fatigue, too, triggered by Apollo's scornful voice and woven into the project in ways I didn't understand.

Not long thereafter, I dreamed that I retrieved a dead child from the underworld. Up into the darkened central hallway of a middle-class home

I carried the shade of some woman's baby. I was in a rage at this woman. I saw my hands close around her beautiful throat just before I woke, tense and shaken.

My family moved to England five years after the end of the Second World War. In London, bright flowers, called fireweed, bloomed in the open cellar holes of bombed buildings. My parents brought with them a 1949 Chevrolet with green fenders thick as dinner plates. "The dollar was strong," and the grounds of the house we rented in a village outside London included a tennis court, an apple orchard, a playhouse with leaded diamond windows, and a bomb shelter, inside of which the gardener forced rhubarb and on top of which sat the landlady's two marble Buddhas, which my brother and I chipped at with a hammer for their fabulous flakes of soapy white stone.

When I was five, my parents had a third child, Edith, born in December of 1950. Twenty months later, she died. A mosquito bite had infected her with the trypanosome that causes the encephalitis they then called African sleeping sickness. One afternoon she began to cry inconsolably, then fell into a coma. During the week or so she lived, I was allowed to go once with my parents to visit her in the hospital. I can still see her lying on the white bed, her lips moving in an odd reflexive way, as if sucking. As I watched, her lips stopped moving and I secretly thought perhaps I had seen her die. At the funeral my older brother Lee wept but I did not. I was jealous of his tears, but felt none of my own. I heard them say I was "too young to understand," whereas Lee "loved Edith very much." After the funeral we sat in the Chevrolet by the churchyard while adults leaned toward the windows to talk to my parents. After that, Mother would sometimes rise from the dinner table, twisting her napkin in her hands, and walk into the darkened living room, Father following behind. Lee and I broke out with boils; I had one on my right calf that soaked its loose white bandage with pus. We were sent away for a while to stay with some woman who owned a guitar, which, if I did not leave the couch where it lay, I was allowed to strum.

I have sometimes imagined that an early experience of death turns a soul toward art. Reading that Flannery O'Connor's father died when she was young, I thought, yes, no wonder she gave herself to those remarkable fictions of loss and redemption. I realize this is simpleminded—no one

claims such vocational causes when death marks the childhood of su-
permarket managers or auto mechanics. But it is *my* simplemindedness;
in my story, death and art have run in tandem. Long after those years in
England my mother, reminiscing, once said to me, "After Edith died I
needed a baby, and you were there." I think we fell into a silent reciprocity, she and I. In return for her renewed attentions, I set out to relieve
her of her sorrow. I became her willing anodyne, and whatever talents I
had in terms, say, of reading subtle signs of grief and pleasure, I gave
over to that end. In retrospect at least, to see how my unconscious choice
of that epigraph in Apollo's mocking voice was followed so quickly by
that dream leads me to wonder whether my adult attentions were not still
bound up in that task, as if at this remove of years I still hoped that the
exercise of my talents might somehow lift Edith's soul from the grave and
return it to sunny England with its lupines in spring and its young queen.

Surely the old sorrow of all this was present as I stood in the wind
that evening, but I now think it was mixed as well with the sentimentality
of a grown man still attached to the child's grandiose mission even as he
longs to be quit of it. The dream, at least, picks up the latter theme and
elaborates it with a vengeance. The situation is adult, sexual (that beautiful throat), and I am in a lethal rage at the woman I have tried to help,
as if when Orpheus walked into the sunlight and turned to look back at
Eurydice it was not doubt that moved him, but resentment. Who is she
to have made him charm old Charon with song, and pacify that three-
headed dog guarding the distant shore? Who is she that he let his art be
drawn into this hopeless enterprise? And yet to imagine this Orpheus-
resentment is to dwell on the anger of the dream, and that seems the
wrong tack, for the anger, after all, wakes me up. Some change of consciousness seems to be called for, some jump in the narrative. Perhaps
there is resentment in the Orphic stories, but the makers of those stories
knew a wider range of feeling than that. In the parallel Coyote story,
when Coyote's impulsiveness sends his wife's spirit back to the Land of
the Dead, the death spirit scolds him: "You inveterate doer of this kind
of thing! . . . Only a short time away the human race is coming, but you
have spoiled everything and established for them death as it is." The
makers of that story knew death as it is, not as we might wish it. They
knew we live in Coyote's world, where sexual impulse and mortality are
one thing, not two. The dreamer who must wake from the dream in anger
does not know this, for he has tried to do what Orpheus never did, what

Coyote never did. Nor can that dreamer find a way out of the plot he's put himself in, at least not so long as he stays inside his dream.

In the coal fields of West Virginia there are abandoned mines—their entrances long closed, the nearby towns long impoverished—that have caught on fire. These fires are impossible to put out; slowly they burn through the seams of coal, thirty or forty years. How wonderful if the writer of a book should happen on a topic with such longevity! At times he'll wish he'd picked some simpler theme, something he could strip-mine in a season, or something that would flash up and die down in a matter of months so that he could publish and get on. Get on with what, though? Better to be enveloped in a matter that darkly feeds itself with hidden fires; better not to know fully where the veins of fascination lead, but to trust that they will slowly give up their heat in recompense for attention paid. Certainly, in considering my topic again with these memories and reflections in mind, I find that they inform one another in several ways. For one thing, I realize that framing my project with Apollo's voice indicates some confusion of purpose, for it was not Apollo, nor those above-it-all Muses, who drew me to this work, but a figure much more earthy. To feel the call of those lofty voices is to be drawn into their scorn, which means to turn against this world, where humans die the way they do. To respond is to hope once more that the dead might return. Small wonder, then, that trying to work out my themes had left me feeling sad and spent, for in my confusion I was working still on a task not really my own (it was my mother's grief, not mine), and impossible besides.

I had forgotten, in other words, that Hermes begins by setting himself against Apollo, that tricksters in general begin by muddying high gods. Returning to such lowliness shifts the work away from idealist or Apollonian artistry (and its effort) and toward some trickster artistry (and its playfulness). Trickster's style is not so heavy, not so elevated. At the meal after the funeral, he makes the first off-color joke. Moreover, to work in his spirit is to be less obedient to "the parents," less likely to be drawn into their tasks. When Hermes returns from his night of thieving, his mother chastises him; she has a clear image of what he is and, by implication, an image of what she'd prefer him to be. But her preferences do not move him. Like the story of the baby Krishna, the *Hymn to Hermes* imagines an infant so fully independent that he never plays a part to please his parents, never puts on a mask his elders have designed. In the story about Coyote going to the Land of the Dead we might get the feeling that a "proper" Coyote would have been able to contain his impulses, but the story is no argument for propriety. It is surely sad when his desires escape him and disaster follows, but it would have been sadder had he contained himself, as it is sad whenever men or women become so well behaved that no "joyous impulse" ever disturbs their lives.

In all this, trickster stories are radically anti-idealist; they are made in and for a world of imperfections. But they are not therefore tragic. After his trip to the Land of the Dead, Coyote is left alone and weeping, but his wider story does not end on that note. In fact, it may be exactly because these stories do not wish away or deny what seems low, dirty, and imperfect that their hero otherwise enjoys such playful freedom. Trickster is the great shape-shifter, which I take to mean not so much that he shifts the shape of his own body but that, given the materials of this world, he demonstrates the degree to which the way we have shaped them may be altered. He makes this world and then he plays with its materials. There is the given of death, the given of waterfalls and sunlight, of sleep and impulse, but there is also an intelligence able to form the givens into a remarkable number of designs. There is no healing for death, but it does not follow that humans must "live witless."

Still, it is the wit to reshape the story that seems unavailable to the frustrated dreamer of my dream, a man trapped in a tale that no longer serves, one he cannot escape—at least not until he wakes, not until some Guide of Souls, some psychopomp, comes along to help him cross the line, out of that dream where the stuff of a life (dead baby, grieving mother, grown man's art) seems so tightly knit together, and into a shiftier consciousness where old stories fall apart so that new ones may form from the fragments. (Maybe that isn't Edith's soul the dreamer retrieves; maybe it's the baby Hermes, or a child of my own, or a returning portion of my youth; maybe it's the "baby, baby" in an old blues song . . .) The Guide of Souls who allows a plot to be deeply rearranged is rarely an obvious actor in the story at hand, for durable stories are self-containing, self-defended against change and fragmentation. The high gods set guard dogs around their sacred meadows. If there is to be a change, its agent will have to hypnotize those dogs and slip in from the shadows, like an embarrassing impulse, a cunning pathogen, a love affair, a shameless thief taking a chance.

PART TWO

TWO-ROAD CHANCE

4

....

AN ATTACK OF ACCIDENTS

The gods' carefree life [is] dedicated to aesthetic pleasures. . . . On
account of this one-sided dedication to their own pleasures, they forget
the true nature of life, the limitations of their own existence, the
sufferings of others, their own transiency. They do not know that they
live only in a state of temporary harmony. . . . They are gifted with
beauty, longevity, and freedom from pain, but just this lack of
suffering, of obstacles and exertion, deprives the harmony of their
existence of all creative impulses.
—A. Govinda

Several stories in the following chapters will feature tricksters once
again stealing food, but it seems a little forced to say that traps of
appetite are what's at stake. As we saw earlier, when the genealogy of
hunger's cunning arrives at the invention of language and lies, the narrative takes a quantum leap. Just as Coyote cannot eat plums until he
realizes the reflected image is not the thing itself, so listeners to that story
cannot get its full sense until they see that it doesn't necessarily contain
any plums, or coyotes for that matter. Sometimes a stomach is just a
stomach, but rarely. Questions of appetite necessarily shadow my argument for the rest of the book, but the field of inquiry must widen if we
are to get an accurate portrait of the intelligence that allows this wandering, hungry, no-way being to make his home in this world.

The rest of the book is therefore organized around themes that are at
once central to the trickster myth, exemplary of the sort of imagination
figured there, and present among us to this day. I begin with chance and
accident. Wandering aimlessly, trickster regularly bumps into things he
did not expect. He therefore seems to have developed an intelligence

about contingency, the wit to work with happenstance. From the point of view of his more settled neighbors, his aimlessness makes him an embodiment of uncertainty—no one knows when he'll show up, or how he'll break in, or what he'll do once he has arrived. Not surprisingly, the stories exhibit some tension around this issue, for these more settled neighbors often tire of trickster's disruptions and set out to bind or suppress him. That turns out not to be so easy, and to have unexpected consequences.

Our main sources for Norse mythology are *The Poetic Edda* and *The Prose Edda*, the former being a collection of Icelandic poems, some dating back to the early years of the Viking Age (as early as 850), and the latter being a book written around 1220 by an Icelandic aristocrat named Snorri Sturluson. (There is debate over what "Edda" means, but it has come to signify a collection of traditional poetry.) The Eddas contain two key moments in which the trickster Loki threatens the Norse gods with old age and death. The first begins and ends quickly. It seems that Loki was once captured by a giant (disguised as an eagle) who agreed to free him on condition that he promise to go to the goddess Idunn ("The Rejuvenating One"), who tended the orchard where the Apples of Immortality grew, and bring her and her fruit out of the Asgard (the gods are Aesir, their home Asgard). In Snorri's version:

> At the time agreed on, Loki enticed Idunn out from Asgard into a wood, telling her that he had found some apples she would prize greatly and asking her to bring her own with her for comparison. Then the giant . . . came in the form of an eagle, and seizing Idunn flew away with her to his house. . . .
> The Aesir . . . were much dismayed at Idunn's disappearance, and they soon grew old and gray-haired.

In later Norse mythology, Loki will take on a more devilish cast, but in this tale he is a mere mischief-monger. When the gods confront him with what he's done, he willingly repairs the wrong, changing himself into a falcon and stealing Idunn back from Giantland.

To reflect on this brief moment of disruption and repair, it helps to know that the Norse gods have a variety of supernatural creatures beneath them (dwarfs, elves, norns), but their greatest enemies are the giants.

Furthermore, though Loki sits among the gods, in many ways he is intimate with these threatening underlings. His father was a giant, for one thing, and though he has a devoted wife, it is by a giantess that he fathers his children. In these and other ways, Loki seems to be a point of contact where giants touch the gods, and thus it makes a certain sense that through Loki a giant manages to expose the eternal ones to time. When Loki tricks Idunn, he breaches the wall around Asgard and two worlds briefly come together. Loki is the creator of that threatening contingency.

A s I say, the ability to create or work with contingency I take to be a mark of trickster's intelligence. To speak of "contingency" or "coincidence" usually connotes a more or less *meaningless* convergence.* It was "just" a coincidence, we say, a "mere" contingency, and by these diminutives we mark our sense that no deep significance, no real meaning, is present. The same import lies behind a classic use of the word "accident." In the *Categories*, Aristotle argued that we ought to be able to look at any group of things, say "apples" or "human beings" or "jazz recordings," and determine what is essential to membership in the category and what isn't. A human being, for example, must have an animal body, that is essential (bronze statues are not human), but it makes no difference whether a person's hair is brown, black, or gray. A human being's hair color is not an essential, it's an accidental. An apple is a fruit, that's essential, but whether it's ripe, green, bruised, wormy, on the tree, or in a bag—all this is accidental. Accidentals are present by chance, essentials by design. Accidentals are changeable and shifting; essentials are stable. The real significance of a thing lies with its essences, not with its accidents.

It may be relatively simple to define the category "apple," but complexities soon spring up with any more markedly cultural term. Jazz, for instance, is an African-American music: is the "blackness" of the mu-

---

* Both "contingency" and "coincidence" contain the image I have just suggested, that of two things coming together. The Latin roots of the former (*con-* + *tangere*) denote two things "touching"; the roots of the latter (*co-* + *incidere*) indicate two things "falling together." (The Latin root of "accident" is *accidere*, to fall to, which comes from *cadere*, "to fall," which turns up in English as "chance" by way of Italian *cadenza* and Old French *chéance*.)

sicians essential to a jazz recording? Racial categories are famously difficult to establish for many reasons, not the least of which is that the races can mix. There being no natural boundaries, what is the essence of "white" or "black"? In America, where social formation depends so heavily on these designations, the bizarre fiction developed that "one drop" of "black" blood consigns an individual to the category "black." One drop makes the essence; fifty drops of "white" blood are accidents. Or take the category "American." After it became clear that American citizens had bombed the Federal Building in Oklahoma City in 1995, a member of Congress gravely pronounced that they "were not Americans," as if building a bomb were essentially not-American, despite a famous history to the contrary.

More to the point for matters of creative intelligence, the complexity of this play between accidents and essences is well illustrated with examples from the arts. Early in his career the American composer John Cage started to question how we differentiate between "noise" and "music," and from that time on, a good part of his efforts went toward allowing supposedly non-musical sounds to enter his compositions. In fact, Cage defines modern art as art which cannot be disrupted by non-art. It is permeable, open at its edges. A baby's cry at a classical music concert is usually a distraction, a noise, a bother. Cage lets it be part of the event, just as some modern painters have let the dust that settles on their canvases become part of the painting (a famous example is Marcel Duchamp, who let his *Large Glass* gather dust for months, then fixed a portion of it with varnish). Put in a slightly different language, Cage takes coincidence seriously (or, rather, he lets it amuse him, lets it be a muse).

To the classic sensibility, the cry at the concert or the dust on the canvas are accidents; they just happen; they aren't the real event. They are impurities, and have no beauty. The noise of the baby and the music coincide, but not in any meaningful way, and if the cry could be erased from a recording of the concert, so much the better, for without that noise the listener gets the "true" event.

To all such assertions Cage might reply with the following anecdote from his book *Silence*:

George Mantor had an iris garden, which he improved each year
by throwing out the commoner varieties. One day his attention

was called to another very fine iris garden. Jealously he made some inquiries. The garden, it turned out, belonged to the man who collected his garbage.

Every category must have its rubbish heap. For the classic sensibility, the problem is to keep the rubbish at a distance, for difficulties will arise if it returns, especially if it comes back with a plausible claim to having been falsely excluded to begin with. If the irises in the garbage are beautiful, then beauty itself is contingent, and not some still point in eternity. If "noise" is suddenly music to my ears, then the acoustical seal around the music hall is broken.

The point is simply that calling something a "mere accident" begs or suppresses the question of significance. Who's to say the rain on the roof of the concert hall is not a part of beauty? Why is a single drop of black blood so powerful? Why not say one drop of white blood makes a person white? If jazz is a black music, what color was Bix Beiderbecke? Or, to come back to one of my opening examples, why not say, as many religions do, that the animal body is an accident, that the soul is the essence of a human being? In creating cultural categories we give shape to this world, and whoever manages to change the categories thus changes the shape. One kind of creative perception is always willing to take coincidence seriously and weave it into the design of things.

A story from the novelist Leslie Marmon Silko:

When I was a little girl and we lost a beloved dog or cat, often strays which people dumped out along Highway 66 would come to us. My father always told us that these strays knew we had just lost a cat or dog and that's why they came. It was a little strange how that used to happen, but coincidence is what you'd have to call it.

A story from science:

In 1978, at the U.S. Naval Observatory, James Christy was working on describing Pluto's orbit. One of his photographs showed an elongated image of the planet; he was about to discard it when he came upon another photo in the archives labeled: "Pluto image. Elongated. Plate no good. Reject." Christy made a collection of such plates and in this way discovered that the elongation was not an accident: Pluto has a moon.

More conservative minds deprive coincidence of meaning by treating it as background noise or garbage, but the shape-shifting mind pesters the distinction between accident and essence and remakes this world out of whatever happens. At its obsessive extreme such attention is the beginning of paranoia (all coincidence makes "too much sense"), but in a more capacious mind it is a kind of happy genius, ready to make music out of other people's noise. Either way, the intelligence that takes accidents seriously is a constant threat to essences, for in the economy of categories, whenever the value of accident changes, so, too, does the value of essence.

L et's return, then, to the Loki story and the idea that he creates a threatening contingency when he allows giants to get hold of the Apples of Immortality. Eternal, divine, and heavenly, the Aesir belong to an elevated category of beings, one from which the giants are excluded. A wall around Asgard assures the distinction. From inside that wall, giants appear to be transient accidentals. But this way of dividing up the universe doesn't sit well with all concerned. That the giants constantly pester the borders of Asgard indicates there's some resentment among the accidentals. Why exactly are they not invited to eat those apples? Why must they be trapped in time? Loki is not unsympathetic to such questions, not just because his family includes giants, but because the Aesir sometimes treat him, too, as if he did not belong among them. Treat someone that way and you will foster skepticism about the shape of things.

Here it will help to note that the language of essence and accident always contains a temporal dimension: accidents happen in time, essences reside in eternity. When Loki orchestrates the coincidence of giantland and godland, the wall between the temporal and the eternal leaks at the point of contact, which is to say the transients get a taste of immortality apples, while the eternals get a taste of time. The gods grow old and gray after this attack of accidents. Change has entered heaven itself, everything is in flux, and a great shape-shifting seems entirely possible.

But it doesn't happen. Something truly new might have emerged from that uncanny coincidence in which time and eternity contaminate and fertilize each other, but no, the whole thing was just mischief. Loki quickly repairs the damage. When he brings Idunn back to Asgard, one of the giants gives chase; the gods build a fire at the Asgard wall and burn him to death. So much for that taste of immortality. The wall is sealed again, and the good-for-nothing drifters of time no longer threaten the eternals (though it should be said that the eternals will be a little more alert after this event; Loki keeps them lively).

No permanent harm is done, then, but the story nonetheless indicates Loki's potential as a cataclysmic change-agent, a capacity we find starkly realized in a later story having to do with the death of the god Baldr. Baldr is the Pure One of the Norse pantheon. Handsome and good, he is associated with the sun ("so fair of face and bright that a splendour radiates from him"). One day, however, Baldr begins to be troubled by nightmares indicating some harm will come to him. His mother Frigg therefore sets about exacting an oath from everything in heaven and earth—from men and beasts, from fire and water, from metals and stones—not to harm Baldr. When everything in heaven and earth has so sworn, it follows that the assembled Aesir amuse themselves by throwing things at their invulnerable companion, watching their darts and arrows drop before they touch his shining body.

All this annoys Loki, who disguises himself as a woman and quizzes Frigg as to the details of her oath-taking. In this way he discovers that she has, in fact, omitted one item. "West of Valhalla," she says, "grows a little bush called mistletoe. I did not exact an oath from it; I thought it too young." Loki immediately shapes a dart from the wood of the mistletoe and, finding the assembled gods throwing their weapons in sport at Baldr, approaches one of them, Hod, who stands doing nothing at the edge of the group. "Why are you not honoring Baldr as the others are?" Loki asks, and Hod explains that he is blind, "and besides, I have no weapon." Loki gives Hod the mistletoe and guides his hand. The dart goes straight through Baldr and he falls dead to the ground.

Much follows upon this tragedy. The gods try to recover Baldr from the underworld, but fail. They capture and punish Loki, binding him beneath the earth with cords made from the guts of one of his own children. They set a snake to drip venom on him for all eternity, though Loki's wife, Sigyn, is allowed to hold a dish and catch the dripping poison. Every so often she must leave to empty the dish, and then Loki writhes in pain as the drops hit his face. The periodic writhing of Loki beneath the earth we now call earthquakes.

As far as I know, none of the Norse literature says that what happens next in these legends happens *because* Loki has been bound, but the sequence of events is always the same and so the cause and effect is always implied. The gods' binding Loki is always followed by the prophecy of Ragnarök, the doom of the gods.* First will come three terrible winters with no summers between them; brothers will kill one another for greed; one wolf will swallow the sun, another the moon. The stars will vanish. All fetters and bonds will be snapped, including the cords that hold Loki to his stone. Released, Loki will pilot an assaulting ship made from the unclipped fingernails of the dead. Odin will battle the wolf Fenrir, Thor will battle the Midgard Serpent, Loki will battle the watchman Heimdall, and all these will die. Fire will consume the heavens and the earth, and mortals and immortals alike will perish.

The prophecy, however, does not end there, for the world is born again, refreshed, from this apocalypse. Two humans will have survived and will repeople the earth, the daughter of the sun will light the sky, and the gods will reappear. In one of the oldest of the Norse poems, the *Voluspá*, we hear the voice of a woman prophet:

> *I see the Earth rise from the deep,*
> *green again with growing things. . . .*

> *The unsown fields will bear their crops,*
> *all sorrows will heal, and Baldr will return.*

• • •

---

* In Icelandic, the gods are called *reginn*, which means "organizing powers." *Ragna-* is the possessive plural of this word. The suffix *-rök* means "marvels, fate, doom." *Ragnarök* thus means "the gods' wonders" or "the gods' fate/doom." R. I. Page, from whom I draw this etymology, says that the second half of the word has become confused with *røkkr*, "twilight," and it is often translated as such, as into Wagner's German: *Götterdämmerung*, "twilight of the gods."

A t this point I want to widen my focus so as to show that the plot of the Loki story appears on yet another level in the Norse setting.* My claim is that the prose *Edda*, the thirteenth-century source for much of the Norse material, is itself an agent in a historical drama of disruption and repair. To see how this might be, consider that in ancient times the deadly weapon Loki discovers, the mistletoe, was used ritually in a manner suggesting that the drama of Loki and Baldr once mirrored the solar or agricultural calendar. It was the custom in northern countries to gather mistletoe at Midsummer's Eve, that is to say, at the summer solstice, the point in time when the sun reverses its course and spends the rest of the year dropping lower and lower toward the horizon. In ritual, then, picking the mistletoe "causes" the sun's decline, just as, in myth, Loki's discovery of that green weapon causes the death of Baldr the Bright.†

By the thirteenth century, however, when Snorri Sturluson wrote his prose *Edda*, the Norse world had changed so dramatically that the stories about gods growing old or dying had taken on new meaning. Snorri was an influential Icelandic farmer, a diplomat, and a speaker in the Icelandic parliament. A learned and cosmopolitan man, he knew the Bible well; he knew saints' lives and other Latin works; he knew about the *Odyssey*. (In fact, he thought the Norse gods were actually descendants of Priam of Troy, powerful kings who had come to be worshipped by ignorant people; at the end of one book he even suggests that Loki is the local name for Ulysses!) Most important, Snorri was a Christian, Christianity having come to Iceland over two hundred years before he wrote his *Edda*. He was a careful scholar and antiquarian who did not believe in the

---

* Another trickster story echoes key details of Loki's career. In Chinese legend, Taoist Immortals have an orchard where their Peaches of Immortality grow. The trickster Monkey invades that sacred precinct and eats the peaches, whereupon angry Taoists capture and bind him, though in fact they cannot do it without the help of the Buddha, who traps Monkey beneath a mountain. There he stays until the Buddha releases him, five hundred years later, so he may help lead a journey to the West (to India from China) in search of scriptures. My analysis of this story is similar to what I have to say in regard to Loki, so I have placed both the telling and the commentary in an appendix.

† The great resistance to change in the Norse myth, and the gravity of the subsequent apocalypse, may be connected to the fact that the story comes from the far north, where the sun actually disappears from the sky in winter as if devoured by wolves. This is a myth for cold climates, where the sun's fortunes are regularly, seriously, and unhappily reversed.

heathen gods and warned his readers against such belief. As one of his translators puts it, he "makes it clear that . . . the pagan religion . . . was a rational but misguided groping towards the truth."

The prose *Edda* is a transition document, then. Snorri is interested in preserving themes and devices from the old oral poetry, but he undercuts the old gods even as he offers them to the reader. His main rendering of the old myths is called *Gylfaninning*, "the tricking of Gylfi," and presents the entire Norse corpus as an illusion foisted upon one King Gylfi, a traveling Swede. The narrative delivers the stories as "deceptive appearances," a conceit that would have been unthinkable in any earlier age of Viking belief. Consequently, as others have pointed out, there are really two eras of Norse mythology, and two Lokis, the Christian lens having turned Snorri's Loki darker and more demonic than the Loki who inhabits the earlier poems. When Snorri says that Loki is the "father of lies," an epithet that does not occur in the poetic *Edda*, he doubtless knows that this is what Christians call Satan.*

The point is simply that when Snorri Sturluson recounts "the fate of the gods" or "the theft of Idunn's apples," he is presenting stories of gods *who have in fact died.* These are no longer narratives that reflect an endlessly repeated agricultural cycle; we are now in history, hearing about a group of eternals who have suffered the accidents of time, grown old, and departed from the hearts of the faithful. After Snorri, the Norse apocalypse is a historical fact. And if for the thirteenth century the old stories record a "misguided groping towards the truth," then Baldr's post-apocalyptic rebirth no longer reflects the cycles of nature—it portends the historical coming of Christ. Snorri reinscribes a cyclic vegetation

---

* The other poem in which Loki seems less the impish mischief-maker and more the devilish destroyer is the *Lokasenna*, also a relatively late text (probably composed around 1200).

This poem recounts how a certain Aegir held a drinking party for the gods. Loki, banished from the party for killing a servant, returns to insult each of the guests. The poem is a long dialogue of vituperation (which is what the word *senna* means; it's an ancient form of the dozens). There is humor in the poem but not in Loki, who seems unredeemably malicious. At the end, having questioned the integrity, sexual fidelity, and toilet habits of everyone present, he lays a curse on the assembled Aesir, calling for fire to consume their hall and all within.

Like Snorri, whoever wrote this poem does not believe in the old Norse gods; he has read Lucian's *Assembly of the Gods*, and is toying with dead belief to amuse his audience.

myth into linear time, where it is not about the same Baldr reborn each year, having suffered and survived the winter, but about a misguided early avatar of Christ who has died to make way for the real thing. In the thirteenth century, the prose *Edda* was a work of modern art that allowed the "noise" of Christianity into its frame.

Cultures regularly suffer from contingency; they bump into things they do not expect and cannot control. By Snorri's time the old Icelandic religion had run into Greek religion, and into a gospel from the shores of the Mediterranean. By 1220 the citizens of Iceland had been comparing apples for two hundred years, and had come to prize imported fruit, not the local crop. Snorri's *Edda* thus enacts the drama it relates. One curious thing about the book is how much of a role Loki plays in it. In earlier Norse poems Loki is a minor character, but Snorri is drawn to him, expanding Loki's role because, I would argue, he identifies with the trickster: they both betray the Norse gods, draw them into time, make them old. Snorri is his own Loki and the book he makes is a lethal-but-vital mistletoe, a creation that subtly undercuts one world while building another.

If there were believers who, hoping to prevent the death of their gods, set themselves against Christians such as Snorri, the problem they faced was the same as the problem facing Baldr's loved ones once Baldr began to have bad dreams. Can eternals be shielded from time and from change? Can essences be protected from accidents? The myth itself suggests the answer. To my mind, the whole sequence that moves from Baldr's baleful nightmares to the Norse apocalypse hinges on the moment when Frigg decides to make the world safe for her son. Baldr's dreams have told him something bad will happen, and so Frigg sets out to suppress every possible contingency. With compulsive thoroughness she tries to restrain all mishap ahead of time; she covers the globe with her oath-taking, so that nothing will come out of the blue and hurt her son.

Frigg, the story says, "decided to seek protection for Baldr from every kind of peril," a line that recalls the earlier story in which Raven's "father tried to keep his son from all danger." Both cases imagine an attempt at control, an imposition of order, so exacting ("*every* peril," "*all* danger") that, were it to succeed, the world as we know it would no longer exist. In *The Fragility of Goodness*, the classicist Martha Nussbaum has produced a long meditation on the questions that such obsessive care-taking inevitably raise. How much control can we have before the good life we're guarding ceases to be good in any conventional sense? Can we reduce contingency to zero, or must we always have some exposure to things we cannot control? Is the life that has no risk a human life? Nussbaum argues that one strain of Greek thought was clearly skeptical of any impulse to order that would close out all contingency. The good life must periodically occupy "the razor's edge of luck," they say, which means that the art of living, in Nussbaum's words, "requires . . . the most delicate balance between order and disorder, control and vulnerability."

The makers of the myth at hand lean toward a similar judgment. It is hardly enough to say that Loki is an evildoer and Frigg a dutiful mother; the problem of "delicate balance" demands an ethical language finer than that. In this story we do not get the green world, growing even as it perishes, fruitful even in decay, without the paired forces of order and disorder. There must be right relationship between these two. The Norse gods are *reginn*, "organizing powers," and by themselves cannot bring that world to life; they need the touch of disorder and vulnerability that Loki brings, a point we see by its reverse: when Loki is suppressed, the world collapses; when he—and disorder—returns, the world is reborn.

The weapon Loki discovers brings these forces back to right relationship after Frigg has tried to banish all disorder. Mistletoe is an evergreen; late in winter, its green ember still catches the light high in the leafless oak. Because of that, as Sir George Frazier once argued at length, this tiny shrub came to symbolize the soul that can survive the body's death and find rebirth. Thus Loki's weapon is ambiguously lethal: it carries the promise of rebirth even as it kills. The world can come back green because an evergreen twig killed Baldr. By themselves the ordering gods do not have sufficient power to bring the sequence about; they need as well what their ordering would leave out, Baldr's fragility and Loki's mischief. Before the eternals can be fertile, they need the mulch of death, disorder, and decay.

This is why I say that the real trouble in the tale starts with Frigg's compulsive oath-taking, for in that we have the end of the balance between control and contingency. If Loki's purview includes accident, happenstance, change, and death, then the binding oaths that Frigg extracts amount to a first attempt to bind the god. No wonder he gets annoyed; no wonder he swiftly moves to penetrate her guard and discover the exception to the rule. In so doing, he is hardly the evildoer he's sometimes thought to be; he is only making sure that a process already in motion gets carried to its end. After all, Bright Baldr *has* had those dreams: his death is prophesied and is, therefore, already present, as it is for each of us. Moreover, Baldr's powers are already in decline, as Georges Dumézil has pointed out. The prose *Edda* calls him "the wisest of the gods," but adds that "it is a characteristic of his that none of his judgments hold or come true." For Dumézil, Baldr embodies the will whose energy is spent, the sovereign whose death is near. He's the irremediable mediocrity of the present age, and must be killed if there is to be any change for the better.

Frigg's attempt to guard her son stands in the way of this necessary end, which is therefore more destructive than it needed to be. Just as violent upheavals increase where no political process allows for change, so here the sneakiness and shock of Loki's deed is proportional to Frigg's exaggerated attempt at control. Moreover, the witless gods learn nothing from that violence, for they immediately increase the stakes, binding Loki and, as the inexorable logic plays itself out, bringing their whole world to its apocalyptic end. There is no way to suppress change, the story says, not even in heaven; there is only a choice between a way of living that allows constant, if gradual, alterations and a way of living that combines great control and cataclysmic upheavals. Those who panic and bind the trickster choose the latter path. It would be better to learn to play with him, better especially to develop styles (cultural, spiritual, artistic) that allow some commerce with accident, and some acceptance of the changes contingency will always engender.

5

·····················

THE GOD OF THE CROSSROADS

Necessity knows no magic formulae—they are all left to chance. If love is to be unforgettable, fortuities must immediately start fluttering down to it like birds to Francis of Assisi's shoulder.
—Milan Kundera

THE PALM-NUT ORACLE

I once lived in a small town where all the employees of the local hotel jointly won the state lottery. The prize divided up, each of them got about $30,000 a year for many years, not a princely sum but handy, very handy. Within a few years, though, one of the clerks managed to go bankrupt. What struck me about this story when I heard it was the capping detail: this clerk *had gone bankrupt once before*. It was his fate to be bankrupt, no matter what good fortune descended upon him. He was a bankrupt sort of person.

C. G. Jung once said that "when an inner situation is not made conscious, it appears outside as fate." A bankrupt sort of person, unconscious of his own nature, may well feel the gods have it in for him. An undisciplined student will feel the fates have dealt him a series of bad teachers; a drunk will be convinced some evil destiny haunts her with a series of automobile accidents. In modern Western countries, of course, such people might end up in a therapist's office, doing the work to uncover what Jung calls "the inner situation." In West Africa, in the Yoruba parts of

Nigeria, the person who wishes to discover "the inner head," as the Yo-ruba call it, goes to the diviner. The Yoruba believe that before we are born we meet the High God and request the life we want. Although the too-greedy may find their requests denied, within limits we can choose our fate. Unfortunately, at the moment of birth the soul forgets all that has transpired; therefore, when men and women feel they've gotten off-track, when the way seems confused and knotted up, they go to the diviner in hopes of seeing once again the design of things as it is remembered in heaven.

Both William Bascom, an American anthropologist, and Ayodele Ogundipe, a Nigerian who studied folklore at Indiana University, have written at length about Yoruba divination and its gods, and from these accounts it is clear that in this setting "destiny" and "fate" refer not only to "the inner head" or matters of temperament and character but to one's whole lot in life. Everything is given shape before birth, from your position in society to the person you will marry and when you will die. Destiny determines whether you will be lucky or unlucky, rich or poor, kind or cruel. It prescribes the occupation you should follow. It includes, says Bascom, "a fixed day upon which the soul must return to heaven"; we enter this world with "a predetermined life span that can be shortened by evil forces, but never lengthened." (We may not say it as openly or describe it in the same terms, but I think a similar sense of fate is not uncommon in the modern West. If you see Michael Apted's film *35 Up*, which follows a group of English men and women from age seven to age thirty-five, it is immediately clear the great degree to which the situation of birth determines the shape of a life. We talk of temper-ament, of genetic predispositions, of class and race and gender, of the family that raised us with its patterns of privilege and abuse going back generations—all of which were "there before birth" and all of which a person may try to uncover and understand when his or her path is mys-teriously blocked.)

In any event, if a person in Yorubaland has questions about present troubles or future enterprises (What is wrong with my marriage? Will I be safe on a journey? Should I take this job? Why am I sick so often?), he or she may take the puzzle to the diviner in hopes of hearing what Ifa, who knows the hidden design of things, has to say. (Ifa is the name given both to the deity who knows about fate and to the method of divi-nation itself.)

In its practice, the Yoruba system of divination is quite a bit like the Chinese system contained in the *I Ching*. With the *I Ching*, to discover a response to your question, you throw yarrow sticks or flip coins to indicate one of 64 hexagrams. A coin flipped six times has 64 possible outcomes and the *I Ching* has 64 texts, each linked to one of the possible results of this chance operation. If, for example, you ask, "Should I leave this love affair?" and your coin comes up heads-heads-tails-heads-tails-tails, you have the hexagram Chien or "Development (Gradual Progress)," and the response to your question begins "A tree on a mountain develops slowly according to the law of its being and consequently stands firmly rooted." They say that divination works best if you come with a "burning question"—it's no use if you just want to know what necktie to wear, but it may be helpful if you're in some anguish about this love affair, for then the oracle's enigmatic responses will work the way so-called projective therapies work (Rorschach tests, for example), calling hidden structure and knowledge to the surface. You ask "Should I leave?" Then you must decide what "the law of its being" means, what "firmly rooted" means.

As I say, Yoruba divination is much like the *I Ching*. It begins with a similar "heads-or-tails," "even-or-odd" chance operation (rather than coins or yarrow sticks, Yoruba diviners cast palm nuts). Then it gets more complicated. First of all, this chance operation is done eight times, rather than six, which means there are 256 "figures of Ifa" and 256 possible responses to a question. Second, as with the *I Ching*, these responses comprise a body of divinatory literature, but in this case it is not written down. Diviners know by heart as many as three or four responses to each figure—folktales, proverbs, poems. A master diviner may know as many as four thousand elements of this oral literature.

The Yoruba credit their trickster figure, Eshu, with the origins of this art.* The story they tell about how Eshu brought divination to humankind reminds me of the Loki story, only in reverse. In that narrative, as we just saw, heaven finds itself attacked from below; hungry giants disturb the garden where the fruits of immortality grow. I read that story partly in terms of an old Aristotelian language: attacked by resentful accidents, heavenly essences grow old. If Baldr is the essence of the Good and the Beautiful, as the Norse myths say, and if these categories are eternal, then Baldr should not be subject to time or change. Certainly he should

---

* "Eshu" is accented on the first syllable and pronounced with a soft "e," as in "essay."

not have to suffer death. But as long as Loki is around, such purity is never safe. All purity comes by refinement, and refineries must leave behind their piles of tailings, slag, dross, rubbish, accidents. There is a wonderful West African story in which one of the gods is being chased by Death and in order to escape ascends into heaven, leaving a rubbish heap behind on earth. The lesson seems to be that becoming pure enough to avoid death depends on having left all dross behind. By the same token, however, "deathless" purity is vulnerable to the return of what it sloughed off, and tricksters, whose "bungling" brought death in the first place, are the agents of that return.

I rehearse all this because in the story of Eshu bringing the art of divination to humankind, it becomes clear that heavenly essences are vulnerable not just to the return of earthly accidents but to their absence as well. The gods need distance from earth, but not too much. They can be wounded by the return of rubbish, but they can also suffer if they have *no* contact with whatever is beneath them. In West Africa as in Greece (in fact, as must be the case all over the world), the gods need to be fed by human beings; gods who aren't, who have no real contact with the lowly time-infected earth, may starve and disappear even as their perfection increases, like anorexics whose lethal idealism forbids all contact with the world of changing bodies. What the gods need, it seems, is some sort of "right distance," neither too much contact nor too little.

The story of Eshu and the origins of divination has to do with establishing this right distance. It begins with a problem raised by appetite:

Once upon a time the sixteen Gods were very hungry. They did not get enough to eat from their wandering children on the face of the earth, who seemed to have forgotten them. Men no longer made them burnt offerings, and the Gods wanted meat. Some of them tried hunting, some fishing. They caught one antelope and one fish, but these didn't last long. The Gods grew unhappy with one another, and quarreled.

They began to wonder how they might get sustenance from humankind again. Eshu set to work on the problem. He conferred with Yamaya, who told him, "Threatening them doesn't seem to work. We've tried everything. The God of Disease has scourged them with pestilence, but still they won't sacrifice. He's threatened to kill them all, but they will not bring him food. The God

of Lightning struck them dead but they won't trouble themselves
to bring him things to eat. They don't seem to fear death; we need
some other method. Try giving them something good, something
they will yearn for and therefore want to go on living."

Eshu had an idea of what he needed, and so he went to Orungan. Orungan greeted him: "I know why you're here. The sixteen
Gods are hungry and we must give something good to humankind.
I know of such a thing. It is a big thing, made from sixteen palm
nuts. If you can get them, and learn their meaning, we will once
more gain the goodwill of humankind."

So Eshu went to the palm trees where the monkeys guarded
the sixteen palm nuts. The monkeys gave him the sixteen nuts,
but once he had them he had no idea what to do. "You got the
sixteen nuts by guile, Eshu," the monkeys said, "but nonetheless
we will counsel you. Travel around the world and ask their meaning in each of the places of the sixteen Gods. You will hear sixteen
sayings in each of the sixteen places. Then, from your place
among the Gods, tell humankind what you have learned. Once
again they will look on you with awe."

In this way the Gods now impart their knowledge to their
descendants on earth. Humankind can know the will of the Gods,
and what will come to pass in the future. When human beings
understood that through Eshu they could escape evil things in the
days to come, they began to slaughter animals again and burn
them for the Gods. In this way Eshu brought the palm nuts down
to humankind, and humankind satisfied the hunger of the sixteen
Gods.*

Eshu is well known for setting people to fighting with each other;
when we read at the outset that the gods themselves have been quarreling
we might suspect that Eshu has been at work (it would be like him to

---

* This is the tale that Henry Louis Gates, Jr., uses to establish a link between Eshu, the
reader-of-hidden-meanings or hermeneut of Yoruba religion, and the "signifying monkey"
(also a hermeneut) of African-American vernacular culture. The link is in the monkeys,
of course, though how they are transmuted into New World monkeys, and why a monkey,
rather than Eshu, becomes the trickster, is, as Gates himself admits, "extremely difficult
to reconstruct."

cause a problem only he can solve!). Whether or not Eshu lies behind it, at the beginning of this story there has already been some sort of "twilight of the gods": the Yoruba deities are in danger of dying out because their children have forgotten them. We are at a nodal point in the unfolding saga of the world: before this the gods had a relationship with humankind, and after this they also do, but at the moment they are in eclipse and trickster must help them out (which is why I say the plot reverses the other "twilight" stories—it's as if Monkey were to reinstall the Taoist patriarchs or Loki to recover Baldr from the underworld).

The opening of this tale, "the . . . Gods were very hungry," links it to the genealogy of cunning for which I argued in Part I: unsatisfied appetite requires a sly intelligence. The gods are grumpy for meat, and Eshu is the hunger artist whose guile will get them fed. The hunger is spiritual now, however, and so the cunning involved has to do with getting humankind to see the point of sacrifice—that is, of trading carnal satisfaction (or actual meat) for spiritual satisfaction. This is post-Hermetic, as it were: we have a trickster who knows that sacrifice of carnal appetite can lead to the quieting of other hungers, and who can jigger the relationship between mortals and immortals to that end. The result is a boon to both sides: the immortals get fed, while a trickster-culture-hero bestows the art of divination on humankind.

The story contains a curious contradiction that I want to lean on a little bit. On the one hand it says "the monkeys gave [Eshu] the sixteen nuts," and on the other hand the monkeys say that Eshu "got the sixteen nuts by guile." If both things are true, then Eshu must have gulled the monkeys into giving him the nuts, and if he did that, then he's a kind of sneak thief or seducer. Whatever the explanation, the monkeys seem to be saying that this is not a pure gift. What more lies behind these lines I cannot say, but remember the story of Prometheus, another tale of a trickster and the institution of sacrifice: in that tale Prometheus tries to improve the lot of humankind, but Zeus resists. If Eshu has to work by guile, perhaps we are meant to see that even as the gods need sacrifice from human beings they resist delivering the return gift, the art of divination. They resist for the same reason Zeus did: a change of circumstance is in the offing. With the reinstitution of sacrifice and the gift of divination comes a cosmic reallotment, a shift in the apportioning of spiritual things; human beings end up with a power they did not have before, and the gods end up fed but a bit less sovereign.

If the gods resist what they also need, then it's clear why they must call on Eshu, too. This cosmos has come to an impasse it cannot resolve on its own terms. Ambivalence binds it and things get stuck until some-one has the wit to call into play a figure who is at home with contradiction and who can do good works by cheating.

The present-day practice of divination preserves the flavor of these origins. To see it in action, and to see more clearly how Eshu op-erates in respect to fate, let us explore a specific case. Imagine that a worried man, thinking of going on a journey, checks with his diviner to help him decide whether or not to make the trip. The diviner casts the palm nuts; the first four casts come up even-even-even-odd, and the second come up odd-even-even-odd, yielding a figure of Ifa called Ogunda-Iwori. The diviner then tells a story that corresponds to the figure. It goes like this:

> This has all happened before. Long ago an Ifa diviner cast the palm nuts for a man named Ajaolele when he was about to make a journey to a distant town. The palm nuts indicated that to assure a safe trip Ajaolele should sacrifice a nanny goat, three cocks, a hen, and a razor blade. He did that.
> When Ajaolele reached the distant town, Eshu took the razor blade that had been sacrificed and put it in Ajaolele's hand. They were in the marketplace where a woman named Oran, a chief's daughter, was in the process of selling the traveler some corn-starch pudding. Eshu pushed the woman against the blade in Ajaolele's hand, and it cut her. A horrible fight erupted and every-one accused the stranger of being a trouble-maker. Eshu inter-vened, however, saying that Ajaolele had not started the fight, and that the people should put the wounded woman under Ajaolele's care.
> And so it happened that Ajaolele nursed Oran back to health. Now it also happened that Oran was already married and living with her husband, but she had not yet borne a child. When she and Ajaolele began living together, they also began sleeping to-gether, and after a few months she was visibly pregnant. When the chief of the town heard about this he said he would give Oran

to Ajaolele as his wife. Likewise the second chief gave Ajaolele one of his daughters, and the third chief did the same.

When Ajaolele returned to his own town he had become a person with followers, and he began to dance and sing, "What was prophesied for my journey has come to pass! What was prophesied has come to pass!"

Having told this story, the diviner might add a conclusion, a brief reading:

"Ifa says that we will be happy about the thing for which this figure was cast. He says we will gain glory; and we will become someone with a following, and that we will be given a wife without having to give bridewealth."

The trickster Eshu plays several roles in this example, a few of them not so obvious. First of all, Yoruba practitioners use as a divining board a wooden platter about eighteen inches around, and Eshu's face always appears on it. The board has a flat center where the diviner marks a record of how the palm nuts fall, and the edge is decorated with carvings, the main and obligatory one representing the face of Eshu. That face is always present during divination, then, a constant reminder that the god who gave this art to humankind is still present as the go-between, both "the gateman" through whom human questions must pass before Ifa can respond and the messenger who carries that response from heaven to earth. When our imagined traveler comes to the diviner, it is Eshu who must open the pore into heaven so that the gods can hear his question, Eshu who brings the answer, and Eshu who helps reveal its meaning.

Second, Eshu is known as "the enforcer of sacrifice." In this story about Ajaolele, it is typical both that the man with the problem must sacrifice at the outset and that Eshu ends up with part of that sacrifice (the razor) in his own hands. Divination involves an exchange: mortals get insight into destiny, and the gods get the fruits of sacrifice. In fact, people say that Eshu starts fights and stirs up troubles so that human beings will have to go to the diviners, have to sacrifice, have to feed the gods. Even if that isn't the case, Eshu is always interested in having sacrifice attend divination, for he always takes a portion for himself (about ten percent, the same as agents take from authors).

So Eshu is present in many ways in my opening example: his face appears on the divining board; he delivers the sacrifice and takes his cut; he delivers the oracular story and helps the traveler make sense of it; finally, he shows up in the story itself as the instigator of its happy accident.

In most of these roles Eshu is connected to the inquiry into destiny, but he's not exactly Ifa's faithful servant—he's more of a complicating factor, a faithful-unfaithful servant. They may call him "Heaven's Revered Gateman," but they also call him "Leather-Clothed Troublemaker." As go-between he's a kind of static on the line, a connector who may or may not connect, a reminder that all responses obscure as they enlighten. One folktale gives a thumbnail description of the relationship between Eshu and his more reliable colleague in divination, Ifa:

> Through the use of divining seeds, Ifa conveyed to men the intentions of the supreme god . . . and the meanings of fate. But Eshu strove to turn the Sky God's meanings aside, so that events would take an unintended course. Ifa smoothed the road for humans, while Eshu lurked on the highway and made all things uncertain. Ifa's character was destiny, and Eshu's character was accident.

In the same folktale we learn that these two who seem so much at odds are nonetheless the best of friends. To find out who were his true intimates, Ifa once staged his own mock funeral. False friends immediately appeared at the house, trying to get something for themselves from the estate; only Eshu was truly heartbroken and wanted nothing. It would seem that accident is fond of destiny, and uncertainty is certainty's intimate companion.

In a polytheistic cosmos, such friendship of opposites allows for contradictory belief. The Yoruba, at least, believe simultaneously that fate is binding and that fate may be altered. They say that the day of one's death cannot be changed, for example, but mothers nevertheless pray to Eshu to extend their babies' lives. One diviner told Bascom, "An individual cannot basically change his own destiny," except to spoil it; yet others say that "destiny is not fixed and unalterable," that "destiny . . . can be modified by human acts and by superhuman beings and forces." Similarly, Ogundipe says that the Yoruba believe in destiny . . . but freewill and accident also exist. . . . The Yoruba say . . . "It is in one's hands to change one's lot." Changes are brought about by individual effort, industry, and will, as well as by chance and accident. And this is where Eshu comes in. He is the complement to fate. He represents the elements of life not accounted for by fate or destiny.

Out of the friendship of Ifa and Eshu (like that of Apollo and Hermes at the end of the *Homeric Hymn*) we get no tragic opposition, then; we get, rather, the creative play of necessity and chance, certainty and uncertainty, archetype and ectype, destiny and its exceptions, the way and the no-way, the net of fate and the escape from that net.*

In the tale about Ajaolele, we see Eshu enacting the latter half of these pairings. Ifa is a different matter: if Ifa's territory is one's lot in life, then a story that begins with a man leaving his hometown leaves Ifa behind at the outset, for a man's "hometown" here stands for all the constraints of family, occupation, and temperament that constitute that lot in life. As one ethnographer has put it, "the Yoruba have a singularly prescriptive culture. . . . At any point in time there is a well-defined pattern of status and role expressed in prescribed behavior." But Eshu offers "escape from the rigidity of social laws." In this case, as soon as Ajaolele hits the road, and especially after Eshu bumps into him in the market, that escape is under way and all that Ifa stands for—law, system, rigidity—is held in abeyance until he returns to town at the end. (Here I should acknowledge that most divination verses are more conservative than the example at hand; most direct the questioner back into the structure of Yoruba society. Nonetheless, all feature Eshu in that all require interpretation, and some feature him directly, and directly suggest release from the rules.)

At the outset, then, Ajaolele enters an area of risk and uncertainty.

---

* Eshu's cousin among the neighboring Fon is the trickster Legba; he has similar functions. Melville Herskovits writes: "What is in store for a man is foreordained. Yet . . . a 'way out' is not denied. . . . This power that permits man to escape his destiny—philosophically the personification of Accident in a world where Destiny is inexorable—is found in the character Legba."

Similarly, Paul Mercier writes: "Man is not a slave. Though his fate binds him strictly to the structure of the world, it is no more than the guiding line of his life. . . . Legba has stratagems . . . to evade the rigid government of the world."

He leaves family and friends with their known rules and enters the realm of ambivalent fortune where things both horrible and wonderful might happen to him. He was wise, then, to pay homage to uncertainty before leaving town, which is to say he was wise to make the sacrifice Eshu asked for. Paying attention to Eshu has an effect on luck. I think of luck as the disposition of chance, and of Eshu as the force that can turn that disposition sunny or sour. Tricksters are masters of reversal, remember, and Eshu is a special case, his stock in trade being the reversal of fortune. He can rob a woman of her children, or make the barren wife fertile. He can turn friendship into hatred, make the moon and sun change places, turn right into wrong, make the innocent seem guilty and the ugly beautiful. In Ajaolele's world, it is certainly *not* the case that a man could get himself a bride without giving bridewealth. Men are destined to give bridewealth; that is the way things *are*. Unless, of course, a man could somehow step outside "the way" and in the less than orderly world of a foreign bazaar suffer some lucky happenstance; then perhaps he could become "someone with a following" despite the rigid rule of fate. Perhaps, if its disposition were right, a chance event could change his lot in life.

PURE CHANCE

At stake in Eshu's interventions is the somewhat larger question of how change might come to any orderly, self-regulating, and self-protecting world. Most enduring structures (in nature, society, the human psyche) are resistant to fundamental change, by which I mean change that alters the givens of those structures themselves. It's almost a matter of logic: no self-contained world can induce its own fundamental change, because self-containment means it knows nothing beyond its own givens. In such cases, accidents are useful indeed.

Some ideas from evolutionary biology will help me explain what I mean here, for those who theorize about evolution have spent a good deal of time pondering the creative force of chance. In *Chance and Necessity*, the French biochemist and Nobel laureate Jacques Monod, for example, argues that there are two kinds of chance, one of which is well illustrated by a roll of the dice or spin of the roulette wheel. The outcomes of such events are impossible to predict, Monod says, mostly because our information isn't fine enough. When we throw the dice (or when Yoruba diviners cast the palm nuts), it is only because the causes are too subtle, the chain of events too long, the sequence too fast, and so forth, that the outcome is an apparent accident. Monod calls this kind of chance "operational" ("in roulette the uncertainty is purely operational and not essential"); I call it "one-road" chance (the event may be complicated but it unfolds along a single path), the better to contrast it with Monod's second kind of chance, which he calls "absolute" and I call "two-road" chance.

Imagine that I set out in my automobile for work at 7:05 a.m., a few minutes late because I went back for my umbrella. Meanwhile, two cats down the street start caterwauling beneath a window. A neighbor throws a glass of water at them, one cat runs into the road, I swerve to avoid hitting it . . . and have an accident. In this case two causal paths cross; each, by itself, unfolds with its own inner logic, but each is wholly unrelated to the other until they meet. After an automobile accident we may search frantically through the preceding events, hoping to find the "cause" (if only I'd skipped the umbrella!), but what makes it a true accident is that nothing connects the one chain of events to the other. The cat's running is no accident and my driving no accident, but their convergence is. Of such cases Monod concludes: "Chance is obviously the essential thing . . . inherent in the complete independence of two causal chains of events whose convergence produces the accident." (As I pointed out in the last chapter, our words "coincidence" and "contingency" contain this image of "two events converging.")

Monod didn't invent the notion of two-road chance, of course. Aristotle devotes three chapters of his *Physics* to things that happen "by accident," one of his examples being a farmer who, digging in his garden plot, happens upon a treasure that another man buried years ago. The farmer intended to grow a crop; the other man intended to hide his gold; when these unrelated intentions meet, we have true accident, the coincidence of unrelated causes. We can go back further than Aristotle, too, out of science into mythology. At the start of the *Homeric Hymn*, Hermes makes the first lyre from the shell of a turtle. When the hymnist of that story says that Hermes "happened upon" that turtle, he is beginning a story about two-road happenstance and the particular kind of changes it can bring. And in Yoruba religion the same phenomenon is well worked out in the figure of Eshu, who dwells at the crossroads, the classic focal point of true coincidence.

To come back to the modern understanding of these motifs, once

Monod has explained why two-road chance is "essential" and "absolute," he goes on to argue that with it comes the possibility of "*absolute* newness." Nothing new under the sun can happen without absolute chance; it "*alone* is at the source of every innovation, of all creation in the biosphere." This is the second idea I want to borrow from evolutionary theory. The role of chance in evolution has often been exaggerated, to be sure, but even when we understand the many ways in which creation is *not* a matter of accident,* accident still remains as the single source of true innovation. A genetic mutation is a two-road chance event in that there is no link at all between it and the world into which its consequences must fit. When a mutation meets its context we have a pure coincidence, a crossroads event. As Monod puts it, "between the occurrences that can provoke or permit an error in the replication of the genetic message and its functional consequences there is . . . a complete independence."

It is this independence that means absolute chance produces absolute newness. If the opposite were the case, if mutations arose in response to an organism's needs or to some hidden intention, they would express things that already exist (the need, the intention) and would not, therefore, be absolutely new. They would be, Monod argues, *revelations* of something already present, not creations of something new. Monod makes this point with the analogy of a sugar crystal forming in a sugar solution. If you dissolve enough sugar in hot water, and then cool the water, crystals will always form. The cooling in a sense "creates" the crystals, but the creation is not "absolutely new" the way the surviving consequences of a mutation are new. In the case of the sugar crystal, "the necessary

---

* Monod and others articulate clear limits on what chance can contribute to evolution. In many instances, mutations don't arise by accident, for example (they are easy to induce with various mutagens). More important, every mutation appears in a set of ongoing contexts—from the context of physical law to the context of the other genes—and must fit each of these if it is to survive.

Finally, over and over again these contexts sort the fruits of chance in a rigorous and predictable way. For Richard Dawkins, the cumulative effect of such sorting means that "chance is a minor ingredient in the Darwinian recipe . . . ; the most important ingredient is cumulative selection, which is quintessentially *non*random." Monod makes the same point: "Natural selection operates upon the products of chance and can feed nowhere else, *but* it operates in a domain of very demanding conditions, and from this domain chance is barred."

information was present, but unexpressed, in the constituents. [Such] building of a structure is not a creation; it is a revelation," while evolutionary creation, by contrast, "arises from the essentially unforeseeable [and] is the creator of *absolute* newness." Like the sugar crystal, the butterfly that emerges from its chrysalis reveals a structure that already exists; in any one species, every chrysalis always reveals the same butterfly. There is no surprise, nothing absolutely new. In ancient days, when the first such metamorphosis took place, however, something absolutely new happened. That first metamorphosis (or, rather, each small component of it), like everything else in the biosphere, was born at the happy crossroads where a shift in the genetic code met a hospitable environment.

These are the claims that raise the hackles of all who believe in divine intention, of course. Feeling ourselves to be the center of things, and witnessing the complexity of the surrounding world, who could believe that creation arose from a series of cumulatively selected accidents? "All religions," Monod writes, "nearly all philosophies, and even a part of science testify to the unwearying, heroic effort of mankind desperately denying its own contingency." "All religions . . ." except the many that preserve a trickster figure. It is perfectly possible to have a system of belief that recognizes accident as part of creation. In Yoruba mythology, Eshu is understood to have gotten one of the creator gods drunk at the beginning of time, and that is why there are cripples, albinos, and all other sorts of anomaly in the world. When geneticists breed fruit flies, a fly sometimes appears with legs growing from the sockets where its antennae ought to be. Clearly Eshu, who delights in mishap as well as good hap, is still slipping palm wine to the high gods. The old Greek wisdom says that "Hermes leads the way or leads astray." If I suffer an accidental loss, that is Hermes the thief, and if there is an accidental gain, that is Hermes the luck-bringer. But, gain or loss, what is constant with Hermes and with Eshu is the presence of accident. Chance is hardly mysterious in such religions; what's mysterious is that there can be people who deny it exists, who have no trickster figure, and who have thus saddled themselves with all sorts of intractable philosophical problems because their cosmology doesn't fit *this* world, the world as it is.

· · ·

onod's ideas help me explain what I mean when I say that accident
is needed for certain kinds of change. Monod covers the case of
change in nature, and before we get back to Eshu, I'd like to add a word
about newness in art, for artists, too, have long known that happenstance
breeds new worlds, that sometimes the creative spirit must abandon its
own designs, the kingdom of our intentions being so cramped and predictable. Leonardo da Vinci used to suggest that art students "look at
any walls spotted with various stains," so as to "arouse the mind to various
inventions." Sandro Botticelli liked to throw a sponge wet with colored
paints against a wall, then search out new landscapes in the resulting
splatter. But it is in this century (perhaps prompted by similar movements
in biology, psychology, and physics) that the role of chance in art has
expanded, especially in Dada and surrealism, where a studied attention
to accident abetted the attempt to baffle logic, convention, and bourgeois
taste. There is much to say about these movements, but I'll limit myself
here to a brief look at Marcel Duchamp, who was involved in both of
them, and who used chance to create what I think of as the "humor of
escape."

Duchamp once made a piece called *Three Standard Stoppages*; it
simply records the undulating shapes produced when he held three
meter-long pieces of thread outstretched and let each one fall in turn.
Asked about the piece, Duchamp explained: "The idea of 'chance' . . .
struck me. . . . The intention consisted above all in forgetting the hand.
. . . Pure chance interested me as a way of going against logical reality. . . ." Turning things over to chance, letting them fall as they may,
means in this case "forgetting the hand," which in turn means, first of
all, getting away from the hand's acquired and habitual gestures. More
figuratively, it means eluding habit in all its forms, and eluding the constant repetition that habit forces on us (Duchamp didn't want to spend a
lifetime painting the same canvas over and over, which is what he thought
most painters, slaves to the remembered hand, had to do). Forgetting the
hand promises freedom from one's own taste both good and bad, an escape
from the rules of causality, and a way to avoid perceptual routine. "Art,"
Duchamp once said, "is an outlet toward regions which are not ruled by
time and space." Chance was one of his tools for creating that outlet. It
amused him, he used to say. To forget the hand and let things happen
made him happy the way that Hermes is happy bumping into the turtle
and Ajaolele is happy returning to his village. It is the happiness of being

released from the known and meeting the world freshly, the happiness of happenstance.

This smiling escape from expected patterns is so consistent a theme in Duchamp that you find it wherever you enter the work. It's initially a matter of attitude, well illustrated by Duchamp's response to the fate of his *Large Glass* (a famously complicated painting executed on sheets of glass). In the late 1920s this piece was exhibited in Brooklyn, then boxed up and returned to the woman who owned it. It shattered in transit. Duchamp eventually restored it as best he could and, standing in front of it thirty years later, had this to say:

> I like the cracks, the way they fall. You remember how it hap-
> pened in 1926 . . . ? They put the two panes on top of one another
> on a truck, flat, not knowing what they were carrying, and bounced
> for sixty miles into Connecticut, and that's the result! But the
> more I look at it the more I like the cracks: they are not like
> shattered glass. They have a shape. There is a symmetry in the
> cracking . . . and there is more, almost an intention there, an ex-
> tra—a curious intention that I am not responsible for, a ready-
> made intention, in other words, that I respect and love.

"Readymade" is a term Duchamp coined to describe the mass-produced goods he plucked from the obscurity of hardware stores or junk heaps and declared to be "art" (the first was a bicycle wheel he mounted on a stool; another was a hat rack). In the production of readymades Duchamp enacts the stance he displays toward the broken glass. In this case the coincidence doesn't happen to him, he makes it happen. He becomes the crossroads where things that habit has assumed must remain apart may meet. Take his *Bottle Rack* of 1914. Duchamp bought this neat bit of mercantile design—a small tower of metal pins for drying bottles—at a street bazaar outside the town hall in Paris. Now it's in the Phila-delphia Art Museum (or rather a copy is; the original has been lost). Duchamp used to speak of a readymade as "a kind of rendezvous," and of this piece as "a bottle-rack which changed its destination." It was on its way to some restaurant kitchen, perhaps, and never made it. It was minding its own business in the marketplace when someone shoved it, and now it lives the elevated life of "art without artwork." It was sitting in the market of useful goods, one universe of value and meaning, when

Duchamp set up a rendezvous with another such universe. The art world hasn't been the same since. Museums once had some sense of what they were, of what belonged in them and what didn't, but then came this unfortunate collision with a bottle rack.

In both spirit and practice, then, I see Duchamp enacting a modern version of an old and continuing drama. He is Eshu in the marketplace, Eshu at the crossroads, Eshu at the gate. He is the mischief-maker for whom the most interesting part of the museum is its front door with the guards in their blue livery. He courted chance for its amusing openings, and left behind a string of accidents that slipped past the guards and changed all the exhibits. It all happened in a matter of decades, art being swifter than evolution.

From the story of Ajaolele's trip to a distant market I turned to these ideas about evolution and about art to expand on the notion that Eshu is a god of uncertainty and accident, and that these functions are necessarily connected to his ability to change someone's lot in life. These are all one and the same thing: leaving the village, the accident in the market, and the change of fortune. Ajaolele's altered situation, his conversion into "a person with followers," would never have come to him in the context of his own village, for the village is rule-governed and no man gets "brides without bridewealth" there. For a fundamental shift of that sort Ajaolele needs a happy accident, and for that it helps if he puts himself "on the road" and "in the market," phrases I put in quotation marks because we should remember not to confine ourselves to their literal reading. At stake here is an attitude toward life, and you do not really need to leave town to have it. Duchamp makes that clear. You can be on the road at home and in the mind, attentive to the plenitude of coincidence that habit and design sometimes obscure. There is an old saying: "Luck is the residue of design." Being "aware of Eshu" means entering a frame of mind in which the eye notices that residue all around it, the plentiful and ready-made world right at hand.

All tricksters like to hang around the doorway, that being one of the places where deep-change accidents occur. Eshu is no exception. He likes especially the doorway between heaven and earth, which is why his face appears on the divination board. The art of divination makes heaven and earth briefly coincident. Eshu is a sort of slippery joint at the point of their contingency, revealing fate or reversing it depending on the disposition of things. It may well be that fate is set in heaven, but it must be played out here on earth, and between heaven and earth there is a gap inhabited by this shifty mediator.

Eshu's desire to keep the commerce across that gap lively means there is one key exception to his love of chance. Humankind *must* sacrifice to the gods; that is the single rule that cannot be left to chance. It's an apt exception to Eshu's otherwise constant uncertainty, for sacrifice maintains the commerce between the worlds and gives the mediator his job. Once there is sacrifice, however, once the commerce is established, Eshu can begin to play, and neither gods nor humans should assume his mediations are sure, trustworthy, and unambiguous. If people refuse to sacrifice, Eshu will certainly bring them suffering, but if people do sacrifice, he will mix luck into fate's designs. If the Yoruba forget the gods, Eshu will certainly cause trouble, but if they remember the gods, he will open a space for surprise and reversals of fortune.

Eshu is aptly called an "enforcer of sacrifice," then, but beyond that he's not very rule-governed. For one thing, the kind of sacrifice he insists upon has contingency built into it. Notice *where* it takes place. One folktale has it that "today" when people sacrifice, "sacrificial food is placed at the crossroads where Eshu lived; birds and beasts partake of this food." Another folktale explains that "any sacrifices found outdoors or at the roadside belong to Eshu. Whenever Eshu is swamped with sacrifices, he asks that they be taken to the crossroads, the town gates, the roadsides, the bush, the mahogany tree, the rubbish heap, and to the beach next to a waterway so that other living creatures—birds, animals, and insects— might share the sacrifice."* Another says that he told human beings "that as long as they sacrificed at the crossroads he would always be with them."

In short, sacrifice connected to Eshu focuses on sites of contingency, places where people might bump into something unpredictable. Eshu sacrifice does not take place on an altar in a protected temple, but in shifty locations; travelers might eat the food of this sacrifice, or merchants, or dogs, or wild birds. This sacrifice opens a pore at the edge of

---

* In Greece, food offerings were left out on the road in a similar manner, at roadside statues of Hermes. According to Carl Kerényi, these offerings "were windfalls for hungry travelers who stole them from the God—in his own spirit, just as he would have done."

the known so that an element of "traveler stuff" or "the wild," or something from the "rubbish heap," might enter. It is two-road or threshold sacrifice, and invokes therefore the possibility of fundamental change.

The chanciness of Eshu's mediations go beyond these matters of location, too. The immortals may give him messages to carry, but from time immemorial they've known he can't be trusted. Remember that he acquired the palm nuts "by guile"; remember that he got one of the gods drunk at the creation. He once got the sun and moon so mad at each other that they quit their assigned orbits. Several stories tell how his constant troublemaking led the gods to force him to live on earth, not in heaven. In one such tale Eshu is so jealous at someone else's good fortune that he goes about making the gods gossip and betray each other. "For his part in these events, Eshu was banished to the crossroads."

Not that Eshu's willingness to betray the gods means he is a sure friend of mortals. His face on the divining board places him *between* heaven and earth, and bespeaks uncertainty on both sides. Praise poems address him, saying: "Your handling of sacrifice makes one doubt your fairness." He "takes money stealthily." He is a "man of considerable means," but he "roams the streets collecting money off sacrifices." He is the "one who dares appropriate sacrificial money." There's much more to say, but this catches the gist of it: with a wealthy kleptomaniac like this on their side of the exchange, humans are no better off than the gods.

Eshu's ancient gift of the palm-nut oracle brought a mediating uncertainty principle to human-divine relations. The gods now have contact with "their wandering children on the face of the earth," but because Eshu cannot be trusted, it is a contact that puts them slightly at risk; they open themselves to disruption whenever they call on him. Humans, on the other hand, now have an institution of prophetic contingency; divination by lots gives them an accidental glimpse of the divine, and no sure way to know what it means. Constrained by neither heavenly nor earthly rules, Eshu stands between the two worlds, or between two of anything trying to communicate, not like some high-fidelity sender-receiver, but more like the atmosphere itself, shifting, cloudy, full of static and the smoke of human fires. This may seem like a problem when humans are desperate for higher meaning, but it is actually a blessing, because if the gap between the worlds were fully closed, fate would be truly binding, there would be no more two-road accidents and no more deep change on either side. "Everything existing in the universe is the fruit of chance and of necessity," wrote Democritus. There are designs in this world, but there are also chance events, which means design is never finished. In artistic practice open to happenstance, or in the West African arts of divination, human beings have a way to enter into the play of fate and uncertainty, and from that play this world constantly arises.

6

....

THE LUCKY FIND

The bottom of the mind is paved with crossroads.
—Paul Valéry

Chance and chance alone has a message for us. Everything that
occurs out of necessity, everything expected, repeated day in and day
out, is mute. Only chance can speak to us. We read its messages
much as gypsies read the images made by
coffee grounds at the bottom of a cup.
—Milan Kundera

A GIFT OF HERMES

Outside my study door a bird has built its nest with the usual twigs and moss but also, in this case, with two strips of paper torn from the sides of my computer printout. The bird did not set out in search of those white strands, but when it happened to find them it knew how to weave a habitable home. "I do not seek, I find": Picasso's famous dictum underlies the wandering portion of his artistic practice. In both cases, an intelligence makes itself at home in the happening world, one not so attached to design or purpose as to blinker out the daily wealth of accidents. "Chance itself pours in at every avenue of sense: it is of all things most obtrusive": I happened on that sentence from the philosopher C. S. Peirce the day I was writing these paragraphs (I happened on that bird earlier, and stored it up). A friend was stuck writing her thesis when, wandering aimlessly through the library, she happened on a carrel where someone had spread out just the article she needed. Antonio Stradivari, walking in Venice one day, came upon a pile of broken, waterlogged oars, out of which he made some of his most beautiful violins. Mozart heard a starling singing in a street vendor's cage, and thus we have the theme of the last movement of the G-major Concerto for Piano and Orchestra. A lucky find gave Picasso one of his famous sculptural creations:

> Guess how I made that head of a bull. One day, in a rubbish heap, I found an old bicycle seat, lying beside a rusted handlebar . . . and my mind instantly linked them together. The idea for this *Tête de Taureau* came to me before I had even realized it. I just soldered them together. . . .

If only preconception does not block the avenues of sense, accidental finds are all about us.

In Yoruba folktales the lucky find is often a "pit of beads" whose chance discovery makes a poor man rich; sometimes Eshu makes these beads appear with a clap of his hands, whereupon we see that accidental gain is a gift-of-Eshu (as was Ajaolele's on-the-road accident). In classical Greece the lucky find is a *hermaion*, which means a "gift-of-Hermes." With both these characters, of course, lucky-find and unlucky-loss lie close together. Hermes is a generous thief, Eshu a rich kleptomaniac; both finding and losing belong to their ambivalent sphere. In a journal entry Carl Kerényi records how a book of his disappeared on a boat trip: "Does Hermes wish to play . . . with me again? . . . I am left with the feeling of being stolen from, something uncanny, a vague sense of change of circumstances—truly something hermetic." Accidental loss, accidental gain—both flow from these figures, the single constant being accident.

And yet that formulation doesn't quite catch the tone of things, for with the right kind of attention it is the *happy* accident, the creative accident, that Hermes or Eshu engenders (Hermes does steal but he's regularly called "luck-bringing," a "ready-helper," "emphatically delighting"). Perhaps Kerényi's use of the word "uncanny" bears attention: in trickster's territory, who's to say what is loss and what is gain? It's hard to get your bearings. There's a "change of circumstance," that's all you know, for in uncanny space the terms themselves collapse, and a sudden loss (my computer crashes, my keys disappear) can flip and become a sudden gain (I slow down, I go walking in the woods).

The idea of "finding" itself bespeaks this indeterminate space. There are many ways in this world to acquire things: you can make something with your labor, you can buy it, you can receive it as a gift, you can steal it. "Finding" occupies an odd position on any such list. If I pocket a $5 bill found in the trash at the edge of a deserted parking lot, am I a thief? How should we describe that farmer who finds buried treasure in Aristotle's example of two-road chance? He gets the gold not by working for it, not as a present from friend or relation, not by stealing it, not by purchase. We are in a shady area here, and shady language is in order. "It fell off a truck" is the American version of the more ancient "I found it at the crossroads."

To speak of happy accident is not to deny the negative side of chance. We all know that accident can bring great loss and grief, contingency can breed great tragedy. I have a recording of a Nez Percé woman telling the story of Coyote going to the Land of the Dead; at the end she says, "When we were children we used to cry and cry over that." Of the death of Baldr, Snorri writes, "This was the greatest misfortune ever to befall gods and men." There is a Job-like story in which Eshu strips a rich man of all he loves with a series of accidents. But these are really exceptions to the dominant tone of the trickster tales, and more often than not, overweening pride or overreaching control is a contributing factor.

For the more typical tone, we could take the first of Hermes' own chance encounters. A newborn babe stepping from his mother's home, "he crossed the threshold of that roomy cave and found a tortoise." At the threshold, at the boundary between under world and upper world, at the Eshu-spot of crossroads chance, like Picasso at the rubbish heap, he "found a tortoise, and got possession of boundless wealth." Not everyone would have made something of that encounter ("What's out there?" "Just an old turtle."), but with Hermes coincidence turns fertile. This was one of the points the anthropologist Victor Turner made in his classic book on liminality, *The Ritual Process*, that the state of being betwixt-and-between is "generative" and "speculative"; the mind that enters it willingly will proliferate new structures, new symbols, new metaphors, not to mention new musical instruments.

The ingredients of such moments—surprise, quick thinking, sudden gain—suffuse them with humor, not tragedy. Hermes laughs when he happens upon the turtle, and a slightly manic mood overtakes him when he realizes how to make the lyre: "just as a swift thought can fly through the heart of a person haunted with care, just as bright glances spin from the eyes, so, in one instant, Hermes knew what to do and did it." Picasso once described his amusement coming upon some sea urchins in a tidal pool: "the sense of sight enjoys being surprised. . . . It's the same law which governs humor. Only the unexpected sally makes you laugh." The agile mind is pleased to find what it was not looking for. Someone once said that Picasso painted to do a kind of "research"; the remark annoyed him, and prompted him to formulate his sense of "finding":

> In my opinion to search means nothing in painting. To find is the thing. Nobody is interested in following a man who, with his eyes fixed on the ground, spends his life looking for the pocketbook that fortune should put in his path. The one who finds something . . . , even if his intention were not to search for it, at least arouses our curiosity, if not our admiration. . . .
>
> When I paint, my object is to show what I have found and not what I am looking for.

Whoever the gods of fortune are, they will drop things in your path, but if you search for those things you will not find them.

Coming from who knows where, a lucky find is potentially unsettling to whatever world it enters. The moralists will be likely to complain, the gamblers will be pleased, while everyone else will wait to see if it really is amusing, this new thing. Whatever the case, before we can have a full sense of the disruptions and delights that come in the wake of a lucky find, we need fuller examples to work with. In 1965 George Foster, an anthropologist who had worked in Mexico and Italy, published an essay that is partly about how peasants respond when their neighbors' fortunes suddenly change. In "Peasant Society and the Image of Limited Good," Foster argues that many otherwise perplexing details of peasant behavior can be understood by assuming that peasants believe there is a fixed quantity of wealth in the community and therefore that if someone in the group suddenly becomes richer it must be because someone else, or the group as a whole, has become poorer. The idea holds if we imagine, as Foster does, a closed community, or—to put it the other way—the idea finds its exceptions in cases in which wealth clearly comes from outside the nominal bounds of the group. Peasants do not feel ripped off if one of their number becomes richer as a result of selling labor as a migrant worker, for it is clear that wages so earned come from across the border. More telling for my purposes are the other ways to get wealth without being subjected to group opprobrium. In peasant communities in southern Italy, for example, the neighbors won't harass someone whose sudden success comes as a "gift of Fortune," as, for example, when "a rich gentleman gave a poor boy a violin," or when "a rich gentlewoman adopted an abandoned child," when a man "hit upon a hidden treasure" buried in the woods, and when "another was lucky enough to win in the lottery."

Foster calls all these "gifts of Fortune," but they could as easily be called gifts-of-Hermes or gifts-of-Eshu. With the lottery we are in the domain of a "change of lot," which both Hermes and Eshu govern (remember that Hermes actually holds a private lottery in conjunction with his sacrifice, dividing the sacrificial meat by chance). With treasure buried in the woods we are back with the pit of beads that Eshu can reveal, and with certain kinds of hermetic gain (in a story from Horace that I'll touch on later, Hermes lets a peasant find gold in his field).

Another ancient example of a gift of Hermes tallies well with this description of the lucky find in peasant communities because it so clearly links hermetic action to Foster's sense that what's really at issue is the neighbors' sense of right and wrong. In one of Plato's dialogues, Socrates talks with his friends about the life after death. "If the soul is immortal," he says, "it demands our care not only for that part of time which we call life, but for all time. And indeed it would seem now that it will be extremely dangerous to neglect it. If death were a release from everything, it would be a gift-of-Hermes [*hermaion*] for the wicked, because by dying they would be released not only from the body but also from their own wickedness together with the soul. . . ."

I realize that Plato may well speak of a *hermaion* here without thinking of Hermes, just as we speak of Saturday without thinking of Saturn. Most translators do not bring the root reference to Hermes over into English, turning *hermaion* into "boon" or, at best, "godsend." Still, if any god were to send this boon it would have to be Hermes: the discussion has to do with release from a morality Socrates feels should contain us, and Hermes' name naturally crops up, for he is the amoral escape artist.

The point is that both Foster and Plato think a lucky find offers a way out of an otherwise restrictive situation. The fabric of social and spiritual life contains, shapes, and binds our lives; a lucky find tears a hole in that cloth so that we can slip free. In the world that Foster's essay describes, for example, the lucky find arrives from outside the knotted nets of community reciprocity. Nets of reciprocity, moreover, bring with them tremendous moral and ethical suasion, so that we might also describe this containing fabric as the weave of morality. We place an ethical grid over most of our experience, sorting events quickly into the good and the bad. In saying that the wicked would certainly be getting a gift of Hermes if there were no afterlife, Socrates is protesting the idea that there might be a way to escape the hold of moral systems. All of which suggests a final way to describe the fabric that a lucky find disrupts or evades, for in many traditions the demands of the collective are felt as a kind of fate, the fates themselves being imagined as weavers whose weaving shapes the lives of human beings.

Against all this—against the nets of reciprocity, the grid of ethics, the weave of fate—we have the find which is a lucky break, a hole in the surrounding cloth. The lucky find is an opportunity, then, a pore or penetrable opening in an otherwise closed design. We saw earlier that the Greeks called such an opening a *poros*; they also called it a *kairós*, a term that comes from the art of weaving and refers to the brief instant when the weaver may shoot her shuttle through the rising and falling warp threads. A *kairós* is a penetrable opening in the weaving of cloth, the weaving of time, the weaving of fate. Through such pores, gaps, and fleeting openings slips the buried gold, the waddling tortoise, the song of a starling—chance encounters that cannot be derived from the structures that surround us.*

---

* This is one of the places where the trickster material talks back to my earlier book, *The Gift*. In the introduction to that book I used the old debater's ploy of declaring off-limits all the things I knew might weaken my argument. "I touch on many issues, but I pass over many others in silence." To speak of trickster's gifts breaks that silence.

In its positive aspect, traditional gift exchange is an agent of social cohesion; group structures can be articulated and solidified by way of a commerce of gifts, a point I argue in Chapter 5 of *The Gift*. That is all very well, unless the structure happens to keep you in a place you'd rather not be, or happens to exclude you from the group.

In the peasant communities that Foster describes there is tremendous pressure to conform and little chance, therefore, for an individual to change his or her lot in life. Ongoing systems of reciprocity and the ethical injunctions they carry give the group great stability, but that very stability can sometimes make people feel trapped. In that context a gift-of-Hermes or gift-of-Eshu is a category-confusing gift, one that promises to upset

• • •

In Plato's *Gorgias*, one of the disputants, Callicles, gets frustrated because every time he misspeaks himself Socrates jumps on the mistake and uses it to his own advantage. Finally Callicles bursts out: "Will this fellow never stop driveling? Tell me, Socrates, are you not ashamed to be captious about words at your age, considering it a gift-of-Hermes if one makes a slip in an expression?" Callicles complains that Socrates takes a slip of the tongue to be a hermetic gift because it lets the philosopher penetrate his opponent's argument. You talk and talk, weaving an enchantment or marshaling the points of your argument like troops on a battlefield, and then suddenly you misspeak yourself. Your tongue betrays you, a *hermaion* for your opponent, who quickly slips through the opening and attacks your hidden weaknesses.

Nowadays, of course, we follow that old charmer Freud and take a slip of the tongue to be a window onto the unconscious, revealing what is beneath the surface or behind the mask, what is hidden sometimes even from the speaker. A friend means to say "one hundred" but she says "one husband," and we know what's on her mind. I mention this because to speak of a pore or opening in what we take to be the order of things raises the old question of what lies on the other side of that order. If fate contains us, what lies outside fate? If Eshu and Hermes are messengers, what message is hidden in their accidental gifts? What does a lucky find reveal to the man or woman who stumbles upon it?

For most ancient or believing peoples, the answer is simple: accidents are no accident, they reveal the will of the gods. What happens on earth follows the designs of heaven, and if it appears to be random chance, that is only because our sight is not capacious enough to see that apparent chance actually follows grand design. Thus the Yoruba will often say that the way the palm nuts fall is not really left to chance but is controlled by Ifa, the god of divination. An expert on Greek oracles tells us that in ancient Greece "the drawing of lots was governed, not by chance, but by the will of the gods." Such has also been the Christian understanding for centuries. In his *Anatomy of Melancholy* (1621), Robert Burton writes

---

the boundary markers of the old system of exchange.

By linking them to tricksters, these cultures acknowledge that these are anomalous gifts, and indicate that there must sometimes be exceptions to the rules of reciprocity.

that "Columbus did not find out America by chance, but God directed him. . . . It was contingent to him, but necessary to God." Even today in the United States, Amish communities elect their bishops by a lottery which they understand to reveal God's will in the matter.

In cases where a character like Eshu or Hermes is taken to be the agent of chance, it now becomes apparent that the trickster who causes accidents is the same as the trickster who brings messages. In these systems, that is, contingency is prophecy, at least to those who have the ears to hear. Eshu's face on the divining board bespeaks all this: it means that apparent chance is in fact an oracle, at least for those who can hear the way Eshu hears (his ears are unusually open, "perforated . . . like a sieve"). Hermes, too, gives his followers acute hearing; they call him "the god of the third ear," the one that can hear an essence buried in an accident. There is a form of divination associated with Hermes called *cledonomancy*, derived from *cledon*, which means an accidental but portentous remark, the language version of a lucky find. Long ago Pausanias described this oracle of "Hermes-of-the-Marketplace": at dusk as the lamps are being lit the petitioner leaves a "coin of local money" at the image of Hermes, whispers the question he hopes to have answered, puts his hands over his ears, and walks away. When he takes his hands from his ears the first words he hears contain the oracle's reply. All the better if the words are uttered by a child or a fool, someone clearly incapable of calculating an effect.

Both Hermes and Eshu, then, are not only agents of luck, they help to draw heaven's hidden meanings out of luck's apparent nonsense. In the modern world we find a similar conjunction of accident and insight, only the discovered meanings now lie in the head rather than the heavens, for we have translated the ancient art of inquiring into the will of the gods into psychological terms. "Divination techniques . . . are techniques to catalyze one's own unconscious knowledge," says Marie Louise von Franz in a typical modern formulation. Von Franz was a student of Jung's, and it was Jung in his preface to the *I Ching* who famously announced that when we find meaning in synchronous events (the uncanny encounter in a distant city, say, or the three of spades turned up on the third of May) we are getting insight into "the subjective . . . states of the observer or observers." Freud was less directly concerned with divination, but his understanding of chance was similar. All his lectures on "the psychology of errors" are addressed to the doubter who would say that slips of the tongue "are not worth my explanation; they are little accidents." On the contrary, Freud argues, what hides in the unconscious only "masquerades as a lucky chance," and we must learn to remove the mask. Slips of the tongue and other errors "are serious mental acts; they have their meanings"; they "are not accidents." Seeming mistakes will appear "as omens" to all those who have hermeneutic "courage and resolution."

I suppose we'll have to say it is no accident how many artists in the twentieth century had a similar understanding at the same time. Picasso believed that no painting can be plotted out beforehand and yet nothing is an accident, a seeming contradiction unless we understand that Picasso believed in the deep self, a personality of which the artist himself or herself is not necessarily aware. "I consider a work of art as the product of calculations," he once said, "calculations that are frequently unknown to the author himself. It is exactly like the carrier-pigeon, calculating his return to the loft. The calculation that precedes intelligence." What leads this pigeon-like artist are his desires, his impulses. In a work of art, "what counts is what is spontaneous, impulsive." "Art is not the application of a canon of beauty but what the instinct and the brain can conceive beyond any canon. When we love a woman we don't start measuring her limbs. We love with our desires. . . ."

One of Picasso's favorite assignments for a young artist was to have him or her try to draw a perfect circle. It can't be done; everyone draws a circle with some particular distortion, and that distorted circle is *your* circle, an insight into *your* style. "Try to make the circle as best you can. And since nobody before you has made a perfect circle, you can be sure that your circle will be completely your own. Only then will you have a chance to be original." The deviations from the ideal give an insight into the style, and thus, Picasso says, "from errors one gets to know the personality."

This, then, is the sense in which an artist both works with accidents yet creates work in which "there are no accidents." "Accidents, try to change them—it's impossible. The accident reveals man." With Picasso as with Jung and Freud, accidents point to the concealed portion of the man or woman to whom they happened.

Ancient or modern, then, one continuing line of thought holds that accidents break the surface of our lives to reveal hidden purpose or design. The carefully interwoven structures of thought and social practice provide stability and structure, but they bring a kind of blindness and stupidity, too. Gifts of Hermes tear little holes in those fabrics to offer us brief intelligence of other realms.

That, at least, is one answer to the question of what a lucky find reveals. But here Hermes himself might come forward to complicate things. When he bumps into the tortoise, he seems to be giving a *hermaion* to himself, and what, we might ask, does *it* reveal? Who is sending a message to whom? Remember, too, that when Hermes butchers the cattle he divides the sacrificial portions by lot. If such lotteries reveal the will of the gods, what is a god doing holding one, and whose will is being revealed?

Similar conundrums arise in some of the Eshu stories. Eshu, after all, brings accident into heaven (getting the creator drunk, for one thing). Moreover, the gods themselves sometimes need the palm-nut oracle. In one tale, the god of thunder and lightning, Sango, finds himself in trouble and begs Ifa to cast the divination nuts and find the cause; in a Cuban–Yoruba story, the "king of the gods," Obatala, is beset with all kinds of problems and turns to Ifa for insight. The tale ends: "Obatala had learned that even the gods cannot live without divination." This conclusion yields the same paradox Hermes led us into. What do the gods learn when they inquire into the will of the gods? If trickster Eshu is the messenger in divination, whose message does he bring when Obatala himself casts the palm nuts?

All this directs us back to an earlier point: from Loki to Eshu, if tricksters are around, the gods themselves must suffer from uncertainty. If heaven itself is not immune from chance, then an accidental find must sometimes reveal something other than heavenly will or hidden purpose. A remark by Carl Kerényi suggests what this might be: "Chance and accident," he says, "are an intrinsic part of primeval chaos [and] Hermes carries over this peculiarity of primeval chaos—accident—into the Olympian order."

In this conceit, the cosmos itself is a containing fabric, and what lies outside is chaos, confusion, muddle. "Opportunities are not plain, clean gifts," writes the psychoanalyst James Hillman; "they trail dark and chaotic attachments to their unknown backgrounds. . . ." It must be that sometimes our assertions about higher order and hidden design are fables we've made up to help us ignore our own contingency. Accidents tear little holes in the fabric of life to reveal, well, little holes. In one of the books he wrote under the general title *Hermès*, Michel Serres, a French philosopher of science, writes skeptically about our assumptions of underlying unity in things. "The real," Serres suggests, may be "sporadic," made of "fluctuating tatters." Perhaps "the state of things consists of islands sown in archipelagoes on the noisy, poorly-understood disorder of the sea. . . ." Perhaps trickster's accidents reveal not hidden realms of greater order but a world of shifting fragments, noise, and imperfection. The fruit fly born with legs where its antennae should be has not received a useful message. Accident is the revelation of accident.*

In all fairness to the nature of hermetic accidents, however, I must here double back on myself one last time and add that in the case of the tortoiseshell lyre and the sacrifice-lottery, when Hermes works with chance he does more than upset the order of things. If Hermes is involved, after a touch of chaos comes another cosmos. Hermes is a god of luck, but more than that, he stands for what might be called "smart luck" rather than "dumb luck." These two kinds of luck figure in Latin mythology, where Mercurius stands for the smart and Hercules for the dumb. "Should a *stupid* fellow have good luck, he owes it to the witless Hercules," Kerényi writes, referring us to a story in Horace in which "Mercurius once

---

* This is a second place where the trickster material talks back to *The Gift*. In that book I took the idea that gifts establish connections between people and therefore have a cohesive social function, and linked it to ideas about the imagination, claiming that imagination, too, has "esemplastic" power. This term comes from Coleridge, who describes the imagination as "essentially vital" and takes as its hallmark the ability "to shape into one," an ability he names "the esemplastic power." Imagination assembles the disparate elements of our experience into coherent, lively wholes.

In *The Gift* I hang many claims about the imagination on this idea of cohesiveness—that, by nature, imagination moves toward unity, for example, and that we can see this if we look at how artists make their work, or if we look at the role that works of imagination play in society. Trickster stories are often at odds with such formulations, of course. Here imagination often seems *dis*ordering, more at home in fragmentation and confusion than in unity, and things get lively exactly when we stop trying to pretend to unities that don't exist. Trickster's imagination works well in a world of "fluctuating tatters," as does the imagination of many of the artists I speak of in this book.

let Hercules talk him into enriching a stupid man. Mercurius showed him a treasure which he could use to buy the piece of land he was working. He did so, but then proved himself unworthy of the hermetic windfall by continuing to work the same piece of land!"

That's "dumb luck," the luck of all gamblers whose winnings never enrich them, the luck of the hotel clerk who hits the lottery and quickly spends himself into bankruptcy. It's sterile luck, luck without change. "Smart luck," on the other hand, adds craft to accident—in both senses, technical skill and cunning. Hermes is a skillful maker of the lyre, and he is canny as well, leveraging the wealth his *hermaion* brings. Hermes "trades up" with his lyre; he doesn't just become a turtle farmer or a lyre-maker with an unpaid small-business loan. Late in the *Hymn* he sings a song with his new instrument and the tune seduces the brother he has recently robbed. After Hermes stops singing, the *Hymn* says, "Apollo was seized with a longing he could do nothing about; he opened his mouth and the words flew out: 'Butcher of cattle, trickster, busy boy, friend of merry-makers, the things you're interested in are worth fifty cows. Soon I believe we shall settle our quarrel in peace.' "

Hermes at this point in the *Hymn* is actually involved in negotiating for certain divine powers; Apollo not only knows that, he accepts the music of the lyre as a part of the exchange. Under the manic spell of this *hermaion*, Apollo cancels the debt that Hermes incurred by his theft. We will return to this moment in later chapters; for now, the point is simply that this lucky find does more than add chaos to Apollo's world. The lyre *is* disruptive, of course—with it, Hermes not only sings the shameless song of his own begetting but gets the spellbound Apollo to abandon his sense of what should properly happen to a thief. So on the one hand a touch of chaos comes into the Olympian order but on the other hand it doesn't endure, because Hermes soon weaves his lucky find into the scene he has disturbed (forever after, Apollo plays the lyre as part of his own repertoire). Thus does Hermes show us how "smart luck" responds to hermetic windfalls.

Perhaps, then, what a lucky find reveals first is neither cosmos nor chaos but *the mind of the finder*. It might even be better to drop "cosmos" and "chaos," and simply say that a chance event is a little bit of the world as it is—a world always larger and more complicated than our cosmologies—and that smart luck is a kind of responsive intelligence invoked by whatever happens.

A story of scientific discovery makes a good illustration. "Chance favors the prepared mind" is Louis Pasteur's famous aphorism,* and his own career abundantly illustrates its meaning. The neurologist James Austin has described one famous case:

> Pasteur was studying chicken cholera when his work was inter-rupted for several weeks. During the delay, the infectious organ-isms in one of his cultures weakened. When injected, these organisms no longer caused the disease. However, this same group of fowls survived when he later reinoculated them with a new batch of virulent organisms. Pasteur made a crucial distinc-tion when he recognized that the first inoculation was not a "bad experiment" but that the weakened organisms had exerted a pro-tective effect.

For chance to "favor the prepared mind" means, first of all, that chance events need a context before they can amount to anything. In evolution, a chance mutation disappears immediately if there is no hos-pitable environment to receive it; more to the point here, in this example Pasteur had a set of ideas about disease and inoculation and was thereby more able to recuperate his botched experiment. But notice that in ad-dition to having a ready structure of ideas, the prepared mind is ready for what happens. It has its theories, but it attends as well to the anomaly that does not fit them. We therefore get this paradox: with smart luck, the mind is prepared for what it isn't prepared for. It has a kind of openness, holding its ideas lightly, and willing to have them exposed to impurity and the unintended.

In a 1920 letter to a friend, James Joyce made a wonderful quick remark on Hermes that links the god to this receptive mind. Joyce is musing on the mysterious plant, the *moly*, that Hermes gives Odysseus on the road to Circe's house. Classicists aren't sure what the *moly* is in fact (wild garlic?) but Joyce has a hunch as to what it is in spirit:

---

* More aphoristic in English; the French is: "Dans les champs de l'observation, le hazard ne favorise que les esprits préparés."

Moly is a nut to crack. My latest is this. Moly is the gift of Hermes, god of public ways, and is the invisible influence (prayer, chance, agility, *presence of mind*, power of recuperation) which saves in case of accident. . . . Hermes is the god of signposts: i.e. he is, specially for a traveller like Ulysses, the point at which roads parallel merge and roads contrary also. He is an accident of providence.

What I like best here is the phrase Joyce underlines: when Hermes is around, his gifts reveal the *presence of mind*. Not some hidden structure of mind, necessarily (not the Oedipus complex or an instinct for beauty), but more simply some wit that responds and shapes, the mind on-the-road, agile, shifty in a shifting world, capable of recuperation, and located especially at the spot where roads, "parallel . . . and contrary," converge. Valéry's enigmatic assertion, "the bottom of the mind is paved with crossroads," speaks to me here, for the mind that has smart luck makes meaning from unlikely coincidences and juxtapositions.

How do we come by this wandering, crossroad mind? We already have it, I suppose, but those who take it seriously awaken and school it through attention to its gods, something as simple as telling the old stories, or touching Eshu's image as one leaves the village gate, or touching the *herm* as one enters the marketplace. At the thresholds where one crosses into territories of increased contingency, such small ritual actions bring to mind the mind contingency demands. Going on a journey (or entering the painting studio) without consulting the god of the roads invites dumb luck; taking the god into account summons the presence of mind that can work with whatever happens. The first lucky find (or unlucky loss!) will reveal whether or not anything has responded to the summons.

A NET TO CATCH CONTINGENCY

In the late 1940s D. T. Suzuki, the Japanese Buddhist scholar, used to lecture at Columbia University, and one of these lectures gave the composer John Cage a key insight into what was already a part of his method. Suzuki drew a circle on the blackboard and sectioned off a bit of it with two parallel lines. The full circle stood for the possible range of mind, while the small part between the lines stood for the ego. Cage remembers

Suzuki saying that "the ego can cut itself off from this big Mind, which passes through it, or it can open itself up."

It is especially by our "likes and dislikes," Cage says, that we cut ourselves off from the wider mind (and the wider world). Likes and dislikes are the lapdogs and guard dogs of the ego, busy all the time, panting and barking at the gates of attachment and aversion and thereby narrowing perception and experience. Furthermore, the ego itself cannot intentionally escape what the ego does—intention always operates in terms of desire or aversion—and we therefore need a practice or discipline of *non*-intention, a way to make an end run around the ego's habitual operations. Zen Buddhism, Cage says, suggests the practice of cross-legged meditation: "you go *in* through discipline, then you get free of the ego." Cage thought his own artistic practice moved in the other direction to the same end: "I decided to go *out*. That's why I decided to use the chance operations. I used them to free myself from the ego."

What do you want for lunch, a hamburger, falafel, or a taco? Flip a coin, and the decision will have nothing to do with your habitual tastes. Would you like silence here, a sustained flute tone, the noise of traffic, or a car alarm? You might hate car alarms, as I do, but with Cage's method "you" and "I" do not get to choose. Cage says:

> I have used chance operations . . . in a way involving a multiplicity of questions which I ask rather than choices that I make. . . .
> If I have the opportunity to continue working, I think the work will resemble more and more, not the work of a person, but something that might have happened, even if the person weren't there.

"Something that might have happened," by haps, per haps. Cage's faith was that this method would, as meditation promises, "open the doors of the ego" so as to turn it "from a concentration on itself to a flow with all of creation." Cage was fond of repeating Meister Eckhart's assertion that "we are made perfect by what happens to us rather than by what we do"; therefore Cage not only allowed things to happen, he developed a practice that encouraged them to do so.

Popular perceptions of Cage tend not to see that for him chance operations were a spiritual practice, a discipline. One kind of courting of chance is exactly the opposite of discipline, of course—the young person putting herself at risk, the gambler on a spree, the speculator playing with a relative's money. Cage was a playful man, but these are not his uses of chance, as he himself often struggled to make clear. In recommending non-intention, he once explained, "I'm not saying, 'Do whatever you like,' and yet that's precisely what some people now think I'm saying. . . . The freedoms I've given [in a musical score] have not been given to permit just anything that one wants to do, but have been invitations for people to free themselves from their likes and dislikes, and to discipline themselves."

In many ways the discipline Cage recommended was as stringent as that of any monk on a month-long meditation retreat. He asked that intention be thwarted rigorously, not occasionally or whimsically. He *worked hard* at chance. He would literally spend months tossing coins and working with the *I Ching* to construct a score. It took so much time, he would toss coins as he rode the New York subway to see friends. One famous piece less than five minutes long took him four years to write. And when a piece was finished, it was not meant to be an occasion for improvisation; it was meant to be played *within the constraints* chance had determined. "The highest discipline is the discipline of chance operations. . . . The person is being disciplined, not the work." The person is being disciplined away from the ego's habitual attitudes and toward a fundamental change of consciousness. This is Cage's version of Duchamp's "forgetting the hand."

We can glean an even fuller sense of the intentions of Cage's non-intention from the several places where he contrasts his own practice with the work of other artists who might seem, at first glance, to be engaged in a similar enterprise. Cage distanced himself from improvisation, from automatic art, and from methods of spontaneous composition, even though such things might initially seem related to his project. The score for Cage's *Concert for Piano and Orchestra*, for example, "frees" the orchestra at one point, and if you listen to the Town Hall recording of this piece you will hear one of the woodwinds improvise a bit of Stravinsky at that point. "You could look at the part I had given him," Cage later commented, "and you'd never find anything like that in it. He was just going wild—not playing what was in front of him, but rather whatever came into his head. I have tried in my work to free myself from my own head. I would hope that people would take that opportunity to do likewise."

For the same reasons, Cage was not drawn to an art like that of

Jackson Pollock. Pollock's working assumption was that the wildness of his paintings expressed his deep, primitive, and feeling self, and Cage would argue, I think, that no matter how "deep" the self is, it's still the self. "Automatic art . . . has never interested me, because it is a way of falling back, resting on one's memories and feelings subconsciously, is it not? And I have done my utmost to free people from that." Cage much preferred the incidental drawings that are scattered throughout Thoreau's *Journals*: "The thing that is beautiful about the Thoreau drawings is that they're completely lacking in self-expression."

The point of Cage's art, then, is not to entertain nor to enchant but to open its maker (and, per haps, its audience) to the world. In one of his oft-repeated stories, Cage tells of a time when he had just left an exhibit of paintings by his friend Mark Tobey: "I was standing at a corner of Madison Avenue waiting for a bus and I happened to look at the pavement, and I noticed that the experience of looking at the pavement was the same as the experience of looking at the Tobey. Exactly the same. The aesthetic enjoyment was just as high." Cage is praising Tobey here, not criticizing him, for Tobey's work had opened its viewer's eyes; he could *see* and enjoy what previously might have been the city's dull and unregarded asphalt skin. Such is one function of twentieth-century painting, says Cage, "to open our eyes," as its music should open our ears. As one of Cage's colleagues, the painter Jasper Johns, says: "Already it's a great deal to see anything clearly."

I should add here that Cage's ideas have some authority for me because I've had the experience they describe. I first heard Cage himself in 1989 when he gave Harvard's Norton Lectures, offering a collage of text fragments—drawn from Thoreau, Emerson, *The Wall Street Journal*, older lectures of his own—assembled and ordered through a series of chance operations. I found the lectures sometimes amusing but mostly boring; I walked out of the first one before it was over. But then a funny thing happened. I couldn't get the experience out of my head; the readings had cocked my ear, as it were, so that situation after situation recalled them to me. Nowadays in any city in the world one constantly hears a complicated sound collage—fragments of the radio, phrases coming out of shop doorways, the passing traffic, the honk of horns, the click of a door latch. From all around us, noises join coincidentally at the ear and, like it or not, this is the world we are given to hear. Having heard Cage, I hear it more clearly.

I spent a summer some years later in Berkeley, California, writing a draft of these chapters and reading Cage's prose pieces and interviews. At the same time I was sitting zazen at the Berkeley Zen Center and often, as I sat, I would become conscious of the sounds around me—of bird song punctuating the drone of a jet plane, for example, with a conversation from a nearby house as a sort of middle theme. These moments of hearing were *amusing*, and I have to wonder if my amusement wasn't the happiness of letting the world happen. I found I could briefly drop my unconscious, reflexive filtering, and when I did, it was as if my hearing had increased twenty percent, or as if I'd had water in one ear for years and suddenly it disappeared. In an interview Cage once described his own struggle with his *dislike* of the background drones of machines like refrigerator motors. "I spent my life thinking we should try to get rid of them. . . . What has happened is that I'm beginning to enjoy those sounds, I mean that I now actually listen to them with the kind of enjoyment with which I listen to the traffic. Now the traffic is easy to recognize as beautiful, but those drones are more difficult and I didn't really set out to find them beautiful. . . . They are, so to speak, coming to me." There is a state of mind that finds the sound of the refrigerator motor interesting, even at 3 a.m.

Cage readily admits that the change of mind that leads to this sort of interest is one of the purposes of his purposelessness. "I think that music has to do with self-alteration; it begins with the alteration of the composer and conceivably extends to the alteration of the listeners. It by no means secures that, but it does secure the alteration in the mind of the composer, changing the mind so that it is changed not just in the presence of music, but in other situations too."

Chance operations can change the mind because they circumvent intention. "Everyday life is more interesting than forms of celebration," Cage once said, adding the proviso: "*when* we become aware of it. That *when*," he explained, "is when our intentions go down to zero. Then suddenly you notice that the world is magical." The Tibetan Buddhist teacher Chugyam Trungpa once said that "magic is the total appreciation of chance." We are more likely to appreciate chance if we stop trying to control what happens, and one way to do that is to cultivate non-intention. To do it totally is to realize how fully the world is already happening inside us and around us, as if by magic.

In one sense, "art" itself disappears as a result of such a practice. In later years Cage felt that his own technique of composition had changed him, "and the change that has taken place is that . . . I find my greatest acoustic, esthetic pleasure in simply the sounds of the environment. So that I no longer have any need not only for other people's music but I have no need really for my own music." An art produced in this spirit is hardly an art at all, at least not in the sense of leaving any durable object behind, any recognizable trace of the ego's intentions. In his book *For the Birds*, Cage tells of a party he once attended: "As I was coming into the house, I noticed that some very interesting music was being played. After one or two drinks, I asked my hostess what music it was. She said, 'You can't be serious?' " It was a piece of his own, as it happens.

Such a piece differs markedly from the creations that an artist like Picasso makes when a lucky find surprises his eye, or at least the artists differ markedly. Remember Jacques Monod's distinction between a creation and a revelation, between what he calls "absolute newness" and a newness that arises predictably from conditions already present. In these terms, Picasso's *Tête de Taureau* is a revelation, not a creation. I'm actually following Picasso himself when I say this: "The accident *reveals* man," he says. In the case of the *Tête de Taureau*, what we see, in case we hadn't seen it before, is that Picasso's "deep personality" is in love with the bulls and bullfighting. Some of his earliest childhood drawings are of bullfights. The bull's head is a part of his mental landscape, so it's no surprise when his eye catches a familiar pattern in the handlebars and bicycle seat. It's an accidental find, to be sure, but it is a symptomatic accident. If there were bottle racks or a face of Christ in that rubbish heap, Picasso didn't see them. Were Matisse to look over the same rubbish heap, he might have found something much more colorful. If the mathematician Benoit Mandelbrot had cast his eye over that rubbish, he might have seen a feathery rill of mud or a paisley oil slick. And John Cage? We could not predict what Cage would find, at least not if he came to the rubbish heap carrying the *I Ching* under his arm.

In Cage's terms, then, Picasso's attention to accident is a way of *exploring* the self, not of *leaving* it, and therefore runs the risk of indulgence and repetition. I'm reminded of the theater director Peter Brook's critique of actors who try to get in touch with their "deep" selves: "The method actor . . . is reaching inside himself for an alphabet that is . . . fossilized, for the language of signs from life that he knows is the language not of invention but of his conditioning. . . . What he thinks to be spontaneous is filtered and monitored many times over. Were Pavlov's dog improvising, he would still salivate when the bell rang, but he would feel sure it was all his own doing: 'I'm dribbling,' he would say, proud of his daring."

The materials in Picasso's accidental find are new, but the art he shapes from them returns us to the same old Picasso. Picasso, of course, was quite happy to work with accident as a tool of revelation ("From errors one gets to know the personality!"), but Cage was not ("Personality is a flimsy thing on which to build an art"), for Cage was after Monod's "absolute newness" of pure chance. He was not out to discover any hidden self, nor did he think chance operations would reveal any hidden, already existing divine reality, as ancient diviners thought. "Composition is like writing a letter to a stranger," he once said. "I don't hear things in my head, nor do I have inspiration. Nor is it right, as some people have said, that because I use chance operations my music is written not by me, but by God. I doubt whether God, say he existed, would take the trouble to write my music."

If the products of Cage's chance operations are not revelations, either of the self or of the divine, then what exactly are they? As I've said, in one sense they are "nothings," experiences whose lack of purpose has as their purpose the creation of a kind of awareness or attention ("Not things, but minds" was one of Cage's aphorisms). Nonetheless, while Cage is clearly more interested in consciousness than in art objects, he does sometimes speak as if he were an object-maker, describing his works as inventions or discoveries, and his process as a labor to "bring . . . new things into being."* This minor theme in his self-descriptions interests me because in it I hear echoes of Monod's idea that pure chance might lead to absolute newness, to creations that could not have been foreseen even if one knew the unrevealed contents of self or cosmos. Almost as a

---

* Cage's father was an inventor, and Cage himself was always proud of the fact that Arnold Schoenberg once described him as "not a composer, but an inventor of genius."

matter of definition, such absolute newness (in either evolution or art) can only arise if the process itself has no purpose, for where there is purpose, creations reveal it and are not, therefore, absolutely new.

Cage once said, for example, that a "happening" should create a thing wholly unforeseeable. In 1952, Cage and a group of friends at Black Mountain College produced one of the first happenings, a mixed theatrical performance whose shape was devised by chance operations (it included Cage reading one of his lectures from the top of a stepladder and the painter Robert Rauschenberg playing records on an old Victrola). Much later Cage would say: "A Happening should be like a net to catch a fish the nature of which one does not know," a remark that resonates nicely with Monod's sense of "absolute" creation, for in evolution, too, the addition of chance to necessity means that creation always "catches fish" the nature of which can never be predicted. Cases of convergent evolution (in which similar species evolve in similar but distant ecosystems) demonstrate the point nicely. In both Africa and South America, for example, fish that must navigate in muddy water have evolved a method of sensing what's around them that involves broadcasting a weak electric field. For such electrolocation to work, the body of the fish becomes a sort of receiving antenna and must therefore be held stiff, which means the fish cannot undulate to swim the way most fish do. Electric fish propel themselves by means of a single large fin that runs the length of the body. In the African species the fin runs along the fish's back, but in South America it runs along the belly. Such beings arise from the play of chance and necessity; the nature of electricity necessarily stiffens the body, but the propelling fin is located by haps. Because pure chance is involved, in the evolution of species and in a John Cage happening, "fish" appear the nature of which no one could have predicted from the original circumstances.

To say this another way, in both cases whatever emerges—no matter how beautiful or useful—is not the fruit of any hidden purpose. Cage, like Picasso, might have been able to say, "I do not seek, I find," but in Cage's case his lucky finds never reveal unconscious motives. One of Cage's early innovations was to stick all sorts of objects into the strings of a piano (screws, bolts, pieces of paper), producing unpredictable and novel noises. "I placed objects on the strings, deciding their position according to the sounds that resulted. So, it was as though I was walking along the beach finding shells. . . . I found melodies and combinations of sounds that worked with the given structure." If Cage was looking for "what works," it might seem at first that he did have purposes here, and that he was allowing his taste to guide him. But if that's the case it's hard to explain why he never made use of his lucky finds. That is to say, when Cage happened upon a melody he liked he didn't then go on to build with it, repeat it, weave it into a climax, and so forth. To do so would be to promulgate his "likes and dislikes," and by that begin again to shape and solidify the ego. Just as the play of chance in evolution is not directed toward any end, even when durable beauty arises from it, so when chance handed Cage an interesting melody he never took it as a sign of his purposes (as Picasso might), nor did he allow it to arouse his intention. He moved on to let chance decide what happens next.*

Thus, and despite the fact that Cage sometimes spoke as if his art produced objects, this line of thought takes us back to his aphorism, "Not things, but minds." Cage was above all dedicated to creating a kind of awareness, believing that if we rigorously allow chance to indicate what happens next we will be led into a fuller apprehension of what the world happens to be. Take what is probably Cage's best-known composition, a piece called *4'33"*, four minutes and thirty-three seconds of silence broken into three movements (each indicated by the piano player lowering and raising the lid of the piano). The same year this piece was written, 1952, Cage had a chance to visit an anechoic chamber at Harvard University, a room so fully padded that it was said to be absolutely silent. Alone in the room, Cage was surprised to hear two sounds, one high, one low; the technicians told him these were the sounds of his nervous system and his circulating blood. At that point he realized that there is no such thing as silence, there is only sound we intend and sound we do not intend. Thus *4'33"* is not so much a "silence" piece as a structured

---

* Cage was rigorous in his devotion to chance, to the consternation even of his friends. The composer Earle Brown once argued for the mixture of chance and choice: "I feel you should be able to toss coins, and then decide to use a beautiful F sharp if you want to—be willing to chuck the system in other words. John won't do that."

Mark Twain's witticism about Wagner—"His music is better than it sounds"—nicely catches the complexity of my own reaction to Cage (walking out on him and then being haunted). Like Earle Brown, I prefer the play of chance and intention to the purity of Cage's method. But I also realize that he cleared a field no one had entered, and set a marker there. Even those who do not follow him into his field benefit from the sight of that marker.

opportunity to listen to unintended sound, to hear the plenitude of what happens. The audience at the premiere of *4'33"* "missed the point," Cage once remarked. "What they thought was silence . . . was full of accidental sounds. You could hear the wind stirring outside during the first movement. During the second, raindrops began patterning the roof, and during the third the people themselves made all kinds of interesting sounds as they talked or walked out."

Theories of evolution have shown us that, even though it is difficult at first to imagine how a process that depends on chance can be creative, nonetheless it is by such a process that creation itself has come to be. I have been following Jacques Monod's picture of the role of chance in the creation of the biosphere partly because his language resonates with Cage's in so many respects. On the one hand, Monod recognizes that there is a kind of self-protective egotism to all living things, which is to say all living things perpetuate themselves through invariance (DNA is remarkably stable) and guard themselves against the "imperfections" that chance might bring upon them. On the other hand, invariance means that living things, by themselves, cannot adapt when the world around them changes, nor change to occupy empty niches of the biosphere. In nature, as in the heavens that Loki pesters, true change requires accidents, happy or not. "The same source of fortuitous perturbations, of 'noise,' which in a nonliving . . . system would lead little by little to the disintegration of all structure, is the progenitor of evolution in the biosphere and accounts for its unrestricted liberty of creation," Monod writes, calling DNA "[a] registry of chance, [a] tone-deaf conservatory where the noise is preserved along with the music."

This echoes Cage's aesthetic quite precisely. He was not blind to the fact that cultures and selves guard and replicate their ideals, their beauties, their masterpieces, but he did not cast his lot with durable structures, he cast it with perturbation. He turned toward chance to relieve the mind of its protective garment of received ideas so that it might better attend to the quietly stirring wind or the rain patterning the roof. He made an art that was a net to catch contingency. He cocked his ear for noise, not the old harmonies, sensing that noise can lead to something as remarkable as this world, and believing that, in a civilization as complex and shifting as ours has become, a readiness to let the mind change as contingency demands may be one prerequisite of a happy life.

PART THREE

DIRT WORK

7

....

SPEECHLESS SHAME
AND SHAMELESS SPEECH

THE IMMIGRANT CHILD

The Interior Salish in Idaho tell this story: " 'I will be the Sun-god,' declared Coyote, and the people allowed him to try. He took the Sun-lodge across the sky. But he watched everything that the people did. Seeing people in secret love, he yelled down to them, much to their embarrassment. He told on those who were hiding. The people were glad when that day was over. They lost no time taking Coyote from the Sun-lodge."

You and I know when to speak and when to hold the tongue, but Old Man Coyote doesn't. He has no tact. They're all the same, these tricksters; they have no shame and so they have no silence. Hermes should bite his tongue when he's hauled before the assembly of the gods, but instead he wiggles his ears and tells a boldface lie, wearing—his mother says— "the cloak of shamelessness." Loki once had his lips sewn shut by an irritated dwarf, but Loki ripped the thongs out and went right on talking.

It's the same with Old Monkey in China. We know that Tripitaka, the venerable Buddhist monk who takes Monkey with him on "the journey to the west," is a good man, because he's regularly "struck dumb by his shame." That's as it should be; shame should steal your voice. Even if you *want* to speak, shame should bind your tongue. Some villagers once offered Tripitaka a woman. "When he heard these words, he bowed his head and fell into complete silence." No such paralysis ever strikes Monkey's loose and apish tongue. In fact, his constant fluency in situations that would silence more sensitive creatures is an ironic boon to Tripitaka on his journey, for it is hard to travel in this fallen world if you lose the power of speech every time evil meets you on the path. Tripitaka is so kindly that when monsters mask themselves as virtuous men he never sees through the disguise. "Master, please put away your compassion just for today!" Monkey begs. "When we have crossed this mountain, you can be compassionate then." Monkey, never blinded by compassion, and certainly never "struck dumb," keeps the pilgrims moving smartly along.

Monkey's spirit, Maxine Hong Kingston once said, is one of the gifts that Chinese immigrants brought with them to America. At first glance, at least, Kingston herself might not seem a bearer of that gift. Concerned with ethical issues and dedicated to beauty in her art, she hardly has a reputation as a "shameless" author. Still, she has had her struggles with silence. (In a memoir she writes: "When I went to kindergarten and had to speak English for the first time, I became silent. A dumbness—a shame—still cracks my voice in two. . . ." She was so quiet she flunked kindergarten.) Moreover, moral sophistication and beautiful prose are qualities of Kingston's finished work, not of her process, and it is in the process that the Monkey spirit is her ally, guiding the pilgrim-artist over the divide from shame's speechlessness into speech. "Mistress, please put beauty away just for today! When we have crossed this mountain, then . . ."

Kingston's first utterance as an American writer comes exactly from this divide. Her memoir of growing up in a Chinese-American home, *The Woman Warrior*, begins with these remarkable words: " 'You must not tell anyone,' my mother said, 'what I am about to tell you.' " The story that Kingston's mother prefaced with this injunction to silence concerned an aunt back in China who bore an illegitimate child and, shamed by the village for her adultery, committed suicide, drowning herself and the baby in the family well. Kingston's mother told her daughter this cautionary tale on the occasion of the girl's first menstruation. " 'What happened to her could happen to you,' she warned. 'Don't humiliate us. You wouldn't like to be forgotten as if you had never been born. The villagers are watchful.' "

The link that most of us feel between shame and silence becomes an actual instruction here. Kingston is not only given to understand that her sexuality is a potential source of shame, she is given a glimpse of what the territory of shame contains, and then told never to speak of it. Her mother's admonitory account of a woman hounded into suicide comes from what is sometimes called a "shame culture," one which preserves its structure by swamping those who step out of line with deadly, smothering waves of shame.* Kingston herself offers a striking image for the valuable thing that a shame culture hopes to preserve by such tactics. A properly functioning Chinese village is like the face of the moon, she says. "The round moon cakes and round doorways, the round tables of graduated size that fit one roundness inside another, round windows and rice bowls," these, says Kingston, remind a family of "the law," the path, the rules that keep the village intact, especially in difficult times, in times of hunger or war. "The frightened villagers, who depended on one another to maintain the real, went to my aunt to show her a personal, physical representation of the break she had made in the 'roundness.' " They threw eggs; they tore out the rice; they slaughtered the stock.

This image asserts, I think, that an orderly world will have areas of

---

* "Shame cultures" are often distinguished from "guilt cultures." A shame culture arises in the kind of face-to-face community where you behave because other people's eyes are always on you. ("The villagers are watchful" is a sentence from a shame culture.) If a man from a shame culture goes on a journey, it is assumed he may do bad things because, after all, no one is looking. In a guilt culture, the moral sanctions are more internalized; you carry the internal eye of your conscience with you wherever you go, and so you will behave on a desert island or in a foreign city. Guilt cultures supposedly follow and improve upon shame cultures (these being the terms, for example, by which E. R. Dodds places Hellenistic Greece above Homeric Greece).

I find this distinction sometimes useful and sometimes not. We certainly have not left shame behind, for one thing (all American high schools are shame cultures; advertising promulgates a culture of shame). The distinction between outside eyes and inside eyes doesn't hold up under scrutiny (even in shame cultures people internalize the group; even in guilt cultures the eye of God watches from above). Douglas Cairns argues, in fact, that the anthropologists who developed these distinctions (Mead, Benedict, Leighton, Kluckhohn) unconsciously assumed their own middle-class, Protestant, American guilt culture to be at one end of an evolutionary path. For Cairns's excellent summary and critique of the whole debate, see his *Aidos*, pp. 14–47.

speech and areas of silence. "You must never tell others what I am about to tell you" seems an odd way to begin a story, at least for those of us who buy our fictions in bookstores. But it has always been the way that one class of narratives begins. In the American Southwest, the stories that the Hopi tell in the kivas are not told to strangers; they are not even told to other Hopi. In ancient Greece it was unlawful to recite the Orphic poems to the uninitiated. Similarly, Greek myth has it that the goddess Demeter personally showed the people of Eleusis "the conduct of her rites and taught them all her mysteries . . . —awful mysteries which no one may in any way transgress or pry into or utter, for deep awe of the gods checks the voice."

We might say, then, that in many traditions the injunction to silence is the speech act by which a particular narrative is made sacred.* The rule of silence separates or cuts these stories off from all other stories and makes them special, holy, sacred. The root of the Hebrew word *k-d-sh*—usually translated as "holy"—contains this notion of separation, so that in fact some versions of the Old Testament translate a line like "I am the Lord . . . ; be ye Holy because I am Holy" as ". . . and I am set apart and you must be set apart like me." Similarly, in the Greek tradition a piece of land dedicated to a god is called a *temenos*, a word derived from a verb meaning "to cut off." A story preceded by the rule of silence is a language *temenos*—speech cut off from other speech and thereby sanctified.

Such rules produce two kinds of speaking and two kinds of silence. "Profane" means *pro fanum*, in front of the temple. I can never think of this without imagining an old European town square with a bustling street market in front of the church or cathedral. In the courtyard outside the church, people speak profanely by definition and, if they've been properly

---

* This means that a book such as this is necessarily made from profane texts. I've mentioned before that Coyote tales were traditionally told only in winter; now they appear in the library no matter the season. Paul Radin points out that when he found an informant among the Winnebago Indians willing to tell the trickster cycle he knew he'd also found a loss of the sacred.

Then again, perhaps the *truly* sacred is still hidden. In an essay on African-American narrative, Bill Hampton speculates that "trickster tales of more sacred character have never been collected from American Negroes, only those of a profane nature either actually being told among the Negroes themselves or told to collectors."

instructed, they are silent about the mysteries. Inside the temple, on the other hand, they speak of the mysteries but remain silent as to the profane. Such spheres of speech and spheres of silence, and recognizable boundaries between the two, are thus intimately tied up with any world organized to distinguish between the sacred and the profane.

Kingston's mother, then, is a kind of Chinese bard, trying to keep the mysteries alive. The phrase "You must not tell anyone" announces that she is initiating her daughter (the American girl Monkey) into an area of special speech. Moreover, the mother doesn't actually mean "anyone": I think Kingston is expected to repeat this story eventually to her own daughter. It is a family or village myth—spoken ritually at the time of a young girl's menstruation, and forbidden to speech in all other times. If we say that narratives marked as special by a rule of silence are not only sacred but mythic, and that the telling of myth is the way in which a society affirms its own reality, then we begin to get a sense of why honoring the silence might be important, and why one might not invite Monkey into the home, or let Coyote ride in the Sun-lodge. If rules of silence help "maintain the real," as Kingston puts it, then one takes considerable risk breaking them.

To put it boldly, one risks destroying the cosmos. And if that is the case, then the shame that binds the tongue is a gift from the gods to protect reckless mortals from their own foolishness. In fact, the current popular understanding of shame (as a sort of disability acquired in childhood) does not invoke fully enough the kind of recognition and caution this gift entails. *Aidos* is the Greek term that often gets translated as "shame," and it has an instructively wide range of meaning, denoting not only modesty, self-respect, and regard for others but, more important, reverence and awe. When you enter the grove of a god (or meet a prophet, poet, or king) these several feelings should rise as one: awe and reverence and the kind of inhibitory shame that keeps you from doing or saying anything profane or sacrilegious. In fact, the person who has no such *aidos*, the person who cannot sense the force fields of the spiritual world, is in danger, like an animal stripped of its protective instincts. Understood this way, the danger isn't really that shamelessness will destroy the cosmos, it's that the cosmos will destroy the shameless.

∙ ∙ ∙

These threats on both sides, to the shameless person and to the world around him, are, I think, what sometimes lead people to ask if the trickster isn't really a psychopath. Certainly there are parallels. Psychopaths lie, cheat, and steal. They are given to obscenity and, as one psychologist puts it, exhibit "a confusion of amorous and excretory functions." They're not just antisocial, they're foolishly so (they "will commit thefts, forgery, adultery, fraud, and other deeds for astonishingly small stakes and under much greater risks of being discovered than will the ordinary scoundrel"). While they are often smart, they have a sort of "rudderless intelligence," responding to situations as they arise but unable to formulate any coherent, sustainable long-term plan. They are masters of the empty gesture, and have a glib facility with language, stripping words of the glue that normally connects them to feeling and morality. Finally, they lack both remorse and shame for the harm and hurt that trail behind them. One way or another, almost everything that can be said about psychopaths can also be said about tricksters.

But the opposite is not the case. It's not simply that trickster operates in myth rather than the real world, though that is an important distinction, of course. It's more that trickster's mythic functions are wider than any psychopath's, and harder to classify. For one thing, trickster stories themselves have typically been told in ways that marked them as "special speech," so that, no matter how profane their content, they belonged to an anomalous category, a sort of sacred lack of the sacred. Furthermore, the cheating, stealing, lying that go along with this sacred/not-sacred position enable tricksters to perform a unique set of necessary tasks, as we've amply seen, from enlivening gods that have been deadened by their own purity to negotiating the otherwise necessary and impermeable divide between heaven and earth. It might be right to say that trickster, like the psychopath, has a "rudderless intelligence," but if so it is a useful intelligence, for it continues to function when normal guidance systems have failed, as they periodically will. Finally, for all his failings and all the grief he authors, trickster is also a culture hero, inventor of fish traps, bringer of fire, the one who turned his own destroyed intestines into foodstuffs for the New People. He is connected to a class of actions no psychopath ever performed. Here it's worth recalling Paul Radin's classic insight: trickster is "at one and the same time creator and destroyer, giver and negator . . . [who] knows neither good nor evil yet . . . is responsible for both." We lose half of this and more (for the quick of the matter is in the ambiguity) when trickster is rewritten as a psychopath.

I have often wondered, then, whether the associative leap that links these two characters isn't really a defense against the anxiety that trickster's methods can produce. There is, of course, good reason to be cautious when glib and cunning human beings appear on the scene. But it must also be the case that a society, to preserve the status quo, will slide an image of the psychopath over the face of the trickster to prevent real contact. Like one of those Styrofoam owls they put on buildings to scare off timid pigeons, the image of the psychopath is a minatory illusion, a threatening mask to keep the conventional from approaching trickster's sacred/not-sacred functions. Trickster is among other things the gatekeeper who opens the door into the next world; those who mistake him for a psychopath never even know such a door exists.

This digression doesn't actually take us very far from Kingston's story, for she, too, when confronting the possibility of breaking her mother's rule of silence, found herself imagining a threatening and frightful image—not a psychopath but the haunting visage of her drowned aunt. That woman had thrown herself into the family well: "The Chinese are always very frightened of the drowned one," Kingston explains, the one "whose weeping ghost, wet hair hanging and skin bloated, waits silently by the water to pull down a substitute." Kingston says that to write her book she had to confront and go beyond this terrifying apparition. Hers was the fear of a woman who *does* feel the inhibitory shame and awe of *aidos*, but feels compelled to speak nonetheless, the fear of a woman who knows that in breaking the moon's roundness by giving voice where silence is supposed to reign she may well be exiling herself to a world without order.

As I've tried to make clear, such exile is one of the plausible consequences of shameless speech, and to understand why someone might risk those consequences I want to focus on one essential detail in Kingston's situation—the fact that she is the child of immigrant parents. Because they live in two cultures at once, such children have an unusual and instructive relationship to shame. Their parents come from China, say, or Mexico or Poland or Tibet. The Old Country inheres in their speech inflections, the spices they put in the cook pot, the stories they tell, and the silences they keep. At home the children live surrounded by all this, but early every weekday morning they also go down the street to the American school, where many things, from the spices to the silences, are different.

Children who live in two worlds are vulnerable to several shames, several sets of eyes watching them. Most obviously, of course, both the parents and the school want the child to know that their way is *the* way, and that all other ways lack true dignity. Immigrant children get to be shamed, first, *by* their parents, and then they get to be ashamed *of* their parents. In *Hunger of Memory*, a memoir of growing up Mexican-American in Los Angeles, Richard Rodriguez gives several vivid pictures of this latter feeling. He remembers times, "like the night at a brightly lit gasoline station (a blaring white memory)," when he stood awkwardly listening to his father, "pressured, hurried, confused," trying to speak English to the easygoing teenage attendant. He remembers winning an award at school and having his parents come to see him receive it. "A few minutes later, I heard my father speak to my teacher and felt ashamed of his labored, accented words."

As for shame *from* the parents, the feeling has an extra confusing twist for an immigrant child because it is so clearly contingent, just one version of things, and yet its authors are the parents themselves: surely they can't be living in a dream world! Both Rodriguez and Kingston spend much of their books struggling against their elders' sense of decorum. (Rodriguez describes his parents as having a kind of "aristocratic reserve." "Of those matters too jaggedly personal to reveal to intimates, my parents will never speak." "I am writing about those very things my mother has asked me not to reveal.") But both these authors struggle to honor the elders even as they betray them. These books are written in the language of the dominant culture and addressed mostly to anonymous readers, but each is formally dedicated to those it disobeys: "To mother and father" (Kingston); "She turns silent to my father, who stands watching me. . . . For her and for him—to honor them" (Rodriguez).

Such elegiac touches aside, in the end these artists decidedly break the family rules of silence, and we are now in a position to understand more fully why they do so despite the large and plausible consequences that might follow. In Kingston's case, her mother's story carries with it the lesson that the villagers set and enforce the rules of sexual conduct.

For Kingston to accept the injunction to silence that prefaces the story is to accept that lesson as well. And much more, for to enter Chinese village society on its own terms is to be placed in a hierarchy in which girl children have almost no value, and are raised either to marry or to be sold as slaves. "I am useless," Kingston used to feel, "one more girl who can't be sold." One grandfather used to call her a "maggot," asking, "Where are my grandsons?"

> When I visit the family now, I wrap my American success around me like a private shawl; I *am* worthy of eating the food. From afar I can believe my family loves me fundamentally. They only say, "When fishing for treasures in the flood, be careful not to pull in girls," because that is what one says about daughters. But I watched such words come out of my own mother's and father's mouths. . . . And I had to get out of hating range.

When Kingston's mother says, "You must not tell anyone what I am about to tell you," she weaves a shame cover. Beneath its rules of silence lies a whole system of gender relationships. Perhaps in China the divisions those rules produced healed into sacred scars, but in Stockton, California, they wound, and the girl who has been marked by them must speak shamelessly if she is to be healed.

As I imagine it, such an immigrant child begins to speak shamelessly on the road between home and school. Both at home and at school she may be enchanted by the local mythology, but on the road between the two she is briefly free to discard and retain parts of each world. She throws things out of her lunch box and crumples up notes from her teachers. On the road between home and school she invents a mediating language or story; she assembles from the fragments of her experience the new story that will be hers, the story that combines what is of use from each world into a new world, crossbred from the two. Furthermore, where this story uses parts of the Old World, its author must overcome her shame of her parents; where it uses parts of the new, she must overcome their shaming. To her parents' ears the result, the mediating invention by which an immigrant child comes to her identity, is necessarily shameless speech. In Kingston's case, its guardian spirit, the one who keeps the tongue lively as it moves through fields of inhibition, is the faithful-unfaithful servant the old Chinese stories call the King of the Monkeys.

SLAYER OF ARGUS

As all travelers discover, the list of things that shame the locals varies from place to place. The claim is always made that *aidos* is inborn in the noble soul, but the traveler who has visited the groves of foreign gods and felt no inhibitory awe soon wonders if that is really so. Shame itself may be universal, but its content is not fixed in heaven. Some places women cover their breasts; some places they do not. Most places men cover their penises, but some places they do not, as in this report from an ethnographer in Indonesia:

> The anus . . . had a special cover. . . . To touch a man's anus was either an appeal to his strength or a very serious insult. . . . The penis . . . or the pubic hair of a man drew less attention. They did not wear any shame cover.

In the United States, we wear many shame covers, but we are not as easy to shame as the Japanese. In the United States, if a man retrieves a stranger's windblown hat, a simple "thanks" repays the courtesy; in Japan, where there is highly elaborated attention to hierarchy and indebtedness, the same simple kindness leaves its recipient deeply abashed, for in Japan a debt to a stranger is strongly felt and impossible to repay. In Japan, if a small boy wets the bed, his mother will hang the yellowed sheets from the window to make him lose face before his friends (while, in the United States, we leave the child alone and look for a bed-wetting gene).

One hardly needs leave home to do the kind of traveling I'm imagining here. All children, after all, are travelers in time, which is to say that the content of shame shifts from one generation to the next. The immigrant child stands metaphorically for all human beings who grow to differ from their parents. Didn't each of us when young recurrently have the feeling that our folks "just got off the boat," what with their odd sense of when people go to bed, their oppressive manners, and their deaf ear for the new language? To the degree that we differ from these people, and especially if they hurt us, we will seek out some other land to call home, in fantasy if not in fact. In China, those who dream of America as a promised land call it the Gold Mountain; there is China and then there is the Gold Mountain. For the rest of us, there is the family of our birth and then there is some Gold Mountain, a more noble world to which we really belong, one whose citizens will recognize us for who we really are. The richness of this ideal world is often proportional to the poverty of the real, as personal grandiosity is proportional to shame. (Beethoven, born into a family where depressed, alcoholic adults regularly beat their children, convinced himself he was actually descended from nobility. John James Audubon thought he was the lost Dauphin of France, stolen from prison during the Revolution and given over to sailors—this rather than acknowledge that he was a Créole, the bastard child of a French sea captain and his Haitian mistress.)

We visit the land of our secret grandeur in fantasy or in books and movies, and on the road between these imaginings and the actual house where we must eat and sleep, to the degree that we are able, assemble a life from the usable fragments of each. An in-fact immigrant artist like Maxine Hong Kingston makes her art at the place where her parents' remembered Chinese village is coincident with the Gold Mountain (or with Stockton, California, at least). Metaphorical immigrant artists, travelers in time, create their art at the point where the ideal is coincident with the real, though in this case, too, there are shame barriers and rules of silence to contend with, and a particular kind of cunning is required.

A case in point would be the poet Allen Ginsberg. Ginsberg grew up with a rather passive and straitlaced father, Louis, and a periodically crazy mother, Naomi (clinically paranoid, she was afraid, for example, that her thoughts were being manipulated by three implanted metal bars that the FBI had wired to her brain during a stay in the hospital). When Ginsberg was in college, the two most troubling areas of his world were this crazy mother and his own homosexuality. If he turned to his father for advice on these matters, what he got was the injunction to silence. Louis Ginsberg dealt with the upsetting parts of his family life by a hasty retreat to convention and denial. We hear the paternal call to conformity in letters sent to his son in college. Here he is lecturing Allen during his sophomore year at Columbia: "The homosexual and the insane person is a menace to himself and to society. Danger and disaster lie that way!" A man must "resign himself to pragmatic values or commit suicide," counsels a later letter. The father here names these two perplexing issues in his son's life and says, basically, "If you insist on pursuing these topics I suggest you kill yourself." (This, by the way, is the standard advice of a shame culture. Because shame is felt as an indelible stain to the whole self, release seems to call for suicide, as in Kingston's aunt's case. In fact, shame cultures sometimes have an ethic of noble suicide; in Japan, if you have two conflicting obligations—a demand made by the emperor, say, at odds with one made by your family—and if the denial of either one would be shameful, the honorable solution is to honor each, then kill yourself.)

If there are homosexuals and crazy people around, Louis Ginsberg would rather deny they exist than know them, even if they are his kin, and even if silence means death. It's worth noting, too, that the younger Ginsberg sometimes shared his father's caution. A later letter from Allen to his father declares soberly that he had stopped cutting classes, was dressing formally in a coat and tie, and had "started to really get an education, making the most of the College by returning unread to the library" all his volumes of Gide and Baudelaire.

Were that the end of the tale, it would be a pure case of speechless shame, but as we all know, Ginsberg not only retrieved Gide and Baudelaire from the library, he left his father's house and spent several decades "wandering in various alternative . . . metaphysical universes," as he once put it. "I went . . . to what my imagination believed true to Eternity." Ginsberg's early work is full of Eternity and Angels, and in such language we hear the shamed boy's dream of traveling out of present time toward some more perfected land. He would leave the muck of father's village and take himself to the peak of the Gold Mountain.

The summit of that mountain is not the source of his art, however, or not the whole of it at least. The art is in the mixing up of time and eternity, the amalgamation of muck and gold. What gives Ginsberg's early poems their durable presence is the way he cuts his idealist visions with great catalogues of actual fact (sick mother Naomi serving him "a plate of cold fish—chopped raw cabbage dript with tapwater—smelly tomatoes— week-old health food"; Naomi exposing herself, "scars of operations, pancreas, belly wounds, abortions, appendix, stitching of incisions pulling down in the fat like hideous thick zippers.") Ginsberg's art oscillates between idealizing the actual and actualizing the ideal. Having been wounded by this crazy mother, he nonetheless found a way to praise and even elevate her in his poetry; having had what he took to be visions of Eternity, in which, for example, the voice of William Blake spoke poems to him, he spent a lifetime singing Blake to college students, federal judges, and TV talk-show hosts.

Here, however, I must admit that to speak of this work as "shameless" does not quite catch the tenor of it. Artists such as Ginsberg or Kingston struggle deeply with shame. The work they create is not an escape from that struggle, but the resolution or fruit of it. Kingston would not allow herself to publish until she had made a thing of beauty to replace the cultural shapeliness that her speaking out threatened to destroy. Unalloyed shamelessness exists in myth, and in our fantasies of psychopaths, but most actual humans cannot uncover their secrets without passing through their shame. Ginsberg's poem "Kaddish" reveals in detail the things that "embarrassed him the most" about his wounded childhood, but the record indicates it took a lot of work to bring about that revelation; the poem itself begins with several hundred lines of anxious stalling and a catalogue of the strategies (staying up all night, doping himself with amphetamines, listening to Ray Charles blues, reading prayers for the dead out loud, weeping) that Ginsberg used to free his tongue from its own inhibitions.

Perhaps it would be better, then, to say that those who work the edge between what can and can't be said do not escape from shame but turn toward it and engage with it. They wrestle with it; they try to change its face; they kill it in one form so as to resurrect it in another. Hermes is a shameless speaker in the *Hymn*, but that poem regularly refers to him as the Slayer of Argus, as if to remind us that he doesn't simply avoid shame, he faces it and fights it if he has to. In fact, the story behind that epithet gives a wonderful picture of how shame was once imagined, and will deepen our sense of the work Ginsberg—or anyone—must undertake to untie the tongue.

In Ovid's version of this story, Zeus has taken a woman named Io as a lover. His wife, Hera, suspects the infidelity and comes snooping, whereupon Zeus changes Io into a heifer to hide his crime. Hera doesn't quite know what to make of finding her husband with a cow, but she's suspicious and asks Zeus to give her the beast as a gift. Zeus does, and Hera then sets a local giant named Argus to watch over Io. Argus is an unusual giant; in Ovid's words, he has "a head set round with a hundred eyes, of which two in turn were always resting, while the others kept watch and remained on guard."

When Zeus discovers that he can't sneak past the guard to see his girl-friend, he sends Hermes to kill the giant. Hermes, disguised as a goatherd, walks past Argus playing his pipes. Argus is charmed by the music and invites the stranger to sit with him. "With many a tale Hermes wiled away the day in talking and playing on his pipe, as he tried to overcome the watchful eyes. But Argus fought to keep the charms of sleep at bay, and although some of his eyes slumbered, yet some remained awake." Finally Hermes adds a story to his song, telling Argus how the pipes were invented, how Pan had chased a young woman who, desperate to escape, changed herself into the reeds from which Pan fashioned his pipes.

As Hermes weaves this tale he sees "that Argus' eyelids were closed, and all his eyes fast asleep. At once he stopped speaking and deepened Argus' slumbers, gently touching those drowsy eyes with his magic wand. Without delay, as the watchman sat nodding, Hermes struck him with his crescent-shaped sword, just where his head joined his neck; then he flung the body down the cliff, all dripping with blood, and spattering the precipitous rocks as it fell. Argus lay dead—the light of his many eyes was quenched, the whole hundred shrouded in a single darkness."

At the start of many of the tales of Zeus' philandering, we find the father of the gods trying to keep himself from sight. He prefers to dally in darkness, under a cloud, deep in a cave—and from this we may infer that he is not entirely proud of his actions. When Hera asks for the heifer as a gift, Ovid writes, "on the one hand shame persuaded [Zeus] to yield, but on the other love made him reluctant." So here we have a god who feels appropriate *aidos*, and also feels constrained by it. In a shame society, the group is a primary source of both of those feelings, and a good image for that watchful collective is this hundred-eyed, unsleeping giant, Argus. In a shame society, no matter where you are, no matter the time of day or night, no matter how many people are sleeping, at least two eyes are always watching you—or at least that's the feeling you have if you've been properly raised. Luckily, if dalliance is your design, there is a spirit who knows how to put the beast to sleep. He can even kill it and throw the body from a cliff, a bloody end to be sure, but better, perhaps, than killing yourself.

Transposing these images to Ginsberg's story will show, I hope, that there's more to them than their antique sexual politics. The devices I listed earlier by which Ginsberg worked himself up for the "release of particulars" that are the meat of his poem about his mother—the way he stayed up all night, doped himself on amphetamines, and so on—all these are Argus killers. They close his father's eyes, and his teachers' eyes, and all the other eyes that led him to feel ashamed of his mother and of his own hurt. As Hermes does, he finds the songs and the stories (he listens to old blues, he reads aloud Shelley's poem about the death of Keats) that put the guards to sleep, so that he might speak what his own otherwise apt inhibitions forbid. In this case, the man is not looking to cheat on his wife but to speak plainly about his wounds. One of the things that differentiates Ginsberg from other so-called confessional poets is that the things he comes to "confess" are not things he wishes to distance himself from, but things he longs to honor. Therefore, he not only wrestles with shame, he remakes its territory, sanctifying what others have called profane.

This sequence I take to be the general case with those who seek to change the face of shame. Refusing their elders' sense of where speech and silence belong, they do not so much erase the categories as redraw the lines. They lift the old shame thresholds and place them in new doorways. They promulgate an altered sense of dignity to replace the constraining dignity that the village urged on them. By the end of "Kaddish," things that had been unspeakable and degrading about Naomi Ginsberg are not only spoken but transfigured, even (the poet hopes) redeemed. At the end of her memoir, Kingston likens herself to a woman in Chinese legend whose kin learned to sing the song she had composed while living with the barbarians. In both cases, this kind of art settles on the line between sacred and profane, opens a commerce between the two, and by that commerce shifts their content, or shifts the line.

And yet, if I may reverse my own reversal, to say that such artists *aren't* shameless doesn't quite do them justice, either. At the difficult moment of first speaking, it is probably impossible for anyone to know if the future holds such noble ends as "changing the face of shame." If shame has bound the tongue, even the most ethical person must pass through a period that has the feel of unalloyed betrayal and risk if he or she is to speak again. The boundary markers cannot be moved unless they are briefly lifted from their footings, and with that the shapely, reassuring world once held together by faithful kinfolk disappears. In its absence, one needs guides whose sense of shame is not too finely tuned. As I said at the outset, moral sophistication and fine writing may be a feature of Kingston's finished work, but in the process of making that work she was surely led by messier and more ambivalent spirits. The published Ginsberg, too, has clear ethical concerns (he regularly calls down shame on his government, for example), but especially to make the early work he sought out a score of tricks to put the beast of shame to sleep. Given clear injunctions to silence both internal and external ("Commit suicide"!), and given that what he hoped to describe was incoherent in terms of the poetry his elders admired, he could take no other path. Creative mobility in this world requires, at crucial moments, the strategic erasure of ethical boundaries. They lose that mobility who cling to beauty, or who suffer from what the poet Czeslaw Milosz has called "an attachment to ethics at the expense of the sacred." When the pilgrim Tripitaka insists too forcefully on righteous action, his Monkey guide goes home sulking and the pilgrimage collapses. When Monkey persuades him to leave his unseasoned and abstract sense of shame behind, they cross mountain after mountain.

During the years I was writing this book, there was an intense national debate over the concern that government funds might be used to subsidize pornographic art. The particulars will undoubtedly change, but the debate is perennial. On the one side, we have those who presume to speak for the collective trying to preserve the coverings and silences that give social space its order. On the other side, we have the agents of change, time travelers who take the order itself to be mutable, who hope—to give it the most positive formulation—to preserve the sacred by finding ways to shift the structure of things as contingency demands. It is not immediately clear why this latter camp must so regularly turn to bodily and sexual display, but the context I am establishing here suggests that such display is necessary.

To explore why this might be the case, let me begin with the classic image from the Old Testament: Adam and Eve leaving the garden, having learned shame and therefore having covered their genitals and, in the old paintings, holding their hands over their faces as well. By these actions they inscribe their own bodies. The body happens to be a uniquely apt location for the inscription of shame, partly because the body itself seems to be the sense organ of shame (the feeling swamps us, we stutter and flush against our will), but also because the content of shame, *what* we feel ashamed of, typically seems indelible and fixed, with us as a sort of natural fact, the way the body is with us as a natural fact. "Shame is what you are, guilt is what you do," goes an old saying. Guilt can be undone with acts of penance, but the feeling of shame sticks around like a birthmark or the smell of cigarettes.

I earlier connected the way we learn about shame to rules about speech and silence, and made the additional claim that those rules have an ordering function. Now, let us say that the rules give order to several things at once, not just to society but to the body and the psyche as well. When I say "several things at once" I mean that the rules imply the congruence of these three realms; the orderliness of one is the orderliness of the others. The organized body is a sign that we are organized psychologically and that we understand and accept the organization of the world around us. When Adam and Eve cover their genitals, they simultaneously begin to structure consciousness and to structure their primordial community. To make the *temenos*, a line is drawn on the earth and one thing cut from another; when Adam and Eve learn shame, they draw a line on their bodies, dividing them into zones like the zones of silence and speech—or, rather, not "like" those zones, but identified with them, for what one covers on the body one also consigns to silence.

Kingston's mother's story also works in this three-level way. It's a homemade Chinese-American Adam and Eve story. It takes a bodily fact—menstruation—and names it as shameful by setting it in the context of a shame story. Then it links the content of shame to particular teachings about a woman's self-image and her place in society. We find the same pattern with different content in Richard Rodriguez's memoir. The "bodily fact" here is the color of his skin, which, as a teenager, he took to be a kind of stigma and tried to keep covered:

> The normal, extraordinary, animal excitement of feeling my body alive—riding shirtless on a bicycle in the warm wind created by furious self-propelled motion—the sensations that first had excited in me a sense of my maleness, I denied. I was too ashamed of my body. I wanted to forget that I had a body because I had a brown body.

In this case, as in Kingston's, an unalterable fact about the body is linked to a place in the social order, and in both cases, to accept the link is to be caught in a kind of trap.

Before anyone can be snared in this trap, an equation must be made between the body and the world (my skin color is my place as a Hispanic; menstruation is my place as a woman). This substituting of one thing for another is called metonymy in rhetoric, one of the many figures of thought, a trope or verbal turn. The construction of the trap of shame begins with this metonymic trick, a kind of bait and switch in which one's changeable social place is figured in terms of an unchangeable part of the body. Then by various means the trick is made to blend invisibly into the landscape. To begin with, there are always larger stories going on—about women or race or a snake in a garden. The enchantment of those regularly repeated fables, along with the rules of silence at their edges, and the assertion that they are intuitively true—all these things secure the borders of the narrative and make it difficult to see the contingency of its figures of thought. Once the verbal tricks are invisible, the artifice of the social order becomes invisible as well, and begins to seem natural. As menstruation and skin color and the genitals are natural facts, so the social and psychological orders become natural facts.

In short, to make the trap of shame we inscribe the body as a sign of wider worlds, then erase the artifice of that signification so that the content of shame becomes simply the way things are, as any fool can see.

If this is how the trap is made, then escaping it must involve reversing at least some of these elements. In what might be called the "heavy-bodied" escape, one senses that there's something to be changed but ends up trying to change the body itself, mutilating it, or even committing suicide, as Kingston's aunt did. Suicide is the extreme case, of course; Rodriguez's memoir offers a good example of the more common manner in which people try to escape the trap while still taking its figurative elements at face value:

> As a boy, I'd stay in the kitchen ... listening while my aunts spoke of their pleasure at having light children. . . . It was the woman's spoken concern: the fear of having a dark-skinned son or daughter. Remedies were exchanged. . . . Children born dark grew up to have their faces treated regularly with a mixture of egg white and lemon juice concentrate.

Egg white isn't really white, of course, just as white people are not really white, but where the figures of thought are invisible, the connections will seem fixed and in a racist society a brown boy will end up scrubbed with egg whites.

These are the beginnings of conscious struggle, but we have yet to meet the mind of the trickster—or if we have, it belongs to the trickster who tries to eat the reflected berries, who burns his own anus in anger, who has not learned to separate the bait from the hook. As we saw earlier, the pressures of experience produce from that somewhat witless character a more sophisticated trickster who *can* separate bait from hook, who knows that the sign of something is not the thing itself, and who is therefore a better escape artist with a much more playful relationship to the local stories. The heavy-bodied, literalizing attempt to escape from shame carries much of the trap with it—the link to the body, the silence, and so on. Inarticulately, it takes the sign for the thing itself, imagining racism inheres in the color of the skin. Wise to the tricks of language, the light-bodied escape from shame refuses the whole setup—refuses the metonymic shift, the enchantment of group story, and the rules of silence—and by these refusals it detaches the supposedly overlapping levels of inscription from one another so that the body, especially, need no longer stand as the mute, incarnate seal of social and psychological order. All this, but especially the speaking out where shame demands silence, depends largely on a consciousness that doesn't feel much inhibition, and knows how traps are made, and knows how to subvert them.

Richard Rodriguez's memoir describes the growth of such a consciousness. He becomes proud, rather than ashamed, of his skin. One summer he got a gardening job and let himself darken:

> After that summer . . . the curse of physical shame was broken by the sun. . . . No longer would I deny myself the pleasing sensations of my maleness. During those years when middle-class black Americans began to assert with pride, "Black is beautiful," I was able to regard my complexion without shame.

This goes only partway, however. The phrase "Black is beautiful" still literalizes. Black is sometimes beautiful, sometimes ugly; sometimes "black" means oil, sometimes it means a business suit. To free "black" from "shame" by tying it to "pride" doesn't go far enough, as Rodriguez eventually comes to see. Nowadays, when he stays at fancy hotels, the clerks assume he is rich and leisured and they read his dark skin as a sign that he's been skiing in Switzerland or boating in the Caribbean. "My complexion," he says, "assumes its significance from the context of my life. My skin, in itself, means nothing." This is the insight that comes to all boundary-crossers—immigrants in fact or immigrants in time— that meaning is contingent and identity fluid, even the meaning and identity of one's own body.

It should by now be easier to see why there will always be art that uncovers the body, and artists who speak shamelessly, even obscenely. All social structures do well to anchor their rules of conduct in the seemingly simple inscription of the body, so that only after I have covered my privates am I allowed to show my face to the world and have a public life. The rules of bodily decorum usually imply that the cosmos depends on the shame we feel about our bodies. But sometimes the lesson is a lie, and a cunningly self-protecting one at that, for to question it requires self-exposure and loss of face, and who would want that? Well, trickster would, as would all those who find they cannot fashion a place for themselves in the world until they have spoken against collective silence. We certainly see this—not just the speaking out but the self-exposure—in Allen Ginsberg, and we see it a bit more subtly in both Kingston and Rodriguez. Neither of them is a "dirty writer" the way Ginsberg is, but to begin to speak, one of them must talk about menstruation (which talk she links to becoming the mistress of her own sexuality) and the other must talk about his skin (which talk he links to possessing his "maleness").

To the degree that other orders are linked to the way the body is inscribed, and to the degree that the link is sealed by rules of silence, the first stuttering questioning of those orders must always begin by breaking the seal and speaking about the body. Where obscene speech has such roots it is worth defending, and those who would suppress it court a subtle but serious danger. They are like the gods who would bind Loki, for this suppression hobbles the imagination that copes with the shifting and contingent nature of things, and so invites apocalyptic change where something more playful would have sufficed. Better to let trickster steal the shame covers now and then. Better to let Coyote have a ride in the Sun-god's lodge. Better to let Monkey come on your journey to the West.

8

....

MATTER OUT OF PLACE

Marcel Duchamp spoke to me, during the course of the Second World
War . . . , of a new interest in the preparation of shit, of which the
small excretions from the navel are the "de luxe" editions.
                                                        —Salvador Dali

HEAVEN'S PRIVY

Once upon a time the gods were closer to this earth; once they walked among us and sat at our tables. But that was long ago, long before the enduring divisions that shape this world were drawn. The Fon in West Africa call the female portion of their androgynous creator Mawu; she is the mother of the trickster Legba. In ancient days when Mawu lived here on earth, Legba was her obedient servant. When he did a good deed the people ignored him and thanked Mawu, but when he did an evil deed the people blamed him directly, as if Mawu had nothing to do with it. Legba complained of this arrangement. Mawu replied that in governing the world it is best if the master be known as good and the servants be known as evil.

"Very well," said Legba.

Now Mawu had a yam garden and Legba told her that thieves were planning to steal her crop. So Mawu assembled all the people and announced that anyone who stole from her garden would be put to death. That night Legba stole Mawu's sandals and, wearing them on his feet, stole all her yams. When the theft was discovered, Mawu assembled the people and searched to find a foot that matched the footprints in her garden. When none could be found, Legba asked if Mawu herself might have come in the night and forgotten about it.

"Who, me? That is why I do not like you, Legba. I will measure my foot with that footprint." When Mawu put her foot down, it fit the print exactly.

The people began to laugh and shout. "The owner herself is a thief!" Mawu was humiliated. She left the earth. She didn't go very far, though— only about ten feet up. And Legba was still her servant: every evening he would come to her and give an account of the day's activity and receive his instructions for the day that followed.

And again, whenever Legba did something wrong the people would blame him, and Mawu herself would join in the reproach. Irritated, Legba conspired with an old woman. Every evening after she had washed her dishes, this old woman would throw the dirty dishwater up into the air and soak Mawu with it. Angered, Mawu soon departed. Now she lives on high and Legba, her son, lives here on this earth.

The detail that interests me here is the dirty dishwater at the very end, but before I can explain what draws me to it, I need to give some sense of how I read its context. At the beginning of the story, Legba is differentiated from his mother on her terms, not his own, and that irritates him. If he is really her obedient servant, executing her will without fail, then she should at least acknowledge that his actions, both good and bad, are her actions. In the little drama that Legba engineers, that might mean acknowledging that the owner of the yams really is the thief (which seems like a lie, but if the mother rules the son, it's a lie that tells the truth). Mawu wants to pick and choose, however; she wants to hide her own duality so that people will think she's good and never bad, high and never low. Legba's ruse forces her to come clean (or dirty): she must differentiate herself from him more fully or else confess their unity. She chooses to differentiate. She completes the separation from her offspring, whereupon Legba is not quite so watched over and can himself become the ambivalent author of what humans take to be both "good" and "evil."

But Mawu doesn't retreat right away. She's the kind of mother who hopes to back off just five or ten feet. Perhaps her son would like a basement room with his own refrigerator? Legba deals with this inadequate distance by forcing his mother to face up to one final ambivalence: is she clean or dirty or some primordial combination of the two? If Mawu made this world, then the dirt in the dishwater is part of her, or, rather, it once was: this story is a later chapter in an unfolding creation, marking the moment when the pure and the impure, the clean and the dirty, the immaculate and the pied, are separated into categories and a line drawn between them. On Legba's earth there is still a great confusion of the dirty and the clean, and we must wash the dishes all the time. But no one washes dishes in heaven. There is no dirt up there, and Mawu can keep her purity intact.

What exactly is this "dirt," this un-cleaning agent so powerful that Legba can enlist it to separate the heaven from the earth? It seems to be shifty stuff. "Dirt" washed from the dishes was "food" not long ago and we sat around putting it in our mouths. As anyone knows who has traveled a little in the world, the line between the dirty and the clean is not fixed by nature. A friend who lived on a small Pacific Island where the locals void their bowels on the beach below the high-tide line found those locals could not believe that Americans actually shit in their own homes (disgusting!). Centuries ago, Native Americans were revolted to find that Europeans kept their snot in pocket handkerchiefs. "If you like that filth so much," said one native ironist of manners, "give me your handkerchief and I will soon fill it for you." In the same line, I'm told that people who are native to hot climates, amused by the excesses of European clothing, sometimes conclude that those from more temperate lands like to keep their farts close to their bodies. In the Mysore state in India, a Brahmin who has been seriously polluted can purify himself with cow manure and water. "Cows are sometimes said to be gods," a traveler writes. "Cow-dung, like the dung of any other animal, is intrinsically impure and can cause defilement—in fact it will defile a god; but it is pure relative to a mortal. . . . The cow's most impure part is sufficiently pure relative even to a Brahmin priest to remove the latter's impurities."

Enough examples like these and we begin to wonder if there is any way to make a general rule about what is dirt and what is not. The anthropologist Mary Douglas (whose book *Purity and Danger* informs my argument here) suggests we go back to an old saying: "Dirt is matter out of place." Egg on my plate is breakfast, but egg on my face is dirt; shoes in the closet are tidy, but shoes on the table are a mess; the farmer in Iowa washes the manure from his hands, the Brahmin in Mysore washes with it. To this first definition of dirt, Douglas adds a second: dirt is the anomalous, not just what is out of place but what has no place at all when we are done making sense of our world.

The Old Testament, for example, divides the world into three parts—earth, water, and sky—and each element, Douglas explains, has "its proper kind of animal life. In the firmament two-legged fowls fly with wings. In the water scaly fish swim with fins. On the earth four-legged animals hop, jump, or walk." Old Testament dietary laws decree that all anomalous creatures, all those that do not fit this scheme, are dirt, "abominations." The lobster is dirty but the scaly salmon is not; the snake is dirty but the frog is not. The rock badger looks like an earless rabbit, has teeth like a rhino, and the little hoofs on its toes seem to relate it to the elephant: clearly an abominable beast.*

In either of Douglas's cases—out of place or anomalous—the point to underline here is that dirt is always a by-product of creating order. Where there is dirt, there is always a system of some kind, and rules about dirt are meant to preserve it. Whether you live in Iowa or in Mysore, if you care about your community, you will respect the dirt commandments that give it structure. As with keeping shame's appropriate silences, honoring the distinction between the clean and the dirty helps make the world an orderly place, while dishonoring that distinction—defecating in the wrong spot or mixing lobsters with the fish—threatens the design, the cosmos.

The Legba story illustrates both sides of this idea. If by cosmos we mean the structure of things before Mawu departs, then Legba threatens it with a strategic application of dirt. But once Mawu has departed, a new cosmos appears, one whose shape is defined exactly by the exclusion of that dishwater. Douglas has it that "dirt is the by-product of . . . system-

---

* I should add that Douglas removes questions of hygiene from her definition of dirt. Our taxonomies and our attempts to avoid pathogens are often connected, of course, but probably less than we assume. Hebrew dietary laws have often been explained in terms of hygiene, but Douglas shows that such explanations don't hold up as well as the taxonomic one.

atic ordering," but it's more that dirt and order are mutually dependent, for in this case the conceit can be as easily reversed: for Legba, the creation of order is a by-product of dirt. Dirt is one of the tools available to trickster as he makes this world, the world in which the heavens are very far away.

I have chosen to open this chapter with the Legba story because it deals with First Things, and first things should come first. But if they are done right, first things need never be repeated, and in many respects the Legba story is an exception to the rule. After those early times, what Legba likes to do, what tricksters in general like to do, is erase or violate that line between the dirty and the clean. As a rule, trickster takes a god who lives on high and debases him or her with earthly dirt, or appears to debase him, for in fact the usual consequence of this dirtying is the god's eventual renewal.*

One of the best versions of this motif of revivification through dirt comes from ancient Japan. In Shinto mythology we find the character known as Susa-nö-o using dirt to disturb the line between heaven and earth and upsetting the way the cosmos has been differentiated. Susa-nö-o is a kind of storm god (when spring storms destroy the rice paddies, Susa-nö-o is to blame). Susa-nö-o's sister is the Goddess of the Sun, Amaterasu, and at the beginning of the episode that interests me here she has just entered into the rituals that bring the agricultural year to its close: in the New Palace she is about to taste the first fruits of the harvest, and in the sacred weaving hall she and her maidens will weave new garments for the gods.

Each of these activities has an air of purity and enclosure about it. The weaving maidens are virgins, and great ritual order attends both the weaving of cloth and the growing of crops. The cultivation of rice, especially, calls for carefully delineated rice paddies, and the several ways

---

* The *Homeric Hymn to Hermes* is more decorous than most trickster tales, but it nonetheless retains a touch of the dirt-rebirth theme, the key moment being when Apollo grabs baby Hermes and threatens to throw him into the underworld if he doesn't confess to his thefts. "Phoebus Apollo picked the child up and began to carry him. At this point the powerful Killer of Argus had a plan. Held aloft in Apollo's hands, he cut loose an omen, an exhausted belly slave, a rude herald of worse to come." At the close of the *Hymn*, Apollo is enchanted and lively, playing a lyre he never had before, but that does not happen until he has descended into Maia's cave and been sullied by a farting, shitting baby.

of tampering with their design are listed among the great "heavenly sins" of archaic Japan.

The stormy Susa-nö-o of course disrupts the orderliness and enclosure of his sister's ritual activities. Even before he arrives at the New Palace and the weavers' hall, he has played havoc in the rice paddies, setting up false boundary stakes, breaking down the earthen dikes, and letting wild ponies loose to play in the water. After that, he enters the palace where the first fruits are tasted and defecates, strewing his feces about the hall. In some versions of the story he defecates under Amaterasu's exalted throne, so that no sooner has she taken her seat than she leaps up in great disgust. As for the weavers' hall, Susa-nö-o tears a hole in its roof and drops a dappled pony that he has skinned "backward" onto the women working inside (backward means from tail to head— a taboo violation and another "heavenly sin"). This sudden intrusion so terrifies his sister the Sun Goddess that she falls against her loom, the shuttle piercing her vagina and wounding her or, in some versions, killing her.

At one level, all this is a story about the life and fortunes of the sun, as told by a people who depend on it to grow their rice. Because of Susa-nö-o's actions the sun declines, or dies (just as, in the Norse tales, the sunny Baldr dies because of Loki). Put another way, Susa-nö-o intervenes to create the pivot upon which the old year can turn into the new year. In versions in which Amaterasu does not actually die as a result of Susa-nö-o's actions, what happens next is almost as bad: she hides herself in a cave, the heavens and earth go dark, and "all manner of calamities" occur. The gods then must work very hard to bring light back to the world, and while there are many interesting details to the way they lured her from her cave (it includes ribald play and much laughter), the point for now is that the dirt and disorder Susa-nö-o has injected into the harvest rituals have initiated some sort of eclipse, which is followed, in turn, by rituals to repair the loss. The sun disappears; then the sun returns.

Susa-nö-o's actions not only turn the year, they add something to Amaterasu's year-end ceremony that makes the world a more fertile place to live, as we see from what happens next. First of all, for his misdeeds the gods banish Susa-nö-o from heaven and he comes to live in this world (by one reading this is the beginning of agriculture on earth, the harvest riches formerly reserved for the gods are loosened by this descent). Second, as soon as he arrives on earth Susa-nö-o kills a "food-goddess" out of whose dead body come seeds: rice, millet, red beans, wheat, soy beans. The story that began with a heavenly harvest thus ends with earthly seeds that can be planted to feed the human race. In between there is a winter's tale in which dirt gets into the house of the sun, fruitfully reversing the year-end impulse to enclosure, order, and purity.

Such reversal is needed because the sun's impulse toward purity will end in another kind of loss if it is not checked. The sequence of this narrative—trickster subverting the sun's intentions and by that leading her into death or decline—implies that one of her intentions was to avoid exactly that end, to avoid death. Winter is coming, and she would like to put it off, or elude its consequences. Susa-nö-o's disruptions mean she can't, and the new seeds that follow show us why, or why her success would have been a worse disaster. In this world, in trickster's world, life and death are one thing, not two, and therefore no one gets rid of death without getting rid of life as well. You get no seeds at all if the sunlight is too pure ever to mingle with the muck of the rice paddies. You get no seeds if shit never enters the New Palace. And because there is always a hunger seeking for those seeds, whenever humans or gods move to purify life by excluding death, or to protect order completely from the dirt that is its by-product, trickster will upset their plans. When purity approaches sterility, he will tear a hole in the sacred enclosure and drop a dead pony on the virgin weavers, or strew his feces under the Sun Goddess's throne. In the Legba story we saw that trickster can create the boundary between heaven and earth, threatening the gods with dirt until they retreat into the distant sky; here we see that once such a boundary exists trickster can abrogate it, importing dirt into the exalted halls until some of heaven's wealth is loosened and the earth is fertilized, the sun reborn.

I am, of course, reading this Japanese story rather literally. While it is a nature myth for an agrarian culture (those seeds are actually seeds, and that pile of shit should properly be called manure), the images resonate at other levels as well. If dirt is "matter out of place," if it is what we exclude when we are creating order, then this and other stories about tricksters and dirt must also speak to the sterility that hides in most all human system and design. The models we devise to account for the world and the shapes we create to make ourselves at home in it are all too often inadequate to the complexity of things, and end up deadened by their own exclusions. Such is the implication of the Susa-nö-o story, and such also the implication of one of the founding narratives of twentieth-century psychotherapy.

One summer day when Carl Jung was a twelve-year-old schoolboy in Basel, Switzerland, he fell to admiring the cathedral in the town square. In his autobiography he recalls his train of thought:

> The sky was gloriously blue, the day one of radiant sunshine. The roof of the cathedral glittered, the sun sparkling from the new, brightly glazed tiles. I was overwhelmed by the beauty of the sight, and thought: "The world is beautiful and the church is beautiful, and God made all this and sits above it far away in the blue sky on a golden throne and. . . ." Here came a great hole in my thoughts, and a choking sensation. I felt numbed, and knew only: "Don't go on thinking now! Something terrible is coming. . . ."

The boy could feel some dangerous image presenting itself and fought to keep it from entering his mind. For several days, in fact, he struggled with all sorts of metaphysical confusions about whether or not God, who controls all things, could allow him to think a thought he shouldn't think. Finally, having worked himself around to believing that God *wanted* him to have the forbidden thought, he relented:

> I gathered all my courage, as though I were about to leap forthwith into hell-fire, and let the thought come. I saw before me the ca-thedral, the blue sky. God sits on His golden throne, high above the world—and from under the throne an enormous turd falls upon the sparkling new roof, shatters it, and breaks the walls of the cathedral asunder.

Even as a boy, Jung found this scatological image redemptive. "I felt an enormous, an indescribable relief. Instead of the expected damnation, grace had come upon me. . . . I wept for happiness and gratitude."

From the start, Jung understood this newfound connection to the deity to be different in kind from anything he'd been offered by his own Church. Jung's father was a Protestant minister but one, we gather from Jung, for whom the Church had become lifeless. As a child he thought his father was reliable but powerless, and after his epiphany, he says, "a great many things I had not previously understood became clear to me. That was what my father had not understood, I thought; he had failed to experience the will of God, had opposed it for the best reasons and out of the deepest faith. And that was why he had never experienced the miracle of grace. . . ."

Jung had been born into a church purified to the point of sterility, and his twelve-year-old imagination provided an initial compensatory or fertilizing instruction: the purity ("the roof of the cathedral glittered") must be mixed with dirt. The dirt is a special kind, of course: it is a *divine* turd that falls, so the ground of re-creation is a part of the divine that has been cast off as excrement. Put another way, Jung's redemptive project required going back into some primal ambiguity—where the dirty and the clean, the high and the low, are not differentiated—and beginning again to sort the *prima materia*, the old stuff.

In Jung's later years, that "going back" took a particular form. As a boy he attributed his scatological fantasy to the God of his father's Church, but I suspect that the older Jung would have argued that the "turd beneath the throne" came from a much more pagan figure, the old Roman god Mercury, or Mercurius in the Latin of the medieval alchemists who fascinated Jung. Mercurius was one of the mature Jung's tutelary deities. When he was almost seventy years old he published a long essay on how Mercurius functions in the alchemical imagination, linking him to the more ancient Hermes, and giving at one point the following capsule description: "Mercurius consists of all conceivable opposites. . . . He is the process by which the lower and material is transformed into the higher and spiritual, and vice versa. He is the devil, a redeeming psychopomp, an evasive trickster, and God's reflection in physical nature."

The main thrust of Jung's argument is that the figure of Mercurius appeared in European thought to compensate for an overpurified Christ. As his image was refined over the centuries by Christian thought and dogma, Christ became the New Sun, the "*Sol Novus* before whom lesser stars pale." Not as a result of his own teachings, "but rather of what is taught about him," he acquired a kind of "crystal purity." But crystals cannot appear until the earth's deep fires have burned off a great deal of dross, and the dross itself is not consumed but accumulates somewhere in the shadows. A loving belief in the purified Christ, Jung writes, "naturally involves cleansing one's own house of black filth. But the filth must be dumped somewhere, and no matter where the dump lies it will plague even the best of all possible worlds with a bad smell."

Jung is here addressing himself to the problem of Christian dirt, of what to do with the by-products of putting a spiritual house in order. The rule seems to be that there is always error, imperfection, and diminishment when human beings set themselves to putting things in order, even if it is a church they are cleaning up. Something will always be excluded that turns out to be needed in a later time or place, whereupon an "occult" science must arise whose task is to reclaim what has been lost. In this light the alchemists' project was a kind of Christian dirt-work. "In comparison with the purity and unity of the Christ symbol," Jung writes, alchemists imagined a philosopher's stone, or "Mercurius-lapis," that is "ambiguous, dark, paradoxical, and thoroughly pagan." For Jung, this Mercurius-stone represents "an aspect of the self which stands apart, bound to nature and at odds with the Christian spirit. It represents all those things which have been eliminated from the Christian model." The alchemists compounded the image of Mercurius from material found in the privies of the cathedral builders. "The texts remind us again and again that Mercurius is 'found in the dung-heaps.' "

Before turning to the content of this excreta, I should say that Mercurius actually has two roles in the history that Jung is imagining: he is Christ's shadow, as it were, embodying the dirt that comes of purifying the New Sun, and he is the agent or the medium through whom that dirt finds its way back into the town square. Mercurius is both the grace-engendering turd that falls on the brightly glazed tiles of the cathedral roof and the force that produces that image, the psychopomp who presents the young boy's mind with the material that dogma has excluded.

I'm obviously making Mercurius out to be a kind of European Susa-nö-o, a figure whose actions not only get dirt under the very throne of god but in so doing bring the figurative new seeds of vivifying grace where before there was only powerless responsibility and arid belief. In this sense, Jung's childhood fecal epiphany and his late-life sketch of Mercurius' powers are both stories about redemption or re-creation through dirt. For the boy the redemptive moment happens the way a dream happens, entirely through images, and the problem of recognition remains, the problem of seeing into the symbols and translating their content into the abstractions that belong to waking consciousness. A half century later, then, the old man produces an essay that decodes the young boy's dream. In turning to alchemical literature, Jung was trying to discern the content of that divine excreta. What are "all those things . . . eliminated from the Christian model"? What will a trip to the Christian dung-heap yield?

Different dirt-workers will come back with different treasures, of course. For Jung the dumps contain, first of all, pagan gods like Mercurius himself, "forced under the influence of Christianity to descend into the dark underworld and be morally disqualified." Moreover, the suppression of the pagan gods entailed the suppression of a particular kind of spiritual complexity. Aboriginal peoples not only imagined and lived with ambivalent characters like Mercury, they imagined them in close relationship to the other gods. Pagan belief has no trouble picturing a friendship between Hermes and Apollo or between Eshu and Ifa; it readily imagines intimate family dramas with Susa-nö-o and his sister or Legba and his mother. Nothing quite comparable remains in Christianity, at least not in the nineteenth century. Jung reminds us that in the Book of Job we hear of a day "when the sons of God came to present themselves before the Lord, and Satan came also among them," but that by the time of the New Testament "this picture of a celestial family reunion" gives way to clear separation ("Get thee hence, Satan"). Jung is not blind to the spiritual advances that come from this greater differentiation of powers, but his point is that every advance has its cost.

In this case, Jung takes pagan "family reunions" to bespeak a lost relationship between consciousness and the unconscious, so that what is weakened when Mercurius is suppressed is both intelligence in regard to the unconscious and the psychopomp himself, the go-between who allows the kind of mental commerce that can, for example, decipher a dream or convert dirt into treasure. There is more (Jung expands on the idea cited above, that Mercurius is "God's reflection in physical nature"), but for now the simple point is that in making this core image of their science the alchemists drew on polytheist paganism and a discarded sense of how the divine operates in darkness and matter. From such sources, "hesitantly, as in a dream, the introspective brooding of the centuries gradually put together the figure of Mercurius and created a symbol which, according to all the psychological rules, stands in compensatory relation to Christ."

I have gone over these ideas not so much to weigh their merits as to give some sense of what it might mean to say that with the return of dirt comes redemption or re-creation. If it is right to say that Jung's father ministered in a moribund spiritual house, and that Jung early on was granted a sense of how to reclaim its energy, then what we're seeing is a man out to revive Christianity by smuggling pagan gods and dark matter from the unconscious into the sanctuary. To do this, he courts an old figure who knows how to make a connection where there has been a separation, who can, in Jung's words, "throw a bridge across the abyss separating . . . two psychological worlds."

At this point, though, it might be better to describe what's going on as creation itself rather than re-creation. Dirt's return *is* a threat to the old order, and in this case the old dirt doesn't just enliven the Church, it replaces it with something new. The alchemical tradition grows up as an alternative to orthodox Christianity. More to the point, Jung's essay is partly a reflection on his own case; he's telling us that in his lifetime the trip to the dung heap created the various forms of psychoanalysis. Imagining a centuries-long exploration and unfolding of consciousness, Jung diagnoses the Christian Church as finally blocked by its own purity, and declares that "it was the medical men who, at the turn of the nineteenth century, were forced to intervene and get the obstructed process of conscious realization going again." Juxtaposing Jung's boyhood fantasy and this late essay, it doesn't seem so strange to say that by making a bridge between the Church and its own excreta, the Spirit Mercurius created a third thing, analytic psychology. If there are "new seeds" at the end of this dirt-worker story, that is one of them.*

But the tale should not end there. "According to all the psychological rules," analytic psychology will eventually have its own troubles with dirt. The Spirit Mercurius is not finished with the Jungians. We've had some decades now of acolytes purifying the master's ideas, a process that must necessarily produce its own pile of slag. If Jung flirted with anti-Semitism, if he cheated on his wife in the name of the archetypes, if he

---

* Freud sometimes describes his work in similar terms. The technique of psychoanalysis, he says, "is accustomed to divine secrets and concealed things from despised or unnoticed features, from the rubbish-heap . . . of our observations." More broadly put, both Freud and Jung practice divination with dung, like hunters of old reading scat on the trail, and psychoanalysts are trained to do what Coyote has always done, get a conversation going with excrement.

overlooked inconsistencies in his own evidence, well, for those who believe, all these are accidents, not the core, not the real Jung. But someone
may differ, of course; someone may want to get the sacred fruit out of the
garden. Even as I sit writing these pages, the newspaper reports that a
pesky researcher is claiming that Jung omitted a few key details when
he first presented his theory of the collective unconscious. More to the
point, in response the Jung family has righteously sealed Jung's archives
against this man's requests for access. So it goes.* I wouldn't be surprised
to hear that at about this time the young daughter of some analyst in
Zurich suffered the forbidden fantasy that something dark and smelly
appeared under the comfortable chair in which her father sat discovering
anima figures in his patients' dreams.

DEMOCRATIC CARNIVAL

All this material, from the ancient tales to these modern psycho-spiritual
battles, raises the question of how any order—spiritual, secular, psychological—should relate to its own dirt. On the one hand, if purity often
ends in sterility, no order should locate its dung heaps too far from town.
Then again, if dirt is the by-product of creating order, no order should
willingly entertain the return of dirt unless it has some self-destructive
impulse.

Given the latter half of this dilemma, we should hardly be surprised
that order often turns violent when threatened by its own exclusions.
Better to kill everything that crawls on the sea floor; better to build huge
incinerators and be done with it. As Mary Douglas remarks, "the existence of anomaly can be physically controlled. . . . Take night-crowing
cocks. If their necks are promptly wrung, they do not live to contradict
the definition of a cock as a bird that crows at dawn." But we hardly need
anthropology to help us find violence turned against the anomalous and
out of place. Close at hand we have the whole grim twentieth-century
history of "ethnic cleansing," or the perennial attempts to keep homosexuals "in their place," to remind us how order can become cruel in the
name of its own imagined purity.

I mention violent exclusion, that pervasive and rather obvious re-

---

* So it went in the Freud archives, too, pestered by the disobedient Jeffrey Moussaieff
Masson.

sponse to dirt, because it is in contrast to brutality and lethal force that
other responses look attractive, especially what might be called ritual
contact with dirt—any sort of sanctioned, structured, and contained involvement with things that are normally out of bounds. In a sense, much
of this book is about such contact, the telling of trickster tales being a
sort of narrative dirt-ritual. In the dark, in the dead of winter, "when the
snakes are below the ground," Native Americans would tell these tales,
entertaining in fantasy all the things (incest, taboo violations, mad egotism, etc.) that could not possibly be part of the center of things. Take
the opening of the Winnebago trickster cycle: "Once upon a time there
was a village in which lived a chief who was just preparing to go on the
warpath." As we soon find out, and as every Winnebago listener would
have known immediately, this "chief" is trickster and what he is doing
lies absolutely outside the order of things (as Paul Radin remarks, "the
Winnebago tribal chief cannot under any circumstances go on the warpath"). By the end of the first episode this faux-chief has slept with a
woman (forbidden to men about to go to war), given a feast from which
he is the first to leave (the feast-giver always leaves last), thrown his
warbundle down and stomped it into the ground ("an inconceivably sacrilegious action"), and so forth.

Not only do trickster's actions invert and disorder the normal pattern
of Winnebago life, but the story itself may well be (if the practice of other
tribes is any indication) a narrative reflection of events actually acted out
in ceremony. In a central Hopi ceremony, for example, ritual clowns enter
the plaza backward, climb down ladders head-first, and talk as if human
beings rather than spirits were at the center of things. In Zuñi dirt rituals,
celebrants drank urine and ate human and canine excrement.

Nor are such unusual rites confined to Amerindians, or even to so-
called primitive societies. During the European middle ages an annual
Feast of Fools exposed the Catholic Church to the profanities usually
kept well beyond the walls of the churchyard. We get a clear sense of
what went on from a fifteenth-century letter in which an apparently more
decorous Parisian churchman complains about a Feast of Fools he'd seen
in the provinces:

> In the very midst of divine service masqueraders with grotesque
> faces, disguised as women, lions and mummers, performed their
> dances, sang indecent songs in the choir, ate their greasy food

from a corner of the altar near the priest celebrating mass, got out their games of dice, burned a stinking incense made of old shoe leather, and ran and hopped about all over the church.

From other descriptions we know that excrement was sometimes burned instead of incense, and that the clergy themselves would sometimes ride in dung-filled carts through the town, eating sausages and tossing turds at the crowds.

In academic circles, these transgressive celebrations are currently discussed under the general heading of "carnival," a term more properly reserved for Catholic festivities that end with Mardi Gras, the "Fat Tuesday" preceding the austerity of Lent ("carnival" comes from *carnelevarium*, "the removal of meat"). The stock anthropological and literary understanding is that carnival celebrations, despite their actual bawdiness and filth, are profoundly conservative. Especially in highly ordered and hierarchical societies, carnival reinforces the status quo because, first of all, it provides the exceptions that prove the rules. We may laugh at men dressed as women, or greasy food eaten at the altar, but when the laughter ends, the normal patterns return all the more solidly. Carnival is, after all, officially sanctioned and clearly contained. The powers that be are in on the game; they give it space in the town square (it never actually reaches into the palace, the Vatican, etc.), and they control its timing. Fat Tuesday never leaks over into Lean Wednesday. When Lent begins, the normal hierarchy reappears with a sheen, the rust of its internal tensions burnished away by their exposure.

Mocking but not changing the order of things, ritual dirt-work operates as a kind of safety valve, allowing internal conflicts and nagging anomalies to be expressed without serious consequence. If everyone secretly knows the Pope is *not* perfect, the secret can harmlessly endure if once a year, for a limited time only, the people make a fool of the Pope. If everyone secretly knows that slaves have powers their masters lack, slavery can continue anyway if once a year, for a limited time only, the masters serve thé slaves at table (as they did during the Roman Saturnalia). Carnival is thus a sort of psychic and social drainage system in which structure's garbage gets expressed only to be carted away when the banners come down.

· · ·

Where we value the old world, carnival's conservative function is one of its virtues, of course. The dirt ritual protects us against our own exclusions, like a kind of vaccination, and in that manner offers a stability that is lively and not particularly violent. After all, it is not just night-crowing cocks who end up dead when violence is the only way for the dominant order to protect itself. Beware the social system that cannot laugh at itself, that responds to those who do not know their place by building a string of prisons.

Where change is not in order, then, ritual dirt-work offers the virtue of non-violent stability. But where change *is* in order, dirt-work also has a role to play, for it simply isn't true that these rituals are always conservative. Dirt rituals may stabilize things for years on end, but when the order is in fundamental crisis these rituals can become the focal points for change, catalytic moments for dirt's revaluation and true structural shifts. Every so often Fat Tuesday *does* leak over into Lean Wednesday, and into the rest of the year as well. Regular dirt rituals are like nodes on a shoot of bamboo, repeating year after year to strengthen the growing stalk, but then, when conditions demand it, splitting open to produce new growth.

Historians have recently provided us with a number of specific cases that demonstrate this general model. It now seems clear, for example, that carnival's ritual debasing of the Pope played a key role in the Reformation in Germany. The ritual container broke, the pollution leaked out, and the Church itself was fundamentally altered. It seems clear also that play with gender roles has sometimes leapt the fences of ritual. The historian Natalie Zemon Davis has argued that the gender reversals of various early modern European festivals served to "*undermine* as well as reinforce" prevailing social structures. The carnival image of unruly women, normally the object of joking and play, sometimes turned out "to sanction riot and political disobedience for both men and women in a society that allowed the lower orders few formal means of protest." Davis is well aware that letting carnival's "woman-on-top" have power during the holidays usually served to keep women on the bottom when the holidays were over, but once such an image exists it is hard to control, and this one sometimes also "promoted resistance," "kept open an alternate way of conceiving family structure," and served as "a resource for feminist reflection on women's capacities."

I assume that trickster tales serve an analogous double role; usually they bring harmless release, but occasionally they authorize moments of radical change. The tales themselves, at least, declare the latter point: the character who can freely play with dirt, they say, is also the culture hero who brings fundamental change. In one of the Raven stories told around Sitka, Alaska, for example, Raven steals water from the stingy Petrel, who has an endless supply but will not share it with the thirsty world. Petrel vigilantly guards the spring where his water bubbles up (he keeps it covered; he sleeps beside it). Raven tries to get Petrel to leave his hut by telling him tales of all the wonderful things happening in the world, but Petrel is suspicious and won't move. That night Raven sleeps in Petrel's lodge; early in the morning, when he hears Petrel sleeping soundly, he goes outside, takes some dog shit, and smears it on Petrel's buttocks. As the sun rises, Raven cries out, "Wake up, wake up, my brother, you've shat all over your clothes." Petrel runs from the lodge to clean himself, whereupon Raven takes the cover from Petrel's spring and begins to drink. As he flies away, water falls from his beak and turns into the great rivers of Alaska and all the little salmon creeks.

Stories like these are not about conservative dirt-work but about the end of one world and the beginning of another (the Susa-nö-o story, remember, can be read as recording dirt-work that led to the invention of agriculture). If trickster's freedom of motion in regard to dirt means that he can acquire water or fire (acquire new energy, new tricks, new technologies, new mental insights, new ways of walking), then his narratives can be road maps for fundamental change. To be sure, imagining tricksters most often lets off steam and enlivens the existing order, but sometimes these imaginings are the beginning of much deeper alterations. If it's right to make a creation story by juxtaposing Carl Jung's fecal epiphany, his later attraction to Mercurius, and his sense that Mercurius is a guide to the unconscious, then we already have a modern case in which dirt-work enables a "theft of fire," a story whose protagonist challenges a weakened spiritual system with its own exclusions and, out of that, acquires a psychological method, a new technology for the human race.

Perhaps this is a good time to pause and summarize the ground we've covered so far. In the Legba story we saw a trickster using dirt to create one of the primordial cosmic divisions, the distance between heaven and earth. Two other stories—about Susa-nö-o and about

Raven—embody the related and more common theme: trickster's free-dom with dirt means he can operate where fastidious high gods cannot and as a result heaven's fertility and riches enter this world. Both cases illustrate the link Mary Douglas makes between dirt and the creation of order. When Legba's mother retreats to keep herself clean, the order of the cosmos as we know it emerges; in the other cases, new orders emerge after trickster's dirt-attacks upon the old. All this material contains a tension between the need for order and the need for dirt's return, and poses the problem of how to resolve that tension. One traditional solution has been to institute periodic ritual contact with dirt, thereby avoiding, on the one hand, the violence and sterility that seem to accompany pu-rified order, while allowing, on the other hand, not only the liveliness of a commerce between order and its exclusions but the possibility of fun-damental change when the old order is dying or in crisis.

Reading the story about Carl Jung alongside the old trickster tales, however, poses another, more modern problem, one I want to focus on in closing. The novelist Flannery O'Connor used to say that she wrote about backwoods churches rather than her own Catholic Church because she found the problems of modern faith more starkly revealed by "home-made religions." Jung's work with his childhood fantasy is homemade ritual. His twelve-year-old psyche spontaneously provided the initial ma-terial, material that would, in a differently developed culture, have found its reflection in already active community rituals. But little such collec-tive understanding remains in the modern world, and a child like Jung, who would have seen immediately that his fantasy belonged to the Feast of Fools if he'd lived in the twelfth century, must create his own psycho-logical system if he's to get any lasting benefit from that early moment of grace.

It's not that the modern world has no ritual—simple rituals are all around us—but we certainly don't have much agreed-upon collective dirt-work. Hopi ritual clowns attract tourists, but they don't climb back-ward into the halls of Congress. The Catholic Church was always ambivalent about carnival, but it was the Protestants who really got rid of it (having seen how unsettling it can be). What remains? What are the modern forms by which order deals with its own exclusions? Where is the dirt-work of democratic mass society? Where has trickster's spirit settled?

My own sense of how to respond to these questions begins by noting that many of our modern fights about dirt are fights about transgressive art, art that is accused of being obscene or blasphemous. Dirty movies, dirty books, dirty photographs, and sacrilegious acts have become the focus of public contestation, especially when someone claims for them the privileges of artistic space. Two cases emerged as I was writing this book, and I cannot help but wonder if they shouldn't be thought of as homemade rituals for a culture that has no good way to respond when faced with its own dirt.

The first of these was the protest that arose because the National Endowment for the Arts had given support to the photographer Andres Serrano, and Serrano had produced an image he called *Piss Christ*. *Piss Christ* is a large Cibachrome print of a crucifix (wooden cross, white plastic Jesus) seen through a jar of urine. The urine has little bubbles in it, so the viewer is well aware of the filter. In other images from the same series the filter is water with the red tinge of human blood or the white tinge of human milk. I've heard friends say that in making these pieces Serrano was surely out to shock, to make himself famous as a bad boy, and perhaps he was. Certainly he did. *Piss Christ* became one of the prime images used by the conservative and Christian right wing to destroy federal support for the arts in the United States in the early 1990s. But the intent to blaspheme that has been imputed to Serrano does not accord with my own response to the work when I first saw it in a New York gallery. To explain that response, I must say a bit about some things I brought to the images.

When I was in my twenties I worked for several years as a low-level attendant in a city hospital. I was working on the ward for alcoholics where men and women came who had gotten themselves so bent out of shape that they needed medical supervision during withdrawal. I found hospital work grounding and invigorating, especially the somewhat me-nial kind that involves hours upon hours of direct contact with sick and suffering bodies. This work has its own kind of propriety, of course, but at the same time much of our careful gentility necessarily drops away in those precincts, so that we may attend to the common life of the body. The drunk ward, at least, always smelled slightly of urine and the acrid sweat of shaking insomniacs. I mostly worked the night shift, and I would occasionally find myself in the early dawn cleaning a man who'd fouled himself while lost in a delirium. In those days I was spending most of the rest of my time engrossed in books and ideas, and hospital work balanced all that with saving gravity.

In the presence of Serrano's work, these memories ended up joined to things that those raised in a Christian milieu always carry—specifically, the sense that Christ's incarnation is key to the Gospels, that the crucifix should remind us that his *body* suffered on the cross. When he wept there were tears; the thorns and spears drew blood. The whole story falls apart if none of that matters, if a purified Christ is a fleshless Christ.

In any event, *Piss Christ* struck me as an experiment with color and embodiment: Serrano made himself a pallet of literal flesh tones, not the million tones of the paint-shop mixing chart, but the primary colors of the organism, the ones to which we all respond reflexively. With body fluids as his filters, he makes us see the crucifix *through* the body. We know this Christ not just through the clear humor of the human eye but through the heavier, more occluding humors of our other organs. The dead Christ has a shroud of urine, a shroud of blood.

In Serrano's photograph the image so shrouded is a plastic dime-store crucifix, a cheapened bit of kitsch we might otherwise pass over without seeing. Serrano seemed to me to be playing with the old problem of recognition. How do we see what's really in front of us? The swineherd meets Odysseus on the beach, but does not know him. Why can't he see what's there? How does the mind recognize the real meaning of what the senses offer up? Conjoining an abstracted Christ and the human body, specifically the body we deny and turn away from, the blood and excreta from which we normally avert the eye, Serrano's image seemed to me to ask what the Roman soldiers asked Peter: "Do you know this man?"

The old wisdom would say that this debasing of the god is a necessary part of his periodic renewal, and that Serrano intervenes, as Susa-nö-o did, to save the divine from its own too elevated purity. But we currently have no collective form, no agreed-upon narrative, to guide us in such an operation, and therefore—because the need for this kind of renewal does not go away—we are periodically forced to make something up. In this light, the whole public uproar around Serrano's photograph begins to look like homemade ritual for a land without carnival. First we have the transgressive artist symbolically sullying the god, and then Senator Jesse Helms and his friends drawing the line and insisting the dirt be carried out of town. It takes both sides to enact this drama, of course.

The team of Serrano & Helms finds the dying god abandoned in the five 'n' dime, exposes him to gross impurity, then raises him up again, newly clean, newly powerful.

The event, then, has the structure of conservative dirt-work. This is partly because Serrano himself is a Christian and sees his art as working inside the faith, not against it. About *Piss Christ* he has had this to say:

> Complex and unresolved feelings about my own Catholic upbringing inform this work which helps me to redefine and personalize my relationship with God. For me, art is a moral and spiritual obligation that cuts across all manner of pretense and speaks directly to the soul. Although I am no longer a member of the Catholic Church, I consider myself a Christian and I practice my faith through my work.

But with this in mind it will be of use to widen our frame of reference a little, because I suspect the controversy over *Piss Christ* was not the "practice of faith" that Serrano hoped for. His experiment may have worked in the privacy of his studio, but when it hit the streets something else happened. The politicians who attacked the National Endowment for the Arts, using Serrano as one of their wedges, were not really interested in their relationship to God. Senator Helms, at least, has an exquisite instinct for how to build a power base and raise money; like any demagogue, he knows how to translate a complicated problem into a simple fear, how to stir up racial animosity, and how to set his constituents at each other's throats. If that's what was actually going on, then this artist's dirt-work fails: he tries to revive a dying god, and revives a politician instead, and a particular kind of politician at that.

Here I find myself led into a bit of historical speculation. I sometimes think that what this event really demonstrated was the way in which Protestantism can renew itself through the suppression of old-style Catholic extravagance. When the Russian critic Mikhail Bakhtin wrote about carnival, he wasn't simply describing how it works, he was arguing that the Renaissance was marked by the "carnivalization of literature." The style of carnival—all its bawdy inversions—left the town square and entered art (entered the novel especially).* Carnival didn't just get aes-

---

* Bakhtin writes: "During the Renaissance . . . the primordial elements of carnival . . .

theticized, it took refuge in art, for the shift was contemporary with the rise of Protestantism and its insistence on more restrained forms of public practice. The aptness of this historical hypothesis aside, in Serrano we have a lapsed Catholic stumbling upon a medieval practice for reviving his faith, and the successful attack on him by Protestant churchmen and their legislators, whose power gets renewed to the degree that they can run the Catholic artist out of town. In trickster terms, what we get is a church and its political allies consolidating their identity by successfully demonizing the mercurial imagination (which is how I read the destruction of the NEA at the end of the century).

Before developing this line of thought any further, I want to turn to a second public fight over dirty art because it differs in several instructive ways from the Serrano case. In 1989 a traveling exhibit of Robert Mapplethorpe's photographs—including graphic images of homosexual sadomasochism (e.g., the artist himself photographed with the handle of a bull whip inserted in his rectum)—appeared at the gallery of Cincinnati's Contemporary Arts Center. The next day sheriff's deputies raided the show, videotaped seven of the photographs, and then got a grand jury to indict the gallery on obscenity charges.

The gallery had actually gone to some lengths to protect the innocent from Mapplethorpe's images: there was an admission charge, no one under eighteen was admitted, and the dirty photos themselves were set aside in a special room with warning signs at the door. You not only had to be a mature person with pocket money, you had to *want* to see these pictures. The whole event was elaborately gated. Getting to that inner sanctum where the dirt was on display was almost as elaborate as getting into the Eleusinian mysteries or the Lele pangolin cult.

Still, local prosecutors took the gallery to court and there ensued a trial in which curators and critics from around the country defended Mapplethorpe's work to a jury of local farmers, secretaries, and bank clerks. The charges hung on the question of whether or not the images were art, and the experts said they were. "If it's in an art museum, it is

---

took possession of all the genres of high literature and transformed them fundamentally." In addition: "The Renaissance is the high point of carnival life. Thereafter begins its decline."

intended to be art, and that's why it's there," explained Robert Sobieszek of the Los Angles County Museum. Jacquelynn Baas of the Art Museum at Berkeley was asked to defend the artfulness of a photograph showing one man with his arm in another man's rectum. "It's the tension between the physical beauty of the photograph and the brutal nature of what's going on in it," she said, "that gives it the particular quality that this work of art has." A Cincinnati newspaper reported the testimony of Janet Kardon from Philadelphia's Institute of Contemporary Art:

> Led through . . . the photographs by [the prosecutor], Kardon carefully defended each . . . in terms of how Mapplethorpe located the human figure in the picture, how lighting was used, the picture's symmetry, the use of lines, how the characteristics of some of these photographs could also be found in Mapplethorpe's more famous pictures of flowers.

In short, the work is art because it appeared in an art gallery and because experts can talk about it in art language, a conclusion that may not be as silly as it first seems if we are in fact witnessing some sort of ritual event and if we remember that ritual and belief often have a tautological core: we draw the *temenos*, the sacred precinct, and what enters it becomes, willy-nilly, sacred; we create spaces for art and educate curators to watch the gates, and, willy-nilly, what gets in is art.

Be that as it may, the "art" issue was key to the trial because the law of the land currently holds that a work is *not* obscene if, taken as a whole, it has any serious literary, artistic, political, or scientific value. "Art" and "obscenity" are distinct categories, the law says—and on these grounds the jury deferred to the critics and voted to acquit. One juror, the manager of a warehouse, explained the decision: "All of them [the experts], to a person, were so certain it was art. We had to go with what we were told. It's like Picasso. Picasso from what everybody tells me was an artist. It's not my cup of tea. I don't understand it. But if people say it's art, then I have to go along with it.' "

Myself, I'd say that Mapplethorpe was certainly an artist, but a minor one whose import was magnified by the historical moment, and it is this last that really leads me to use him as my example here. The trial of Mapplethorpe's gay-sex photographs coincided with the first decades of the AIDS pandemic (Mapplethorpe himself died of AIDS in March of

1989), and that context gave the whole event different weight as ritual dirt-work, for the presence of the AIDS virus has challenged the ways in which we imagine sexual behavior and integrate it into the rest of our lives. It's as if the "cunning" of the AIDS virus lies precisely in its having located its passage in socially invisible sites—in homosexual acts and illegal intravenous drug use. Or rather, there is no cunning here at all, only witless contingency, the coincidence of a parasite and a particular style of social organization. The virus happened to appear in the dirt pile, as it were, and we cannot work with it without working with dirt, which is to say, without altering that style. To take it seriously we are forced to reimagine social space; we have to do such things as give away sterile needles to drug addicts, and allow a formerly closeted eroticism to have a different and fuller public presence.

There may have been a time when American democracy could afford to treat homosexual sex as an excluded anomaly, but once the AIDS virus was among us, that way of patterning social/sexual space no longer served. If we are to live with this virus, everyone needs to be able to imagine gay sexuality. The jurors at the trial, at least, had apparently not imagined what Mapplethorpe had to show them. As one of them said, "I sure didn't know this stuff existed. It surprised me completely that they did those kind of things. So that was an education in itself." Another juror, a secretary, told reporters "I learned more about that type of life-style than I ever thought I could possibly know."

Which is to say that the dirt ritual of this art trial was not the kind of carnival that releases the excluded only to contain it again. This was rather the dirt-work that threatens to alter the order of things by exposing that order to its own exclusions. Eighty-one thousand people attended the Cincinnati exhibit, leading the public prosecutor to wonder on the day he lost the case, "Who *were* those people? Were they just people from the arts community? Were they people from Columbus, Cleveland, New York and Los Angeles? You have no idea who they were." The poor man couldn't believe that something had changed in Cincinnati itself, that before this exhibit the dominant community could not imagine "that type of lifestyle," and after it they could.

At this point I want to come back to the question of Mapplethorpe's artistry, minor or not. Writing in *The New York Times* at the time of the trial, and freed from the constraint of explaining seven photographs taken out of their larger context, the critic Andy Grundberg made a plausible case for where Mapplethorpe's real innovation lies.

> The contested, fleshy subject matter of the pictures featured in the Cincinnati trial coexists with such "innocent" contents as the faces of celebrities and calla lilies. By placing them all in a single continuum, Mapplethorpe's work suggests that society's traditional moral values are less important than the Platonic ideal of beauty. This is the essential key to his art. . . .

I'm not sure about that "Platonic ideal," but something along these lines seems right. Faced with the received distinctions between the beautiful and the ugly, the clean and the dirty, the male and the female, the normal and the anomalous, Mapplethorpe levels the terrain; he produces an image-series based on a different set of rules. If he succeeds in creating that "single continuum" he becomes a dirt-worker in the classic trickster lineage, one who usefully disturbs the shape of things by crossing or reworking the line between the elevated and the excremental. A measure of his success is the degree to which his opponents helped move the drama to its classic conclusion. It's touching, actually, how those sheriff's deputies signed on as part of Mapplethorpe's posthumous crew, making that videotape of the dirt, carrying it to the courthouse, and presenting it with juridic formality to their fellow citizens. This modern shit finally found its way into the sacred throne room, and because in that setting the law of the land imposed certain constraints, the elevated powers had to let it lie there.

If we think back on Serrano it may become clear why, in most respects, Mapplethorpe's dirt-work is more subversive than his colleague's. First, it had the luck of getting into court, where the game had to be played by pre-established rules. Second, when it comes to the content of his images, Mapplethorpe's work defies its context in a way that Serrano's doesn't. As I said, Serrano works inside of Christianity, not against it; in a nation still enchanted with heterosexual romantic love, however, Mapplethorpe is truly transgressive, a challenge to the received order. Finally, that challenge spoke to and coincided with the AIDS epidemic, which meant this "dirt" had to be reckoned with. For all these reasons and more, in this case when conservatives rallied to put the artist and his dirty pictures in their place the rally came up short, and the citizens of Cincinnati had their maps redrawn, if only a little.

I'd like to close by widening the focus. If dirt is a by-product of the creation of order, then a fight about dirt is always a fight about how we have shaped our world. (A fight about obscenity is a *serious* fight, the Latin roots of "obscene" meaning "really dirty.") The end-of-the-millennium obscenity arguments in the United States centered on quite specific topics—mostly feminism and homosexuality—the implication being that in these areas the country was debating some serious re-alignments. But for now it is not the content of these battles that inter-ests me so much as the wider question of how any community should structure itself so it can have such fights in the first place. In a large democratic nation, at least, several things need to be in place before we have the possibility of the periodic dirt-work that these cases em-body. We need the right to free speech, of course, but because we have obscenity laws we also need the clarification that those laws do not ap-ply where there is artistic, scientific, or political value. Finally, then, we need that value; more to the point, we need the artist (scientist, pol-itician) who can create it. We need to tolerate if not welcome the mer-curial imagination.

One of the ironies of America's public dirt battles in the early 1990s was that they coincided with the collapse of Soviet-style Com-munist regimes, regimes made fragile precisely because they never developed a way to work with the many things they had excluded. Put the other way around, the real danger in democratic societies comes not from fights about obscenity but from attacks on the rules that al-low these fights to proceed. It comes from those who, when they find professionals disagreeing with them, attack the professions; those who, when they find that the Constitution prohibits the total suppression of excreta, attack the Constitution itself; and those who, when they find themselves blocked by "artistic value," attack artists. The old wisdom, at least, suggests that such attacks are more dangerous than the dirt they seek to purge. Cultural longevity lies in a more tolerant course. One does not put Raven or Legba or Susa-nö-o in the center of things year round—these boundary-crossers belong at the edges most of the time. But unless we think we've perfected this world and come to the end of history (especially if we think that) we cannot do away with dirt-workers, either. Their labors promise a communal life that is flexible rather than repressive, that can tolerate and draw on its own exclusions, laugh at its own designs, and above all adapt itself to the contingencies this world will regularly offer up.

PART FOUR

TRAP OF CULTURE

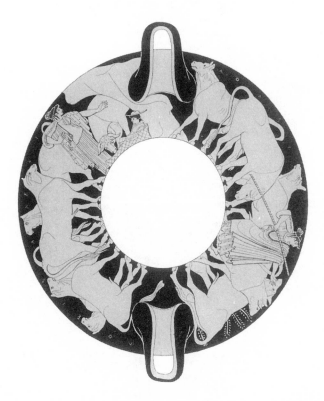

9

....

HERMES SLIPS THE TRAP

HERMES OF THE LIGHT, HERMES OF THE DARK

When Hermes comes home after stealing Apollo's cattle, he and his mother Maia have the archaic mom-boy argument over his behavior. In reply to her scolding, Hermes explains to her that he doesn't believe they should go on living obscurely in a cave. They deserve better:

> "I'm ready to do whatever I must so that you and I will never go hungry. . . . Why should we be the only gods who never eat the fruits of sacrifice and prayer? Better always to live in the company of other deathless ones—rich, glamorous, enjoying heaps of grain—than forever to sit by ourselves in a gloomy cavern. And as for honor, my plan is to have a share of Apollo's power. If my father won't give it to me I intend to be—and I mean it—the Prince of Thieves."

When he speaks of "Apollo's power" Hermes may be referring to the art of prophecy or to the guardianship of the herds, but however we read the line, the general point is not obscure: if his father won't give him honor and wealth, Hermes will steal them.

This opposition between gift and theft was one of the things that initially drew me to trickster figures, and to this story about Hermes especially. There have always been communities in which some wealth circulates through the exchange of gifts, rather than through purchase and sale. Tribal groups are the typical case; in many tribes it is thought improper to buy and sell food, for example; instead of a market, an elaborate system of gift exchanges assures that every mouth has food to eat. Such a circulation of gifts is an agent of social cohesion; it can even be argued that a group doesn't become a group until its members have an ongoing sense of mutual indebtedness, gratitude, obligation—all the social feelings that bind human beings together and that follow automatically in the wake of a system of gift exchanges. Nor are these phenomena limited to tribal or "primitive" situations. Individual scientists are drawn together into a "scientific community," for example, only to the degree that they treat their data and ideas as contributions to the group (while, conversely, the community fragments when ideas become proprietary, guarded by secrecy and fees).

All of which is very fine if you are one of the in-group. But what if you're an outsider, or what if you're inside but the customary commerce always leaves you beneath your "betters"? All the wonderful gift exchange in tribe A is little help if you've had a crop failure and belong to tribe B. The small-business club down the street may have a fine program for start-up capital, but what if it's for white folks only? What if all the male scientists swap data and you happen to be a woman? What if students at your high school always get scholarships to trade schools, never to elite universities? In cases such as these, you may have to resort to some form of subterfuge to get ahead; if the others won't give, you may have to steal.

By his own description, some such tension lies behind Hermes' thefts. For this and other reasons I read the *Homeric Hymn* as the story of how an outsider penetrates a group, or how marginalized insiders might alter a hierarchy that confines them. Hermes has a method by which a stranger or underling can enter the game, change its rules, and win a piece of the action. He knows how to slip the trap of culture.

His thieving is only one part of his method, of course, just as exclusion from gift exchange is only one way a group might keep someone in his or her place. There are many more. I opened this book with a discussion of actual traps attributed to trickster's intelligence, but it soon became clear that tricksters work with more ethereal snares than those that hunters use. The webs of signification by which cultures themselves are woven are the more complex and enduring sites of trickster's labor. To look at Hermes debating gift and theft is to watch a trickster disturbing but one knot in the almost unlimited number of knots that hold such a web together. Cultures take their shape from distinctions such as "gift and theft" or, to recall others we have seen, "the clean and the dirty," "the modest and the shameful," "essence and accident." These exactly are the joints of the cultural web and therefore the potential sites of trickster's play.

There are as many tricks as there are traps, of course, and I mean to use Hermes' stealing only as my point of departure, adding as we go along the other cunning wiles by which he unravels a particular cultural artifice and weaves a new one in its stead. In this way, by describing it carefully, I would like to abstract from Hermes' method a pattern or template with which to look at other cases of the marginalized undoing the snares that bind them.

As for other cases, I will turn my attention in the next chapter to the story of an African-American slave freeing himself from the plantation culture into which he was born. As I address myself to the *Homeric Hymn* I am therefore going to juxtapose language from the classic *Narrative of the Life of Frederick Douglass, an American Slave*. I shall quote Douglass without much comment, as the connections are not obscure, though it will help at the outset to know the simple facts of his life. Douglass was born in 1818 in Talbot County, Maryland, on the eastern shore of Chesapeake Bay. His master (and probably his father) was a small landowner, Aaron Anthony, who worked as overseer on the plantation of one Colonel Edward Lloyd. Douglass was sometimes a field slave in Talbot County and more often a house slave in the Baltimore home of Aaron Anthony's in-laws, Hugh and Sophia Auld. He escaped from slavery in 1838 and settled in New Bedford, Massachusetts, where he became active in abolitionist circles, giving a famous first speech about his experiences to an anti-slavery convention in Nantucket in 1841.

With this in mind, let us return to Hermes and the *Hymn*.

• • •

As is apt for an interpretation guided by Hermes, I want to read the *Hymn* on several levels, to take it as a story about creativity, about the psyche, about social change, about an actual history. To begin with this last, the question is: If tricksters disrupt cultures that exclude or confine them, is there a particular historical context to which the *Hymn* itself belongs, and if so, what historical changes does it record? Norman O. Brown proposed one answer to these questions in his 1947 book, *Hermes the Thief.* Brown set out to chart the ways in which the mythology of Hermes altered from one era to the next, from the Helladic to the classical periods, a thousand years—1500 to 500 B.C.—during which Greek society moved from tribalism through a long period of agrarian kingship to end, for Brown's interest in Hermes, with fifth-century Athenian democracy. Brown places the *Hymn* during the last of these shifts, arguing that it was written down in Athens around 520 B.C., toward the end of a long tension between agrarian kingship and mercantile democracy.

He therefore proposes this parallel: just as Hermes acquires a place alongside Apollo in the course of the *Hymn*, so in the course of the sixth century the "Athenian industrial and commercial classes achieved equality with the aristocracy." That equality was not easily won; it required the resolution of a whole series of differences. In the aristocratic era, wealth came from herding and farming the soil; in Athenian democracy those sources of wealth still existed but were increasingly challenged by a craft economy and commercial exchange with strangers. Agrarian aristocracy was organized around hierarchical kinship ties; Athenian democracy retained such ties but added a new ethic of equality symbolized by the fact that many political positions in Athens were filled by a lottery in which all citizens could participate, regardless of family or status. Most important, the emerging cosmopolitan democracy brought with it a "new ethics of acquisitive individualism [that] conflicted with the traditional morality which the Greeks called Themis—the body of customs and laws inherited from the age of familial collectivism." The older morality took *any* deviation from "the archaic form of commerce by mutual exchange of gifts" to be an immoral thieving (even what we would now call fair trade was taken to be robbery). In short, during the sixth century, a world organized through kin relationships and a collective ethic of gift exchange gave way to a world in which hierarchy could be periodically revised and social relations were increasingly articulated through the individualist (which is to say, thieving) ethic of the marketplace.

As for those who were excluded or marginalized, we should remember that, in a society where the dominant values are kin ties and agrarian wealth, those whose identity is bound up with trade are typically consigned to a subordinate place in the order of things. They are, so to speak, "low caste" (as they have been historically in India, where merchants and artisans fall into the lower two of the four *varnas*). If, in the Greek case, such people hope to place themselves on an equal footing with the warriors and family farmers of ancient days, they will have to subvert that order and reshape it on their own terms. Such, Brown argues, is exactly what happened: the "regime of the landed aristocracy was overthrown, its agrarian economy yielding to a new economy based on trade and handicraft industry, its political oligarchy yielding to the politics of ancient democracy." The *Hymn* reflects that change: "The theme of strife between Hermes and Apollo translates into mythical language the insurgence of the Greek lower classes and their demands for equality with the aristocracy."

Brown's claims cover a lot of ground and his talk of class conflict gives off an air of retrospective Marxism, but the *Hymn* itself, however we fit it into actual Greek history, sets up a tension in accord with the one that Brown suggests. There is little doubt that in the classical period Hermes is associated with artisans, merchants, and thieves, and the poem itself makes it clear that some kind of "outsiderness" is at issue, and that Hermes hopes to change it.

To effect that change he has, as I said earlier, a method by which the excluded can enter a group, change its structure, and give themselves a place at the table. A whole range of cunning tricks makes up this method, but its underlying structure is quite simple: no matter what he does, Hermes is either an enchanter or a disenchanter. The simplest way to imagine him in this double field of action is to picture him at that moment, early in the story, when he emerges from his mother's cave:

He didn't lie around in his sacred cradle, no, the minute he slipped from his mother's immortal arms he leapt up and set out

to find Apollo's herds. As he crossed the threshold of that roomy
cave he happened on a turtle and got himself an endless source
of wealth.

"He crossed the threshold": here is the boundary-crosser on the boundary
itself. He is leaving his mother, his cradle, the earth, the underworld, the
private, the dark; he is entering the sunlight, the public, the uncovered,
the outer and upper worlds of the sky gods (Zeus, Apollo, Helios). Poised
on the threshold, he is in *his* world, the crepuscular, shady, mottled,
ambiguous, androgynous, neither/nor space of Hermetic operation, that
thin layer of topsoil where all these things are not yet differentiated. From
this position Hermes can move in either direction or, more to the point,
act as the agent by which others are led in either direction.

It is this double motion that makes Hermes at once an enchanter and
a disenchanter. In his enchanting phase, he often begins by going after
the border guards, for if they have their wits about them he cannot operate. Earlier we saw how he cast a lazy forgetfulness over the watchdogs
guarding Apollo's cattle. In speaking of shame, we saw how he mesmer-
ized Argus with song and story, then sealed the giant's sleeping eyes with
a magic wand. Hermes drops the sentinels who watch the peripheries
into a stupor, and impermeable boundaries become porous.

This is only the beginning of his enchanting/disenchanting power,
too, for once the border is breached, Hermes will deliver a soul into
whatever world or mental state lies across the line. He carries his charges
into the underworld or out of it, into dreams or into wakefulness, into
mythologies or out of them, into foreign countries or back home. When
Odysseus has slain the suitors, it is Hermes who carries their souls down
into Hades; in another story, it is Hermes who guides Persephone out of
Hades and into the daylight. In one story, it is Hermes who puts to sleep
the watchmen encircling Achilles's camp; in another, it is Hermes who
awakens Odysseus as he walks toward Circe's house, so as to be sure
that her magic cannot touch him.

Depending on which way he is moving across the threshold, I call
him Hermes of the Dark or Hermes of the Light. Hermes of the Dark is
the enchanter or hypnagoge who moves us into the underworld of sleep,
dream, story, myth. This darkening motion is a precondition of belief;
with it Hermes delivers you to one of the gods and puts you under his or
her spell. He dissolves time in the river of forgetfulness, and once time

has disappeared the eternals come forward. Hermes of the Dark is the weaver of dreams, the charmer who spins a compelling tale, the orator who speaks your mother tongue with fluid conviction.

Hermes of the Light is the disenchanter or awakening angel who leads you out of the cave. There the bright light prepares the ground for doubt. There he kills and roasts the sacred cattle. He dissolves eternals in the river of time, and when they have disappeared, the world becomes contingent and accidental. Hermes of the Light translates dreams into analytic language; he rubs the charm from old stories until they seem hopelessly made up and mechanical. He walks you inland until you stop dreaming in your mother tongue.

Hermes himself is neither one of these alone but both at once. He is neither the god of the door leading out nor the god of the door leading in—he is the god of the hinge. He is the mottled figure in the half-light, the amnigoge who simultaneously amazes *and* unmazes, whose wand *both* "bewitches the eyes of men to sleep and wakes the sleeping," as Homer says in the *Iliad*. I sometimes wonder if all great creative minds do not participate in this double motion, humming a new and catchy theogony even as they demystify the gods their elders sang about. Pablo Picasso had that double motion, disturbing classical perspective while presenting a strange new way of seeing, one so hypnotic it shows up decades after his death on billboards and children's printed pajamas. Sigmund Freud had that double motion, dragging slips of the tongue into the daylight, or "explaining" Moses, while simultaneously retelling the old story of Oedipus in a manner so compelling that, decades after his death, Ivy League literary critics can't get it out of their heads. Or there is Vladimir Nabokov: if you think his deft language magic is serious, you're wrong, and if you think it's just a game, you're wrong.

To see how this double motion serves Hermes' purposes in the *Hymn* itself, let's begin by watching him disenchant the world into which he has been born. He has several ways to drag it into the light. Theft necessarily comes first. Somehow he must make an entry; few groups go out of their way to embrace the marginal or foreign. All cultures set watchful dogs around their eternal cattle. All cultures guard their essences. If Hermes hopes to create a new home for himself against the grain of the old, he can only begin by stupefying those dogs and making a raid on the middle. And so he steals the cattle, moves them to Pieria, slaughters two of them, and so on. This theft alone is a disenchantment, for with it Hermes, like Loki and Monkey, brings time and death to what was formerly timeless and immortal. (In the situation of archaic Greece by which Brown reads the *Hymn*, the "sacred cows" are kingship, gift exchange, and the like; in the classical period, Hermes types "steal" these eternals and drag them into time where they become history.) Hermes' theft proves the boundary between his world and Apollo's is porous; it implies that the rules by which Apollo operates are contingent and arbitrary. Deftly done, a trickster's thieving calls into question the local property rights. Who gave Apollo those cattle in the first place? Who decided he could set guard dogs around that field?

> [From Frederick Douglass's *Narrative*:] Colonel Lloyd kept a large and finely cultivated garden. . . . It abounded in fruits of almost every description from the hardy apple of the north to the delicate orange of the south. This garden was not the least source of trouble on the plantation. Its excellent fruit was quite a temptation to the hungry swarms of boys, as well as the older slaves, belonging to the colonel, few of whom had the virtue or the vice to resist it. Scarcely a day passed, during the summer, but that some slave had to take the lash for stealing fruit.
>
> All the education I possess, I may say, I have stolen while a slave. I did manage to steal a little knowledge of literature, but I am now in the eyes of American law considered a thief and robber, since I have not only stolen a little knowledge of literature, but have stolen my body also.

To call the local property rights into question, one must forgo the pleasures of conforming to the local moral code. Hermes willingly submits to being seen as a thief in local terms, even if in his own amoral space or by some different morality the term does not apply. When the local code is insufficient to describe the situation (is stealing from Colonel Lloyd "virtue or . . . vice"?), the creative person is the one who will readily endure that insufficiency and, from an "immoral" position, frame a new set of rules.

Such willing immorality brings us back to questions of shame. As we have seen, communities often establish shame thresholds to mark their internal boundaries; for those contained in them, a network of such boundaries is either empowering or confining, depending. For Hermes the net confines—or, rather, it would confine but for the shamelessness by which he cuts the knots of its authority. And where do the shame thresholds lie in the *Hymn*? What is the content of shame where Hermes is concerned? To begin with the historical reading, we may find an answer in Hesiod, whom Brown offers as nostalgic spokesman for the older era of agrarian collectivism, a golden time that, for Hesiod, has died and been replaced by an age of iron. Brown summarizes the complaint:

> "Robbery," "Shamelessness," "Force," "Strife," are the harsh realities of life in the iron generation; "Shame" and "Justice," the daughters of Themis, the ideal patterns of human behavior, exist only in heaven. Hesiod recommends agriculture as the best way of life because it offers the maximum self-sufficiency, the maximum isolation from the new economy; his calendar of *Works and Days* is designed to make the farmer as self-sufficient as possible, as independent as possible of the craftsman, even when such a policy is economically irrational. Hesiod is an isolationist: "it is better to stay at home, since the outside world is noxious"; he firmly turns his back on the new commercial culture.

Hesiod's shame threshold, then, would separate (among other things) market "robbery" from gift exchange, the sacred commerce of kinship. Those with appropriate shame will not cross that line. Hermes, of course, does. As Brown points out, the poet of the *Hymn* has put in Hermes' mouth a parody of Hesiod's advice to "stay at home": carrying the turtle into the cave, Hermes says, "It's safer inside, you could get in trouble out there." Then he kills her. So much for pastoral wisdom. Hermes firmly turns his back on Hesiod and—crafter of the lyre, patron of trade—embraces "the new commercial culture" without feeling the recommended embarrassment. Quite the contrary, as merchants in archaic times must have done, he assumes a willing "immorality" and proceeds from there, unencumbered by the received ethical grid.

In the situation of Hermes' birth we find the tale's second shame threshold. It is not just "robbery" that is out of bounds here; Hermes is meant to feel ashamed of his origins. The first part of the *Hymn* establishes this: Zeus and Maia conduct their affair in deep and mutual shame; their every move is secret, retiring, enacted in the dark. Hermes is therefore a child of stolen love; his kin ties are not clear. His birth poses a question of legitimacy and illegitimacy; to what family does this child belong? (When Hermes finally addresses Zeus, he keeps naming his father *as* his father, making his otherwise unestablished paternity a matter of public record.)* Hermes is like the child of a black slave woman and a white slaveholder; he will be confined forever to the slot the system has assigned him unless he can scheme some way to enter into his father's estate.

[Douglass:] The whisper that my master was my father, may or may not be true; and, true or false, it is of but little consequence to my purpose whilst the fact remains, in all its glaring odiousness, that slaveholders have ordained, and by law established, that the children of slave women shall in all cases follow the condition of their mothers; and this is done too obviously to administer to their own lusts, and make a gratification of their wicked desires profitable as well as pleasurable. . . .

---

* Carl Kerényi maintains that the language of the *Hymn* suggests that Maia is a courtesan. Whether he's right or not, Maia is certainly not Zeus' wife. To read from the myth to the social situation, one would then want to ask about the status of a child born of a citizen and his concubine, or of illegitimate children in general.

The inquiry leads to no simple answer. Under Pericles, both parents had to be citizens for their child to be a citizen, but the law was not strongly enforced. At the end of the fifth century, Aristophon proposed that the child of a male citizen and a female alien could not inherit property, but the proposal itself implies that some such children *did* inherit.

The very fact that the rules might not have been clear supports the point I want to make, however: a child such as Hermes is in a potentially ambiguous position, and might want to get it clarified. Of even more bearing here is a point made by Jenny Strauss Clay, that this Olympian scene reflects the classical Greek family in which "the father retains the sole right to acknowledge his children as his own, to legitimize them, and to admit them into the family."

Finally, to come back to myth, not all of Zeus' extramarital children become Olympians. Herakles, Perseus, Helen, Minos, Dardanus, and Castor and Pollux: Zeus sires all these but none does what Hermes does, get his father to recognize him on the mountain before the other gathered gods.

Against Hermes' possible "shame of origins" we soon get the boy with his new-made lyre "broadcasting the story of his own famous conception," famous *now*, that is, now that he has made an instrument and found his voice. Often the powerful (or the proper) tease and taunt the powerless (or the impudent), invoking Legitimate and Illegitimate as if they were categories of nature, then tying illegitimate tongues so they cannot speak to their own condition. Apollo and Maia both play this role here, reminding Hermes of his place. If he had a proper Hesiodic sense of right and wrong, they seem to say, he'd stay in the cave where he belongs. He's a boy from the slums—to reformulate it a bit—and were he not so uppity he would be content to stay there and be quiet.

> [Douglass:] The truth was, I felt myself a slave, and the idea of speaking to white people weighed me down. I spoke but a few moments, when I felt a degree of freedom, and said what I desired with considerable ease. From that time until now, I have been engaged in pleading the cause of my brethren. . . .

A kind of collective magic activates a shame threshold. The group marks a boundary and those who try to cross it, if they feel the communal Argus eyes upon them, will suffer shame's physical seizure, the flushed skin, the bound tongue. Perhaps when Maia says that Hermes "wears the cloak of shamelessness" we are meant to imagine a garment that shields him from this collective spell. Whatever the case, he has the freedom of motion and the freedom of speech that leaves the collective magic powerless. The hooks of shame can find no purchase on this lad with the trick shoes. He refuses absolutely the picture of the world implied by his elders' morality, and refuses also the hierarchy that goes with it. Where others might sit quietly, he improvises a new song, "the way teenagers sing out insults at a fair."

Hermes' shamelessness is not the only device by which he erases thresholds, disturbs boundary markers, and muddies up the clear divisions that once organized Apollo's world. Tricksters sometimes speak in a way that confuses the distinctions between lying and truth-telling or (to preserve the useful words "true" and "false") undercuts the current fictions by which reality is shaped. The statement "Hermes did not steal the eternal cattle" is a lie in the initial context of the *Hymn* when Apollo's world is still intact, but afterwards—when they are no longer eternal, when Hermes has the herder's whip—it feels a little quaint to call it a lie. Similarly, the assertion "The slaves didn't steal Colonel Lloyd's fruit" might be a lie in the fictive world of plantation culture but true in a world that takes slavery itself to be a form of theft. Before that shift can take place, however, the old story must lose its charm. It must be moved into the space where its design is perspectival and temporal, not eternal. To make that happen, trickster enters the old story in a way that makes its former clarity collapse into befuddling contradiction, like the octopus filling a transparent sea with obscuring ink.

> [Douglass:] It is . . . plain that a very different-looking class of people are springing up at the south, and are now held in slavery, from those originally brought to this country from Africa; and if their increase will do no other good, it will do away the force of the argument, that God cursed Ham, and therefore American slavery is right. If the lineal descendants of Ham are alone to be scripturally enslaved, it is certain that slavery at the south must soon become unscriptural. . . .

Much like Hermes' lies and thefts, the creation of the lyre from the shell of the tortoise produces its own befuddlement, its own confusion of categories. Archaic Greeks assumed that if wealth was not earned by the sweat of the brow or received as a gift from a friend, then it must have been stolen. Earned or stolen, gift or theft: by such oppositions agrarian kinship understood the acquisition of riches. A lucky find, a *hermaion* such as the lyre, eludes these categories. The *Hymn* says that Hermes "happened on a turtle and got himself an endless source of wealth"; that wealth is neither kin gift nor immoral theft but a third thing, created in a manic moment out of chance and mental insight. Like any such combination of technique and accident it seems, therefore, to come out of nowhere and, at first, to have no clear place in the order of things. It seems a bit shady, like the sudden fortunes of oil barons in the early twentieth century, like the sudden fortunes of software developers more recently.

Applying smart luck to the tortoise is, in a sense, the first of two disenchanting chance operations that Hermes performs on the design of the world that confronts him at birth. The second is the private lottery he conducts as he sacrifices the cattle, the moment when he cuts the meat into twelve portions, "distributed by lot, each one exactly right." To sketch the unsettling effect of this act, I probably need only restate earlier conclusions. With it, we have the trick of reapportionment and the cancellation (or remaking) of hierarchy. Hermes symbolically makes himself a player (he aspires to be one of the twelve gods, so to make twelve portions is to deal himself in); he subjects existing order to an attack of accidents, letting things fall as they may; and if the existing order had an air of necessity about it, he dispels that air, making it clear that any order is partly a matter of chance. No wonder trickster is sometimes the god of those who do not control their own lot in life, but hope to.

[Douglass:] My old master, Captain Anthony, died. . . . He left no will as to the disposal of his property. . . . I was immediately sent for, to be valued with the other property. Here again my feelings rose up in detestation of slavery. . . . Prior to this, I had become, if not insensible to my lot, at least partly so. . . .

After the valuation, then came the division. I have no language to express the high excitement and deep anxiety which were felt among us poor slaves during this time. Our fate for life was now to be decided. We had no more voice in that decision than the brutes among whom we were ranked. . . . I fell to the portion of Mrs. Lucretia [Auld], and was sent immediately back to Baltimore. . . .

To see Hermes as a god of reallotment fits nicely with the way Brown connects the *Hymn* to Greek social life. "Hermes . . . was the patron of lottery . . ." Brown writes, "and lottery was one of the characteristic institutions of Greek democracy; the extensive use of lottery in the selection of Athenian public officials was the supreme expression of the democratic principle of the absolute equality of all citizens." Not that all *were* citizens, of course, but for those who were, the lottery canceled potential hierarchies of wealth and family.*

---

* The question arises whether trickster might not be the god of democracy. He isn't, is the short answer: Hermes, as Brown's book shows, can align himself with any political system (he is the servant of Zeus under kingship, the meat-thief in hunting times, and so

As for those who were not (slaves, foreigners, women*), if they hoped to reshape the world and reapportion its goods, they would have to await their own lucky finds, contingencies, loopholes. There can be no sleight of hand until you have a hand to play. Hermes, by his thieving and finding, gets himself a hand; he becomes a player with a game of his own. It's a *hidden* game, of course, rather like a child's secret ritual in which something is played out in safety as a precondition of some later, more public action. As a consequence of its privacy, that is, the scene in which Hermes apportions the meat has the air of a symbolic or mental reallotment presaging an actual one; we're watching a change of consciousness (the *mind* playing with stolen goods) that portends a later, actual escape from the trap of culture.

> [Douglass:] I was not about twelve years old, and the thought of being *a slave for life* began to bear heavily upon my heart. Just about this time, I got hold of a book entitled "The Columbian Orator." Every opportunity I got, I used to read this book. Among much of other interesting matter, I found in it a dialogue between a master and his slave. . . . In this dialogue, the whole argument in behalf of slavery was brought forward by the master, all of which was disposed of by the slave. The slave was made to say some very smart as well as impressive things in reply to his master—things which had the desired though unexpected effect; for the conversation resulted in the voluntary emancipation of the slave on the part of the master.

CHANGE THE RAP AND SLIP THE TRAP

For a human community to make its world shapely is one thing; to preserve the shape is quite another, especially if, as is always the case, the

---

on). That said, if trickster is a this-world, vernacular figure, if he is the low and the common, perhaps he moves more to the center in democracy, where the "common" may periodically upset and reshape power. Moreover, in this particular case, there is a link between Hermes and democracy, for the lottery of elections is a way of breaking aristocracy.

* In Athens, women were sometimes citizens to the degree that their children inherited citizenship; beyond that, they had no political rights.

shape is to some degree arbitrary and if the shaping requires exclusion and the excluded are hungry. So along with shapeliness comes a set of rules meant to preserve the design. "Do not steal. Do not lie. Do not blaspheme. Do not gamble. Do not pick things up in the street. Behave yourself. You should be ashamed. . . ." Whoever has the wit to break these rules, whoever puts the guards to sleep, slips across the threshold and floods the sacred meadows with contingency, whoever steals the boundary stones of clear distinction, that person strips design of its protective glamour. Hermes does all this and by it he disenchants the world into which he was born.

Having done so, having dragged design into the light where its seams appear and fray, he turns in his tracks and moves toward the dark, weaving a new world in place of the old. After all, his disruptions in no way get Hermes the honor he tells his mother they deserve. Mischief alone will likely leave a boy outcast and outlawed, even more excluded than he was to begin with. Therefore, we find Hermes reversing himself to play as well the smooth-tongued enchanter. Or perhaps I should say he plays the double-tongued enchanter, for he can move the conscious mind in one direction and the unconscious in another. When Apollo accuses him of theft, for example, his response combines a surface message with a subliminal one. Even as he denies the theft, he hints at something else. "I'd advise you not to talk like this in public," he says at one point. "The deathless gods will think it odd indeed." Twice he declares a readiness to swear his innocence in front of Zeus; at one point he leaps up, asking Apollo, "Where are you taking me?" and finally he begins to walk quickly across the sand, leading Apollo toward Mount Olympus.

Highlighted in this way we see that even as Hermes overtly protests the charges, covertly he hopes to move the quarrel to Mount Olympus so it can be held before the other gods. By my reading, he wants the shift for two reasons, one of which I've already mentioned (to have Zeus recognize his paternity). The other is that Hermes wants a change of venue. He's like a petty criminal who seeks to get his case into federal court so as to increase his status. If he's going to be a thief, at least he should be charged at the Olympic level. And he gets Apollo unwittingly to help enact the script that leads to this end. Left to his own devices, the older brother would have thrown the baby into darkest Tartarus, but under the spell of that young and silver tongue, Apollo accompanies him to heaven, where Hermes becomes a kind of royalty (the *Prince* of Thieves, not a crook from a cave), and where he stakes public claim to his lineage.

But these are only minor fruits of Hermes' enchanting powers; his acquisition of the herder's whip and of other offices is far more substantial, for with these gains come changes in the social order itself. Here again the lyre is his tool. When Hermes is ready to stop fighting and establish a connection with Apollo, he takes his instrument out and sings a theogony, a

> story of the gods . . . and of the dark earth, and how each came to be at the beginning of time, and how each came to have what now is theirs. . . . [Hermes] praised the . . . immortals, each in order of age, and he told how each was born, naming one by one in order as he struck his cradled lyre.

The song emphasizes honor, order, and rank, in marked contrast to all the earlier disordering moments (it is especially the opposite of Hermes' initial shameless song). This trickster whose transgressions have revealed the artifice of Apollo's world is not, for all that, the enemy of artifice; he can sing a shapely cosmos if he wants to.*

Hermes' performance initiates an exchange with Apollo that eventually brings the newcomer into the order of things. By the time the song is done, Apollo has fallen in love with the lyre. With a narrative set to music Hermes has amazed (he mazes) the great archer. Story and song: these are two of the hypnotics by which social orders maintain their self-enchantment, the radio playing all day in laundries and gas stations, a background hum of catchy ballads to keep an agreed-upon reality in place and seemingly alive.

After the song is sung, Apollo is as if hypnotized:

---

* In the Indo-European tradition, the order of sacrifice and the order of the cosmos were meant to reflect one another and, therefore, sacrifice and theogony belong together. "Such is clear . . ." Bruce Lincoln tells us, "in . . . Persian rites in which the Magi are said to have chanted a 'theogony' . . . during the dismemberment of an animal victim." In the *Hymn*, then, the separation of the two events bears out the idea that, in his sacrifice, Hermes is disordering an existing world and, in his theogony, ordering a new one.

And Apollo was seized with a longing he could do nothing about; he opened his mouth and the words flew out: "Butcher of cattle, trickster, busy boy, friend of merry-makers, the things you're interested in are worth fifty cows. Soon I believe we shall settle our quarrel in peace."

Apollo not only responds to and longs for the lyre, he makes it clear that he's willing to come to some agreement about the cattle. Soon he suggests an exchange of gifts ("By my dogwood staff I swear I shall make you the renowned guide of the deathless gods. . . . I will give you wonderful gifts"). Hermes then gives Apollo the lyre and Apollo "ordain[s] him Keeper of the Herds." By the end of the *Hymn* there is much more: Hermes is given his magic wand and his own art of prophecy; he is put in charge of lions, boars, and dogs, as well as the herds; he is appointed messenger of the gods and guide to Hades.

In short, the outsider seems to have become an insider. An insider with a difference, that is, for he changes the center as he enters it. At the simplest level, the inside has him in it, and that's a significant change. When Hermes sings his catalogue of gods and how "each came to have what now is theirs," does he include himself? I expect he does, just as he made himself an object of sacrifice. It isn't any old melodic narrative he sings, either; it's a new story, a new song ("change the rap and slip the trap"). Moreover, he accompanies himself with a new instrument, and that also means a change. A bit of luck and a trick of craft gave Hermes something to trade with that was not part of the old economy. Like the person who has found buried treasure or like the craftsman who has dreamed up a new technique, Hermes appears with a kind of wealth that eludes the received moral grid, and patron of smart luck, he turns it to good advantage and exchanges gifts with Apollo.

With all this enchantment and disenchantment, then, Hermes manages to resolve the dilemma he posed in the speech to his mother ("either they *give* me honor or I *steal* it"). He resolves it with a theft that confuses the definition of theft, with lies that muddy the truth, with speech that shifts the thresholds of shame, with chance operations that dissolve hierarchy—*and* with a musical tongue that casts new spells even as the old ones are undone. When he is finished, the reallotment he dreamed of is actual, not just mental. The fictive designs that faced him at birth are altered so as to include him and his creations. The thief has come into the gift community. The outsider has become an insider.

A final question arises at this point. Having rewritten the script, will Hermes stick to it, or will he go on being a pest? Will he enter the house of the gods or linger on the threshold? There comes a moment soon after Hermes and Apollo swear their mutual fealty when Apollo suddenly has second thoughts. True, Hermes has given him the nod, traditional sign of a serious oath, but still, this is a shameless liar, boy inventor of the slippery sign, master of the empty gesture. What can possibly assure Apollo—and us—that he means it when he says he won't break into his brother's house and steal his caldrons?

To answer, I must say a bit about the general shape or plot of trickster stories.

The literary theorist Vladímir Propp once sought to show that all Russian folktales could be seen as variations of a few underlying plot elements. In one general case, a preliminary situation is followed by "Misfortune or Lack" and then by a sequence of events that repairs what Misfortune or Lack disturbed. By such a model, the mischief-maker and thief is one of the prime movers of narrative. The original plotter of plots, he gets the story moving and it comes to an end only when he and his mischief have been dealt with.

There are only a few ways to deal with him, too, only a limited number of plots. From the edge of a group or the threshold of a house there are only a few ways a trickster can move: he can come inside, he can leave entirely, or he can stay exactly where he started, resisting all attempts to civilize or exile. From trickster's point of view, this last, staying on the threshold, must be the ideal type; it gives us the plot that never resolves itself, the endlessly strung-together Coyote tales each linked to each with the phrase "Coyote was going along . . ." or (in Europe) the picaresque narrative in which the pícaro, the knight of the roads, wanders from town to town, individual episodes ending but not the tale itself because the pícaro never changes, never settles down in fact or in spirit. Collodi's *Pinocchio* is an endless picaresque in this way until the puppet gets a conscience, at which point the story hurries to closure (just as the Monkey narrative ends when Monkey becomes a good Buddhist). Awakened conscience is the potential end of narrative; without it, the tale can go on and on, another night, another season.

In a second kind of story, trickster is eventually domesticated. He comes in from the edge of town and agrees to play by the rules. Paul Radin says that if we read the Winnebago trickster cycle carefully we can see places where the narrator himself seems to get upset at his hero's bizarre exploits and so inserts moments of settled home life. Thus, after one of the strangest episodes (a transvestite marriage in which trickster wears a fake vulva made from elk liver!) the tale turns sharply toward the proper: "Our raconteur has expressed [his] shock by bringing his narrative to a full stop. . . . Suddenly, and for the first time in the cycle, [trickster] is pictured as a normal man with a wife to whom he is legally married and a son for whom it is still necessary to provide. In short, he is suddenly represented as a good citizen, as a thoroughly socialized individual." It would seem that human communities find it hard to live with the chaos tricksters portend, or the ambiguity and anomaly they bring, and so there is always this pull to get trickster off the threshold and into the house, not just to get Wakdjunkaga married but to get Eshu away from the crossroads and into Ifa's house, to get Monkey out of the Peach Garden and make him bow to the Buddha, to get Loki to be a proper guest when there's a drinking party at Aegir's house, to get Coyote to take a bride so he will not keep his tobacco to himself but swap it around, the way proper people do.*

The third possible plot ends in the exile, destruction, or binding of the trickster. If only Coyote could be driven farther west, into the wilderness, away from the settled villages! Or, for the more violent resolutions, think of the end of the movie *Easy Rider* in which the bothersome, rootless, hungry road trippers are simply blown away, a shotgun appearing at the window of a truck and blasting them from their motorcycles. End of movie. Many trickster tales have at least a moment of this impulse (Apollo threatening to throw Hermes into darkest Tartarus, all the times Coyote is "killed"). In an Alaskan story, Wise One gets tired of Raven's incessant thieving and burns him to death. Unfortunately, all the human

---

* In the last chapter we saw how to combine these two plot types—domestication and staying on the threshold—which is to have annual ritualized periods of misrule, contained but endlessly recurrent touches of the picaresque.

beings immediately disappear, and Wise One must resurrect Raven in order to recover them. More often, the plot stops short of trickster's death and settles for attempts to bind or contain him, as we saw with Loki, tied beneath the earth.

With certain reservations to which I'll turn shortly, I would argue that Hermes in the *Hymn* is domesticated. His promise, his nod to Apollo, is the real thing. To begin with, he seems to domesticate himself at certain points. If he includes himself in the new theogony he sings, then he makes himself part of a cosmos, not chaos. Or take his moment of restraint, *not* eating the meat of sacrifice, hungry as he is. Here Hermes doesn't just erase an old boundary; he draws a new one. By the old rules he is *not* Olympian, *not* an insider, *not* an object of sacrifice; Hermes cancels that "not" and, in secrecy and stealth, includes himself in the circle. Once he's in, however, he needs to draw a new circle, he needs to remake the boundary on his own terms, which he does by not eating. With that "not" he produces the symbolic meat-not-eaten and rearticulates the cosmos with himself in the pantheon.

More broadly, if we step out of this particular story and look at Hermes in other Homeric texts, we find a domestic strain. Very often he is the faithful servant of Zeus. At the end of the *Iliad*, for example, Priam must go to Achilles to ransom Hector's body, and Zeus sends Hermes to guide the old man past the guards. This he does surely. He faithfully executes the will of Zeus. It is not hard to imagine an unfaithful servant or messenger, a drug courier, for example, who sneaks through customs but then cheats his employers as well. But that is not how Hermes is pictured. Zeus asks him to do something and he does it reliably; there is never any anxiety about what he'll do. Every year he brings Persephone up from the underworld; in the *Odyssey* he faithfully conducts the suitors' souls into Hades. He is the trusted guide.

That said, I must refine the point a bit, for there are certain areas in which Hermes is not to be trusted at all. First of all, when the gods themselves are at odds, Hermes is still the trickster, siding with stolen love, theft, and shameless behavior. In this patriarchy, he will kill Argus to help Zeus deceive Hera (or, in a less patriarchal moment, to help the grieving Demeter, he will sweet-talk Hades into freeing the captive Persephone). Second, to the degree that he is domesticated, his *domos*, his home, is with the gods, but he is never brought into line where mortals are concerned: the closing lines of the *Hymn* say that "most of the time, when night has fallen, he deceives the race of those who must die."

In addition to all this, even if Hermes in some sense becomes a faithful servant in the world of the gods, it's important to remember an earlier point: even if he behaves, he does so in a world he has altered. The art of sacrifice, a new way of making fire, the pan pipes and the lyre, a messenger to Hades, new forms of wealth, new boundaries of exchange—so many things change when Hermes arrives that it hardly seems right to say he is "domesticated" when he makes peace with the other gods. Better to say he is a culture hero who comes to terms with the group, and that the terms are partly his own.

A nd yet, to complicate the question one last time, I should point out that the *Hymn* seems to say that all of Hermes' mischief takes place "in the mind of Zeus," as it were; it appears that the old man has foreseen and authorized everything. Hermes' conception and birth are described as Zeus' "purpose" being fulfilled; when he comes home from his night of thieving, Maia says, "Your father meant you to be a great bother, both to the gods . . . and to humans." Apollo later says, "Zeus has given you the honor of initiating deeds of exchange trade among human beings all over the fruitful earth." Most telling of all, when Zeus settles the quarrel between his two sons we read: "Then [Zeus] nodded his head and good Hermes obeyed, for the will of Zeus . . . persuades without effort." Like a parent who tolerates a certain amount of misbehavior, knowing its outcome better than the children who believe they're free, or like a politician who allows particular disruptions, knowing they will in fact serve his own ends, it begins to feel as if Zeus had imagined the whole plot from the outset. In some sense he "contains" all the changes that Hermes brings, and they are not, therefore, a deep disruption.

Here it will help to remember once more that the Hermes story may reflect actual history. Brown surmises that the *Hymn* was written down around 520 B.C., and if he's right then this narrative comes *at the end* of a period of tension and change. That being the case, it may come as no surprise that one way to articulate the change—admitting the new but preserving the old—is to say, "Well, this is what we had in mind all along." Whether we think of the *Hymn* as recording changes wrought by a mythic culture hero or by an actual class of merchants and artisans in Greece at the end of the Archaic age, to say that the whole disruptive story has taken place "in the mind of Zeus" may be a way, after the fact, of framing change so as to contain it. To have the lying, thieving Hermes spring from Zeus' loins is to figure Zeus as the ultimate author of hermetic inventions, as if Hermes had never really been an outsider, as if there weren't a period in Greek history when a shame threshold kept traders at a distance from aristocrats. To have Zeus father Hermes is to claim that the changes he brings are a part of the eternal and *not* contingent, relative, or dependent on historical situations. It draws history back into myth.

Such may be the frequent fate of radical change-agents, to be co-opted, outflanked, and contained by the larger culture, to be brought up short of a full apocalyptic reallotment. But what exactly are the options? A remark by Claude Lévi-Strauss offers a way to imagine the possible fates of those who threaten a group with fundamental change. Lévi-Strauss contrasts two types of societies: "those which practice cannibalism—that is, which regard the absorption of certain individuals possessing dangerous powers as the only means of neutralizing these powers and even of turning them to advantage—and those which, like our own . . . adopt what might be called the practice of *anthropemy* (from the Greek *emein*, to vomit)." The latter eject dangerous individuals; they leave them in the woods, or build special jails to cut them off from the group and keep them isolated. In short, groups can either expel or ingest their troublemakers. The most successful change-agent avoids either fate and manages to stay on the threshold, neither in nor out, but short of that difficult balance the next best fate may be to be eaten, to be incorporated into the local myth.

Let us say, then, that the *Homeric Hymn to Hermes* records an incorporation; it is an after-the-fact record of a disruption that has been contained and re-presented as something Zeus "had in mind all along," not an apocalypse. Trickster's disruptions are always potentially apocalyptic, but in this case they are converted into manageable mischief. For apocalyptic action, one needs turn to Monkey disrupting the Taoist immortals or to the medieval Loki after whose disruptions the Norse gods are *not* reborn in Scandinavia but supplanted by Christianity.

The *Hymn* is not so apocalyptic and that may be the more common case. It is what might be expected when an outsider penetrates the group:

at some point there must be an understanding, a series of compromises that formalize the move, a negotiated living together. In this case the terms are to a large degree set by Hermes, but they do not upset the entire order of things; the order adapts to contain the introject, the foreign thing it has swallowed, and at that point we should divide the "domestication" plot into two forms. It is one thing to submit to an old set of house rules, quite another to enter a house that you yourself have helped to build.

10

....

FREDERICK DOUGLASS
AND ESHU'S HAT

ANSWERING BACK

*To all these complaints . . . the slave must answer never a word.
Colonel Lloyd could not brook any contradiction from a slave.*
—Frederick Douglass

*When Hate-to-be-contradicted was dead, Ananse cut up his flesh in
little pieces and scattered it about. That, the Ashanti say, is how
contradiction came among the people.*
—Robert Pelton

I realize it may seem odd to seek out a vein of trickster consciousness
in a person as serious and moralizing as Frederick Douglass. There
are certainly more obvious cases of tricky Americans. One could take
Douglass's contemporary, P. T. Barnum, if one wanted a playful and creative public figure. Or, if one wanted a canonical artist who imagined
disruptive creativity in great detail, one could look at Herman Melville

and his portrait of the confidence man. But neither Barnum nor Melville was situated so clearly at the margins. The birth of a Hermes-like threshold consciousness is partly a matter of temperament and partly a matter of setting. Put on the threshold, trickster mind may awaken in almost anyone. Those who are given to the pleasures of liminality may actively seek out such settings (as have artists like Duchamp or Ginsberg), but such settings will also leave their mark on persons not otherwise predisposed.

Frederick Douglass, in any event, may have been a moralist by temperament, but he was born into a world where two distinct moral systems conflicted, and found himself forced to mediate between them. He was the child of a white man and a black woman in a world where the races were radically separated. After his escape he was a "free slave," a remarkable contradiction in terms. He also had a strong will to test the forbidden, and it kept him on the edge, where others might have accepted the portions they had been offered. When he writes that his master's "bitter opposition" goaded him into learning to read, we witness his willfulness and at the same time see its fruit, for it was by his reading that Douglass produced a second miscegenation: through access to books he became the child of two cultures, not just two races.

In short, Douglass dwelt on the boundaries of plantation culture, and in that setting he became a cunning go-between, a thief of reapportionment who quit the periphery and moved to the center. An artist like Melville or a con man like Barnum never needed to effect a change of that magnitude, but Frederick Douglass did.

To slip a trap of culture, Hermes both enchants and disenchants the world around him. Where, in Douglass's case, are the sacred cattle whose theft might begin the disenchantment? Much of his story has to do with property rights and determining who is or is not a thief, from the slaves stealing fruit at the Great House Farm to Douglass stealing himself out of slavery. But none of these is the central object of the raid Douglass makes on plantation culture. His central theft is literacy.

Reading and writing were first offered to the eight-year-old Douglass as gifts: his mistress in Baltimore, Sophia Auld, taught him "the A. B. C." and how to spell simple words.

Just at this point of my progress, Mr. Auld found out what was going on and at once forbade Mrs. Auld to instruct me further, telling her, among other things, that it was unlawful, as well as unsafe, to teach a slave to read. To use his own words, further, he said, ". . . A nigger should know nothing but to obey his master—to do as he is told to do. Learning would *spoil* the best nigger in the world. Now," said he, "if you teach that nigger (speaking of myself) how to read, there would be no keeping him. . . . He would at once become unmanageable, and of no value to his master. . . . It would make him discontented and unhappy."

These words sank deep into my heart. . . . It was a new and special revelation, explaining dark and mysterious things. . . . I now understood what had been to me a most perplexing difficulty—to wit, the white man's power to enslave the black man. It was a grand achievement, and I prized it highly. From that moment, I understood the pathway from slavery to freedom.

Douglass knows he's at the edge of a sacred meadow because the alarm goes off, the watchdogs start barking. Now he understands what he wants and why; in secrecy and stealth over the next years he "steals" literacy from the world around him. (He gets white boys on the street to help him learn to read and, in an essential lucky find, comes across Caleb Bingham's book, *The Columbian Orator*, a collection of eloquent speeches, including a dialogue Bingham himself had written, in which a slave cunningly demolishes each of his master's pro-slavery arguments.)

In stealing literacy it is as if Douglass stole all printed books in the Great House and carried them to the slave quarters. The prohibition on teaching a slave to read was meant to prevent exactly such movement. Remember that when Odysseus moves his oar inland it is eventually taken for a winnowing fan; the motion itself, the shift in context, creates the multiple meanings. As I earlier argued, a rule that classifies certain appropriations as "theft" and forbids them is therefore a prohibition on the creation of new meaning. Douglass violates such a rule and in so doing makes a world of sense where sense was previously absent. The Bible, for example, reads differently in the dirt-floored cabin than it does in the Great House. A reading of Genesis 9 in the slave quarters might find little sense in the cursing of Ham, but a meaningful model in Ham's frank disclosure of Noah's drunkenness.

This is not all, though, for Douglass's theft does something at once simpler and more complex than shifting the site of reading. Having learned to read and write, having studied eloquence, Douglass proceeds, simply enough, to write and to speak, and these acts *by themselves* undercut plantation culture, for that culture had as one of its "eternals" the notion that writing and speaking belonged inherently to whites, that their absence was inherent to blacks. In one of his essays, Henry Louis Gates, Jr., offers a good summary of places where this racist division is asserted in high European philosophy; it appears in Hume, in Kant, and in Hegel; in America we find it in Thomas Jefferson. To take but one example, Hegel says that Africa "is no historical part of the World; it has no movement or development to exhibit. . . . What we properly understand by Africa, is the Unhistorical, Undeveloped Spirit, still involved in the conditions of mere nature. . . ." For Hegel, black Africans are part of nature and different in kind from whites because they have no written history. "The absence and presence of writing," says Gates, "of a collective black voice that could in some sense be overheard, were drawn upon by European philosophers to deprive African slaves of their humanity." No wonder Hugh Auld panicked when he saw his wife teaching Douglass to read. By these assumptions, her success would have made the black child as human as their own white child, and confounded distinctions essential to the whole enterprise of slavery.

A s the stealthy Hermes initially operates under cover of his ally the night, so Douglass schools himself in secret. But in both cases, once the theft is done, the plot cannot proceed without its revelation. If Douglass hopes to be the active disenchanter of his master's world, he must speak and write in public, even though in a good slave a proper sense of decorum, of shame, would still the tongue and hand.

It is not quite right to call plantation culture a "shame culture"; it was first and foremost a culture of terror, bloodshed, and fear. And yet the whip produced a system of shame barriers as its ancillary product. Corporal punishment was always ready, but acquired inhibitions alone could often be relied upon to hold the line. Douglass's repeated use of the word "impudent" bespeaks this internalized threshold (impudence is shamelessness; the Latin root is *pudere*, to feel shame). A few examples will suffice, beginning with the exception that proves the rule: it was the naïve Sophia Auld who, not knowing how to treat a slave, gave Douglass his first sense of the arbitrary nature of plantation decorum: "She did not deem it impudent . . . for a slave to look her in the face." Elsewhere, of course, ʷʰat Douglass got was the rule itself, a constant schooling in locally appropriate silence. Thus he reports that slaves were forbidden to ask "questions . . . concerning their ages," as "such questions were regarded by the masters as evidence of an impudent curiosity." He tells us that a slave who tried to justify his conduct when he had been censured for it would be thought "guilty of impudence,—one of the greatest crimes of which a slave can be guilty." A certain cruel overseer would even make sport with these rules: "He was one of those who could torture the slightest look, word, or gesture, on the part of the slave, into impudence, and would treat it accordingly. There must be no answering back to him." It should be added, too, that these rules of silence were also a matter of law in plantation culture. The word of a slave (and of a free black) had no legal standing; slaves could not testify in court; no warrant could be issued on their word, and so forth. In law as in practice, slaves were supposed to stand mute, and plantation culture—like others we have seen—thus organized itself through spheres of speech and spheres of silence. Slaves were taught that "a still tongue makes a wise head."

Frederick Douglass presents himself in the *Narrative* as a person rarely bound by such rules; he comes before us as the heroic, unabashed speaker; his book itself proves his boldness. But if we look closely, the book also shows that he had to struggle before he found the necessary impudence. His description of the first time he spoke at an abolitionist rally in Nantucket rewards attentive reading:

> I . . . never felt happier than when in an anti-slavery meeting. I seldom had much to say at the meetings, because what I wanted to say was said so much better by others. But, while attending an anti-slavery convention at Nantucket, on the 11th of August, 1841, I felt strongly moved to speak, and was at the same time much urged to do so by Mr. William C. Coffin, a gentleman who had heard me speak in the colored people's meeting at New Bedford. It was a severe cross, and I took it up reluctantly. The truth was, I felt myself a slave, and the idea of speaking to white people weighed me down. I spoke but a few moments, when I felt a degree of freedom, and said what I desired with considerable ease. From

that time until now, I have been engaged in pleading the cause of my brethren—with what success, and with what devotion, I leave those acquainted with my labors to decide.

It is the mention of "the colored people's meeting" that strikes me in this account. To flag the phrase is to foreground what Douglass passes over quickly: he is *not* describing the first time he spoke against slavery in public; he is describing the first time he spoke to *whites*. The shame threshold which forbade such speech did not disappear when the whip disappeared. Douglass, in the North almost three years, still feels the internal prohibition, and must work to break it. (Douglass revised his autobiography several times; his 1855 version of the same scene is even more graphic: "It was with the utmost difficulty that I could stand erect, or that I could command and articulate two words without hesitation or stammering. I trembled in every limb.") Douglass could speak freely in "the colored people's meeting," but that speaking did not make him feel free (it had never been prohibited). It is only when he can speak across the color line, when he can break the rule of silence and contest the white world's fictions about slavery, that he truly feels himself free.

In a sense it is simply by refusing plantation culture's rules of silence and speaking from and across its internal boundaries that Douglass dispels its enchantment. His main tool in this enterprise is a form of speech expressly forbidden to slaves, "contradiction" or "answering back." Contradiction is the verbal analogue to Hermes walking the cattle backward, or Coyote trapping his dinner in a tunnel with a fire at each end. It confuses polarity; it baffles those who were moving in a pure, straight line; it uncovers hidden duplicity. We hear the contradictory strain of Douglass's voice partly in his constant irony and in his regular antithetical constructions,* but more subtly and importantly in his ap-

---

* Of the many rhetorical tricks that Caleb Bingham recommends, "an antithesis, or a sentence consisting of opposite parts," seems to have been Douglass's favorite. Antithesis produces the prose of contradiction, as in this example from the *Narrative*: "What [Auld] most dreaded, that I most desired. What he most loved, that I most hated. That which to him was a great evil, to be carefully shunned, was to me a great good, to be diligently sought; and the argument which he so warmly urged, against my learning to read, only served to inspire me with a desire and determination to learn."

232 .... TRICKSTER MAKES THIS WORLD ....

parently simple descriptions of plantation life. Consider these few sentences from the first page of the *Narrative*:

> By far the larger part of the slaves know as little of their ages as horses know of theirs, and it is the wish of most masters within my knowledge to keep their slaves thus ignorant. I do not remember to have ever met a slave who could tell of his birthday, they seldom come nearer to it than planting-time, harvest-time, cherry-time, spring-time, or fall-time.

As Henry Louis Gates, Jr., shows in an essay on the opening chapter of the *Narrative*, these lines and those that follow lay out a series of oppositions particular to plantation culture: blacks tell time by the seasons, whites by the calendar; blacks do not know their ages, whites do; blacks are set in nature, whites in culture; blacks belong to night and the earth, whites to daylight and the heavens. Blacks, in short, are like beasts, and whites are human beings. The shape of plantation culture follows from this network of oppositions. When whites deny blacks access to calendrical time, they create a difference between blacks and whites, and an interlocking system of such "barriers of difference," as Gates calls them, produces the articulated world, the cosmos, the cultural weave, of this society, a fiction that will begin to seem real as soon as everyone forgets that human beings made it.

But Douglass contradicts this cosmos merely by describing it: coming from the supposed sphere of silence, any diction is contradiction. From the sphere of silence, speech itself is impudent regardless of its content, and threatens the design of this world. The proof of that assertion lies in the immediate response of Southern planters to Douglass's voice: they claimed that it didn't exist. After the *Narrative* was published, for example, a man from Maryland who said he knew Douglass as a slave wrote to the newspapers to say that the book was a forgery: "I indulge no animosity against the fabricators of the *Narrative*, neither do I know them, but I positively declare the whole to be a budget of falsehood, from beginning to end." Douglass and his friends knew this would happen, thus the framing material peculiar to slave narratives—the subtitle, *Written by Himself*, and the earnest introductions in which white men declare that the book "is essentially true in all its statements . . . ; nothing has been . . . drawn from the imagination."

But once the reader accepts that a black slave is in fact speaking, then, as I say, simple diction leads to contradiction. The voice slowly occupies the "white" portions of the culture's oppositions, and in doing so renders the categories of plantation culture *self*-contradictory. Here simple diction passes to a fuller register, joined by contradiction's cousins, irony and scorn. We have entertained these tones already, in Douglass's remarks about how slavery will be "unscriptural" if white men continue to beget black children, for example, or in the description of "thieves" stealing the Colonel's fruit. There is much more, of course, such as an explanation of why it is best for white women to sell their husbands' mulatto children, but the point is that before too long readers discover they are in a world where civilized men are savages, Christians are pagans, impudence is genteel, genteel women are beasts, illegalities are embodied in the law, thieves are noble, and honest men are thieves.

In this way, the cultural pattern collapses. It becomes senseless. As Gates puts it, having entered into all these oppositions, Douglass has worked "as mediator and as trickster to reverse [their] relations." His reversals make the reader more and more aware of anomalies and ambiguities, the denial of which is essential to preserving the purity of plantation culture. Contradiction, that is, reveals the material whose exclusion created the order in the first place, and its illusion of purity. Its dirt exposed, the code of plantation culture no longer makes sense; it no longer "means" the way it used to. What seemed like noble truths (the gentility of the women, the piety of the men) are discovered to be local and contingent fictions, if not outright lies. The longer we listen to Douglass's voice, the more eternals turn into accidents, unities into confusions, and purities into obscenities. No wonder "Colonel Lloyd could brook no contradiction from a slave."

Earlier I sketched some plots typical to trickster stories, contrasting those that end in domestication with those in which trickster remains on the edge or threshold—the endless picaresque, for example, or festivals of misrule that recur regularly but are contained in a ritual calendar. To assign the vein of trickster intelligence in Douglass to one of these plots, I want to begin with his own analysis of periodic misrule. It was the custom in plantation culture to give slaves a holiday between Christmas and the New Year.

This time we regarded as our own, by the grace of our masters; and we therefore used or abused it nearly as we pleased. . . . The staid, sober, thinking and industrious ones of our number would employ themselves in making corn-brooms, mats, horse-collars, and baskets; and another class of us would spend the time in hunting opossums, hares, and coons.

But by far the larger part engaged in such sports and merriments as playing ball, wrestling, running foot-races, fiddling, dancing, and drinking whisky; and this latter mode of spending the time was by far the most agreeable to the feelings of our masters. A slave who would work during the holidays was considered by our masters as scarcely deserving them. He was regarded as one who rejected the favor of his master. It was deemed a disgrace not to get drunk at Christmas; and he was regarded as lazy indeed, who had not provided himself with the necessary means, during the year, to get whisky enough to last him. . . .

This custom conforms almost exactly to the pattern of the Saturnalia in Ancient Rome. The Roman calendar included festivals for the major deities; the holiday dedicated to Saturn ran for a week in late December and was the most festive—unusual generosity was supposed to prevail, moral restraints were loosened, and slaves were temporarily free to do and say what they liked. This last is of note here: Roman Saturnalia included permission, limited in time, to "answer back," to contradict.

Douglass is astute on the social function of such contained release:

From what I know of the effect of these holidays upon the slave, I believe them to be among the most effective means in the hands of the slaveholder in keeping down the spirit of insurrection. Were the slaveholders at once to abandon this practice, I have not the slightest doubt it would lead to an immediate insurrection among the slaves.

These holidays serve as conductors, or safety-valves, to carry off the rebellious spirit of enslaved humanity. . . . Woe betide the slaveholder, the day he ventures to remove or hinder the operation of those conductors! I warn him that, in such an event, a spirit will go forth in their midst, more to be dreaded than the most appalling earthquake.

This language offers a way to rethink the moment in the *Homeric Hymn* when Hermes does not eat the meat in favor of later access to the food of the gods. Might the scene record the memory of a historical shift, one in which ritual carnival (the carnivore's meat-holiday) was forgone in favor of a shift in social status? Such, in any event, is how Douglass figures the slaves' Saturnalia and his own relationship to it: to indulge the appetites is to tame dissent; to remove that indulgence is to court rebellion.

Douglass knew from his own experience how Saturnalia operated. During the year-end holidays of 1834, enslaved on the farm of one William Freeland, Douglass had been one of those who accepted the master's liquor. The local drink was applejack and the sixteen-year-old Douglass found he liked it very much. He drank his own share, and then drank all he could beg or sponge from companions less interested. Liquor "made me feel I was a great man," he later wrote. "I used to think I was a president." Not surprisingly, the feeling was at odds with the actual effects; apparently on one occasion Douglass woke after a day of drinking to find he'd spent the night passed out in the sty with the pigs. Later he wrote of these holidays:

> [The] object seems to be, to disgust . . . slaves with freedom, by plunging them into the lowest depth of dissipation. . . . Many of us used to think there was little to choose between liberty and slavery. We felt . . . that we had almost as well be slaves to man as to rum. So, when the holiday ended, we staggered up from the filth of our wallowing, took a long breath, and marched to the field.

Despite the distancing "we," this is the voice of experience. And Douglass had not only been in the wallow himself, he had somehow figured out that to slip the trap and enjoy an authentic taste of freedom he would need to restrain the thirst that predatory slaveholders were all too willing to whet.

His choices may call to mind the Greek tricksters and their struggles with appetite. Remember that both Prometheus and Hermes try to change the way the cosmos had been apportioned, but with differing results. Prometheus' trick fails; forever after, his heirs get to eat meat, but they are, for that, "mere bellies," recurrently hungry and confined to a lower sphere. Hermes, on the other hand, denies his own belly and thus exchanges terrestrial for heavenly feeding. In the American South, if the masters had their way, slaves would never know this latter option. Douglass himself had occasionally been wildly hungry (as a child he was forced to fight other children for corn mush in a pig trough), but he had also known the satiation of those who eat regularly and are confined to a lower sphere: Freeland fed his slaves well and supplied them with booze, which is to say that on Freeland's farm Douglass was in danger of entering the Promethean plot, trading the desired higher allotment for a full belly and an annual applejack binge.

But he didn't take that path. On the first of January 1836, precisely after a second drunken holiday, Douglass resolved to turn his back on transitory pleasures and risk the more enduring satisfactions that escape might bring. He refused the endless ritual of contained release in favor of something a little more apocalyptic. He abandoned the cyclical time of ritual in favor of linear time where individuals know their birth dates and where what was in fact an "appalling earthquake"—a civil war— would soon mark the calendar with such dates as January 1, 1863 (Lincoln issues the Emancipation Proclamation); November 1, 1864 (slavery is abolished in Maryland); and November 17, 1864 (Douglass returns to Baltimore, a free man in a free state).

Earlier in this book, I proposed that a trap of shame appears when cultural patterns get linked to the way the body is imagined, especially if the links are rendered invisible. Given such links, a person's experience of his or her own body "proves" the cultural pattern, and changing the pattern seems as impossible as changing the body. In the case at hand, think of Douglass saying that the point of the year-end holiday was to "disgust slaves with freedom," to "plunge them into the lowest depth of dissipation," to get them "wallowing" in filth. He is describing a self-disgust derived from bodily appetite. Playing to that appetite, the masters create the trap's inexorable logic: a slave craves applejack, his boozing shames him, and thus his station in life is part of nature.

How does one unmake such a constellation? One could, of course, simply declare it false (pointing to drunken whites, or sober blacks), but often one needs to enter the myth and change its terms from within. Hermes slips the trap by restraining his appetite, after which the cultural associations to meat-hunger, whatever they are, no longer apply. Douglass does the same thing. Refusing his own craving, he cuts the link between the social artifice and the body. To put it another way, because world and body are meant to pattern one another, when he reimagines his body he reimagines his world.

Thus, to listen to Douglass tell the story of plantation drunkenness and his own relation to it is to hear an enchanter offer new eternal truths to replace those he would destroy. To see how these eternals emerge, remember that it is by restraint of hunger that Hermes makes himself a god. His private lottery erases the line separating him from the other gods; his restraint draws a new line joining him to them. Thus the boundary markers move; thus he becomes an eternal. To believe his story is to enter a new fiction, a new shaping of the world.

In Douglass's case, all who refuse applejack also refuse the contained contradiction of Saturnalia and thereby create the possibility of *uncon*tained contradiction. Plantation culture's spheres of silence enabled the "eternal truth" that the races are essentially different. Refusing Saturnalia, Douglass breaks both the link between appetite and subordination and the link between subordination and silence. In place of all that, he offers a voice that promises to "answer back" at any time and any place, and that voice portends a new world shaped not by racial difference but by the "eternal truth" of racial equality. If we were to end Douglass's story here, we could assign it to that plot in which the marginalized one successfully unravels the trap of culture that contains him and weaves another in its stead.

THE COLOR LINE

A protean Douglass has not been desired by any of his biographers.
—Peter F. Walker

As long as you think you're white, I have to think I'm black.
—James Baldwin

By the time Frederick Douglass died in 1895, much of plantation culture had collapsed, its organizing distinctions erased. But no utopia had arisen from its ruins; Yankee culture had its own organizing divisions, some of them odious and remarkably indelible. I am thinking especially of the way that America divides its population into black and white, and the question of where Douglass belonged in regard to that color line. The answer might seem obvious (Douglass was black; he belongs on the black side), but the more closely one looks, the less obvious it becomes.

Before turning to this subtle story, I want to interleave a famous West African trickster tale, the Yoruba account of two friends who forgot about Eshu. This old-world story provides a useful way to speak about the traps and snares of color in America. Among the Yoruba,

everyone knows the story of the two friends who were thwarted in their friendship by Eshu. They took vows of eternal friendship to one another, but neither took Eshu into consideration. Eshu took note of their actions and decided to do something about them.

When the time was ripe, Eshu decided to put their friendship to his own little test. He made a cloth cap. The right side was black, the left side was white.

The two friends were out in the fields, tilling their land. One was hoeing on the right side, the other was clearing the bushes to the left. Eshu came by on a horse, riding between the two men. The one on the right saw the black side of his hat. The friend on the left noticed the sheer whiteness of Eshu's cap.

The two friends took a break for lunch under the cool shade of the trees. Said one friend, "Did you see the man with the white cap who greeted us as we were working? He was very pleasant, wasn't he?"

"Yes, he was charming, but it was a man in a black cap that I recall, not a white one."

"It was a white cap. The man was riding a magnificently caparisoned horse."

"Then it must be the same man. I tell you, his cap was dark black."

"You must be fatigued or blinded by the hot rays of the sun to take a white cap for a black one."

"I tell you it was a black cap and I am not mistaken. I remember him distinctly."

The two friends fell to fighting. The neighbors came running but the fight was so intense that the neighbors could not stop it. In the midst of this uproar, Eshu returned, looking very calm and pretending not to know what was going on.

"What is the cause of all the hullabaloo?" he demanded sternly.

"Two close friends are fighting," was the answer. "They seem intent on killing each other and neither would stop or tell us the reason for the fight. Please do something before they destroy each other."

Eshu promptly stopped the fight. "Why do you two lifelong friends make a public spectacle of yourselves in this manner?"

"A man rode through the farm, greeting us as he went by," said the first friend. "He was wearing a black cap, but my friend tells me it was a white cap and that I must be tired or blind or both."

The second friend insisted that the man had been wearing a white cap. One of them must be mistaken, but it was not he.

"Both of you are right," said Eshu.

"How can that be?"

"I am the man who paid the visit over which you now quarrel, and here is the cap that caused the dissension." Eshu put his hand in his pocket and brought out the two-colored cap, saying, "As you can see, one side is white and the other is black. You each saw one side and, therefore, are right about what you saw. Are you not the two friends who made vows of friendship? When you vowed to be friends always, to be faithful and true to each other, did you reckon with Eshu? Do you know that he who does not put Eshu first in all his doings has himself to blame if things misfire?"

And so it is said,

> "Eshu, do not undo me,
> Do not falsify the words of my mouth,
> Do not misguide the movements of my feet.
> You who translates yesterday's words
> Into novel utterances,
> Do not undo me,
> I bear you sacrifices."

In Africa, this story is known in many versions, and many locations. During the slave trade it traveled to the Americas, where it necessarily took on different features. According to Lydia Cabrera, there is a Cuban version in which Eshu "had shaved off the hair on one side of his head, and kept beard and coiffure intact on the other. To compound the confusion, he changed himself into a white man on the side with the hair, thus appearing fundamentally different to each friend." When the friends argue, one says he saw a black man, the other a white.

Frederick Douglass assumed that his first master, Aaron Anthony, was his father; his mother, Harriet Bailey, was Anthony's slave. The Baileys were a close-knit kin group, old inhabitants of Maryland's Eastern Shore. Douglass's mother reportedly could read, and *her* mother, though a slave, was relatively independent (married to a free black man, she had a cabin to call her own). Douglass's great-great-grandfather had been born in colonial Maryland in 1701. His people, in turn, had probably been brought to America not from Africa but from the English colony of Barbados, which means, among other things, that the Bailey family had been English-speaking for at least five generations. In short, through his mother, Douglass was heir to an unusually stable and enduring African-American tradition.

Aaron Anthony had been born of poor and illiterate parents whose forebears had come from England. Anthony himself learned to read and write (poorly); he worked on cargo schooners—first as a deckhand, eventually as a captain—until the local rich man, Colonel Lloyd, made him chief overseer of his farms. Anthony married a woman from a prominent family, through whom he acquired his slaves. His considerable self-discipline was regularly disturbed by melancholy and lust; his small library contained a book called *The Pleasant Art of Money Catching* and a nine-dollar Bible.

So, what color was that hat? And where should we stand to say what color Douglass was? Where should *he* stand? Having inherited his father's "white" blood, may he inherit as well a portion of all that "white" is meant to signify? Or, to drop the biological language, in which tradition may Douglass make his home? When speaking of Maxine Hong Kingston, I imagined an immigrant child who creates an original life-story on the road between her family and her school. If such storymaking is a struggle, what Douglass must do is more so, for in this case the family itself is divided and no public thoroughfare connects its parts (they join only in rape, and in the child of rape). Can the child nonetheless fashion an identity that partakes of both the mother and the father? Can he help himself to portions of the Anglo-Saxon, Poor Richard, marry-up, family Bible and money-catching Big House, or must he confine himself to the Afro-Barbadian, dirt-floor, root-magic, sweet-potato home of Harriet Bailey?

He must confine himself, would be plantation culture's flat response. Where white paternity is nothing but a whisper, where law and custom bid the child "follow" the mother, any such mixed identity is absurd, unthinkable, and unreal. Pestering his public for their blindness to the new and original, Herman Melville once wrote, "When the duck-billed beaver of Australia [the platypus] was first brought stuffed to England, the naturalists, appealing to their classifications, maintained that there was, in reality, no such creature." In Talbot County, Maryland, there were, in reality, no black Englishmen, no Afro-Saxons, no sweet-potato captains.

That absence follows no dictate of god or nature, of course, nor can we find inscribed anywhere outside of human culture the inventive mathematics whereby black + white = black. The question then arises whether or not Douglass, born on the boundary and possessed of a disruptive wit, would be able to unsettle the color line. Could he drug the guards and so move freely, as it were, between his mother's house and his father's? Could he alter the taxonomy that excludes him from reality?

Not legally, he couldn't, but as Hermes says, "If my father won't give . . . I will steal." In this context, that is, by his theft of literacy, Douglass doesn't just acquire a voice, he acquires a white one. In taking Caleb Bingham's book as his primer, he makes a raid on Anglo-Saxon patrimony. Bingham's models are Sheridan, Washington, Philo, Franklin, Cato, Milton, Socrates, Cicero, Fox, Pitt, and Addison. Bingham himself wrote the argument between master and slave, and it comes directly out of the European Enlightenment. Greek, Roman, and European classics: for Douglass to learn the speeches in Bingham's book was to make himself at home in his father's house even before he left Baltimore.

In Hermes' case, such theft was eventually followed by the Olympian chuckle, Zeus' amused acceptance of "his child." To see if Douglass was ever graced with such release of tension, we must follow him north to New Bedford and Nantucket, where he was first befriended by white men and women. The historian Peter Walker has written a fine book on nine-teenth-century abolitionists, *Moral Choices*, whose chapters on Douglass focus on his involvement with the group that formed around William Lloyd Garrison's newspaper, the *Liberator*. Walker argues that in his relations with the Garrisonians, and in the way that he fashioned himself in their circle, we see a not surprising impulse on Douglass's part to abandon the world available to him through his mother and increase his claim to all that was not black.

Take, for example, the story of his self-naming. At birth he had been Frederick Augustus Washington Bailey; as he moved north, he renamed himself first Frederick Dailey, then Frederick Stanley, then Frederick Johnson, and finally Frederick Douglass, this last after a hero, Douglas, in Sir Walter Scott's poem *The Lady of the Lake*. "The basic characteristic of Scott's Douglas," Walker writes, "is his unflinching fortitude in adversities brought about by the wrongful loss of his patrimony," and the plot of the poem leads to the restoration of that patrimony.

Douglass's identification with the Scottish hero went beyond a simple name-taking and imaginary reclamation. In 1846 when traveling in the British Isles ("to visit the home of my paternal ancestors," he said), he spent six months in Scotland. He traveled alone. For a while he dropped his anti-slavery work. He learned Scottish ballads and songs, singing and playing them on the violin for the rest of his life. "If I should meet you now," he wrote to Garrison, "amid the free hills of old Scotland, where the ancient 'black Douglass' [*sic*] once met his foes . . . you would see a great change in me!"

In addition, Walker reads Douglass's move into the Garrisonian camp as an escape from blackness, or at least from the artifice of race-language. The Garrisonians seemed to promise an erasure of the color line itself. On the boat going to the Nantucket convention, for example, "there was a row . . . about separate accommodations for the Negroes that was not settled until all the abolitionists, black and white, agreed to share the weather deck." And, as we have seen, Douglass's speech at the convention showed him that the threshold between black and white could be breached. To speak and to be heard in that group was to cease being defined by his auditors' whiteness and his own blackness.

In sum, Douglass's early years of freedom offered a shining hope that there might be such a thing as a community that did not shape itself in terms of color. How Douglass responded to that promise Walker surmises from the way he later revised his account of the Nantucket visit. In the 1855 autobiography a more seasoned Douglass looks back and describes his younger self:

> Young, ardent, and hopeful, I entered upon this new life in the full gush of unsuspecting enthusiasm. The cause was good, the men engaged in it were good, the means to attain its triumph, good. . . . For a time, I was made to forget that my skin was dark and my hair crisped.

What is striking here is that Douglass does not say "my dark skin no longer defined me," but "I forgot I had dark skin." What color is the man who has forgotten his skin? What Walker argues is that, under the sway of this forgetfulness, it must have seemed to Douglass that "for the first time in his life he was able to repeal the Maryland slave code, 'The children of slave women shall . . . follow the condition of their mothers.' He was 'made to forget' that he was Harriet Bailey's son. He was divested of his dark skin and crisped hair. He had ceased to be a Negro."

If that is the case, it turned out to be a costly forgetting, even for a man surrounded by abolitionists. "I found full soon that my enthusiasm had been extravagant," his memoir quickly adds. Even the passive voice of his telling ("I *was made* to forget") seems indicative: in his enthusiasm he became an actor in a Garrisonian drama, not one of his own. In the years after Nantucket, it become clear to Douglass that the color line held. In a thousand ways, subtle and brutal, the world around him defined him as not-white. White ship-caulkers in New Bedford refused to let him work his trade; white churches in New Bedford made him sit in a separate pew; he was forced to ride in Jim Crow railroad cars on Northern trains, and forced to travel steerage when he went to Great Britain; in Indiana he was attacked by a mob that broke his right hand; and on and on. More galling certainly was the racism of white abolitionists. In many respects the Garrisonians treated Douglass as a specimen for their cause, and let him know how they thought the specimen should act. "Give us the facts," they said, "we will take care of the philosophy."

> It was impossible for me to repeat the same old story, month after month, and to keep up my interest. . . . "Tell your story, Frederick," would whisper my revered friend, Mr. Garrison, as I stepped

upon the platform. I could not always follow the injunction, for I was now reading and thinking.

"It is not best that you seem too learned," they told him. One Garrisonian writing to another described Douglass as suitably modest "for a 'nigger.' " Another wrote that she wished he was a "full blood black [without any of] the white blood that is in his veins." They cautioned him about his friendships with white women. They weren't even happy with his hard-earned eloquence: a newspaper once reported that Douglass's "language . . . possesse[d] none of the characteristics of the colored man," but the Garrisonians told him they'd rather he left "a little of the plantation speech" in his lectures. They wanted a "black" speaker, not a "white" one, and certainly not some anomalous Afro-Saxon, the duck-billed beaver of Talbot County.

At the start of this book, I said that trickster is a mythological character; there are no human tricksters. Human beings participate in this mythology, but they simultaneously participate in others, and in history. History favored Frederick Douglass with an opportunity to participate in the unraveling of plantation culture; it did not so favor him when it came to the color line in America. A mythological trickster might find a way to breach that barrier, but what is a man in history to do, a man whose hands are broken by mobs and whose friends begrudge his mixed blood and his absent dialect?

What Douglass did was to leave the threshold where black and white mix, where he had been born, where several cultures touch on each other, and submit to the artifice of race language. He took up residence in his mother's house. He became a black man.

One place to see this move clearly is in the changing story of his childhood. Douglass wrote his autobiography three times, and he allowed himself to revise his life, and especially his origins, with each edition. In the first (1845), he names his father as a white man; in the second (1855), his father is "shrouded in mystery" and white, "or," he strangely adds, "nearly white"; in the third (1881), we find only the flat "Of my father I know nothing." As the white portion of his parentage was thus erased, the black portion was filled in. In the first autobiography, Douglass's mother was a stranger to him; he had never seen her in the daylight, he cannot picture her, and he felt no grief when she died. In the third autobiography, thirty-seven years later, he can picture her vividly. Her image is "ineffaceably stamped upon my memory," he tells us, and recounts a time when she brought him food and sheltered him from cruelty. Above all, by this final version he has discovered in his mother the source of his own talents.

> I have . . . learned that she was the only one of all the coloured people of Tuckahoe who could read. . . . In view of this fact, I am happy to attribute any love of letters I may have, not to my presumed Anglo-Saxon paternity, but to the native genius of my sable, unprotected, and uncultivated mother. . . .

Whereas in 1845 Douglass claimed his white parent and elided the black, by 1881 he elided the white and claimed the black. To see him reshape his early life is to see him spinning himself a new myth of origins; in changing his story he changes what he wants us to take as his "true self." That self is not the child of a white man but the child of Harriet Bailey the slave; that self is black.

In addition, we see Douglass withdrawing from the Anglo-Saxon portion of his being if we look at the "color," as it were, of his public voice. As we have already seen, in 1855 Douglass revised the story of his Nantucket speech, adding a retrospective sense of his naïve enthusiasm. When I first described that speech I underlined the fact that the tension of the moment had to do with speaking to *white* abolitionists; "in the colored people's meeting" Douglass had no problem finding his voice. In keeping with his later sense of misplaced enthusiasm, I would now underline a second detail in his account: Douglass spoke because he was "much urged to do so by Mr. William C. Coffin." The fact is that in the early years of his freedom a circle of white men and women prompted, sanctioned, introduced, and authorized Douglass's voice; they were also his sympathetic audience, his listeners. That being the case, we might ask to what degree it is Douglass himself speaking. And, if we could find the ideal spot to stand, could we assign that voice a color?

That Douglass himself had to struggle with such questions is clear from a curious event that took place in the fall of 1847. Douglass and William Lloyd Garrison were then traveling together in northern Ohio, speaking against slavery; but some Eshu must have ridden a horse between them, for they argued and their differences brought them to an irreconcilable break with each other. (The precipitating issue was Gar-

rison's opposition to Douglass's desire to publish his own newspaper.)
Peter Walker writes:

> The break was painful for both. They became physically ill. Gar-
> rison was laid up for weeks with his "brain terribly oppressed."
> Douglass suffered what seems to have been a more obvious psy-
> chosomatic ailment. . . . As the full force of Garrison's "betrayal"
> descended on him, Douglass lost his voice. He was literally dumb-
> founded. . . .

We can return now to the crucial moment in the story of Hermes'
transgressions, the moment when Zeus laughs and the oppositions of the
story dissolve. Suddenly Apollo and Hermes are the best of friends; the
old world is gone, the new world born. No such moment lightens Douglass's life; no father laughingly acknowledges his paternity, neither his
biological father nor a spiritual/political father such as Garrison. Without
that, Douglass lacked as well any form for paternal "inheritance," any
structure in which his particularity could stop seeming anomalous and
become part of the "real."

On his trip with Garrison, Douglass discovered he didn't have the
audience he thought he had (and to lose one's audience is dumbfounding).
No Garrisonian was interested in a polytropic Frederick Douglass. In
New England in the 1840s, a man with dark skin and crisped hair who
acts as if he were heir to the white estate, who sings Scottish ballads on
the moors, who excises plantation dialect from his oratory, may find no
one willing to give him a hearing. On the contrary, he may find they want
that darky speech, and with that revelation wake to find himself in a land
where the color line persists. I have imagined Douglass standing on that
line, hoping to cross or erase it, when he spoke in Nantucket; remember
his own description: "It was with the utmost difficulty . . . that I could
command and articulate two words without hesitation and stammering."
We see there a man moving from speechlessness into speech as he enters
what he thought was a world organized to include him. Now, in 1847, he
has discovered that that world does *not* include him, and so he is forced
back to the threshold where, struck dumb, "a wet bandage round his
throat," he must find his voice again.

It seems telling in all this that the issue at hand was Douglass's desire
to publish his own newspaper. That he did so the next year, and that he

eventually called it *Frederick Douglass' Paper*, makes it clear that he not only found that voice but intended to claim it *as his*. As to how it was received, Peter Walker has found a remarkable letter from 1847 in which one black colleague of Douglass's describes him to another: "You will be surprised to hear me say that only since his Editorial career has he seen to become a colored man! I have read his paper very carefully and find phase after phase develop itself as in one newly born among us." From where that reader stands, Frederick Douglass has a "colored" voice.

If Eshu is the god of uncertainty, the god who can tear a hole in the fabric of fate so a person might slip from one life into another, then Eshu was present when Douglass took on the culture of slavery. But no such opportunity appeared when it came to the line that Americans draw between black and white. It is not often we see a trickster insisting on a boundary, drawing a line, but in the story of Eshu's hat we have such a tale. The mistake the two friends have made is to think that their friendship unites them, when they are, as the Buddhists say, "not one, not two." To say they are two distinct men is not quite right (they *are* close friends), but to say they are one is not quite right (their fields have a road between them). They are not-one and not-two. Eshu reminds them they are not-one; he rides his horse down the line that separates them, and shows how their claim to friendship has made them unconscious of their attachment to particular points of view.

To say that Douglass was black is not quite right; to say he was white is not quite right either. After Nantucket, he was like the immigrant child trying to fashion a home, and an identity, out of two worlds that had no common place to stand. Though slavery eventually came to an end, the separation between those worlds did not. Here it would seem that the Eshu-spirit could find no rip in the fabric of fate. Historical contingency cuts both ways—sometimes opening up new worlds, sometimes drawing an impervious horizon. Where the community at large can maintain the fiction of its color line, a man forgets the color of his skin at his own peril. If he thinks he is William Lloyd Garrison's close friend, the Eshu-spirit will ride between them and remind them of their unfortunate twoness. After that, after 1847, Douglass no longer forgets; he becomes black, reimagining his family history and redirecting his voice to a more receptive audience.

There are signs that this was a reluctant rebirth (a post-war letter complains: "I shall never get beyond Fredk Douglass the self educated fugitive slave"), but what were his choices? If there is no way to stay poised on the edge, which is the better fate, cannibalism or anthropemy, to be eaten by ideology or vomited into exile? Unless he wanted to leave the country, he would have to work with the hand that history had dealt. As Walker writes, soon after breaking with Garrison, Douglass "accommodated himself to his fated place in American society. . . . He educated himself to the thought and ways of the free Negro community, assimilating them with . . . rapidity and facility . . . ," just as he had earlier assimilated Caleb Bingham. From that time on, he subordinated his own contradictions in favor of presenting a new "essential self" and articulating a position for his race. No longer a voiceless subordinate or stuttering anomaly, he made himself into Old Man Eloquent, the Representative Colored Man of these United States.

If we want now to return to the question of which trickster plot best matches up to Douglass's story, we must first ask from whose point of view the judgment is being made. The man may well seem to be one thing if you are a pre-war plantation owner and quite another if you are a post-war Yankee. For the former, I'd say Douglass was a true Loki, a faithless go-between who, adding strategic self-binding to his already tight fetters, wished apocalyptic changes on the land of his birth. But in terms of the wider American culture that survives the Civil War, Douglass is a little more like the Hermes of the *Hymn*, a willing disenchanter of confining artifice, but also a Hermes of the Dark who can sing a new theogony when he wants to, converting the accidents of his own life into essences where need be, and mingling them with the unchanging portions of the world around him.

It is not simply that he is willing to pretend to a mythic and essential blackness, though that is part of it. When it comes to creed and country, he also leaves the threshold and moves toward an established center. Douglass had been converted to Christianity as a young man and while he could be witheringly sarcastic in regard to Christian hypocrisy he usually made it clear that he spoke not from outside the Church but from the vantage point of a "pure" Christianity. As a child he once found some pages from the Bible in the gutter; he took them home, washed and dried them, and kept them with his secret collection of printed matter. That nicely catches his urge to improve, not quit, his church, as does a typical remark from the end of the *Narrative*: "I love the pure, peaceable, and impartial Christianity of Christ: I therefore hate the corrupt, slaveholding . . . Christianity of this land."

Douglass similarly attacked the hypocrisies of his homeland from the point of view of a purified America. Though he had for a while followed some abolitionists in rejecting the U.S. Constitution as a pro-slavery document, by the early 1850s he was convinced that the Constitution was a useful tool for black emancipation. Douglass never agreed with those who said blacks should refuse to vote, or emigrate to Africa: American-born blacks were Americans; they had helped to build this country and should therefore live here, share political power, and share the wealth. On these issues he was not an apocalyptic change-agent. I mentioned in the last chapter that it is frequently the fate of those who seek fundamental change to end up contained by the larger culture, their demands reformulated as things that "Zeus had imagined . . . from the outset." Douglass allows something along those lines to happen to him. Breaking with other abolitionists and supporting the Constitution, he threw in his lot with "the founding fathers"—or rather with the *ideal* of those men. We can almost hear him saying, "I love the pure democracy of America: I therefore hate the corrupt democracy of the slaveholding Founders."

The words "pure" and "ideal" here alert us to the fact that we are no longer watching someone pull eternals down into time—we are watching a new cosmos emerge with its obligatory higher truths. The man who collapsed the shaping categories of plantation culture with irony and contradiction has no trouble promulgating his own set of organizing dualities. Sacred and profane, heavenly and demonic, savage and civilized, just and unjust, decent and indecent—with these and more, Old Man Eloquent shaped and published his vision of a *true* and *real* America. As Hermes remembers the gods in song, how each came to have what belongs to each, so Douglass asks that Americans join him in remembering their original homeland where Christianity and democracy were not corrupt. He asks them to remember him as a black man whose love of letters sprang directly from his "sable" mother's "native genius."

I cast all this as a kind of domestication because it doesn't just offer new enchantment but willingly participates in some old American "verities." From trickster's threshold, none of these purities exist; they are useful fictions perhaps, but fictions nonetheless. On the threshold, everything is more ambiguous and the pure is wed to the impure (Jung's church has a turd falling on its gleaming roof, the Founders' wisdom is mixed with stupidity, the Constitution is both racist and not-racist, white men speak in dialect and black men sing Scottish ballads.)

And yet, as with Hermes, it doesn't feel quite right to say that Douglass is "domesticated." As much as he may have accommodated himself to American ideology and religion, he did so in a world he had helped to change. If Douglass got himself eaten instead of exiled, we should recognize that American ideology was altered for having had to absorb him. A truly domesticated Frederick Douglass would have remained a slave in Maryland; truly domesticated, he would not have seen in his lifetime the abolition of slavery and the Constitution so regularly amended.

The point is simply that Douglass enters a house he helped to build. Like Hermes, when he moves from periphery to center, he changes the center. For the flavor of that change, for the feel of what it means to be a former slave residing in the altered heart of his nation, let me close with a small and representative incident from late in Douglass's life. One of the direct descendants of Douglass's second master, Thomas Auld, was a physician named Thomas Sears. Around 1883, this Dr. Sears needed to borrow $500 to secure a mortgage. Where did he go? He did not go to the bank, he went to Frederick Douglass, at that time the Recorder of Deeds for the District of Columbia under President Garfield, and the owner of a fifteen-acre estate in Anacostia. Over fifty years earlier, when Thomas Auld's brother forbade his wife to teach the young Douglass to read, he warned that a literate slave "would at once become unmanageable, and of no value to his master." He was right. A great reallotment had taken place in that half century. The chattel slave who once ate corn mush from a trough on the ground *had* made himself "of no value" to his master, had in fact helped so much to alter his country's sense of how its wealth should be embodied that he lived to see one of his master's heirs come knocking for a loan.

The story of Eshu's hat ends with Eshu telling the two friends, "You are both right." The hat is black and the hat is white. It would seem, then, that the conflict of the perspectival truths into which the two friends fall might be eliminated by a higher point of view, a bird's-eye declaration such as "Eshu's hat is black on one side and white on the other." But I doubt that Eshu's spirit can be contained with so simple a closure. There are, for one thing, other versions of the story in which the hat has *four* colors. But even if it has only two, what color is it on the inside? Only the fleas on Eshu's head know for sure (unless it's dark under there, and then what color is a color in the dark?). Or again, isn't it the case that white snow turns pale blue in the moonlight, and the darkest African is not the black of coal? The terms are contextual, and there is no end to context. And even if there were, the idea that the hat has two halves is a kind of storytelling simplification. What color is the *boundary* between the black and the white? How wide is the boundary? What if Eshu, like some modern mathematical topologist, took to stretching his hat, then squeezing it, then folding it—stretching, squeezing, folding, stretching, squeezing, folding—a hundred or a thousand times? How then to trace the divide between black and white? Sometimes a simple boundary becomes unimaginably complex.

To leave our own story with a touch of American complexity, a last bit of turbulence in this historic masquerade, let me note that considerable evidence suggests that Frederick Douglass was the descendant of Native Americans through his maternal grandmother. After all, he *looked* a little bit Indian. And there was a cousin Tom who said it was true. And Aaron Anthony used to call him "my little Indian boy." And then there was the time, during a speech given at the Carlisle Indian Institute, when Frederick Douglass looked out over the crowd and said: "I have been known as a Negro, but I wish to be known here and now as Indian." What color *was* that hat?

II

....

TRICKSTER ARTS AND WORKS OF *ARTUS*

Humans . . . could not budge because they had webbed, jointless limbs,
so the hero [Maui, the Polynesian trickster] extricated them from their
impeding membranes and created connecting joints.
—*Laura Makarius*

That science of apportionment, division, discontinuity,
I refer to . . . as "arthrology."
—*Roland Barthes*

The word "art" interests me very much. If it comes from Sanskrit, as
I've heard, it signifies "making." . . . Everyone makes something.
—*Marcel Duchamp*

GO FOR THE JOINTS

To place these reflections on Hermes and Frederick Douglass in the larger frame of my project, it may be useful at this point to step back and sketch a single unifying image of the work that tricksters do in regard to traps of culture. My intention has been to write not simply about mythological tricksters but also about the disruptive imagination and the art it gives us. The term "art" covers a lot of ground; what portion of that ground intersects with what tricksters do? And where in that ground should Hermes or Douglass be placed now that we see how they operate? If Frederick Douglass is a trickster in some ways but not in others, what are those ways, and to what other artists might we turn to better describe the trickster spirit at work in actual cases of art-making?

• • •

In 1948 the French folklorist and historian of religion, Georges Dumézil, suggested that the Norse story of Loki killing Baldr with the mistletoe is connected by a common root to a group of legends told by the Ossetes in the Caucasus mountains of southern Russia. Among the Ossetes, the Loki-like trickster is named Syrdon, and the Baldr-like hero—pure, good, beautiful, and associated with the sun—is Soslan. As the story goes, the handsome Soslan is invulnerable except for a secret weak spot in his knees, a weakness which the sly Syrdon, disguised as a woman, manages to discover. The other Ossetic heroes are much amused by Soslan's invulnerability and for sport they roll a saw-toothed wheel down a hill just to see it bounce away from Soslan's body. Syrdon, of course, inspires them to aim the wheel at Soslan's knees, and so the pure one is cut down.

From this brief story I would like to entertain the following generalization: the eternals are vulnerable at their joints. To kill a god or an ideal, go for the joints.

The Loki story contains no knee joint, but it has joints nonetheless and they are instrumental in Baldr's death. To see them, consider the deadly mistletoe. When Baldr's mother tried to protect him from all harm, she asked "everything in heaven and earth" to refrain from hurting him; she didn't ask the mistletoe because it seemed so small, and because *it is neither of heaven nor of earth.* A parasitic plant that grows in the branches of trees, the mistletoe lives between high and low and belongs to neither, not unlike the trickster. Moreover, as I mentioned in Chapter 4, there is one moment in the year when this plant is especially important: in Northern European countries, mistletoe was ritually gathered on Midsummer's Eve, which is to say, on the summer solstice. In a solar year or in a vegetation cycle, the solstice is one of the nicks in time by which the annual cycle is articulated; it marks the crisis or turning point in the life of the sun when it seems to stop growing and begins to die.

The spot *between* heaven and earth, and the moment when the sun must reverse itself: the mistletoe stands for these and they in turn stand for Baldr's vulnerability. He may be attacked at the seam between heaven and earth (it is when we put ideals into practice that they reveal their flaws), and he is vulnerable at the solstice. We call those places where the sun must turn "the tropics"; in a Northern summer, the sun turns at the Tropic of Cancer, and at that point any polytropic one, knowing the secret that time itself has joints, can turn a trick and wound the god of light. These then are the senses in which Loki goes for Baldr's knees; he knows how to read the mistletoe and so he is privy to the hidden joints where purity may be cut down.

I gather that if the Loki and Syrdon stories were translated into Latin, we could find ourselves talking about a "knee joint" and a "summer solstice" using the same terms, for a single Latin word, *articulus*, can mean both a joint in the body and a turning point in the solar year. Why exactly this word has such reach becomes clear if we do a little digging in the history of Indo-European languages. *Articulus* belongs to a large group of related terms preserving an ancient root, *-*ar*, that originally meant "to join," "to fit," and "to make." Many words in Greek, Latin, and modern languages come from this root, all of them having to do with joining in one sense or another. To describe the uses of these words is to begin to sketch the unifying image I want for the work that tricksters do in regard to traps of culture.

There are two Greek words that can mean "joint." The first is *árthron*. "The *árthron* connecting the hand and arm is the wrist," says Aristotle. An *árthron* can also be a connecting word in language, an "and" or a "but" for example, as if the flow of speech required its own little wrists and elbows to become intelligible. The second word, *harmós*, also means a joint in the body (especially the shoulder joint), but more commonly it denotes the joints made by artisans: the mason building a wall, the ship-wright fitting planks, the metal worker soldering a seam, the carpenter fastening a door—all these craftsmen are making *harmoí*.

The two related nouns in Latin are *ars* and *artus*. Though the first of these derives from the *-*ar* root, it doesn't refer so much to "joints" as to all that we mean today by "arts": *ars* is skill, artifice, craft, and crafty action; it is a liberal art, a trade, a performance, and a work of art. The Latin term that more properly means a joint in the body is *artus*. (The word I started with, *articulus*, is a diminutive of *artus*.)

A number of current English words still echo these classical proto-types. We have, for example, "artisan" (a "joiner" or maker of things), "artifice" (a made thing), and terms having to do with bodily joints such as "arthritis." "Articulate" nowadays usually has to do with speech, but it also means joining bones together, as in this description from an old anatomy book: "[The body's] most movable joints are those in which the adjacent bones are articulated on the principle either of a pivot or of a hinge."

In most of the Greek and Latin cases, the joints these words describe are not loose, like the wrist or elbow, but stiff and fixed. No one wants flexible joints when a stone mason builds a house. Even in reference to the body, the joints in question are sometimes inflexible: a fixed seam between plates of the skull, for example, is an *árthron* or *artus*, as is the joint that forms when a broken arm heals itself. From such fixed joints come all that is well fitted, well knit, well set; in both classic tongues, the language of "jointing" connotes stability and order. The Greek *harmonía* comes from *harmós*, and as with the modern word, it over-whelmingly implies firm and pleasing design. With *harmonía* comes the well-made ship, the well-tuned lyre, the house of good stone, "each block cut smooth and well fitted," the planets aptly disposed in their orbits, and the stable framework of the body, the mind, the government, the cosmos.

When these words describe joints in language, they again connote clarity and precision. "Jointed" speech has clear divisions to it, just as a good masonry wall has clear lines between the bricks; these divisions turn the sounds that any animal can make into intelligible human language. Aristotle writes:

The dolphin . . . makes a squeak and moans when it is out of the water and exposed to the air. . . . This animal possesses a voice, since it has both lungs and windpipe; but as its tongue cannot move freely, and as it has no lips, it has no articulation of the voice.

In human speech, the tongue and the lips are the organs of articulation. They do the joint-work in a stream of sound. In written language there is joint-work to be done as well. To break an uninterrupted flow of letters into words, sentences, paragraphs, and chapters (or the older "articles"), to divide it with spaces, commas, periods, and indentations, is to artic-ulate it, to make evident the places where thought itself has joints or points of demarcation.

• • •

From this etymology, and from the Loki and Syrdon stories, I would like to suggest that we think of trickster artists as *artus*-workers, joint-workers. Not that they are much involved with making the firm and well-set joints that lead to classical harmony, of course. What tricksters like is the *flexible* or *movable* joint. If a joint comes apart, or if it moves from one place to another, or if it simply loosens up where it had begun to stick and stiffen, some trickster has probably been involved. In several different ways, tricksters are joint-disturbers. One of these ways we have just seen: tricksters will sometimes kill an immortal by attacking the joint that is his hidden weakness.

A second kind of disturbance we have also seen: tricksters often do the work of rearticulation. The stories about meat sacrifice make the best examples here, because sacrifice involves actually carving an animal body along its joints. In Part I, I spoke of Prometheus and Hermes as tricksters who try to change the way the world is apportioned. Prometheus hoped to change the human portion, but failed; Hermes hoped to change his own portion and succeeded. In each case there is an effort to rearticulate the cosmos and each case begins with the carving of an animal body. Prometheus is said to be the first carver, and the ancient term for carver, *artamos*, refers to "the one who cuts along the joints." When Prometheus divided that aboriginal ox, he articulated (jointed) an animal and a cosmos simultaneously, as did Hermes when he carved his butchered cows.

The wider implications of these stories, then, lie not so much in how the animal is jointed but in the claim that one jointing reflects others in a meaningful way. The stories symbolically knit the animal's articulated body to larger social and spiritual articulations. In the ritual of sacrifice, the animal is first cut apart: its viscera are removed and separated (liver, lungs, kidneys, etc.); the legs, shoulders, hooves, haunches, and so forth, are carefully cut one from another. All these pieces are then distributed to humans and to gods. The presiding priest may receive one of the kidneys; choice pieces of meat—thigh, hindquarter, shoulder—may go to the king or high magistrates of the city; the entrails may be made into sausages and given to those at the periphery of the sacrificial meal. The gods receive the bones and blood, and sometimes also specific organs (the tongue went to Hermes, for example). In this way, the shape of the animal comes to represent the shape of the social and spiritual worlds.

There are two orders of articulation here, then. At one level, we have

the shapes of the animal body, the group, the spiritual world; at another
level, we have the second-order shape created by the distribution that
knits these three worlds together. The patterns correspond significantly,
the ritual implies, each being sign and proof of the others. The ritual
holds the articulated animal up against the articulated social and spiritual
worlds and means to demonstrate by their congruence that these various
levels of existence participate in a single grand and stable harmony. A
stable harmony, that is, unless some trickster alters the way the portions
are handed out, disrupting the second-order articulation and so changing
the manner in which nature, community, and spirit are joined to one
another.*

Because Greek sacrifice involves actual animals carved along their
joints, it makes a particularly good case for talking of tricksters as joint-
workers, but I do not mean to limit this image to something so literal. In
many cultures, as we have seen, much of the play of tricksters amounts
to a reshaping (disjointing, rejointing) of the world around them. Eshu,
for example, standing between humankind and the gods, represents the
possibility of reallotment, the chance that the links between things on
earth and things in heaven may be loosened. Once Eshu has been summoned, fate itself is not so tightly bound to events on earth; the pattern
cut in heaven need not determine how things fall out here below.

In all such cases, trickster's art involves playing with what I'm calling
the second-order articulation; trickster shifts patterns in relation to one
another, and by that redefines the patterns themselves. Where one great
harmonía joins together nature, society, and heaven, trickster meddles
with the *harmoí*. In this he is not the killer we saw with Loki and Syrdon,
but he is an *artus*-worker nonetheless, unmaking old harmonies and

---

* The claims of congruence with body joints are often extended to thought and speech as
well. A carver dismembering an animal "proceeds along the skeletal joints," Jean-Louis
Durand remarks, adding that "in the *Phaedrus* Socrates finds no better comment on the
dialectic method: 'It is . . . to be able to separate the details to the natural joints . . . ; it
is to strive not to break any part and avoid the ways of a poor carver.' "

Not that those equipped with mental knives will always agree on how best to carve
the world. There is a moment in the *Posterior Analytics* when Aristotle dismisses Plato:
"So goodbye to the Platonic Forms. They are so much la-la-la, and have nothing to do
with our speech." To Aristotle at that moment, Plato's metaphysical jointing reveals a
clumsy butcher. The old man's speech is not articulate; his lips and tongue have not put
him much ahead of the moaning dolphin.

sometimes, especially if he has a lyre of his own, singing new ones to fill the ensuing silence.

A ttacking the joints to actually destroy something, or attacking the joints so as to change the shape of things: these are the first two senses in which tricksters are *artus*-workers and their creations works of *artus*. There is one more. In an essay on the *Hymn to Hermes*, Jenny Strauss Clay asks why, of all the gods whose stories the *Homeric Hymns* recount, Hermes is the last one born and the last to get his "share of things," his honors. The hymns indicate that by the time Hermes appears all the other gods have their prerogatives and spheres of influence; the cosmos would appear to be complete.

Yet something essential to its functioning is still lacking. The nature of the missing element emerges as soon as we observe that the fully articulated Olympian system of divisions and boundaries remains static and lifeless unless it acquires the possibility of movement between its spheres and limits. Introduced only after the hierarchical configuration of the cosmos has been achieved and its boundaries defined, Hermes embodies that principle of motion. Hermes thus allows the cosmos to retain its ordered structure while simultaneously *instituting movement between its articulated components*.

It is as if a human body were assembled, each of the organs duly in place—liver, heart, brain, and so on—and each duly separated from the others, protective membranes sheathing the bones, impervious barriers protecting the brain against stray blood, and so on. But what if the barriers were such that no organ could communicate with any other? Before a body can come to life, every separation, every boundary, must be breached in some way; each organ must have its pores and gateways through which something (lymph, blood, bile, urine, electricity, neurotransmitters) may flow. Unless they can incorporate internal forces of transgression, organic structures are in danger of dying from their own articulation.

In the Olympian case, it would appear that each of the gods has a tendency to perfect herself or himself and, in that perfecting, to solidify all boundaries. The goddess of chastity allows no licentiousness, the god of reason allows no muddle, the goddess of the hearth allows no strangers in the kitchen, the god of war allows no cowards. To the degree that each sphere is thus perfected, it will draw apart from the others, and the larger structure lose vitality. It is in Hades' nature to seal the gates of the underworld; no soul escapes. But when the full expression of his nature means that Persephone cannot return to earth, springtime never comes and the world begins to die. Then the gods send Hermes to bring her back.

The Olympian system is hardly the only example of a trickster connecting an articulated cosmos. The same pattern appears in West Africa—with some interesting variations. Take, for example, the Yoruba story of how Eshu brought the palm-nut oracle to humankind (the one discussed in Chapter 5). The sixteen gods were hungry because their wandering children on earth had forgotten them and no longer offered sacrifices. In their hunger the gods grew angry and quarreled. To overcome the growing fragmentation, Eshu gave human beings something that would make them *want* to offer sacrifice, the art of divination. This art involves sixteen palm nuts, one for each of the gods, and to learn it Eshu himself had to travel around the world, going to each of "the sixteen places" to "hear sixteen sayings."

A detail latent in this Yoruba tale—that the quarreling gods have a problem communicating with each other—is figured more sharply in a parallel narrative from the peoples who neighbor the Yoruba to the west, the Fon. In the Fon cosmology, the high god bore seven sons at the beginning of time. The first six of these reign over specific domains: the earth, the sky, the sea, the animals, the hunt, and iron. Each son speaks a different language, a tongue unique to his territory. They cannot speak to one another, nor, it seems, can they remember how to communicate with the high god who is their mother. The seventh and youngest son is the trickster Legba. There is some indication that Legba causes the estrangement of the other six sons. Like Eshu, Legba is a god of quarrels. In one story, it was Legba who caused heaven and earth to fight and separate; in another, we learned that the high god who used to walk the earth withdrew because of Legba's double-dealing and dirty ways.

Whatever its origins, the Fon imagine a cosmos so well divided into spheres of influence that it has broken into domains that no longer speak one another's language—or rather, it would have broken were it not for Legba, who translates among the spheres. He is the cosmic linguist: he knows each of the languages that his brothers speak, and he knows the language of their mother as well. If any of these wishes to speak to another, he or she must go through Legba. Human beings are in a similar position; like Eshu, Legba is a god of divination, the gate through which we must pass if we wish contact with the gods. In Haitian Vodoun, the petitioners ask, "Papa Legba, remove the barrier for me," for only with Legba's help can the other deities manifest themselves.

These stories widen our sense of what can happen if there is no figure to move among the articulated components of a cosmos. First, there will be spiritual hunger ("the gods were hungry" is the opening problem of the Yoruba story). Second, when articulation becomes fragmentation the gods don't just quarrel, they begin to speak languages so distinct as to need a translator. Finally, these two details join in a new twist on the genealogy of sacrifice, for here sacrifice not only feeds the hungry gods but the trickster who is its agent must also be the translator, the go-between who crosses linguistic barriers. Both translation and sacrifice, then, are situated, or come into being, exactly at the points of articulation, and keep those points open; they are the creations of a trickster *artus*-worker, the hunger-artist who inhabits the cracks between languages or between heaven and earth.

Tricksters who do this sort of interior *artus*-work may seem to enliven the cosmos without really threatening it. Hermes, according to Clay at least, makes the Olympian system more flexible "*within* the established order"; his boundary-crossings neither undo hierarchy, she says, nor overcome "Apollo's insistence on orderly limits." Likewise, the Fon do not imagine Legba's "daimonic explosiveness" ever getting to the center of home or kingdom. As Robert Pelton says, Legba's "power to open passages and to shut them will serve human life, and not debauch it, provided that he not be allowed to assume control over its center."

Both these portraits seem apt to me if we shade them by imagining that the life stories of tricksters fall into two parts: there is a past period of "first deeds," and then there is a present of ongoing actions. The first deeds of most tricksters *do* undo hierarchy, overcome limits, assume control over the center, disorder the cosmos. In Hermes' case, to take but one example, if it is right to say that the cattle, once stolen, become domestic beasts, henceforth to reproduce sexually and be slaughtered and eaten by human beings, or if it is right to say that when Apollo hands over the herder's whip to the cattle thief there is a significant reapportionment of powers, or if Hermetic sacrifice moves Hermes himself into the pantheon, then several of the newborn god's "movements of passage and penetration" change the structure of the cosmos. In the West African example, Legba clearly got into the center of things when the world was being made, separating earth and sky, this world and the heavens. Whether they bring death into the world, steal fire, or embarrass a modest creator, in their first deeds tricksters upset the old cosmos and create (or reveal) the lines of demarcation that shape the new one, this world.

After that, however, if they are the kind of inner *artus*-worker I am here describing, they may well leave those old divisions intact and turn their attention to keeping them porous and flexible. A trickster might foolishly bring death into the world, but then, rather than abrogating the distinction between the living and the dead, he will take his place as one of the few characters who can negotiate that boundary. The telling detail that supports Clay's sense of Hermes as, finally, a non-disruptive boundary-crosser is his friendship with Apollo at the end of the *Hymn*. Clay sees Apollo as Hermes' natural opponent in the *Hymn* because, "in Apollo, the Greeks recognized the god who maintains order and observes hierarchies and distinctions, especially those separating gods and mortals." For Hermes and Apollo to move from antagonism to friendship implies therefore a kind of balance or poise between these two functions.* In the West African case, Legba surely helps precipitate the quarrels that set the world at odds, but then he turns and joins what he has put out of joint. He separates earth and sky but then induces the rain to fall so that the two are connected even as they are disconnected. He causes the high god to retreat from this world, but then becomes the agent of divination so that there is some commerce across the divide. A remark of Pelton's nicely catches the ambiguity of these actions: "To become a mediator Legba must create a distance that only he can span. . . . His achievement is to join by separating."

At first, then, tricksters create separation, setting others at odds or placing boundary markers in new and unusual places. Initially, they are the non-domesticated *artus*-workers who make or remake the articulated world. Once that work is done, and once they have made a place for

---

* The parallel in the Yoruba pantheon is the friendship between Eshu and Ifa. If Ifa is order and design, then a similar balance is figured by having the more uncertain Eshu be his "best friend."

themselves, they may settle down to be the more domestic figures who keep things lively through a kind of behavior we call mischief. In the *Hymn*, Hermes moves from the first phase to the second: at the start there are deep disruptions and cosmic changes, but once he and Apollo make peace, he becomes an internal change-agent whose actions no longer alter the shape of the cosmos (he never kills Zeus; he never brings an apocalypse). The same is true of Legba: at the beginning of things he deeply disrupts the world, but after that, he plays in the structure he helped to make.

Such play does not exactly assure stability, however. Mischief always holds the seeds of more dangerous disruption. Just as any animal is at risk for having pores in its body and joints between its bones, so any cosmos is at risk for having even a domesticated *artus*-worker around. If there are historical moments during which large changes are in the offing, it may be exactly the otherwise benign *artus*-workers who bring them. The domesticated trickster is like domesticated fire. Fire contained in a well-built chimney will warm the house, but over the years the mortar between the bricks may crack and fall away and then, on that coldest day of the year, when someone heaps the kindling to get a blaze going, the flames reach between the bricks, ignite the lath and framing, and set the house on fire. A Viking museum in Denmark owns a Danish forge stone in which some Norse blacksmith carved the face of Loki with his lips sewn shut, a vivid image of wild fire well contained. But in the larger framework of Norse myth, there comes a time when Loki gets free of the binding thongs and joins the forces that bring that cosmos to its end.

· · ·

This idea that lively articulation requires a kind of built-in ambivalent force that can "join by separating" suggests a new way to describe trickster's inventions and activities. To take the invention of sacrifice as a first example, one striking thing—at least in the Greek tradition—is that the ritual simultaneously separates and connects. Greek ritual sacrifice links humans to the gods but at the same time, because it reenacts the Promethean trick (separating the meat from the bones), it once again divides them. Prometheus is thus a separator-connector and in sacrifice, as Marcel Detienne puts it, "the consumption of the meat effects a distance between gods and men in the very movement that accomplishes communication between this earthly world and that of the divine powers."

A similar sort of connecting/not-connecting may be found in most of the other places where we have seen trickster's imagination at work. Where he is the first thief, for example, his thievery is usually *stealthy*, which means it moves from one sphere to another without actually disrupting the boundary (when Raven steals sunlight he doesn't eliminate the line between heaven and earth, he finds a hole in the line; Hermes doesn't break down the door to his mother's cave, he slips through the keyhole).* Where trickster is the author of market exchange, he creates a form of commerce that allows strangers to come together without becoming kin; people come into contact in his marketplace but they are not as a result connected. Finally, in West African stories where trickster translates for the gods and divines for human beings, both these arts—translation and divination—connect without connecting. Each one builds a bridge, but in so doing reveals a distance. Neither one involves *union*, the pure overcoming of a separation. In divination, humans glimpse heavenly purpose, but the revelation is always enigmatic. Divination simultaneously reveals and obscures, as does one of its modern forms, the psychoanalytic interpretation of dreams. These are tricky arts, and it should be no wonder Yoruba savants carve Eshu's face into the borders of their divining boards (as it should be carved into the analyst's coffee table, alongside the box of Kleenex).

---

* Describing thievery as a connecting/not-connecting art clears up something that puzzled me for a long time: Why don't the gods simply give to humankind the things we need to live on this earth? Why must trickster *steal* from heaven? The answer is that a commerce of gifts might erase the distinction between the two realms, and the gods would cease being gods; stealthy theft, on the other hand, allows for both commerce *and* a boundary. With trickster in play, heaven and earth may touch without touching.

Likewise, translation from one language to another is Eshu-work, Legba-work, Hermes-neutics, and while it may seem to connect two speakers or communities, it can never really do so as long as a translator earns wages in the space between. If Legba's mother and six brothers were really an intimate family, they wouldn't need the seventh son in order to talk to one another. We may sometimes assume that a translation provides a window onto the original, but just as often, as Derek Walcott says, "to translate is to betray." An old Italian pun—*traduttore, traditore* / translator, traitor—reminds us that the translator who connects two people always stands between them.

Translation, divination, sacrifice, theft, and more: these are the connecting/not-connecting arts, and each is therefore well figured as the *artus* that is a flexible joint or the boundary that is a permeable membrane. To say this is, in a sense, merely to restate the old idea that tricksters and their actions embody ambivalence, but it restates it in a language that makes it clear why we may call the tricksters who practice these things artists in an ancient sense and their creations works of art.

"THE ONE THEY CALL THE SEVENTH SON"

These various ways to imagine making or remaking joints offer us a chance not only to redescribe the *Homeric Hymn to Hermes* and Douglass's *Narrative* but to clarify their differences. The Hermes of the *Hymn* is an *artus*-worker in two of the three senses I have sketched. He is no Syrdon, going for the joints to kill the eternals, but he does rearticulate the cosmos and, having done so, he keeps its articulated shape lively. To the first of these tasks he brings the bag of tricks with which he can unsettle the shape of Apollo's world or even remake its joints if he so desires.* Apollo's laughter at Hermes' cheeky lies marks the moment at which it becomes clear the newcomer will be able to move from outer to inner *artus*-work. Apollo's laugh holds the promise of their friendship, after which Hermes, with the same bag of tricks, will make sure that no

---

* To recast but one example of rearticulation in this new terminology, I would say that the meat Hermes hangs in the barn as a "sign of his youthful theft" not only marks the fact that he does not eat meat but is, therefore, a new *artus* or point of demarcation in relation to which he becomes one of the immortals. It's like a new bit of punctuation, a new joint in the expanse of this plentiful world, whose placement changes the way the terrain is read.

Olympian boundary turns into a barrier, no joint or point of articulation freezes up or calcifies. By the end of the *Hymn*, in fact, Apollo himself realizes this promise by naming the particular offices in which Hermes will operate as an approved interior connector/not-connector: he has the honor of overseeing the marketplace; he is the messenger of the gods and messenger to Hades; he even has his own form of divination, the oracle of the Bee Maidens, who sometimes lie and sometimes tell the truth.

Moreover, now that I'm framing trickster's operations in terms of joints I should point out that another work of *artus* and another *artus*-worker are hidden in the *Hymn*, hidden like the purloined letter, that is, for the work is the *Hymn* itself and the worker is its hymnist. A number of lines of the poem direct us toward this conclusion by calling attention to their own maker and equating him with his subject. In the beginning of the hymn, for example, the poet describes Hermes trying out his newly created lyre ("He sang the song of Zeus . . . and Maia . . . ; he broadcast the story of his own famous conception"), an exact description of what any audience watching a hymnist perform this song has just seen and heard. Second, if we understand that the *Homeric Hymns* were sung at various Greek celebrations as preludes to longer performances, then we will hear another conflation of Hermes and the hymnist when we come to the line that says Hermes sang the theogony to Apollo "prelude-style." The hymnist is singing a prelude in which he describes Hermes singing a prelude. Finally, this song about how Hermes was born and came to have his powers contains a description of Hermes singing about how the gods were born and came to have their powers. In each of these passages the *Hymn* is self-reflecting, like a drawing that contains a drawing of itself, or like the Native American tall tale which contains Coyote telling a tall tale, or like the African-American blues musician who sings, "I'm the one, the one they call the seventh son," so his listeners might know that his art springs from Legba, the trickster whose labors keep the joints of creation limber.

If we accept these internal hints and see the trickster in the artist, then where is his antagonist? If Hermes is the hymnist, then where shall we find Apollo? Apollo is the audience listening to the *Hymn*, and the hymnist's performance is a sort of Hermes raid on their Apollonian side. Imagine that audience for a moment. They have come to some festive event from the orderly, everyday world with its hierarchies, rules, and shame attacks for those who step out of line. As with any of us, a part of their psyche is Apollonian; a part of them follows the rules of the game, does nothing to excess, hopes to get exact weights and measures in the marketplace, holds itself at a distance from the merely human, maybe has a touch of the compulsive hand washer, and so on. Then, before such citizens there comes a singer who strikes up his lyre and weaves a melodic tale about a charming, harmless baby.

What happens to the audience as they listen may be something like what happens to Apollo late in the *Hymn*. He himself calls the lyre "a cure for hopeless care"; he says it combines "delight, eros, and sweet sleep"; clearly it is the agent of lolling and loosening, not of sunlit differentiation and discipline, and as it works its magic it draws whoever will listen away from Apollonian limits and into a dilating world of Hermetic possibility. Under its spell, one becomes "Apollo dreaming of Hermes." With this I am reminded that psychoanalysts sometimes welcome the dream of the thief: if a guarded and proper man or woman dreams one night of some shadowy sneak breaking into the house, well, excellent!—now there is the possibility of psychic movement; now those things the ego has denied itself may come forward. In the same line, an analyst friend once told me that when she has patients who seem unable to imagine how life might be different, she suggests they buy a lottery ticket: it is very hard to keep the wings of fantasy clipped when the hope of lucky gain sits in your pocket. Enchanting with his song, the hymnist invokes these (the thief, the gambler) and other psychic movers. This particular song is a fantasy of freedom from collective demands, a fantasy of stealing from relatives and having them laugh, of the gods made happy by happenstance, of amorality in the service of the belly, of speaking true desire in front of mother, father, and that bright, successful older brother. It is a compact advice manual on how to stay in motion when the world puts barriers in your path. Have you tried the trick shoes yet? What about walking backward? What about the strategic fart?

Moreover, the advice manual seems to indicate that the rules can be broken without destroying the Apollonian. The story moves from order to disruption to a balance between the two, figured by the friendship of the protagonists. In this way, the *Hymn* enacts a ritual of inversion, a sort of psychic festival of misrule followed, as such festivals are, by the return of design, or rather by design revitalized by contact with all that it normally excludes. Ideally the experience of such a story leaves the listener not so much freed from all constraints as freed from their tyranny and therefore more flexible and open to change. The teller of the tale offers up "Apollo and Hermes" (or "the Chief's Son and Coyote" or "Yasoda and Krishna") as open-ended symbols into which any listener can pour her own drama of transgression and containment and explore its possible resolutions. The audience listening to any trickster tale undergoes a kind of inner *artus*-work, then, a loosening and breathing of the psychic boundaries. Just as Hermes and Apollo end up related to one another and the articulated pantheon thereby enlivened, so the listener's psyche may have its functions related to one another (connected/not-connected, articulated without being divided) and thereby enlivened. It is not so much that trickster unifies the soul as that his polytropic commerce puts its powers in touch with one another across their necessary divides.*

In short, it is not only in Hermes that we find various sorts of *artus*-work; trickster narratives themselves do the double task of marking and violating the boundaries of the cultures where they are told. The trickster in the narrative is the narrative itself. It creates and inhabits ambivalent space. One of the few places where Claude Lévi-Strauss commented directly on tricksters speaks to this point. "Why is it," he once asked, "that throughout North America [trickster's] role is assigned practically everywhere to either coyote or raven?" His answer begins with the assumption that "mythical thought always progresses from the awareness of oppositions toward their resolution," a resolution which requires discovering a third or bridging term. As an example, Lévi-Strauss offers a set of parallel oppositions—life and death, agriculture and warfare, herbivore and carnivore—and then suggests some resolutions: "hunting" bridges the distance between "agriculture and warfare"; "carrion eater" mediates between "herbivore and carnivore" (the carrion eater grazes like a herbivore but eats meat like a carnivore). And "carrion eater" provides the key to Lévi-Strauss's trickster puzzle, for Raven and Coyote are both carrion eaters: "mythic thought" therefore discovers them in the space

---

* This line of thought converts into psychological terms the image of the trickster who is the necessary *artus*-worker of polytheistic religions. The image could also be translated into political terms, in which case trickster becomes the agent of polycultural situations, those in which groups have a kind of commerce between them that neither turns to conflict nor brings unity, so that they may have separate identities without ever becoming wholly separated from one another. Most debates over "multiculturalism" split into two camps: those who argue for unity (we have to be one nation!), and those who argue for separation (we must preserve our identity!), and thus fail to find the third position (*e pluribus unum*).

between plant- and meat-eaters and from this, in the North American case, assigns them the general role of cultural mediator.

This is a cunning explanation and though it doesn't work as well as Lévi-Strauss might have hoped,* I'm attracted to the idea that trickster narratives appear where mythic thought seeks to mediate oppositions. Just as Raven eating carrion stands between herbivore and carnivore (or, in my own earlier version, just as Raven stealing bait stands between predator and prey), so there is a category of mythic narrative, a category of art, that occupies the field between polarities and by that articulates them, simultaneously marking and bridging their differences. In the tale in which Coyote tries to retrieve his wife from the land of the dead but fails and creates death as we know it, Coyote *does* go to the underworld and so overcomes the barrier between life and death, but at the same time his impulses overcome him and the barrier remains. The narrative itself is a kind of flexible joint showing that the two poles that are its topic can and cannot be linked. The story of Krishna stealing butter overcomes but also preserves the division between the boy and his mother; the story occupies that middle ground where the ambivalence of family dependence and independence may be enacted.

In the case of the *Homeric Hymn*, both Hermes and the hymnist singing his story show that there will always be hidden passageways through any Apollonian barrier, but they do not do away with Apollo; they *play* with the oppositional mind so that when the tale is done, as at the end of a good session with the chiropractor, the auditor's psychic joints have all been manipulated, unkinked, and loosened. All trickster tales are works of *artus* in this sense. They are not, as is sometimes asserted, simply prophylactic narratives meant to show transgression so that people will avoid it; they are invigorating experiences of transgression, salutary dunkings in ambivalence. If flexible articulation is a necessity, so are these stories; if they are suppressed, if there is no place for enacted contradiction, the gods themselves will grow hungry and quarrelsome, or better, the gods themselves will dream of stealthy, thieving babies slipping past the sleeping border guards.

• • •

---

* Coyotes are not only carrion eaters, for one thing, and for another, the third major North American trickster animal, Hare, is not a carrion eater at all.

O f course, if one of the "gods" in question is a slave owner who hates to be contradicted and the baby is Frederick Douglass, the story that results will be something more apocalyptic than any salutary dunking. I have, I hope, dwelt amply on the similarities between Douglass's *Narrative* and the *Hymn*; these reflections on various kinds of *artus*-work help to mark the differences, the ways that Douglass is not, in fact, like Hermes. Douglass is first and foremost a Syrdon or Loki, a one-trick trickster attacking plantation culture at its joints. The *Narrative* is a toothed wheel thrown at the knees of slavery's eternal truths. Douglass does not address the design of plantation culture to reconcile its opposites; instead, he means to penetrate that culture's code and render it senseless. He mediates between his home plantation and his Northern readers, and between the master's and the slave's understanding of their common lives, not as a neutral agent who connects two communities while leaving their differences intact, but as a translator/traitor, the one whose mediations leave the world of his birth disjointed, unspeakable.

Above all, then, Douglass is never the inner *artus*-worker who keeps the articulated cosmos lively. He never entertains the playful mischief that would leave the whole intact while giving its joints a therapeutic stretch. We saw this clearly in his refusal of year-end holiday-making. American slavery's Saturnalia was never as full an inversion as the Roman festival, where masters might actually change places with slaves and wait on them at table, but its effects were similar, as Douglass discovered: at the end of license, the old articulation returned with renewed authority. Having twice participated in this contained release of tension, Douglass restrained himself in favor of the earthquake of historical change. Here again he is more a Loki than a Hermes, for it is the restrained Loki whose struggles bring on earthquakes, and worse. There was an earlier Loki whose pranks enlivened Asgard, but that is not the earthquake Loki, and that is not Douglass.

In fact, Douglass's youthful refusal of Saturnalia is a clear early sign that he is not kin by temperament to those tricksters who lubricate the inner joints, who border on the clown. In America we would have to turn to someone like P. T. Barnum to find that function. A visit to Barnum's museum tickled the ribs; a reading of Barnum's autobiography still does so today. Little in Douglass does. There is wit in his work, but it is always oppositional rather than convivial. No moments of communal humor mark the *Narrative* as they do the *Hymn*. Frederick Douglass was never drawn to amoral play, nor, like the mythic trickster, did he do "good and evil without knowing the difference." His work always has clear intentions; it never courts the fertility of happenstance. On issues of equality he was a gadfly all his life, but in other ways he was strikingly conventional, operating inside Christianity and democratic capitalism, participating wholeheartedly in the American myth of the self-made man, and taking his sense of manliness itself from his oppressors. For Douglass a "man" was always defined in terms of physical force, never, say, in terms of intimacy, tenderness, or whimsy. He was no prophet of the love of comrades and certainly not the cross-dresser we get in Coyote or Duchamp. There were some lifelong threshold men in the nineteenth century, those who perennially sought out the cracks in American gentility, but Douglass was not one of them.

To say all this is really to claim more fully the limits implied at the outset of the last chapter. My position is not that Frederick Douglass is a trickster but that there are veins and moments of trickster consciousness in his life. They appear, as we might expect, where history placed him on multiple thresholds—between slavery and freedom, between South and North, between black and white. The boundary-crosser awakes in Douglass mostly during those years just before and after his escape when he was in fact a part of two worlds and in motion between them, when both of those worlds were still contending for authority, when plantation culture still made claims to being natural and pure, and when he himself was that double anomaly, a free slave and a white-black native son. Once he became in fact free, once he reconciled himself in regard to the color line, once, that is, he was no longer situated at these multiple crossroads, the trickster portion of his spirit recedes.

It recedes but it is always with us, for from those crossroads came that enduring work of *artus*, the *Narrative of the Life of Frederick Douglass, an American Slave*. Just as trickster tales themselves do trickster work, so Douglass's *Narrative* itself works in the joints of racist culture like an attack of arthritis. In it, the old shaping divisions (black and white, calendar time and season time, etc.) come apart and are replaced by new ones (true and false Christianity, honorable and dishonorable theft, etc.). In the clarity of that new articulation one community's impudent and insolent speech turns suddenly into another's proper and communal speech. The book itself is the mark of that reversal, the turning point. Moreover, like all slave narratives, the book jams the old system simply by its presence, for it presents plantation culture with a lethal anomaly, the articulate black voice. In these several ways the *Narrative* is the work of *artus* of Douglass's trickster moment. Like Loki's mistletoe, it wounds the old purities; like the Promethean carver or Plato's clumsy butcher, it reslices the plentiful universe into new portions for a new world; like the "sign of youthful theft," it is hung out for the world to see, a new boundary marker in reference to which African-Americans must be read as self-possessed free agents, not slaves, as Hermes must be read as a god, not an illegitimate cave child. If the book still engages an audience today it must partly be that the drama of rearticulation it envisioned continues to be enacted. It was never a work to enliven with mischief, but one that raised more substantial questions about the living and the dead, saying, in effect, that "America" cannot be a vital collective unless it can incorporate (unless its body can contain) works of *artus* such as itself.

A CORRIDOR OF HUMOR

When I said just now that Frederick Douglass took his sense of manliness from his oppressors I was thinking especially of his description of a physical fight he once had with a cruel overseer named Edward Covey, and how he took considerable pride in having bloodied the white man ("He had drawn no blood from me, but I had from him"). In his *Narrative*, before he tells of this fight, Douglass makes blood the mark of slavery itself: his Aunt Hester had been whipped with a "blood-clotted cowskin," and the sight of her beating was, for Douglass, "the blood-stained gate, the entrance to the hell of slavery." To juxtapose the two moments is to see that when Douglass draws Covey's blood he reverses the system but he doesn't escape it. He becomes a man on terms that slavery itself has set. Doing so engages in a kind of contradiction, to be sure, but in this case we can see that contradiction, as long as it is simply the negation of a positive, is only the beginning of rearticulation. It doesn't reshape things deeply enough. If it only mirrors the thing it opposes, it discovers no secret passage into new worlds.

If we turn, at this point, to a story about one of black America's actual folk trickster figures, we will not only find a model for slipping free of the limits of contradiction, we can at the same time turn from the human and historical Douglass back to the way that mythological trickster intelligence works in regard to traps of culture. Down to the present day,

African-American vernacular culture retains a story about a Lion, an Elephant, and a trickster Monkey who is the master of "signifying," that is, of all the thousand figurative tricks that can be performed with language. In the typical plot, this Signifying Monkey works the Lion into a blind rage at the Elephant by reporting with relish things the Elephant supposedly said about the Lion's family.

> *"He talked about yo' people till my hair turned gray.*
> *He say yo' daddy's a freak and yo' mama's a whore,*
> *He say he saw yo' brother going through the jungle selling*
>   *assholes from door to door."*

Et cetera. The Lion eventually gets so mad he dashes off to attack the Elephant, whereupon the Elephant beats the Lion to a bloody pulp. In some versions, the Monkey subsequently gets so carried away teasing the beaten Lion that he slips and falls from his tree. The Lion pounces on him and is about to tear him to shreds when the Monkey quickly suggests they should start over and have a fair fight (after all, he slipped and fell). The Lion agrees, but of course the Monkey dashes back into his tree as soon as he's released. Sometimes the beaten Lion wounds the cocky Monkey, but usually the Monkey sits safely up on his branch at the end.

> *In the distance you could hear the monkey say,*
> *"As long as these weeds and green grass grow,*
> *I'm going to be around to signify some more."*

Built into this story is a sort of one-sided game of the dozens, a kind of verbal dueling in which antagonists publicly insult one another with elaborate rhyming couplets.* The winner is the player who improvises quickly, who most deftly turns the other's rhymes around, who always responds to wit with greater wit, and who in all this outlasts the other and most delights the gathered audience, for the game is always played to a crowd. The loser is the player who breaks the form and starts a physical fight. The point of the game is to play with language, not to take it seriously, or better, to stay in *balance* on the line between the playful

---

* Loki plays the dozens in the Norse poem called the "Lokasenna": he engages the gathered gods and goddesses in a *senna* or *flyting*, a running dialogue of vituperation.

and the serious while trying to tip one's opponent *off* that balance, dizzied with a whirl of words. The word "dozen" in fact has nothing to do with the number twelve; it is a modern survival of an English verb—"to dozen"—dating back at least to the fourteenth century and meaning "to stun, stupefy, daze" or "to make insensible, torpid, or powerless." The object of the game is to stupefy and daze with swift and skillful speech. The loser who starts a fight has been "put in the dozens," lured into a kind of unconsciousness in which he or she grows deaf to the figurative portion of language and takes everything at face value. The winner is a Signifying Monkey, a polytropic language master whose method with the Lion is (the joke goes) to "trope a dope," stupefying with swift circles of signifying. To be dozened is to be dazed into a kind of simplemindedness, a loss of language in which one stops being a signifying creature and turns into a muscle-bound beast that hasn't a clue about lying or metaphors, a beast that could be a carnivore or a herbivore but never a mediator.

A game of the dozens is built on insults to family, and to mothers especially. The Signifying Monkey story must come, then, from a world in which these things are taken seriously, where a child is admonished to "defend your family," to "respect your Mamma," and where these injunctions, even as they shape and secure the child's world, must confine in some way. Why play the game if there is no ambivalence about the rules it toys with? That the game exists at all indicates that the rules sometimes deaden and constrain rather than enable and enliven. Where the trap of such constraints is felt, the Signifying Monkey's antics point to a way out: wake up, they say, to the symbolic portion of all cultural mandates and by that consciousness stop taking them so seriously. The Monkey of the Mind wakes us to the web of mutable signs that shapes and toys with us until we get the wit to shape and toy with it. To climb into the Monkey's tree is to detach from the bedrock categories of one's own culture and "signify" with them, and that means to recognize that they are serious (there's no insult if this isn't serious) but that their seriousness can be infused with humor (the game demands wit and more wit, not the Lion's muscular response).

The antagonists in a game of dozens play with the difference between meaning something and just saying it, between fact and fiction, between love of family and disregard, between the sacred and the profane, between yo' mamma in fact and yo' mamma in a rhyme. The game requires equilibrium in the force field where all these things join one another. It demands poise in the joints, as it were, balance at the threshold. The loser, the person whose poise fails and who commits himself to the culturally approved side of this string of dualities, slips from the signifying mind with its speed and lightness and falls into the body. The loser is overcome with gravity; he gets serious, attached, defensive of his mamma in fact; his sense of humor evaporates, while the light-bodied winner stays perched in his tree, his humor intact.

Where there is real ambivalence, then, where one can truthfully say both "I *am* attached to my mamma" and "I am *not* attached to my mamma," the loser is that person who chooses a single side of the contradiction. The sign of such singlemindedness is contradiction without humor rather than contradiction with a smile. Here it may help to resurrect the old meaning of "humor": the word once referred to fluids (thus the bodily "humors") and comes ultimately from a Latin root (*umor*) having to do with moisture, liquid, dampness. To treat ambivalence with humor is to keep it loose; humor oils the joint where contradictions meet. If humor evaporates, then ambiguity becomes polarized and conflict follows. We saw this in the story of Eshu and the two friends; the friends will take their sides seriously and fight *unless* they recognize Eshu, unless they honor and welcome the smiling light-bodied figure on the road that both does and does not divide their fields.

A remark by Marcel Duchamp provides a wonderful image for the balance I'm trying to describe, and its creative consequence. Once, in talking about the history of the art movements he and his painter friend Francis Picabia had been involved in, Duchamp noted that laughter adds something useful to contradiction: "While Dada was a movement of negation and, by the very fact of its negation, turned itself into an appendage of the exact thing it was negating, Picabia and I wanted to open up a corridor of humor that once led into dream-imagery and, consequently, into Surrealism." The idea, I think, is that Dada worked *against* French bourgeois culture, but, just as Douglass derives his "manliness" from his oppressors and so does not escape them, in its very opposition Dada could never be more than a response to terms set elsewhere. The escape from this trap of mere opposition is some third thing (bait thief, carrion eater), here called a "corridor of humor," a pore through which fluid may move into new areas. And it should be added that once Duchamp got himself through that corridor of humor and into surrealism he soon began looking for the corridor out. Surrealism itself became programmatic very quickly.

André Breton was angry at Duchamp for years because Duchamp abandoned surrealism and started playing chess; the Pope of Surrealism
wanted no fully polytropic artists slipping free of his dream world, but
Duchamp was a man always looking for the door.*

A touch of humor or levity, then, is one mark by which we know that a
creative spirit working in the force field of contradictions has kept his poise, has not fallen from his tree, and so might actually move beyond the
enclosing oppositions. To take another example, consider a line like the
one with which Allen Ginsberg ended his early poem "America": "America I'm putting my queer shoulder to the wheel." This voice does not oppose "America" and does not oppose "queer," but settles directly in the
joint. It is the utterance of a patriot/ex-patriot, an insider/outsider who
doesn't want to get caught at either pole. This balancing act was part of
Ginsberg's talent, appeal, and art. In politics he managed to be one of the
few modern artists to unsettle Communists and capitalists alike. The FBI
and the CIA kept large files on him, but police agents expelled him from
Cuba and Czechoslovakia as well. In the United States, the Federal Bureau of Narcotics once framed an attack on Ginsberg by borrowing language from an attack printed in Czechoslovakia (both sides declared
Ginsberg had "manners . . . which a normal man—sorry to say—spits
upon"), a rare collaboration of cold-war enemies united in their fear of
anomaly.

The point is that when we hear Duchamp speak of this "corridor of
humor" or hear Ginsberg play the patriot-queer we hear the voice of the
light-bodied Monkey who hopes to stay poised at the joint, not fall into
sober negation and thus end up contained in the very thing being opposed. It isn't that there can't be contradiction, but that contradiction
cannot nourish without the waters of laughter. "Contradiction is a lever
of transcendence," Simone Weil once wrote, but that lever will not work
unless accompanied by some oil to keep it loose, a fluid we call "humor,"
the smile of early surrealism, the laughter of Apollo listening to Hermes
lie, the smile of Yasoda listening to Krishna, the smile of Athena meeting

---

* Duchamp maintained his style to the end, here described by Francis Naumann: "Almost
every evening before retiring . . . [Mme Duchamp] and her husband were in the habit of
reading funny stories aloud to each other. The joke would leave both of them laughing
just before going to bed. On the evening of Oct. 2, 1968, it was his turn to read and, as
usual, when the punch line came, they both laughed exuberantly. But on this particular
evening, while laughing, Duchamp quietly closed his eyes and expired."

Odysseus on the beach, the smile of that naturalist cited early on who says, "It is difficult to escape the conclusion that coyotes . . . have a sense of humor," when the hunter finds his trap has caught nothing but the varmint's smelly calling card. The rapper who perfects a Signifying Monkey story, the blues singer who calls himself the Seventh Son, Duchamp opening a corridor of humor, Ginsberg slipping through the humorless corridors of police bureaucracy—these are not the Lions of History, they are the Monkey *artus*-workers who keep the articulated world lively, at the very least, and who sometimes pull off the more complicated trick of stealing the boundary markers so that new worlds might appear from the plenitude that particular worlds necessarily hide.

In the first part of this book I interpreted a story in which other animals keep saying "That's my way, Coyote, not your way," as being about an intelligence stripped of, or escaped from, any instinctual way of living in the world, and left to weave its own "way" by imitating others and making up creative lies/fictions. In the Signifying Monkey story the Lion has a "way," and that is part of his problem. He's attached to a code by which fights are held, for example, and a code of honor about his family, and he hasn't the Monkey wit to think of these as invented and mutable.

In another kind of story, the Lion's dedication to his "way" would be a virtue, of course, as such dedication was Frederick Douglass's virtue. When Douglass was not the agile signifying rhetoric master (changing his surname three or four times, calling himself an Indian, disenchanting the white man's code of honor) he was the muscular Lion insisting that the code of the Christian Church be honored and telling the world that his "sable" mamma was as beautiful as a pharaoh and bookish to boot. He became an actor in history and, like the Lion, he got beat up for his troubles. There's a poem by Ishmael Reed about Ralph Ellison that could as well be about Douglass:

> i am outside of
> history. i wish
> i had some peanuts; it
> looks hungry there in
> its cage.

i am inside of
history. its
hungrier than i
thot.

It's as if they said to the man, "Frederick, you wouldn't believe what America's been sayin' about yo' people! Frederick, you can't imagine the tales they're tellin' about yo' mamma!'" It made him mad; he went after the beast, and broke himself against it. History ate him. To juxtapose the Signifying Monkey story and the Frederick Douglass story is to come back to the image I took from Lévi-Strauss two chapters ago: once the bothersome Douglass has made his way to the center of things, he is *not* expelled, *not* vomited out, but incorporated, eaten. He's inside "America" now. He got his picture on the postage stamps. After toying with the white man's rhetoric, he promulgated a rhetoric of his own with which he identified, and with that identification the Monkey turns into the Lion, a beast willing to act and suffer in the carnal world.

But to follow the plot in which a real human moves from liminality to action takes us away from the Monkey at hand, and his critique of the Lions of History. To the Signifying Monkey the Lion has foolishly let himself become ensnared in his own cultural code. To the Lion it probably isn't "code" at all, it's The Way Things Are, and the Monkey, for whom that is not the case, can therefore toy with the Lion by toying with words. The Lion is like the fish that does not see the layers of meaning in a baited hook and so ends up as someone else's dinner. Monkey can stampede him into a fight with mere images, just as Coyote can stampede buffalo over a cliff with straw men, trapping them with their own instinctual defenses, their ingrained way.

Better to operate with detachment, then; better to have a way but infuse it with a little humor; best, perhaps, to have no way at all but to have instead the wit constantly to make one's way anew from the materials at hand. Such wit is, in fact, the gift African-Americans attribute to their trickster figures, an unusual talent for making "a way out of no-way," as the saying goes. Brer Rabbit, says Robert Hemenway, is "the brier-patch representative of a people living by their wits to make a way out of no-way." Another African-American trickster, High John de Conquer, does the same, according to Zora Neale Hurston: "Old Massa and Old Miss and their young ones laughed with and at Brer Rabbit . . . and all the time there was High John de Conquer playing his tricks of making a way out of no-way." I once heard Eugene Redmond, poet laureate of east Saint Louis, say that diasporic blacks, those who have been scattered and whose traditions have been frayed, tell their children, "You have to make a way out of no-way."

There could easily be an internal debate in the African-American community about how seriously to take such advice, an argument between those who labor to discover and recuperate tradition and those who find fruitful free play in this black take on the American ability to thrive in the context of no context. In any such debate, the Signifying Monkey story falls on the side of free play. It implies, for one thing, that following the way of no-way will be of particular use to black men and women in a racist world. When every available way of life has a hierarchy of color woven into it, where "black" can literally mean "powerless" or "unemployed," people of color might well teach their children the freedom of the figurative. Knowing that those who take language literally must suffer bondage to its artifices, they might well tell the story of the Signifying Monkey as a primer in rhetoric, a teaching tale to cut open the third ear that hears the multiple meanings in every utterance.

But to read this as a story about race alone is to fall into the very trap it warns against. It's a story about reading the world, a useful skill no matter your skin color. The inexorable and punishing Elephant that the Lion runs into might be white folks, of course, but it might also be the violence of anyone who fails to read the world deeply enough, no matter the racial situation. African-American trickster stories, in one context, are about a particular oppressed people's refusal to be marginalized; in another context, they are about the freedom of the awakened human mind, a freedom those in power have not necessarily acquired. The Monkey is like a martial-arts master who uses the brutishness of the Lion's fundamentalism to flip him, to show him with what cruelty his own flat readings contain him. This is a teaching story, then, meant to remind its audience that the symbolic world into which each of us is born and which, in one sense, has created us, is, in another sense, our own creation. Just as linguists say that individual words derive their meaning from the context of the whole language but that the whole language derives its meaning from the words it contains, so human beings are created by their culture and yet that culture is also their creation. The way we live exists apart from us, but it does not exist unless we live it. We always inhabit a story that others have shaped, but we also always participate in the shaping. Great poets have come before us, but we can still be the poets of individual lives. The gods are above us, but they need us to protect them from hunger.

When we have forgotten the latter portion of these paradoxes, when the way we live closes in around us, feeling like a web woven by strangers, a deadening pattern and not an enlivening one, then, if we are lucky, the Monkey of the Mind will begin his mischievous chatter to wake us from our torpor. For those who are particularly thickheaded he will begin with the trope-a-dope routine, showing them how taking the code too seriously leads them again and again into a kind of self-torture (whose pain will leave as soon as they see that the code itself is theirs to play with).

In an essay on the similarly disruptive young Krishna, John Stratton Hawley asks at one point why any community might actually make these unruly characters into gods and culture heroes. To find the answer, he suggests we turn the question around: maybe it is not the trickster who is unruly; maybe our own rules and need for order are the true authors of misrule and cruelty.

We live in an era of savage order. We have seen bureaucratic finesse used to cause and at the same time justify unimaginable extremes of human suffering, and we are daily aware that with every further winding of the technological clock the possibility of our total destruction draws nearer. These realities, though especially terrifying in their twentieth-century form, have deep roots in history and are as endemic to India's society as our own.

But India's longer experience with the structural oppression of society has produced a notion of God that is peculiarly liberating. To perceive God as the sort of being who roams about outside our walls of reason and discretion, looking for a chance to make a raid, is to question the ultimate sense and authority of the structures we erect in such glorious and proud detail. These machines of the mind, these boundaries and perimeters, often cost us dear; hence it seems little wonder that as we watch them crumble in the mythology of Krishna, we register a certain glee.

In this model, when human culture turns against human beings themselves the trickster appears as a kind of savior. When we have forgotten that we participate in the shaping of this world and become enslaved to shapings left us by the dead, then a cunning *artus*-worker may appear, sometimes erasing the old boundaries so fully that only no-way remains and creation must start as if from scratch, and sometimes just loosening up the old divisions, greasing the joints so they may shift in respect to one another, or opening them so commerce will spring up where "the rules" forbid it. In short, when the shape of culture itself becomes a trap, the spirit of the trickster will lead us into deep shape-shifting. If the old Chinese village code of appropriate silence no longer serves, then a shameless Monkey (this one called Sun Wu-K'ung, "Awake to No-Way") will appear to the children of immigrants and help them articulate their new world. If the Bible's story of Ham has been used to justify human chattel slavery, then a Frederick Douglass will appear with the cunning reversal that shows how, by its own internal logic, slavery itself "must soon become unscriptural." If for some reason the otherwise venerable injunction to honor your mother begins to deaden rather than empower, the Signifying Monkey will appear to transmute Yo' Mamma the Pure into "yo' mamma" the piece of code, in whose presence you need no longer react with unconscious reflex as if you were foolish Coyote diving after berries in a stream. The Monkey of the Mind knows that human beings had a hand in articulating the world they inhabit and so knows that human beings can remake it when they need to. To wake that Monkey is to wake the possibility of playing with the joints of creation, the possibility of art.

CONCLUSION

12

....

PROPHECY

I'm no prophet. My job is making windows where there were once walls.
—Michel Foucault

A poeticized culture . . . would not insist we find the real wall behind
the painted ones, the real touchstones of truth as opposed to
touchstones which are merely cultural artifacts. It would be a culture
which, precisely by appreciating that all touchstones are such artifacts,
would take as its goal the creation of ever more various and
multicolored artifacts.
—Richard Rorty

PLENTY

Traveling from China to India, the Monkey King and the good pilgrim
Tripitaka enter town after town in which evil monsters hope to eat
them. The monsters are always in disguise, often dressing up as wise old
Taoists, and kindly Tripitaka is always fooled. But not Monkey. When
the monsters lie, Tripitaka thinks he is hearing the truth (like the swineherd listening to Odysseus' Cretan lies), but Monkey cries out, "There's
someone here who recognizes you!" "I, old Monkey, can with this pair of
fiery eyes and diamond pupils discern good and evil." Monkey is "the
one who has perception." He has special sight that can dispel "demonic
miasma" and distinguish the perverse from the real.

There is a recurring theme throughout this book, the suggestion that
tricksters might help someone see into the heart of things, and that they
therefore have a touch of the prophet about them. In closing, I want to
pluck this one thread of my narrative, as candle-makers pull a single

thread of the wick so it will bend as it burns and better carry the flame. At the end of Part I, for example, I argued that tricksters offer special insight with "lies that tell a higher truth." Part II touched several times on the idea that there is a kind of "prophetic contingency"; with both Hermes and Eshu, for example, chance events bear messages, opportunities for seeing into the hidden design of things. Even shamelessness can have its prophetic side. The Gnostic *Gospel of Thomas* reports the following of Jesus: "His disciples said: When will you be revealed to us and when will we see you? Jesus said: When you unclothe yourselves without being ashamed." This is a theme well developed in stories about Saint Francis (who asked to be stripped of his clothes as he lay dying), the implication being that the divine lies beyond any distinction between shame and shamelessness, so that an apparently shameless uncovering is a precondition for entrance into heaven. Thus, all the stories in which tricksters "steal the shame covers" or, more literally, steal the clothing of modest persons (as Krishna, Eshu, and Monkey do), may be read as tales of prophetic shamelessness.*

There has been a theme of prophetic insight, then, but it is a theme apparently at odds with itself. If we associate prophecy with righteousness, morality, and unmediated knowing, then it is rather odd to speak of an amoral, lying, thieving, mediating prophet. Some distinctions need to be teased out. In the *Homeric Hymn*, Hermes wants a share of Apollo's prophetic powers, but Apollo refuses. Hermes *does* have special insight, but if he is a prophet, he is not a prophet in the style of Apollo and Zeus. Similarly, Krishna's lies may point to the truth, but prophets don't usually operate in that backward fashion. This is prophecy with a difference.

The stories of the young, butter-thieving Krishna turn out to be a good place to start if one wants a sense of where trickster's insight converges with that of traditional prophecy, and where the difference lies. As I mentioned many chapters ago, Krishna as a child is famous for sneaking into the larder when his mother is away and breaking open the forbidden

---

* "Prophetic" here does not refer to telling the future. Traditional prophecy has a distinct relationship to time, but telling the future is only part of it. The prophet does not say that the stock market will fall next October, or that some celebrity will soon marry. Rather, the prophet speaks of things that will be true in the future because they are true in all time. The prophet disrupts the mundane in order to reveal the eternal.

jars of butter. When Yasoda later confronts the thief, he lies and says he didn't eat any butter, sometimes adding the question, "How could I steal it—doesn't everything in the house belong to us?" There are later adventures I haven't yet mentioned: when this child gets older, the breasts of the milkmaids remind him of pots of sweet butter, and his wiles turn sexual. Apparently lovelorn, the young god wanders the woods at night, singing and playing his flute to lure the village women out.

> *A flute, a tuneful bamboo flute*
> *—or is it a fisherman's pole?—*
> *The name is the same and so is the goal;*
> *to tangle, lure, and snare.*

The fish trap, the oldest trick in the book, is now a flute whose melody respects no garden wall, no window or door, and when the otherwise loyal and chaste women of Braj hear it they abandon their sweeping and water hauling, they turn rudely from their mothers-in-law, they rise from their marriage beds (some leaving the very embrace of their husbands), and go dance with Krishna in the moonlight. The night culminates in a circular dance during which Krishna multiplies himself sixteen thousand times so as to appear fully to each of the women, gratifying each one's desire to be his lover. Then, at dawn, he disappears.

In neither butter thievery nor love, by the way, is Krishna's disruption prompted by scarcity. He is hungry and concupiscent, to be sure, but his appetites bespeak something other than lack. There is no story of Krishna having trouble attracting women, and as for hunger, in the typical butter-thief story, Krishna's mother has been trying to get him to eat all morning. Only when she gives up and leaves does he rouse himself and sneak into the larder.

If food and love are readily available, why all this trickery, this disrupting of settled homes, this breaking-and-entering? Because the abundance that Krishna wants (or symbolizes) is available only when structure has been removed. The foods that Yasoda would feed her child are prepared foods, and they thereby contain a goodly portion of local rules and customs, and of the mother's sense of how things should be (we eat this and not that; we eat now and not later; these spices are special, those are lower-class; you may have a sweet only after you finish your lentils). Prepared foods are sustenance filtered through a net of cultural conditions. Stolen butter, on the other hand, is unconditioned, immediate, concentrated. Like the bait deftly lifted from a trap, it feeds without confining.

As for sexual love, one could here say that marriage is the prepared food of erotic life. In the arranged marriages of Hindu culture especially, the union does not express private attraction so much as the wider social settings of family alliances, property, land, and inheritance. In fact, in some parts of India, John Stratton Hawley tells us, love "should never be the basis of marriage, since to introduce attraction into the realm of structure would lead to a confusion of its very nature, weakening and even polluting it. It is the nature of attraction to contradict what structure decrees, to produce connections that cross boundaries rather than reinforcing them." Similar distinctions are reflected in the way that commentaries read the image of Krishna as a thief of hearts. What we are supposed to understand, they say, is that Krishna will steal the heart of anyone who has been foolish enough to think her heart belongs to her and not to god.

The prepared food, the arranged marriage—these may have their plenty, but more plentiful still is the stolen food, the stolen love. Convention can deliver sufficiency, but beyond its walls, beyond "the structures we erect in such glorious and proud detail," lies a spiritual plenitude that human structures necessarily obscure. In fact, it is because this fullness lies beyond design that Krishna's revelation must come through disruption: if it came any other way, it would have to come through some sort of structure, and all structure—no matter how "good"—exists by excluding something. If there is a love that lies beyond the law, only a thief can be its prophet (though from his point of view he is no thief at all; the real thieves are those who lock the doors, those who guard their hearts).

On the one hand, then, if traditional prophecy involves disrupting the mundane so as to reveal the higher truths of heaven, then Krishna works in that tradition: his lies and thefts point to divine expanses beyond the routines of everyday life. But of course tricksters are not traditional prophets, and one of the details in the stories I just touched on will help to mark the difference. At the end of the woodland dance with the sixteen-thousand milkmaids, Krishna disappears, leaving his lovers bereft, mystified, longing. The thief's last theft is to steal himself away. Now, what sort of revelation is it that follows loss? What does absence signify? There is a negating strain to trickster's actions; he erases mundane law and propriety, but not in order to replace them with something else. Thus, if we say that Krishna's disruptions offer insight into the fullness of the divine, we should at least note that the reading is ours, for the messenger himself left without delivering any message. All he did was break the butter jars, send the flute tones over the garden wall, steal some clothing, uproot a few arjuna trees—he never said what it all meant. He is not the declarative speaker of traditional prophecy, but an erasing angel who cancels what humans have so carefully built, then cancels himself.

If Krishna has a prophetic side, then, his disappearance makes it clear that this is not prophecy as it is normally described. Normally, the prophet can speak declaratively because the divine has intervened directly in the human order. "God himself is the speaker" when the prophet opens his mouth, says Plato. "In preexilic Israel," says a biblical scholar, "the prophet was a man with a message straight from God." In mystic Islam, a prophet is "the union of a divine Name and of the sensible form . . . in which this Name becomes visible," says Henry Corbin. Hellenistic, Hebraic, Islamic—there is a wide tradition in which prophecy is unmediated revelation, the divine coming forth as a presence, not as an absence.

But Krishna never declares in that way and it is therefore difficult to draw positive sense from his erasures. Like the heap of stones over a grave, the symbol that stands for a thing that has been lost (not "Krishna" but "Krishna-gone") belongs to an odd class of symbols. We cannot "read through it" to its sense, because what it stands for is missing. It operates not as a point of entry into meaning but paradoxically as a breeder of multiple meanings. That is to say, when we try to find the sense of one of these "symbols of loss," we discover only senses that we ourselves bring to it, and we can easily bring new ones each time we approach. (A famous example is Thoreau's remark in *Walden*: "I long ago lost a hound, a bay horse, and a turtle dove, and am still on their trail." A hundred and fifty years after this line was written, what one notices is not that its readers have slowly settled on its true meaning but that meanings have proliferated each time someone looks at it.) Symbols of absent things draw interpretive minds the way the flute music draws the gopis. If multiple meanings are what you want, a lost hound is a better breeder than any real Fido. Krishna erases the mundane, then erases himself, and these removals—precisely because they do *not* declare—open the field for human beings to spin out endlessly their sense of what has happened.

A fine modern image of this non-declarative (and therefore meaning-multiplying) aspect of the kind of prophecy I want to describe can be found in the famous parable that Kafka offers in a late chapter of *The Trial*. In his book about the art of interpretation, *The Genesis of Secrecy*, Frank Kermode gives a good synopsis:

> A man comes and begs for admittance to the Law, but is kept out by a doorkeeper, the first of a long succession of doorkeepers, of aspect ever more terrible, who will keep the man out should the first one fail to do so. The man, who had assumed that the Law was open to all, is surprised to discover the existence of this arrangement. But he waits outside the door, sitting year after year on his stool, and conversing with the doorkeeper, whom he bribes, though without success. Eventually, when he is old and near death, the man observes an immortal radiance streaming from the door. As he dies, he asks the doorkeeper how it is that he alone has come to this entrance to seek admittance to the Law. The answer is, "This door was intended only for you. Now I am going to shut it."

Kermode is interested in the problem of how we know the meaning of a parable, and particularly in the common division between "insiders" who know and "outsiders" who don't; and he is especially interested in the outsider, the hermeneut whom Hermes guides through the door so as to apprehend the otherwise hidden sense of things. Though Kermode is skeptical about the luck outsiders can hope to have, he excepts himself in regard to Kafka's striking tale, and declares its meaning: Kafka is saying that meaning (the truth, the Law, the single sense) is like a brief radiance glimpsed on the far side of a door that one cannot go through. The things we try to understand nowadays have "intermittent radiances" only, and these are "uninterpretable."

Note that it isn't necessarily the case that there is no truth, nor that we never have intimations of it, only that we can't in any sense finally arrive at it. We can orient ourselves, but we cannot arrive.

> We glimpse the secrecy through the meshes of a text; this is divination, but what is divined is what is visible from our angle. It is a momentary radiance, delusive or not. . . . When we come to relate that part to the whole, the divined glimmer to the fire we suppose to be its source, we see why Hermes is the patron of so many other trades besides interpretation. There has to be trickery. And we interpret always as transients. . . .

Kermode says "text" here but his sense of hermeneutics is not confined to language. We are transients in the world, "which resembles the book. The world is our beloved codex." We read books, yes, but we also read the swaying pine boughs, the turtle swimming below the ice, the dream fragment brought back by the smell of eucalyptus leaves, the unused bits of code on strands of DNA, the wobble of the flying Frisbee—and each has its radiance to offer, a sense that there are surely secrets yet to be revealed if only the gates would freely open. But in Kafka's parable they will never swing freely; a distant light is all there is, and that only briefly seen.

Let me retrace the thread of my argument. I began by noting that some sort of special insight is regularly attributed to tricksters, implying that they might have a touch of the prophet about them. The Krishna stories make a good example, for in them we find someone who does what prophets do, who breaks through the crust of mundane affairs and conventional morality to reveal higher truths. By the customary reading of the stories, Krishna's actions point toward the spiritual world, to the plenitude and complexity of the divine.

That traditional gloss can be complicated, however, if we dwell on the way Krishna disappears at the end of the forest dance. If he steals away without saying what it all meant, perhaps it would be better to say that Krishna disrupts the mundane and the conventional to reveal no higher law, no hidden truth, but rather the plenitude and complexity of this world. Addressing the problem of how to read the image of something that disappears, how to impute meaning to our longing for absent things, turns out to be a way of expanding this point about plenitude: in Krishna's case, or Thoreau's or Kafka's, the absence of a revealed truth produces a plurality of readings. Erasing the mundane and then leaving things alone opens the books. When Krishna disappears, it is as if the gopis had seen a brief radiance but now have no way of getting its "true" meaning, or it is as if they had woken from a striking dream of fulfilled desire whose nighttime presence evaporates in the daylight. And what does such a dream, such radiance, mean? There will be as many answers as there are human longings. Trickster reveals the plenitude of this world; if he then disappears, we see the same revelation repeated in the multiple ways human beings understand the plenitude of things once conventional understanding has been lifted.

The idea that prophetic tricksters offer a revelation of plenitude lies at the center of what I want to say here, but it is not the whole story. There is a pattern of events that leads up to and goes beyond the revelation of plenitude, and I now want to back off and describe the way I see that pattern from the beginning. In Krishna's case, the first part of the action is not revelation, it's desire. The butter thief is hungry for unmediated food, and that is why he upsets the local rules. The gopis desire Krishna, and that is why they disregard all propriety. Hunger and lust, not their restraint, are the first events in this prophetic journey. Monkey has "diamond pupils" that can see beneath the surfaces, but before the story reveals that fact, it has Monkey feasting on forbidden peaches. Before Hermes becomes a hermeneut, he "longs to eat meat."

In fact, I can widen this assertion about appetite by turning again to the *Homeric Hymn* with the question of prophecy in mind. In the *Hymn*, Hermes gives the lyre to Apollo precisely because he wants a share of Apollo's prophetic powers. But Apollo will only give the newcomer a minor oracle, the so-called Bee Maidens, whose powers recall a time when seers drank fermented honey to induce their mantic enthusiasm. Apollo describes them:

> "There are certain sacred sisters, three virgins lifted on swift wings. . . . They teach their own kind of fortune telling. . . . The sisters fly back and forth from their home, feeding on waxy honeycombs. . . . They like to tell the truth when they have eaten

honey and the spirit is on them; but if they've been deprived of that divine sweetness, they buzz about and mumble lies."

The *Hymn* makes it clear that Apollo's powers are greater than the Bee Maidens'. How are we to understand the difference? In Chapter 3, I outlined how the classicist Gregory Nagy distinguishes two kinds of ancient Greek poets, one who varies his repertoire as he moves around, telling "lies" (or at least "local truths") to fill his belly, and another whose song remains constant as he moves from city to city—this latter type having figuratively freed himself from the belly and therefore having access to a kind of truth that doesn't depend on his situation. Odysseus fits the former pattern; the poet Hesiod, lifted above his former shepherd state, fits the latter. Nagy himself extends this distinction to the case at hand:

> Hermes cedes the lyre to Apollo and confines himself to the primitive shepherd's pipe. In this way, Apollo . . . takes over the sphere of the prophet on a highly evolved pan-Hellenic level (his oracle at Delphi), leaving Hermes the more primitive sphere of the prophet as a local exponent of the sort of "truth" that is induced by fermented honey.

It should be pointed out that the honey that the Bee Maidens eat is a special food, the food of the gods, so that we are not exactly in the realm of human bellies who must eat meat and die an early death. And yet we aren't exactly free of those bellies either, for the rest of the details here fit the old pattern: it is a shepherd's pipe that Hermes now plays (like Hesiod *before* his transformation), and no matter how elevated their diet, the Bee Maidens lie if they are hungry.

We have no extended story about the Bee Maidens, but what we have offers enough for the point I'm after. Pure prophecy belongs to Apollo and some sort of impure or liar's prophecy belongs to Hermes, and this latter, moreover, is *not* free of appetite. Hermes himself may have refused to eat meat, but his oracle preserves a connection between a full belly and speaking the truth. That tells us something about truth-claims in a world with Hermes in it. Do the hungry Bee Maidens tell lies like the lies that Hermes tells? Do they lie the way Legba and Krishna lie? If so, we should return to a point made earlier in the book, understanding the assertion that "mere bellies" tell lies by its converse: when the well fed speak of truth, they are passing the artifice of their situation off as an eternal verity. In that case, the lies that come from empty stomachs serve to strip the "eternal" from the "verity," exposing it for what it is, a human creation subject to change. Where "truth" does not satisfy appetite, an *artus*-worker will find the weak joints in supposed essences and open them up. In trickster's world, appetite is a pore-seeking power, and thus the appetites prophesy. Their prophecy reveals the hidden joints holding an old world together, the hidden pores leading out. If you don't believe it, try keeping Hermes away from your cattle; try keeping Monkey out of the orchard when the fruit gets ripe.

This is the first part of trickster prophecy—appetite seeking the pores of artifice—and it brings directly the second part, the revelation of plenitude. Remember that Krishna, the thief of butter and of hearts, does not steal because the objects of his desires are intrinsically scarce. He steals because they are abundant but human order has reduced their circulation. There is love in marriage, but it is necessarily rule-governed. There is plenty of food in Yasoda's house, but it is laced with local rules about who gets to eat when and under what conditions. The butter laid up in its jars is sealed-off nourishment, a force contained by convention that becomes everywhere available only after Krishna breaks the jars.*

He is himself quite like those broken vessels, for the child not yet disciplined has the same uncontained potential. The local women to whom Hawley spoke in Braj, Krishna's reputed birthplace, told him that they would worry about a young child who never stole or told a lie:

Any mother, they felt . . . would be sorely disappointed if her young child did not display an element of mischievousness (*saitani*, literally "devilishness"). This feeling is particularly strong in regard to boys, but it applies to girls as well, at least up to the

---

* A similar motif appears in regard to Eshu, who is known for breaking calabashes. In other West African contexts, the calabash symbolizes contained creation (and small calabashes are used to hold powerful medicines). Eshu breaking them is a sign of catabolic energy, "not of contained power," says Joan Wescott, "but of potentiality let loose."

age of five, when a child is usually thought to become morally accountable.

A mother, that is, would be disappointed if her child did not have a touch of Krishna, for that child is pure potential crawling among us. It could grow up to be any of the things a human being can possibly be.

This is the child who will eat *anything*, who crawls the floor reflexively putting whatever it encounters into its mouth. In one of the more famous stories, Krishna's playmates come running to tell his mother that the naughty boy has been eating dirt. When she confronts him, he first denies the charge but finally opens his mouth for her to see. Immediately she falls into a swoon, for inside Krishna's mouth she sees the entire universe swirling. The child eating dirt has not yet suffered the fall into structure that begins after the age of five. He has not yet refined the likes and dislikes that will set the ego's boundaries. His mouthful of dirt is therefore anagogic to any eye that loves him, though what the eye will see is not heavenly purity but the fullness of this world before order demanded dirt's exclusion.

So now we have two things that the prophetic trickster reveals, the hidden pores that lead out of the mundane world, and the plenitude that lies beyond. There is a third thing, which I will come at from a little distance.

In 1964, Mac Linscott Ricketts finished a doctoral thesis that is a remarkably wide-ranging survey of North American trickster tales. There and in later essays Ricketts has argued that the tales locate the trickster in opposition to the practice and beliefs of shamanism. To Ricketts's way of thinking, humankind has had two responses when faced with all that engenders awe and dread in this world: the way of the shaman (and the priests), which assumes a spiritual world, bows before it, and seeks to make alliances; and the way of the trickster (and the humanists), which recognizes no power beyond its own intelligence, and seeks to seize and subdue the unknown with wit and cunning. "The trickster . . . embodies [an] experience of Reality . . . in which humans feel themselves to be self-sufficient beings for whom the supernatural spirits are powers not to be worshiped, but ignored, to be overcome, or in the last analysis mocked." The shaman enters the spirit world and works with it, but "the trickster is an outsider. . . . He has no friends in that other world. . . . All that humans have gained from the unseen powers beyond—fire, fish, game, fresh water, and so forth—have been obtained, by necessity, through trickery or theft. . . ." In obtaining these goods, the trickster, unlike the shaman, "did not also obtain superhuman powers or spiritual friendship. . . . He seems to need no friends: he gets along very well by himself. . . ."

To explore this idea, Ricketts shows how a number of trickster stories can be read as parodies of shamanism. In shamanic initiation, for example, the spirits kill and resurrect the initiate, often placing something inside the resurrected body—a quartz crystal, for example—which the shaman can later call forth from his body during healing rituals. If someone in your group claims such powers, you might find wry humor in stories which have Coyote, when he needs advice, calling forth (with much grunting) his own excrement. Likewise, dreams of flying are said to be premonitions of shamanic initiation, and the shaman in a trance can supposedly fly into the sky, into the underworld, into the deepest forest. With this in mind, it's hard not to hear the parodic tone in the almost universal stories of trickster trying to fly with the birds, only to fall ignominiously to earth. Trickster's failure implies that shamanic pretensions are daydreams at best, fakery at worst. "Humans were not made to fly. . . . Trickster, like the human being, is an earth-bound creature, and his wish to fly (and to escape the human condition) is . . . a frivolous fancy."

Similarly, the "bungling host" stories may be not only about the instinctual ways of animals, as I argued in an earlier chapter, but about the shaman's claim to be able to acquire the powers of other beings. Trickster fails to acquire powers because it flatly can't be done. "The trickster, in trying to get his food in the manner of the Kingfisher, for instance . . . is reaching for superhuman abilities. He is, in fact, attempting to transcend the human condition and live in a mode different from that which is proper to humans. Blundering efforts to do what the animals do," Ricketts concludes, "may be viewed as mockery of shamans and all others who think they can get higher powers from the animal spirits."

If the shaman in touch with higher spirits is the prophet of Native America, then trickster, his laughing shadow, is a prophet with a difference. Over and over the stories call attention to the actual constraints of human life: humans can't fly like the birds; the dead do not return. These are a species of "eternal truth," but pointing them out draws attention to this world, not another. It is a revelation of fleshy bodies, not heavenly bodies. Beyond this, where parody is able to strip the things it mocks of their charm, it opens up spaces in which something new might happen. It is true that when trickster breaks the rules we see the rules more clearly, but we also get a glimpse of everything the rules exclude. Commenting on Navajo stories, Barre Toelken writes: "Coyote functions in the oral literature as a symbol of that chaotic Everything with which man's rituals have created an order for survival." Mocking the rituals opens the door for the return of that chaotic Everything. From the shaman's point of view, the rules that trickster breaks articulate the ideal world, but from trickster's vantage point, if we think the ideal is the real we are seriously mistaken and won't see half of what is right in front of us. We may wish our bodies produced quartz crystals, but the bowels regularly tell another story.

In this fashion, a look at Coyote as a shaman-with-a-difference can bring us back to the earlier point about a revelation of the plenitude otherwise hidden behind conventional form. I have not introduced Ricketts's idea to elaborate that point, however, but rather to broach the question of what happens after this plenitude, this "chaotic Everything," appears. Part of the answer lies in the consequences of trickster having created the category "false shaman" to set against the category "real shaman." As when the simple addition of a fishhook produces the categories "true worm" and "false worm," the presence of a trickster in a shamanic tradition calls for recognition of the complexities of recognition itself. If there are false shamans among us, we had better learn to read, and therein lies the final element in the pattern of trickster prophecy. The revelation of plenitude calls for a revelation of mind.

I may be able to clarify what I want to say here by coming at the point from a different tradition. In Hebrew the word for "prophets" (nebî'îm) can have two senses: it can refer to those who bring forth, unmediated, the revelation of the most high, or it can refer to those who speak to the people through the medium of the imagination. The scholar Alan Cooper argues that unmediated prophecy is a special case; Moses is the only example. In the Hebrew Bible, all non-Mosaic prophecy is "imagined," and prophets who speak in this way can be either true or false, for the imagination itself can create both true and false forms. Jeremiah's imagination was clear and he was a true prophet; Hannaniah ben Azzur's was clouded and he was a false prophet.

But how are the listening people to know which is which? The point for now is not so much to answer that difficult question as to mark what it assumes, that the possibility of false prophecy means prophecy is mediated by imagination, and that a listener needs at least to be conscious of imagination itself if he or she is not to be deceived. Likewise in Yoruba divination, the friendship of Eshu and Ifa tells us that insight into heavenly things is never unmediated, so there needs to be insight into insight's vehicles as well (language, imagination, symbolic consciousness, etc.), and those vehicles, as I said in the chapter on Eshu, are not exactly high-fidelity instruments but are more like the atmosphere, shifty, cloudy, full of static.

In related fashion, Gary Lindberg, in a fine book on confidence games as an American literary theme, has offered a useful definition of a confidence man: a confidence man is someone who is in the business of creating belief. That is to say, the confidence man is *not* necessarily a crook, which is why he is so problematic. Some creators of belief are the real thing—prophets, idealists, charismatics, inspiring politicians, and so forth. Land speculators in the nineteenth century were in the business of creating belief ("Come to New Jerusalem, Minnesota, where the town square will soon bustle, the fountains flow, the children laugh in the spacious parks!"). Some were the real thing (P. T. Barnum created East Bridgeport, Connecticut, this way), and others were con men in the criminal sense, creating only rude awakenings. The awakenings are the point: if there is false belief among us, we need to become conscious of how belief is created; we need to be aware of what makes the mind move from doubt to credulity.

One interesting thing about Barnum, by the way, is that his museum in New York made a public game out of the problem of differentiating the real and the fake. Many of the museum's wonders were authentic, many were not, and the visitor was left to figure out which was which. The exhibits could make fools of both the too gullible and the too skeptical, for each would misjudge a portion of the exhibits. Skeptics never saw what the duck-billed platypus really was, and the credulous never saw what the Fiji Mermaid really was. Barnum translated a problem of American urban life—how to know what's going on in such a shifty setting—into a form of entertainment. Those who went to Barnum's museum got their wits sharpened for city life.

But whatever "city life" stands for, it must be very old, for the point is the same in each of these settings. The trickster among the shamans, the false messenger in a prophetic tradition, the confidence man in a world of strangers: each situation requires that the wits sharpen the wits, imagination imagine itself, mind wake up to mind. Not every mind can do these things, of course. The alligator snapping turtle with its lure tongue has a cunning trick, but it doesn't have a cunning mind. The young girl on a spirit quest who goes to sit on a certain pink mushroom because Coyote told her to—that girl has a mind, but she is not yet awake to its complexities. The shaman may well have the strong belief that allows him to operate in the world of spirits, but belief is single-minded and cannot do what trickster does, open the corridors of humor that allow the mind to toy with itself and with its creations. Along with the revelation of plenitude, then, comes revelation of a complex, joint-working consciousness, one that can always find those corridors of humor, one that will play with any concept, no matter how serious it seems (play with shamanism, with the truth, with the apples of immortality), and one that can create new artifice if need be, that can turn to shaping when it tires of shifting.

A somewhat simple analogy will help me summarize the argument I've been making about structure and plenitude, and about the consciousness that the latter demands. Structures always arise from exclusion. Think, for example, of how one might go about designing a flag. This world has endless color; the palette of greens in field and forest is boundless, as is that of water under changing skies. To make a flag, we select only two or three of the colors available and from the infinite ways we might arrange them we settle on a single one. Only by such narrowing can the flag acquire identity. Then it means something. Then we can recognize it, salute it, be its heroes, keep it out of the dirt. Even if we abuse it, we are responding to it as a vessel of meaning, as a particularity struck from the vastness.

The opposite of such structure is motley—the pied, the dappled, the maculate, the gillyflower, the real displaying itself as "fluctuating tatters." Once a mottled surface appears, it has a particular structure, of course, but the sense is always that it got that way haphazardly, by patchwork, and that it may not last. Motley bespeaks a lack of identity. Pied skin sometimes stands for the tattered flesh of the decaying dead, those whose identity is fast dissolving. Among the living, the character in motley is never the hero, never the king, though he or she has a freedom of motion those others lack.

The image of motley's destructuring force runs through the trickster stories. It is in the piebald ponies that Susa-nö-o releases into the rice paddies; it is in the no-design of the Milky Way that Coyote placed in the sky; it is in the unreadable footprints Hermes leaves with his twig-soled sandals, in the pockmarked face of Eshu, in Krishna's dark cheeks smeared with butter. Each of these is a figure of larger possibility—not the fixed constellations but the smear of stars from which constellations may be made, not the ordered rice paddies but the overflowing rain that nourishes all life, not Apollo's sunlight but the cave-mouth light where dreams and reason mix, not the contained energy of design but the catabolic heat given off by compost piles.

Even motley fails to figure the fullest extremes of plenitude, however. For that we need what might be called motley-in-motion, as with the wandering octopus that can shift the pattern of its skin to fit its ever-changing backgrounds. And inside that skin lives something even more fluid. In Aristotle the octopus is an image for its own "many-coiled intelligence," and in Homer it stands for Odysseus' mind, that much-traveled faculty that can shape itself to whatever situation it happens upon in this expansive world. The landscape is constant potential for that traveling intelligence, because the present situation is always dissolving and things that the horizon once obscured are coming into view.

That intelligence belongs to the wanderer who has heard the same object called by different names in different cities. It belongs to the time traveler, the immigrant child in each of us. When Maxine Hong Kingston was young, her family used to say that her mother had cut her frenum, the tissue that connects the tongue to the floor of the mouth. "I was the one with the tongue cut loose . . . ," she says and, as if to demonstrate the effect, proceeds to read the story several ways, imagining at one point that her mother did this deed to keep her daughter quiet, and elsewhere thinking the opposite, that she was cut so she could speak, in particular so she could translate between Chinese and English. Circumstances had put Kingston in a situation of linguistic multiplicity. The immigrant child forced to translate when shopping with her parents: that should be the origin myth of hermeneutics. It is a traveler's story, a story *not* of finding the one true language, the lost original, the unbroken amphora, but of being forced to mediate between incommensurate situations ceaselessly arising. "You just translate," the mother told her, as if it were that simple. "My mouth went permanently crooked with effort. . . ."

Here I can draw to the surface something that lies implicit in all this, that if there is a revelation of plenitude it will include a plenitude of languages. Motley-in-motion can be refigured as the babel of tongues, and its mental reflection as the polyglot mind. Regularly we hear of tricksters being involved in the origins of linguistic multiplicity. In North America, the Bella Coola believe that "the creator thought that one language would be enough, but Raven thought differently, and made many." The Paiute believe that when Coyote became hungry for meat, the other animals learned to be suspicious of one another, and each took up a separate tongue: "The common language was lost." Both Legba and Eshu seem to have caused the fights that mean the various gods no longer speak each others' languages and so need the trickster to move among them, translating.

In fact, the story of Eshu getting the two best friends to fight indicates that by "language" we shouldn't think only of things as large as English, French, Yoruba, Paiute. The friends that Eshu tricks think they speak each other's language, only to find that they don't, and come to blows. Eshu invents a situation that creates a distinct utterance in each man, and—not having taken Eshu into account—each is unable to hear the sense of what the other says. This happens on the road, out at the cross-roads, where novel experience arises contingently and so novel speech must also arise. Plato thought not only that Hermes invented language but that he did so in relation to "bargaining," which implies that a prime site of linguistic invention is the marketplace, another place where we are likely to meet strangers with strange goods, and, crossroads-wise, find ourselves forced to articulate newly.

Moreover, the market at the crossroads may be a metaphor for metaphor itself, or for any original speech, the linguistic flowers that sprout at the crossroads of the mind. The mind articulates newly where there is true coincidence, where roads parallel and roads contrary suddenly converge. This world is suffused with time and space, and therefore fresh speech is always appearing, always being invented. The world is teeming, so mind is teeming, so speech is teeming. There is no end to contingency, and so no end to language. We poeticize as transients. It would be the death of us should some Royal Academy ever succeed in codifying the language. The nation builders who insist on a single, official language are out to bind the trickster again, hoping to stop time, hoping to get Eshu off the road. But if they ever got their language utopia, their hoped-for Esperanto, what police force would enforce the law? If there were a single, unchanging language, the world would be hard upon us, the heavens would be hard upon us, the government would be hard upon us, and we would long for a traveling poet to tell the old story, how Coyote went to sleep during the council of all the animals, and dreamed of eating meat.

The Hebrew story of the Tower of Babel is about the loss of an original unitary and divine language, and it is background for much discussion of both translation and prophecy. Some say that both translator and prophet hope to recover that original language and so get at the real sense of things behind the current noise. The standard prophetic tradition imagines a kind of bard who is able actually to enter again the Golden Age and speak without interference from the noise of time, uttering essential truths in an essential language. The prophetic trickster relates to that imagined situation in two different ways. Either there *is* higher truth but our only access to it is this untrustworthy fellow, so that the messages we get are muddied and ambiguous. Or else "higher truth" is itself an unfortunate fantasy which only serves to obscure what is actually happening.

The prophetic trickster points toward what is actually happening: the muddiness, the ambiguity, the noise. They are part of the real, not something to be filtered out. Many messages arrive simultaneously, each in a different tongue. Inexhaustible meaning, inexhaustible language, inexhaustible world, it's all the same. Christian and Jewish hermeneuts have thought that there are four levels of meaning in a text; in the Cabalistic tradition there are forty-nine levels. But these are small numbers for readers who wear the *petasos*, the traveler's hat. Complexity has been with us since the beginning of time, and a mind as supple as the skin of an octopus arose to work with it. In the last part of his prophecy, trickster reveals himself, for he is that mind. When a human mind recognizes what has been revealed, it is recognizing itself. The hunter finds two things at once when he finally sees the octopus hidden on the rock.

FRAGILE BEAUTY

When Allen Ginsberg's *Howl and Other Poems* was published in 1956, United States customs officials initiated an obscenity trial in San Francisco. Many literary luminaries spoke in defense of the book, including Kenneth Rexroth, who told the District Attorney:

> The simplest term for [Ginsberg's] writing is prophetic, it is easier to call it that than anything else because we have a large body of prophetic writing to refer to. There are prophets of the Bible, which it greatly resembles in purpose and in language and in subject matter. . . . The theme is the denunciation of evil and a pointing out of the way out, so to speak. That is prophetic literature. "Woe! Woe! Woe! The City of Jerusalem! The Syrian is about to come down or has already and you are to do such and such a thing and you must repent and do thus and so." And . . . the four parts of ["Howl"] . . . do this very specifically. They take up these various specifics seriatim, one after the other. . . .
>   "Footnote to Howl" . . . is Biblical in reference. The reference is to the Benedicite, which says over and over again, "Blessed is the fire, Blessed is the light, Blessed are the trees, Blessed is this and Blessed is that," and [Ginsberg] is saying, "Everything that is human is Holy to me," and that the possibility of salvation in this terrible situation which he reveals is through love and through the love of everything Holy in man. So that I would say, that this just about covers the field of typically prophetic poetry.

But of course the context of this assertion was that carnival of mass democracy, an obscenity trial, and most prophetic writing does not find its way into such courts. "Howl" belongs to but is also distinct from the tradition (which never speaks of being "fucked in the ass by saintly motorcyclists"). "Howl" may join the Benedicite to say "The world is holy!" but the latter doesn't add "The tongue and cock and hand and asshole holy!" Rexroth is certainly right as far as he goes, but now that the Collector of Customs has released the book we may refine the description. Ginsberg is prophetic the way that Coyote is, getting out of his cage by calling down the chaotic Everything.

A friend once heard Ginsberg lecture on prophecy; at the end of the talk a young man asked, "Mr. Ginsberg, how does one become a prophet?" Ginsberg replied, "Tell your secrets." Uncovering secrets is apocalyptic in the simple sense (the Greek root means "an uncovering"). In this case, it lifts the shame covers. It allows articulation to enter where silence once ruled. "Tell your secrets" is a practice for loosening the boundaries of the self, for opening up the ego. "The striving for the right to have secrets from which the parents are excluded is one of the most powerful factors in the formation of the ego," the psychoanalysts tell us, but once that right has been acquired, there you are inside the ego, which may well take its job too seriously, pre-tasting all your food and telling friends who phone that no one's home. The teller of secrets I'm trying to describe hopes to create a more porous container to live in. To write his brand of prophetic poetry, Ginsberg went to the West Coast, a good three thousand miles from his parents, and convinced himself he was writing in secret for a few selected friends. That's a good and usually necessary beginning, but in the end it only produces a roomier cage ("we" have a secret), not freedom. Publishing your secrets so that strangers on the street might know them (not to mention those parents)—that is what makes Ginsberg's work prophetic in the sense I'm after.

As we saw some chapters back, the early Ginsberg's "secrets" had to do with his mother's craziness and his own sexuality; as he matured, his revelations became more capacious, so that the older man seemed like the ideal Freudian analysand risen from the couch to walk among us, articulating freely what freely comes to mind. Most such talk is not poetry, of course, excepting if the talker is a poet, and excepting especially if he is the kind of poet who has trained himself for decades to work with the patterns of his own cognition, believing that "if mind is shapely, art will be shapely" (one of Ginsberg's aphorisms). If these are the cases, then this apocalyptic method is a key to prolific art. Vast territories of silence are opened up to articulation. The artist who is not always guarding his or her words has more materials available than the one who must feed a troop of customs officials. Think, for example, of Anatole Broyard, who, for almost all his adult life, kept his black ancestry secret—from his friends, even from his children—and who never finished the novel he hoped to write. Some ego structures stand in the way of creative plenitude and need to be suspended or punctured if the work is to proceed. The poet who is *not* wedded to the structures that secrecy engenders has a wealth of materials at hand. Speech bubbles up. The ready voice itself is part of what he has to profess.

What sort of poem does this ready voice make? If the shapely mind is the mind of a joint-worker or shape-shifter, can its art be shapely, too? If it is regularly drawn to the excluded noise, what harmonies can it possibly offer? Can it make durable beauty if it is so dedicated to transgression? In what sense is the art of *artus*-workers a prophetic art?

To frame an answer to such questions, I would begin by recalling the earlier description of Hermes as enchanter and disenchanter. There I suggested that one kind of trickster tries to stay on the threshold always; he would be neither Hermes of the Light nor Hermes of the Dark, but Hermes the God of the Hinge. This is not quite what we have in the *Homeric Hymn*, however, for there Hermes sings a new theogony to enchant his older brother. He leaves the threshold where noise and harmony mingle, and gives himself to beauty. A tension of this sort informs the practice of those artists who have the boundary-crossing style to begin with. Should they stay in the joints, or should they go through to beauty? Should they be like John Cage, who thought "the highest duty of the artist is to hide beauty," and who met any emerging harmony with chance, so that something fundamentally new might constantly happen? Or should they be like Frederick Douglass (to move from art to politics), who helped destroy plantation culture but then gave himself to the structure of an amended Constitution, who got the rules to change but then took the new ones seriously?

I will briefly place Ginsberg in this range of possibility before I'm done, but before I can do that, it will help to flesh out the substance of these choices with remarks on two other modern artists I've already touched on, Marcel Duchamp and Maxine Hong Kingston. One of these stays in the joints; the other goes through to beauty.

Duchamp is a famously complicated and elusive artist, but it turns out that a few representative moments can take us quite quickly to the heart of his concerns. In 1913, Duchamp wrote himself a short meditation on the topic of window shopping in the Paris suburbs. The cultural historian Jerrold Seigel sets the context: "In France before World War I there was much discussion about how modern commerce sought to harness the powers of desire and fantasy for the lowly purpose of selling goods. Merchandise displays of all types . . . enveloped things in search of buyers in an aura of exoticism and sexual suggestion." Duchamp touches on this, saying (rather enigmatically):

> When one undergoes the interrogation of shop windows, one also
> pronounces one's own sentence. In fact, one's choice is "round
> trip." From the demand of shop windows, from the inevitable
> response to shop windows, the fixation of choice is determined.
> No obstinacy, ad absurdum, of hiding the coition through a glass
> pane with one or many objects of the shop window. The penalty
> consists in cutting the pane and in gnawing at your thumbs [feel-
> ing regret] as soon as possession is consummated.

This means, I think, that the displays in shop windows initiate a kind of trial. Window shoppers are on trial, and those who respond to the allure of the goods convict themselves by acting on their aroused desire. Acquiring the goods amounts to a kind of sexual congress, and is followed by regret.

To unpack this a bit further, note that the glass of shop windows separates the customer and the goods, but ambivalently so, allowing visual and mental possession while preventing actual taking. The glass is a permeable membrane, connecting/not-connecting. For Duchamp, cutting the glass and possessing the goods would remove this ambiguity, moving the window gazer from fantasy to fact to regret—regret, because possession is often smaller and more constrained than fantasy. Fantasy has free play; possession has its single, limited object. Literalized desire is therefore a kind of trap of appetite. You get your meat, but then meat is all you get. Just as the Signifying Monkey gets trapped if he takes the game too seriously, the consummation of desire circumscribes one's freedom to move and change. Better to balance at the boundary itself, to be in and out of the game simultaneously. At the gambling tables in Monte Carlo, Duchamp used to try to play so as neither to win nor to lose.

For an expanded sense of how such poise operates, consider the *Large Glass*, one of Duchamp's most famous creations. Actually called *The Bride Stripped Bare by Her Bachelors, Even,* the work is a painting on two large panes of glass set one above the other. The title and Duchamp's notes and comments ask us to imagine that the abstract painting on the upper panel depicts a "bride," and that the lower panel depicts the "bachelors." There is a horizontal "horizon" between them, a thin strip of glass set at right angles; they communicate with one another, this bride and these bachelors, but they never connect.

"Bride" is a key term in Duchamp's work, and may be best understood as part of the sequence virgin-bride-wife.* A "wife" has known coitus; a "virgin" hasn't. And the bride? She is the category between categories. To continue the sexual analogy of the window-gazing note, the bride represents a kind of arousal without consummation. The preferred state lies between the wedding ceremony and the consummation of the marriage, a state best marked by one of Duchamp's favorite terms, "delay."

The Bride Stripped Bare, Duchamp said, is a "delay in glass." A "delay" both suspends and does not suspend activity. (If you are delayed on a journey, you do not exactly stop traveling—you are still on a journey—but you don't continue, either.) The window gazer who responds to the allure of the goods but does not act on the response knows how to delay in glass, how to hover between fantasy and fact. The *Large Glass* articulates a similar state. As Seigel says, the bachelors, the male figures who occupy the lower panel, "remain forever in the condition of the window-gazer, whose state of being is expanded and animated by desire without ever experiencing the regret and disillusionment that follow from material possession. . . . They never have to complete the 'round trip' that is the penalty of breaking the glass." The female figure remains forever a "bride."

Both the *Large Glass* and the window-gazer note point toward a kind of equilibrium or poise between desire and fantasy, between acting in the material world and taking it as a field for detached symbolic play. It is important not to ignore the material side of this poise; as intellectual as Duchamp can become, his concepts are always connected to the physical world, and especially to desire (he called his female alter ego Rrose Sélavy, "*éros c'est la vie*," Eros is Life). He wanted a viewer of the *Large Glass* to see "something from nature" on the far side. On the other hand, it is also important to note how, for Duchamp, the poise of detached desire awakens the play of fantasy. In this, Duchamp is, like Hermes, hungry

---

* There is another possible sequence: virgin-groom-husband. In Duchamp's world we don't hear anything about the groom and the husband. The artist here is a man, a bachelor much of his life. The erotic energy arises when bachelors consider the bride.

for meat but not eating, a mythic image I earlier read as "a little *nóos* creation story," a description of how symbolic intellect itself comes to life. Reading that image back into Duchamp's work suggests that the work is only partly about bachelors and brides; it is largely about the mind.

Putting the mind back into painting was one of Duchamp's lifelong projects. He hated the French saying, "*bête comme un peintre*," stupid as a painter, and he felt that something had been lost with impressionist sensuality, its delight in eye-smacking surfaces. "Since Courbet, it's been believed that painting is addressed to the retina. That was everyone's error. . . . Before, painting had other functions: it could be religious, philosophical, moral. . . ." "I wanted to put painting once again at the service of the mind."

But what kind of intellectual expression does art contain, and how best to describe the mind of the artist? If religious painting wasn't about the paint, it was about belief and doctrine, but Duchamp's art "at the service of the mind" was not exactly about ideas; it is not didactic; it has no lesson to teach. His work is so suffused with irony that one feels a bit the fool for trying to state its "point," unless one looks to irony itself, or rather to irony as another kind of poise between two poles.

The mind that has this poise is the hinge-mind. Describing the *Large Glass*, Seigel says that it is "as if the two halves of the picture were joined by an invisible hinge. . . . In their original form the two halves were not rigidly held in place." This invisible hinge is a key symbol, and related to what I have already described—"bride" is the hinge between virgin and wife; the window glass is the hinge between the thing on sale and the fantasy. Nor were the hinges always invisible. In 1927, Duchamp had a studio at 11, rue Larrey, in Paris, and there he hired a carpenter to make him a curious door in the corner of a room, a door that, in Seigel's words, "swung on its hinges in such a way that when it blocked the entrance to one room it opened up access to another. . . . Many people saw it as a way of defying the commonsense of the French proverb, 'a door must be either open or shut.' "

Nothing attracted Duchamp like a chance to poke a hole in the platitudes of common sense—his own or his culture's. "I force myself to contradict myself," he famously said, "so as to avoid conforming to my own taste." As we saw in the last chapter, he was not just a contradictor; he was an *amused* contradictor, someone looking for "a corridor of humor" that might get him beyond the set polarity of doors open and doors shut.

In the doorway on rue Larrey, a corridor is always open because the door swings back and forth. The humor is in the hinges. So long as their pins are greased, the work will always elude the cages of common sense.

(Here, too, is where I would place Allen Ginsberg, in the vicinity of the well-oiled hinge. Like Duchamp, he prefers to settle in the joints. A single example: "Kaddish," Ginsberg's long elegy to his mother, ends with a scene in the graveyard where Naomi Ginsberg was eventually buried, a scene in which a voice praising God mixes with the cries of the crows who actually live in the graveyard. The last line of the poem reads: "Lord Lord Lord caw caw caw Lord Lord Lord caw caw caw Lord." The poem seesaws back and forth; the poet himself seems located at the pivot point between "Lord" and "caw." Each phrase immediately calls up its opposite. If you think everything belongs to the Lord, you are wrong, for the crows own this graveyard; if you think everything belongs to the crows, you are wrong, for the material world hides the spiritual. The dead are with us; the dead are carrion for the blackest birds. Between such assertions is where we find Ginsberg himself, the ironic prophet, hoping the universe itself will tell its secrets, but turning on them if they congeal into mundane human truths.)

Duchamp's well-oiled contradiction—like his use of chance, his addiction to puns, or his turn to mechanical drawing—was a tool not simply for avoiding mundane consumer regret but for avoiding the regret of living a life derived from unexamined language, tradition, and habit. Individuals who never sense the contradictions of their cultural inheritance run the risk of becoming little more than host bodies for stale gestures, metaphors, and received ideas, all the stereotypic likes and dislikes by which cultures perpetuate themselves. As Carl Andre once said, "Culture is something that is done to us. Art is something we do to culture." When the thing "done to us" ceases to satisfy and empower, it becomes a kind of parasite, an ichneumon fly depositing its eggs in the soft bodies of children learning to behave. Better, then, if one of those children can outwit the parasite; best if he turns out to be an *artus*-worker, a Hermes of the Hinge, whose mischief keeps the protective barriers surrounding cultural forms porous and open to change.

Duchamp was notoriously unconcerned about many things—fame, money, politics, marriage, preserving his own work—but his indifference left him whenever something promised the kind of fluid identity, personal or cultural, that can escape itself so that there is at least the possibility of real discovery and change. Talking of the time he had sketched a coffee grinder as a gift for his brother and found that "mechanical" drawing freed him, he said:

> Without knowing it, I had opened a window onto something else. ... It was a sort of loophole. You know, I've always felt this need to escape myself. . . .

> I began to think I could avoid all contact with traditional pictorial painting. . . . Fundamentally, I had a mania for change. . . .

Duchamp liked John Cage because Cage thought to put silence into music; "no one had thought of that," he said. He liked Francis Picabia because the man "had the gift of total forgetting which enabled him to launch into new paintings without being influenced by the memory of preceding ones." Of the artist who manages to produce something no one has seen before, Duchamp says, "That is the only thing that brings admiration from my innermost being—something completely independent—nothing to do with the great names or influences."

"A mania," "my innermost being": these will seem like strong words for the artist who supposedly once flipped a coin to decide whether or not to move to the United States. They seem like strong words until we see that they are exactly what motivates the coin toss, a constant search for ways to open loopholes so that he and his friends might regularly get out of whatever cage they were in (though not with any goal in mind).

In short, Duchamp's is an artistic practice dedicated to keeping the corridors open or, as I put it earlier, staying in the joints. Let others arrange the rooms of art; let André Breton take care of the philosophical foundations of surrealism; Duchamp would rather sleep in the hallway, his salesman's grip (his *Boîte en Valise*) packed, ready to move to the United States, South America, Paris, wherever he can get free of the "givens" of whatever logic is most in fashion. He has no program except to grease the hinges and see what happens.

For other artists, this is not enough. For whatever reasons of temperament or historical circumstance, others hope to combine disruption with repair. Hermes can move in two directions—into the light to take things apart, and back into the dark to stitch them together again. Sometimes the noises that disrupted the old harmony should be gathered into a new music. In Maxine Hong Kingston's work, for example, we are not left standing on the threshold, not left with a plenitude of ambient sound, but carried over into a new and shapely world. Though she praises the Chinese who brought the Monkey spirit to America, and though in that spirit she herself once betrayed her elders and told their secrets, Kingston is nonetheless an ardent idealist. She has peach gardens of her own to protect. She cares for beauty and for truth ("The strong imagination imagines the truth," she says). She once said she hoped to write a novel with a Confucian hero, "one who comes into a chaotic scene and brings order, community, truth, harmony."

In her art she is a sort of combination of the Monkey King and the good pilgrim Tripitaka (or perhaps Monkey and Kuan Yin, the female divinity who watches over the journey to the West). As a young writer, she knew that refusing the old shame barriers meant dismembering " 'the law,' the path, the rules that keep the village intact"; but she also knew that not refusing meant giving up speaking for herself. Unable to go forward without betraying her kin and unable *not* to go forward without smothering herself, she found resolution in the process of art.

> At the beginning of [*The Woman Warrior*], I write ... about a community that's broken by a woman who breaks taboos. . . . When I wrote that I thought, "I'm not going to publish this; I'm telling family secrets." I told myself that because then it gave me the freedom to write it. But when I got through writing it—maybe ten, twelve drafts—and pushing it toward form, then I knew I had resolution. I had a beautiful story, and most important of all I gave this woman's life a meaning. Then I felt O.K. "Now I can publish it."

There are two strategies here, privacy and shaping. Privacy means going forward without going public. In Kingston's case, this is the season of the Monkey King, who will break whatever taboos need to be broken, no matter. "Master, please put away your compassion just for today!" But the privacy that allows this freedom can turn lonely, and finally sterile. "It is a joy to be hidden," says the child psychologist Winnicott, "but disaster not to be found." There is great freedom to working in secret, but it is powerless freedom if the enclosure never breaks. The second part of Kingston's process, then, involves "singing a new theogony." Having broken the shape of village life, Kingston works the fragments (the Chinese fragments and some new American ones) until she finds new shape and new meaning, until she comes to beauty. Knowing that circumstances demand shamelessness if the journey is to go on, but unwilling to ignore her own sense of *aidos* (shame-reverence-awe), Kingston settles into a process that allows the double motion anciently figured by the companionship of Monkey and Tripitaka.

Such artistic practice creates a creole beauty. The hero of Kingston's novel, *Tripmaster Monkey*, is much taken with African-American blues and jazz, and when Kingston herself was asked about equivalent music in her own situation she spoke of trying "to take this Chinese-American accent and making it part of America." The immigrant project is not merely to learn English but to infuse the local tongue with one's own inflections. Rather than dropping her own accent, this translator wants to sing a creole tune so captivating that local speakers unconsciously adopt its rhythms. Such music lies at the heart of the parable Kingston constructs to close her first book, *The Woman Warrior*, the retold story of a second-century Chinese woman who lived captive for twelve years among barbarians, finally to be ransomed and returned to her own people:

> She brought her songs back from the savage lands, and one of the three that has been passed down to us is "Eighteen Stanzas for a Barbarian Reed Pipe," a song that Chinese sing to their own instruments. It translated well.

Here, however, we must ask what, in terms of "truth" or "beauty," is the status of the creole tune, or of Hermes' new theogony. Having had the experience of unmaking an old world and redescribing its parts for his or her own purposes, the new singer must at least suspect that the creole song, beautiful and true as it may be, is an artifice and subject to the same kind of *artus*-work that allowed it in the first place. I imagine the hymnist of the *Homeric Hymn* smiling at the audience as he sings of Hermes enchanting Apollo with a new song about the gods, for at some level the hymnist is mocking Hesiod and his above-it-all claim to having sung the one true belly-free theogony (it's Coyote doing a parody of the shaman again). This new song may enchant but not because it is true in the old sense. Similarly, the beauty Kingston has made was born of fundamental change and must carry with it a sense of its own mutability. Once the shame barriers have been moved, once the wall around paradise has been breached, there can never again be the beauty of the Taoist peach garden, the Norse apple orchard, the unmown meadows where Apollo's cattle graze. Hermes sings so sweetly that Apollo forgives the theft, but those cattle do not then walk back to their old enclosure. Hermes is an enchanter but if his enchantments were to take on the trappings of eternity he would move his listeners back toward the threshold where eternals meet the accidents of time.

On Calypso's island Odysseus is allowed to choose whether to return to his mortal wife or live on with the deathless goddess, a choice between two kinds of beauty, really, and he chooses the human kind, the kind which is all the more beautiful to us mortals because it will pass away, as we will pass away. When Kingston continues the Chinese talk-story tradition in a new language, when she plays *her* barbarian reed pipe, she must know, having herself broken an old "roundness," that there is no way the fine harmony of her work can protect it from future noise. True and beautiful it may be, but no immigrant child would claim it lies outside time. That understanding, in fact, is what makes Kingston an American author, "America" here meaning the fabled land of immigrants, of betrayal of the last generation, of opportunity, blues at the crossroads, and confidence games; the land whose government appeared "in the course of human events" and whose flag has changed its design a dozen times.

I have obviously gone into these examples of artistic practice because I think they often overlap with the pattern of revelation I claim for prophetic tricksters. There is an art-making that begins with pore-seeking (lifting the shame covers, finding the loophole, refusing to guard the secrets), that uncovers a plenitude of material hidden from conventional eyes (readymades are everywhere), and that points toward a kind of mind able to work with that revealed complexity, one called, in these last cases, the hinge-mind, the translator mind.

When it comes to the ways in which such minds work with received cultural patterns, there are some whose pleasure it is simply to settle in the cracks; like the inner *artus*-workers of the last chapter, these, at the simplest level, create the possibility of movement between spheres, and of movement out (not *to* something, just out). There are others who disjoint what they have found themselves born to, but then go on to make new harmony in place of the old ("I had a beautiful story"). Even in this latter case, however, the new harmony does not copy here on earth some unchanging music of the spheres. The artist may take her song seriously, but her seriousness is not the same as that of the gods who try to bind the trickster. Hers is a this-world harmony, made by a translator who knows that there is no final language, that once the tongue has been cut loose it will endlessly invent new speech, new articulations complex enough to fit the shifting scene. Where this artistic practice creates beauty, it is a fragile and perishing beauty.

Because he travels, Odysseus knows that what is an oar at the seaside is a winnowing shovel in the hills. As I mentioned many chapters back, these two senses do not exhaust the meanings of that fertile object. A winnowing shovel planted by its handle in a heap of grain means that the harvest is done. An oar planted in a mound of earth marks a sailor's grave. In fact, tradition has it that Odysseus' tomb was marked by his own oar planted in the ground. I suggested at the end of Part I that maybe when an oar has come to mark a grave it has also come to the end of its meanings. But things seem less finished as I finish here. How complicated are the markers over graves! They stand for loss and for memory. They are boundary markers between the living and the dead. Sometimes they remind us there is no passage back from that other world, and sometimes they hint that there is a gate if only one can find the gate-man to open it (his name is hidden in the heaps of stones travelers leave on graves). The oar that marks Odysseus' tomb is not there for him to read; it is planted for future travelers so they might call to mind the one who has been stolen away. As a sign of what has disappeared, it will offer up new meanings as long as there are readers to look on it. It is therefore a gateway back to the fullness of this world. The beauty we make will perish, but not the world from which we make it, nor the wit to do the making. "Rabbit jumped over Coyote four times. He came back to life and went on his way."

ENVOI

The fish trap exists because of the fish; once you've gotten the fish, you
can forget the trap. . . . Words exist because of meaning; once you've
gotten the meaning, you can forget the words.
—Chuang Tzu

Toward the end of the nineteenth century, a certain Father J. Jetté, Jesuit missionary to the Athabascan Indians, lived among the Ten'a in the lower Yukon. In those days the Ten'a told the old stories in the dead of winter, from early December to the middle of January. The group with whom Father Jetté lived would go to bed in the early evening, a dozen or more rolling themselves in blankets on the floor around the cabin, their heads to the wall. The last one blew out the light, throwing the room into complete darkness (every chink and crack was caulked against the cold, and gunnysacks hung outside the windows to keep the window panes from frosting over). Before long, someone would start a story—"In old times, it is said . . ."—the listeners responding *anni! anni!* to keep the voice going. "A strange thing had occurred: the sun had disappeared, and all was in the dark. What was to be done? the old women asked. Who will get back the sun for us?" Peals of laughter as Raven is lured from seclusion by the promise of dog meat.

Father Jetté wanted very much to make a collection of tales, but there were difficulties. The Ten'a were reluctant to let the Raven stories be put in writing, for one thing (though another group of tales—

"the inane stories," Jetté calls them—could be had for the asking). Jetté tried to transcribe tales as they were being told, but the utter darkness frustrated him. Nobody would repeat the stories in daylight, and at night whenever he struck a match to light a candle, the storyteller fell instantly silent.

THE HOMERIC HYMN TO HERMES

THE HOMERIC HYMN TO HERMES

Translated by Lewis Hyde

For Danielle Arnold

HERMES IS BORN

Muse, sing in honor of Hermes, the son of Zeus and Maia, lord of Kyllene, lord of Arcadia with all its sheep, bringer of luck, messenger of the gods. His mother was Maia with the wonderful hair, a shy and shamefaced nymph who stayed in her shady cave, avoiding the company of the blessed gods. In the darkest night, when sweet sleep held white-armed Hera fast, Zeus, the son of Kronos, used to lie with the nymph with the fabulous hair. No one knew about it, neither the gods, who do not die, nor human beings, who do.

Now, when he had finished what he had in mind and when ten moons had risen in the sky, Zeus led his notorious child into the light. Maia gave birth to a wily* boy, flattering and cunning, a robber and cattle thief, a bringer of dreams, awake all night, waiting by the gates of the city— Hermes, who was soon to earn himself quite a reputation among the gods, who do not die.

---

* Or "cunning," "versatile," "much traveled," "polytropic": *poútropon* (literally, turning-many-ways). In all of Greek literature, three characters are polytropic: Hermes, Odysseus, and Alcibiades.

As the sun rose on the fourth day of the month, lady Maia bore him; by noon he played the lyre and by evening he had stolen the cattle of Apollo, who shoots from afar.

HERMES INVENTS THE LYRE

Indeed, he didn't lie around in his sacred cradle, no, the minute he slipped from his mother's immortal arms he leapt up and set out to find Apollo's herds. As he crossed the threshold of that roomy cave, he happened on a turtle and got himself an endless source of wealth. For you should know that it was Hermes who first made the turtle into something that could sing. Their paths crossed at the courtyard gate, where the turtle was waddling by, chewing the thick grass in front of the dwelling. Hermes, the bringer of luck, took a close look, laughed, and said:

"Here's a bit of luck I can't ignore! Hello there, you shapely thing, dancing girl, life of the party. Lovely to see you. How'd a mountain girl with a shiny shell get so playful? Let me carry you inside! What a blessing! Do me a favor, come on, I'll respect you. It's safer inside, you could get in trouble out there. A living turtle, they say, keeps troublesome witchcraft away. And yet, if you were to die you'd sing most beautifully."

So saying, Hermes picked up the turtle with both hands and carried his lovely toy into the house. He turned her over and with a scoop of gray iron scraped the marrow from her mountain shell. And, just as a swift thought can fly through the heart of a person haunted with care, just as bright glances spin from the eyes, so, in one instant, Hermes knew what to do and did it. He cut stalks of reed to measure, fitted them through the shell, and fastened their ends across the back. Skillfully, he tightened a piece of cowhide, set the arms in place, fixed a yoke across them, and stretched seven sheep-gut strings to sound in harmony.

When he was finished, he took that lovely thing and tested each string in turn with a flat pick. It rang out wonderfully at the touch of his hand, and he sang along beautifully, improvising a few random snatches the way teenagers sing out insults at a fair. He sang the song of Zeus, the son of Kronos, and Maia with the wonderful shoes, how they used to chat in comradely love; he broadcast the story of his own famous conception. And he sang in praise of Maia's servant girls and stately rooms, of all the tripods and caldrons she had to her name.

HERMES STEALS APOLLO'S CATTLE

As he sang, however, his mind wandered to other matters. For Hermes longed to eat meat. So, taking the hollow lyre and tucking it in his sacred cradle, he sped from the sweet-smelling halls to a lookout point, a tricky scheme brewing in his heart, the kind that mischievous folk cook up in the middle of the night.

The chariot and horses of Helios were going down below the earth toward Ocean when Hermes came running to the shadowed mountains of Pieria. There the divine cattle of the blessed gods have their stable and graze in lovely, unmown meadows.

There and then, Maia's son, the keen-eyed slayer of Argus,* cut fifty loudly lowing cattle from the herd and drove them zigzag across the sandy place. He thought to drive them backward, too, another crafty trick, mixing up their footprints—the front behind and the hind before—while he himself walked straight ahead.

And right away on that sandy beach he wove himself fabulous sandals, such as no one ever thought or heard of. Tying together the newly sprouted myrtle twigs and tamarisk, he bound them, leaves and all, securely to his feet, a pair of shoes for those who travel light. (The glorious slayer of Argus had picked those shrubs in Pieria when getting ready for this trip, inventing on the spot as one will do when packing in a hurry.)

But as he was hurrying through the grassy fields of Onchestus, he was seen by an old man setting up his flowering vineyard.† The notorious son of Maia spoke first:

"Hey, old man stooping over the hoe, you're sure to have barrels of wine when all those vines bear fruit. If, that is, you listen to me and bear in mind that you haven't seen what you've seen, and you haven't heard what you've heard, and, in general, keep your mouth shut as long as nobody's bothering you personally."

Having said all this, Hermes gathered the excellent herd of cattle

---

* Argus Panoptes (the bright one, all eyes) was a watchful giant. He had a hundred or more eyes all over his body; some of his eyes would sometimes close for sleep, but never all of them. I take him to be an image of the watchfulness of a shame society. The story in which Hermes kills Argus is discussed in Chapter 7.

† From other versions of the story we know this man's name is Battus.

and drove them through many shadowy mountains and echoing gorges and fields in flower.

And now divine night, his dark helper, was almost over and the dawn, which forces mortals to work, was quickly coming on. Bright Selene— daughter of Pallas, lord Megamedes' son—had just climbed to her watch- post when the sturdy child of Zeus drove Apollo's wide-browed cattle to the river Alpheus. They arrived unwearied at a high-roofed barn and watering troughs standing before a remarkable meadow.

A SACRIFICE TO THE GODS

Then, having foddered the bellowing herd and packed them into the stable, chewing fresh lotus and sweet ginger, he gathered a pile of wood and set himself to seek the art of fire, for Hermes, you should know, is responsible for fire-sticks and fire.*

He took a stout laurel branch, trimmed it with a knife, and spun it on a block of wood held firmly in his hand until the hot smoke crept up. Then he piled thick bunches of dry sticks in a sunken trench. The flames caught and spread fiercely.

While the power of glorious Hephaestus kindled the fire, Hermes, full of his own power, dragged two lowing longhorns out of the stable and up to the flames. He threw them panting on their backs, rolled them over, bent their heads aside, and pierced their spinal cords.

Then Hermes set about his chores in turn. First he cut up the richly marbled flesh and skewered it on wooden spits; he roasted all of it—the muscle and the prized sirloin and the dark-blooded belly—and laid the spits out on the ground.

The skins he stretched over a rippling rock (still today, ages later, those hides are there, and they will be there for ages to come). Next he gladly drew the dripping chunks of meat from the spits, spread them on a stone, and divided them into twelve portions distributed by lot, making each one exactly right.†

And glorious Hermes longed to eat that sacrificial meat. The sweet

---

* Hermes does not invent fire; he invents a method of making fire, a trick, a *techne*.

† The twelve portions are *moîras* or "lots," "allotments." Hermes makes one for each of the twelve Olympian gods (Zeus, Hera, Poseidon, Demeter, Apollo, Artemis, Ares, Aph- rodite, Hermes, Athena, Hephaestus, and Hestia).

smell weakened him, god though he was; and yet, much as his mouth watered, his proud heart would not let him eat. Later he took the fat and all the flesh and stored them in that ample barn, setting them high up as a token* of his youthful theft. That done, he gathered dry sticks and let the fire devour, absolutely, the hooves of the cattle, and their heads.

And when the god had finished, he threw his sandals into the deep pooling Alpheus. He quenched the embers and spread sand over the black ashes. And so the night went by under the bright light of the moon.

HERMES COMES HOME AT DAWN

As soon as the sun rose, the god set out for home, the bright peaks of Kyllene. No blessed god, no mortal man saw him on that long journey, and no dogs barked as he sped by.†

And at his mother's home, Hermes, bringer of luck, son of Zeus, slipped sideways through the keyhole like fog on an autumn breeze. Making none of the noise you might expect, he walked straight to the sumptuous heart of the cave. Then glorious Hermes leapt to his cradle, wrapped his baby clothes around his shoulders as if he were a feeble infant, and lay there, picking at the blanket around his knees and clutching his lovely lyre safe at his left hand.

But the god didn't get past the goddess, his mother. "Hello there, you double sneak!" she said to him. "Where exactly have you been at this hour, you who wrap yourself in shamelessness?‡ I believe I'd rather see Apollo carry you out of here, bound hand and foot in unbreakable ropes, than have you grow up to pester the woods with your sneaking thievery. But go ahead! Who am I? Your father meant you to be a great bother, both to the gods, who do not die, and to human beings, who do."

Hermes answered her, his eye on the bottom line:§ "Mother, why are you trying to frighten me, a feeble babe who's never heard such big words, a timid child shaking at his mother's wrath?

---

* *Sêma* or "sign."

† There is another version of the story in which dogs were guarding Apollo's cattle. Hermes silenced them by putting them into a stupor.

‡ Or "wearing the cloak of shamelessness": *anaideien epieimene.*

§ Or "with crafty words": *kerdaléoisi.* A root of this word is *kerdos,* "gain," "profit." Hermes has his eye on the main chance.

"But seriously, I'm ready to do whatever I must so that you and I will never go hungry. You're wrong to insist we live in a place like this. Why should we be the only gods who never eat the fruits of sacrifice and prayer? Better always to live in the company of other deathless ones— rich, glamorous, enjoying heaps of grain—than forever to sit by ourselves in a gloomy cavern.

"And as for honor, my plan is to have a share of Apollo's power. If my father won't give it to me, I intend to be—and I mean it—the Prince of Thieves. If Leto's glorious boy comes after me, he'll soon be in more trouble than he is now. I'll go to Pytho, break into his big house and steal all his wonderful tripods, his caldrons and his gold, all his gleaming iron and his fancy clothes. See if I don't!"

And so they argued back and forth, the son of Zeus, who holds the shield, and lady Maia.

APOLLO SEARCHES FOR THE THIEF

Now Morning, the daughter of Dawn, was rising from deep Ocean's currents, bringing light to men, when Apollo passed through Onchestus, the lovely grove, sacred to the god who makes the earth quake.* There he found an old man grazing his beast along the path by the garden fence. Leto's glorious son spoke first, saying:

"Old man, you who've spent your life weeding thistles from grassy Onchestus, I have come here from Pieria looking for cattle from my herd—cows, all of them, with curving horns. The slate-black bull was by himself, grazing away from the others. Four of my sharp-eyed hounds, as smart as men, chased after the cows, but all were left behind—the bull and the dogs—which is quite uncanny. The cows left the soft, sweet pasture just as the sun was setting. Now tell me, old man born so long ago, have you seen anyone go by driving these cows?"

Then the old man answered him, saying, "Well, sonny, your eyes see so many things it's hard to know where to begin. So many people go down this road, some good, some bad. No telling who's who.

"However, I was up in my little vineyard working my hoe yesterday from dawn to dusk, and as the sun was going down I had the impression, dear sir, though it's hard to say for sure, that I saw a child—I couldn't

---

* Poseidon.

really identify him—following a herd of longhorned cows, a baby with a
staff who zigzagged side to side, and made the cows walk backward, their
heads toward him."

As soon as he heard what the old man said, Apollo hurried on his
way. Before long, he noticed a wide-winged bird and knew immediately
that the thief was a child of Zeus, the son of Kronos. So the lord Apollo,
himself a son of Zeus, covering his broad shoulders with a dark cloud,
hurried on to holy Pylos looking for his footloose cattle.

And when the Great Archer made out their footprints, he cried out:
"Well, well! This is remarkable, what I'm seeing. Clearly these are long-
horn-cattle tracks, but they all point backward, toward the fields of daffodils! And these others, they are not the tracks of a man or a woman,
nor of a gray wolf or a bear or lion. And I don't think the shaggy-maned
centaur leaves such prints. What swift feet took these long strides? The
tracks on this side of the path are weird, but those on the other side are
weirder still!"

THE CONFRONTATION

So saying, lord Apollo, the son of Zeus, hurried on until he came to the
forested mountain of Kyllene and the deeply shaded cave in the rocks
where the divine nymph gave birth to Zeus' child. A sweet smell lay over
the lovely slopes, and many spindle-legged sheep grazed in the grass. Over
the stone threshold and into the dark cavern stepped bright Apollo himself.

Now, when the son of Zeus and Maia saw the archer Apollo in such a
rage about his cattle, he wiggled down into the sweet-smelling blankets. Just
as dark ashes hide the embers of burnt tree stumps, so Hermes slid snug-
gling under the covers when he saw the Great Archer. He bunched his head
and hands and feet together like a newborn child overcome by sweet sleep,
though in fact he was wide awake, his lyre tucked under his armpit.

The son of Leto saw all this. Immediately he spied the beautiful
mountain nymph and her dear son, a tiny child wrapped in crafty subterfuge. He looked into every corner of their great home; with a shiny
key he opened three inner sanctuaries full of nectar and sweet ambrosia.
The closets were filled with gold and the nymph's silvery clothes, as is
the fashion in homes of the blessed gods. Then, having searched every
corner of the dwelling, Leto's son addressed himself to glorious Hermes:

"Little boy lying in the cradle, you had better tell me quickly what happened to my cattle, or you and I will soon be in an unseemly fight. I've a mind to take and throw you into the awful, hopeless dark of gloomy Tartarus. Neither your mother nor your father will be able to free you and bring you back to earth. You will walk out your days beneath the ground, a leader of dead babies."

Hermes answered him, with his eye on the bottom line: "Son of Leto, why are you yelling like a bully? You've come here looking for cows from your pasture? I haven't seen them. I haven't heard a word about them. No one's told me a thing. I can't give you any information, nor could I claim the reward for information.

"Do I look like a cattle driver? A big strong guy? That is not my kind of work. I am interested in other things: I care for sleep above all, and the milk of my mother's breasts, and a blanket over my shoulders, and warm baths.

"I'd advise you not to talk like this in public; the deathless gods would think it odd indeed, a day-old child bringing field animals into the courtyard. You're talking wildly. I was born yesterday; my feet are tender and the ground is rough beneath them.

"Still, if you insist, I am willing to swear a great oath by my father's head, and vow that I didn't steal your cows and that I haven't seen anyone else steal your cows—whatever 'cows' may be, for, to tell you the truth, I only know of them by hearsay."

Hermes' eyes twinkled as he spoke and he kept arching his brows, looking side to side and making long whistling noises as he listened to his own lying words.

Far-working Apollo laughed softly then, and said to Hermes: "My dear boy, what a tricky-hearted cheat you are! The way you talk, I'm quite convinced you broke into many fine homes last night, quietly swiping all the goods, leaving many a poor soul without a chair to sit on. You're going to be a great nuisance to lonely herdsmen in the mountain woods when you get to hankering after meat and come upon their cows or fleecy sheep. For the rest of time the gods, who do not die, will surely award you the title of Prince of Thieves. But come on, O friend of the black night, unless you want your latest nap turned into endless sleep, get out of that cradle."

So saying, Phoebus Apollo picked the child up and began to carry him. At this point, the powerful killer of Argus had a plan. Held aloft in Apollo's hands, he cut loose an omen, an exhausted belly slave, a rude herald of worse to come. At the same time he sneezed and Apollo, hearing all this, dropped him on the ground. Eager now to be on his way, still he sat beside Hermes, mocking:

"Never fear, little baby, son of Zeus and Maia. I'm sure these omens of yours will eventually lead me to my cattle. Why don't you lead the way?"

Hermes of Kyllene leapt up, his blanket around his shoulders and his hands covering his ears. "Where are you taking me, Far-Worker, most impatient of the gods?" he said. "Are you so angrily provoking me all because of your cattle? Oh dear! I wish all the cattle in the world would drop dead! I didn't steal your cows, and I didn't see anybody else steal them either, whatever cows may be, for I've only heard reports. No, do the right thing. Take this to Zeus, the son of Kronos."

And so, with their hearts at odds, Hermes the shepherd and Leto's glorious son argued the quarrel, point by point. Apollo, sticking to the facts, tried to snare glorious Hermes (who really was a cattle thief), while Hermes of Kyllene tried to lead the god of the silver bow astray with rhetoric and wheedling arguments.

THE ARGUMENT BEFORE ZEUS

But when he found Apollo able to match his every ruse, Hermes began to walk quickly across the sand, leading the son of Zeus and Leto. Soon these fine children of Zeus came to the peaks of fragrant Olympus, to their father, the son of Kronos. There, for both of them, the scales of justice were set. And there on snowy Olympus, after Dawn had settled on her golden throne, the gods, who do not die, had gathered to talk.

Then Hermes and Apollo of the Silver Bow stood before Zeus' knees and Zeus, who thunders in the heavens, spoke to his glorious son, asking, "Sunshine, where have you been to capture this fabulous prize, a newborn babe with a herald's face? This is some serious business you bring before the council of the gods!"

The far-working lord replied, "Father, you can tease about my love of spoils, but this is not a silly story I have to tell. Here is a child, an accomplished thief, whom I found after a long search through the hills of Kyllene. As far as I'm concerned, for catching folks on earth off-guard, I've never seen anyone, god or mortal, as brash as he.

"He stole my cows from their meadow and drove them off in the evening along the shore of the loud-roaring sea, headed straight for Pylos.

The tracks were double, quite remarkable, the puzzling work of a clever spirit. Preserved in the dark dust, the cow's prints led back to the fields of daffodils, while this weird creature crossed the sandy ground, not on his feet and not on his hands, but as if—can you believe it!—he were walking on little oak trees. When he drove the cattle across sandy ground, the tracks stood out quite clearly, but when he left the wide stretch of sand and hit hard ground, all tracks disappeared, both his and the cattle's. Still, a mortal man saw him driving the wide-browed beasts straight to Pylos.

"Quietly he hid them away, then sneaked home by some devious route to lie—as still as the blackest night—in a cradle in the dark of a darkened cave. Not even a sharp-eyed eagle could have seen him there. Constantly rubbing his eyes with his fists, he fabricated falsehoods, and spoke up boldly, saying, 'I haven't seen them; I haven't heard of them; no one has told me about them. I can't tell you about them, nor can I win the reward for telling.' "

When bright Apollo finished speaking and sat down, Hermes turned to Zeus—son of Kronos, lord of all the gods—and answered, saying: "Zeus my father, of course I will tell you the truth, for I am an honest boy. I cannot tell a lie. Apollo came to our house today at dawn, looking for his ambling cattle. He brought no witness with him; not one of the blessed gods had seen this theft. Instead, he tried to torture a confession from me. He kept threatening to throw me deep into Tartarus. He is in the powerful bloom of youth, while I—as he is well aware—was just born yesterday.

"I'm no cattle thief, no big strong guy. You tell people you are my dear father, so please believe me. I've not had the pleasure of driving cattle to my home. I haven't even left the house. I'm telling the truth. I greatly revere Helios and the other divinities; you I love; Apollo fills me with awe. You yourself know I'm not guilty. I will even swear this great oath: *Verily, by the gods' richly decorated colonnades, I am innocent!*

"Someday I'll get back at this bully, strong as he is, for his pitiless inquisition. But for now, please help your youngest son."

As he spoke, Hermes of Kyllene, the slayer of Argus, winked and clutched his baby blanket tightly in his arms. Zeus laughed aloud at the sight of his scheming child so smoothly denying his guilt about the cattle. And he ordered them both to come to an agreement and go find the cattle. He told Hermes the guide to lead the way and, dismissing the mischief in his heart, to show Apollo where the cattle were hidden. Then the son of Kronos nodded his head and good Hermes obeyed, for the will of Zeus, who holds the shield, persuades without effort.

HERMES AND APOLLO EXCHANGE GIFTS

Then Zeus' two fine sons hurried to sandy Pylos; at the ford of Alpheus they came to the fields and the roomy barn that sheltered the cattle at night. And as Hermes drove the sturdy cows out of their stony enclosure and into the light, Leto's son, glancing aside, noticed the cowhides spread on the rocks. Right away he questioned glorious Hermes:

"And how were you able to flay two cows, you crafty rogue, you little newborn baby? Looking back on it, your powers amaze me! You don't need to spend much time growing up, Kyllenian boy, son of Maia!"

As he spoke, Apollo twisted together strong willow bands, intending to tie Hermes up. But the bands could not hold the boy; they fell away at a distance and from the ground where they landed at once began to sprout, intertwining as they rose and quickly covering the roving cattle, as Hermes the thief intended. Apollo, watching, was astounded.

Fire flashing in his eyes, the strong killer of Argus looked furtively around, hoping to elude Leto's glorious son. Subtly, then, he began to soften that stern, far-shooting archer.

Cradling the lyre in his left arm, he struck each string in turn with the pick, and the instrument rang out awesomely. Bright Apollo laughed for joy as the sweet throb of that marvelous instrument stole into his heart, and a gentle longing seized his listening soul.

Playing sweetly upon the lyre, the son of Maia plucked up his courage and stood at the left hand of bright Apollo. And, letting the lyre introduce him, he raised his voice and sang,* and his voice was lovely.

He sang the story of the gods, who do not die, and of the dark earth, and how each came to be at the beginning of time, and how each came to have what now is theirs. Mnemosyne, the mother of the Muses, was the first among the gods he honored in his song, for the son of Maia was one of her followers. Then this good son of Zeus praised the other im-

---

* Literally, "he began to sing in prelude fashion, with a lovely voice." Scholars assume that Homeric hymns such as this one were sung as preludes to longer performances. At this point, therefore, a bard singing the *Hymn* describes Hermes as the bard himself would be described, "singing in prelude fashion."

mortals, each in order of age; he told how each was born, naming them one by one in order as he struck his cradled lyre.

And Apollo was seized with a longing he could do nothing about; he opened his mouth and the words flew out: "Butcher of cattle, trickster, busy boy, friend of merry-makers, the things you're interested in are worth fifty cows. Soon I believe we shall settle our quarrel in peace. But come now, tell me, wily son of Maia: was this marvelous thing with you at birth, or did some god or mortal man give you that noble gift and teach you such heavenly song? For this is a new sound, a wonder to my ears; I swear, neither men nor Olympian gods have ever heard anything like it, except for you, O thieving son of Zeus and Maia.

"What skill you have! What a cure for hopeless care! What style! Honestly, three things seem mixed together in this music: humor and eros and sweet sleep. I am a follower of the Olympian Muses—those who love the dance and the bright sound of poetry, full-voiced song, and the lovely call of the pipes—and yet nothing has ever struck my spirit like this, not even the flashiest songs of young men at festivals. In short, I'm amazed, son of Zeus, at how well you play the lyre.

"But now, since you have such remarkable talent, sit down, little boy, and show some respect for the wisdom of the old. Know that you shall now be famous among the immortal gods, you and your mother both. These words are true: by my dogwood staff I swear I shall make you the renowned guide of the deathless gods. Luck will follow you. I will never deceive you; I will give you wonderful gifts."

Then Hermes answered with his eye on the bottom line: "You have an inquiring mind, Far-Shooter. I do not mind your learning this art. Today you shall be its master! For I want to be your friend in both thought and word.

"You have inner knowledge of all things, for you sit at the front of the deathless gods, both good and strong. Wise Zeus loves you, as well he should, and has given you formidable gifts. They say you know from his own mouth the honors that will come to the gods; you know his oracles, O Archer, and you know his laws. From all this I'm already aware of your great fortune.

"And, clearly, you are free to learn whatever strikes your fancy. Since it seems you've set your heart on playing the lyre, go ahead—play it and sing, give yourself over to joy. Do me the honor, my friend, of taking it as a gift from me.

"You have a talent for apt and orderly speech; take my clear-voiced friend in your hands and sing. Carry it freely with you when you're off to a fabulous feast, a charming dance, a famous party. Day and night it brings joy. It's easy if you play it casually; it hates hard work and drudgery. If a wise man takes it up with skill, its sound will reveal all sorts of pleasure to his mind. If an ignorant man strikes it violently, however, it will chatter flighty foolishness in his ear.

"But you can choose to learn what you want to learn, noble son of Zeus, and so I give this lyre to you. As for me, I will see that the free-roving cattle feed in the high meadows and the grassy plains. The cows will mate easily with the bulls and litter the fields with heifers and bullocks.

"You always have your eye on the bottom line, Apollo; well, now you don't need to be so rough and angry."

Having said all this, Hermes held out the lyre; bright Apollo took it and willingly placed his shining whip in Hermes' hand, ordaining him Keeper of the Herds. The son of Maia gladly accepted the gift, while Leto's fine son, lordly far-working Apollo, cradled the lyre in his left arm and tested each string with the pick. It made a wonderful sound, and as it did the god sang sweetly.

Afterward, these charming sons of Zeus drove the cows back to their sacred meadow, and themselves hurried to snowy Olympus, amusing themselves with the lyre as they went. Wise Zeus was glad, and confirmed their friendship. Hermes then loved Leto's son with constant affection, even as he does today. The gift of the lyre was a token of this love for the Great Archer, who played it skillfully, resting it on his arm. As for Hermes, he was eager to know another art, and made himself the shepherd's pipes, whose music carries great distances.

Then Leto's son said to Hermes, "Son of Maia, cunning boy and guide, I'm still afraid you might steal both my curving bow and my lyre, for Zeus has given you the honor of initiating deeds of exchange trade among men all over the fruitful world.* Please set my heart at ease; swear one of the gods' great oaths, either nodding your head or calling on the powerful waters of the river Styx."

---

* Note that Apollo assumes that someone involved in the marketplace will also be a thief. The world of this *Hymn* does not make a clear distinction between stealing and making a profit.

Then Maia's son nodded his head and promised he would not steal anything the Great Archer owned, nor would he ever approach his well-built home. And Apollo, son of Leto, swore he would be Hermes' friend and companion. Of all the immortals—be they gods or human children of Zeus—he vowed to love none better than he loved Hermes.

APOLLO GIVES HERMES HIS OFFICES

Apollo then swore a serious oath: "For mortals and immortals alike, I would have this instrument be the sure and heartfelt token of our bond.

"Moreover, I now bestow on you the marvelous wand with three gold branches. It brings good fortune and wealth, and will protect you from harm as you effect the good words and deeds that I have learned from the mind of Zeus.

"But, noble child of Zeus, as for the other thing you have asked about, the art of prophecy, neither you nor any of the deathless gods may learn it. Only the mind of Zeus knows the future. I've made a pledge, I've vowed and sworn a great oath, that only I of all the undying gods might know his intricate plans. And so, dear brother, bearer of the golden wand, don't ask me to reveal the things all-seeing Zeus intends.

"As for me, I will sorely puzzle the unenviable race of men, destroying some and helping others. If a man comes to me guided by the call and flight of ominous birds, he will profit from my words; I won't deceive him. But the man who believes in birds that chatter idly, who invokes my prophetic art against my will, who tries to know more than the deathless gods, his journey will be useless, I swear. Still, I'd be happy to receive his offerings.

"I'll tell you one more thing, however, son of glorious Maia, son of Zeus who holds the shield, luck-bringing helper of the gods. There are certain sacred sisters, three virgins lifted on swift wings; their heads have been dusted with white meal; they live beneath a cliff on Parnassus.* They teach their own kind of fortune telling. I practiced it as a boy traipsing after cattle; my father doesn't care. The sisters fly back and forth from their home, feeding on waxy honeycombs and making things happen. They like to tell the truth when they have eaten honey and the

---

* These are called the Bee Maidens. Apollo gives Hermes a minor prophetic art.

spirit is on them; but if they've been deprived of that divine sweetness, they buzz about and mumble lies.

"I give them to you, then. Question them well and please your heart. And if mortal men you should instruct, they may have good fortune and follow you.

"And, son of Maia, tend, as well, the ranging, twisted-horned cattle, the horses, and the hard-working mules. May glorious Hermes be the lord of fire-eyed lions and white-toothed boars, and dogs; may he be lord of all the flocks and all the sheep the wide earth feeds. And Hermes alone shall be appointed messenger to the underworld, where Hades gives the ultimate gift and takes none in return."

In this way, with the blessing of the son of Kronos, lordly Apollo showed friendship and good will toward the son of Maia.

So it is that Hermes moves among the gods, who do not die, and human beings, who must. And though he serves a few, most of the time, when night has fallen, he deceives the race whose time runs out.

And so farewell, son of Zeus and Maia; I will think of you often as I go on to other songs.

APPENDIX II

TRICKSTER AND GENDER

TRICKSTER AND GENDER

All the standard tricksters are male. There are three related reasons why this might be. First, these tricksters may belong to patriarchal mythologies, ones in which the prime actors, even oppositional actors, are male. Second, there may be a problem with the standard itself; there may be female tricksters who have simply been ignored. Finally, it may be that the trickster stories articulate some distinction between men and women, so that even in a matriarchal setting this figure would be male.

There needs to be one clarification before I can expand on each of these responses. It is often said that the well-known tricksters are not male but androgynous, or at least of indeterminate sexuality. The anthropologist Victor Turner says, for example, "Most tricksters have an uncertain sexual status: on various mythical occasions Loki and Wakdjunkaga transformed themselves into women, while Hermes was often represented in statuary as a hermaphrodite." This seems to me to overstate the case. The classical hermaphrodite is born of the union of Hermes and Aphrodite; to say the figure represents Hermes is an insult to Aphrodite.

The other cases are a little more complicated. Wakdjunkaga, the

Winnebago trickster, once disguises himself as a woman, marries the son of a chief, and bears three sons. Loki once transformed himself into a mare in heat so as to distract the stallion that was helping to build the wall around Asgard. Not only that, but this stallion and mare mated and Loki thus bore a foal, the eight-legged horse, Sleipnir. There is also one obscure reference to Loki's having eaten the half-cooked heart of a woman and by that becoming sufficiently female as to give birth to monsters.

These are the best, and I think the *only*, examples of tricksters being both male and female. They do not, however, seem to me to indicate "uncertain sexual status." In both cases, *a male figure* becomes briefly female and then reverts to being male. The male is the ground, the point of departure. In the Winnebago case, in fact, the sex-change episode ends with Wakdjunkaga losing his disguise and saying to himself, "Why am I doing all this? It is about time that I went back to the woman to whom I am really married. [My son] must be a pretty big boy by this time." As Radin points out, this is the only mention of Wakdjunkaga having a family; the narrator is underlining trickster's framing maleness, within which there has been an episode of femaleness.

The best we can do, I think, is to modify my opening assertion: the standard tricksters are male, some of whom on rare occasions become briefly female.

A s for trickster being part of patriarchal mythology, I'd like to approach the topic from the other side, by way of a possible female trickster figure, Baubo. In Greek Eleusinian mystery religion, Baubo was a woman (sometimes a queen, sometimes a nurse) who managed to make Demeter laugh in the midst of her grief and anger over the loss of her daughter Persephone. Demeter's bitter sadness had caused fertility to withdraw from the world; the corn seed would not germinate in the ground. Whoever could break her grief was also, therefore, the bringer of spring and fertility. And how did Baubo make Demeter laugh? By lifting her skirts and exposing her pudenda, a shameless and im-pudent act by definition.* Baubo was also associated with the dirty jokes, the

---

* There is a similar motif in Japan. After Susa-nö-o's attacks, the sun goddess Amaterasu hides in a cave and the world grows dark, the seasons stop. To draw her from the cave, a playful goddess (Ama No Uzume) dances by the door, exposing her breasts and genitals.

obscene badinage, women made during Demeter's fertility rites. During the Eleusinian festival of Demeter, ribald remarks were called out on the "bridge of jests" between Athens and Eleusis. (Such joking is a common feature of fertility festivals, meant to arouse the earth and humans alike.)

In any event, we have here a female figure of great antiquity, a female flasher as it were, whose shamelessness is linked with fertility and the return of the dead, all of which are part of the trickster's mythological territory.

But in fact we have very little *story* about Baubo. The earliest record occurs in the seventh-century B.C. *Homeric Hymn to Demeter*, where Baubo is called Iambe and where the critical interaction between her and Demeter is described with restraint: "Careful Iambe . . . moved the holy lady with many a quip and jest to smile and laugh and cheer her heart."

The standard commentary on this hymn, while explaining that in "the Orphic version" of the story "Baubo by an exposure caused Demeter to smile," allows that "the epic dignity of the poet of the hymn" has erased that shameless image, a circular remark since the *Hymn* acquires its "epic dignity" exactly by such erasures. We know the fuller "Orphic version" of the story from Clement of Alexandria, a Church father who cites the crucial lines from an ancient Orphic poem ("She drew aside her robes, and showed a sight of shame"), but not without a prefatory apology: "[The] Athenians and the rest of Greece—I blush even to speak of it— possess that shameful tale about Demeter."

Thus, with both the poet of the *Hymn to Demeter* and Clement of Alexandria, we not only hear an old story which features a shameless female reversing a moribund situation, we get to witness the old story losing its details. Cases such as this (or of Sheela-na-gig, another female flasher whose image appeared on churches in Ireland up into the middle ages) suggest that there may have been a tradition of female tricksters that disappeared over the centuries during which Zeus worshippers and Christian "fathers" were shoring up their dignity. There has, of course, been much speculation in recent decades about gender relations in the

---

The other gods laugh, which arouses the sun's curiosity, and she begins to emerge.

These two examples add a corollary to the idea that tricksters revive high gods by debasing them. If the high one is a goddess, it may take a female trickster to do that work.

pre-history of mythology. A remark by Charlene Spretnak in regard to Demeter's story is typical: "It is likely that the story of the rape of the Goddess [Persephone] is a historical reference to the invasion of the northern Zeus-worshippers, just as is the story of the stormy marriage of Hera, the native queen who will not yield to the conqueror Zeus." Spretnak takes the *Hymn to Demeter* to be a retelling of much older stories about Isis and Gaia, a retelling in a new context where Zeus is the high god and Baubo has become "careful Iambe," and it is getting harder and harder to remember what exactly she did to make Demeter laugh.

The Baubo case suggests that perhaps the traditional literature on tricksters hasn't cast a wide enough net, that there are female figures out there; we just need to look more widely to find them. My own reading has turned up two or three, but before I speak of them I should say that my own sense of the category "trickster" calls for a mythic figure with an elaborated career of trickery. I say this because it is not hard to think of women who have pulled a trick or two; lying, stealing, and shameless behavior are not masculine essences. But one or two episodes do not make a trickster.

Maxine Hong Kingston once suggested to me that the Chinese woman who pretended to be a warrior so that her father would not have to go to war, Fa Mu Lan, was a trickster. I'm skeptical; her ruse is certainly a trick, but it's the only one; she's not like the Monkey King whose deceptions fill a hundred chapters. Similarly, there has been some attempt to describe certain women in the Hebrew Bible as female tricksters. Rachel tricks Laban, for example, when she and Jacob are leaving Laban's house. They leave without announcing their departure, and as they go Rachel steals the teraphim, the household idols. She prevents Laban from searching for the missing goods by telling him "the way of women is upon me." From this event, one critic concludes: "She is the trickster who dupes the one in power! She is a trickster by means of role reversal." Again, I'm not convinced. She has a trick, surely, but there is no elaborated career. These are examples of female trickery, not of female tricksters.

As for female tricksters, there are several, one of which I'll comment on. There is Aunt Nancy of African-American lore, though she is actually a version of Ananse, the Ashanti spider trickster, and the corpus of tales about her is small. There is Inanna, the "deceptive goddess" of ancient Sumeria. There is a figure from the Chiapas Highlands of Mexico called Matlacihuatl (also known as *Mujer enredadora*, the Entangling Woman). She has what looks like a mouth at the back of her neck, but it turns out to be a vagina. If a man seduces her, *he* becomes pregnant, not she. And finally—the case I want to expand on—in the American Southwest there is a female Coyote trickster.

Reading through hundreds of Native American trickster stories, Franchot Ballinger found about twenty that had a female Coyote, almost all of them from two Pueblo Indian groups, the Hopi and the Tewa. In these settings the female Coyote exists alongside the male Coyote, and the majority of the stories are still about the latter. Nonetheless, she does exist, and she differs from her male counterpart in several ways. She is as hungry as he, but she is not driven by his insatiable sexual desire. The male Coyote occasionally has children, but they are usually incidental to the tale. The female Coyote's children play a more significant role, as Ballinger explains:

> Sometimes [the story] opens with a reference to her hunting food or carrying water for her children. Sometimes when she decides that she wants something that is not rightfully hers (for example, pretty spots, a song, an improved scheme for hunting), she wants it (as least ostensibly) for her children. In other stories, her children are active participants in the events that demonstrate or reveal their Trickster mother's foolishness, lack of self-control, or unnatural desires. . . .

Finally, Ballinger found no stories in which the female Coyote is a culture hero. She is not known as a thief of fire, a teacher of dances, or an inventor of fish traps.*

As for why the female Coyote stories appear in these settings, Ballin-

---

* Here we should acknowledge how much the anomalies of collecting can affect the evidence. The absence of published stories does not mean there are no such stories. A collector of tales must suspect something exists and be interested in it before he or she is likely to find it, and even then, if the tales are sacred, they may be withheld, or withheld from certain people. When women anthropologists went to the Trobriand Islands, they heard many things that Malinowski never heard.

ger suggests that it is a consequence of the ways in which power and gender are connected in Hopi and Tewa life.

The most obvious fact we should note about stories with female Tricksters is that they are *all* from tribes that were or are yet matrilineal and/or matrilocal. In most, and maybe all, of the tribes I've named, women have traditionally had significant *de facto* or official authority and power. For example, among the western Tewa and the Hopi, women traditionally control the economic system and the home which is at the core of that system. Women own the houses, the fields, and the fruits of cultivation through their clans, with the clan mothers having final say in matters of distribution. Furthermore, strong ties among mothers-daughters-sisters create a solidarity of opinion which in turn carries much authority. Among the Tewa, it is the women who have traditionally cared for family ritual possessions. . . .

In short, we find this female trickster in the context of female power, a fact that, in the end, supports the idea that the canonical tricksters are male because they are part of patriarchal mythology.

At this point it could be asked why, if tricksters are disruptive and oppositional, they wouldn't be female *especially* in patriarchy. The answer might be a version of Sacvan Bercovitch's point (elaborated in the notes to Chapter 9) about how ideologies contain dissent. Any system does well to figure its problems in terms of its own assumptions. If power is masculine, best to have the opposition be masculine as well. In the history of Greek religion, there was once a cunning goddess named Metis. Zeus ate her. So much for the really threatening opposition. Later Zeus fathered Hermes and by one reading of the *Hymn*, as we saw, Hermes becomes Zeus' faithful-unfaithful servant, not an opponent. This manner of containing dissent does not itself belong to patriarchy; surely a matriarchy would do the same thing. Having a female Coyote in the Hopi tradition may be a good way to protect women's powers from fundamental change.

Be that as it may, having considered the female Coyote stories, it should be said that they are not so much a gateway into an ignored territory as the exception that proves the rule. Unless the problem lies with unrecorded tales, even among the Hopi and the Tewa, the male Coyote is the primary trickster. Furthermore, if in North America there are less than two dozen female trickster stories, then the Native American trickster is primarily male. Finally, these stories come from groups where significant forms of power belong to women, but here, too, they are an exception. There are many matrilineal Native American groups—the Tsimshian and the Tlingit on the North Pacific coast, for example—and in all of them the trickster is male. We do have two clear cases in which a female trickster is associated with matrilineal descent, but the latter is not a sufficient cause of the former. In North America, where significant forms of power belong to women, the trickster is still usually male.

Which brings us to the final line of inquiry into the roots of this gendering. Perhaps some part of this myth is about men, as the myths about Isis or Gaia or Demeter are about women. Perhaps the gendering of trickster derives from sex differences.

There are several ways in which this might be the case. First of all, at least before the technology of birth control, the consequences of the kind of on-the-road opportunistic sexuality that trickster displays were clearly more serious for the sex that must gestate, bear, and suckle the young (it makes sense that the Hopi mute trickster's sexuality to get the female figure). Second, these might be stories about non-procreative creativity and so get attached to the sex that doesn't give birth. It should be noted that trickster's fabled sex drive rarely leads to any offspring. Tricksters do not make new life, they rearrange what is already at hand.

Finally, this mythology may present a (non-Oedipal) narrative about how boy children separate from their mothers. John Stratton Hawley's remarks about Krishna and his mother set me to thinking in this line. Hawley argues that in the Hindu culture that gave rise to the butter-thief stories, the nurturing of boy children involves an intimacy between the sexes that tends to erase sexual polarity; this erasure produces a problem for boys later, when it comes time to claim their separate sexual identity. On the one hand, there is a strong bond between Krishna and his mother, Yasoda. "Her consistent desire is that Krishna remain in her world, remain a child," and to a large extent, he does. On the other hand, he wants to be free of her. As I pointed out earlier, the butter-thief stories enact the doubleness, the ambiguity, of this simultaneous dependence-independence. "Although his appetite is large enough to make him totally dependent on all the women surrounding him, he remains totally independent. At no moment does he become bound by obligation." Hawley at one point contrasts Krishna with Siva, a male deity who avoids dependence by containing himself, by self-restraint. Krishna, on the other hand, gets it both ways, which requires trickery. "Siva's method involves a radical curtailment of activity—ascetic stasis—whereas Krishna's is a product of his constant, lithe, even crooked movement. It is that irrepressible activity of both body and mind, rather than an inner concentration, that renders him invulnerable to the claims of the women who would domesticate him." Invulnerable, but not distanced. His trickery allows him to be connected/not-connected to the female sphere.

This part of the myth *does* seem to be about male psychology, then, about that charming male type who can be maddeningly present and not present to women.* It's a type not confined to India, too. Hawley's formulation is all the more striking because something similar appears in other contexts. Remember that one of Legba's early problems is to get his mother, Mawu, into the distance, and he does so by creating a separation that he then proceeds to bridge. The Signifying Monkey story, too, especially the part in which the Monkey plays the dozens, involves coming to a balanced or poised understanding about "mamma," one that simultaneously takes her seriously and doesn't take her seriously. Hermes may steal Apollo's cattle, but it is his mother Maia who first catches him at it and tries to discipline him. He refuses to display any need for her, but promises to take her with him when he becomes the Prince of Thieves. (One point of the "Interlude" between Parts I and II, by the way, was to describe a place where trickster stories touch me personally, one that lies exactly in this area of dependence on and independence from the maternal.)

In sum, there is at least one place where the trickster material is about issues particular to young men, and in that case there should be no mystery why the protagonist is male. Even in situations where women hold significant power, a story about men negotiating their connection to

---

* Trickster is a non-heroic male, by the way. If by "hero" we mean someone who muscles his way through the ranks of his enemies, whose stamina and grit overcome all odds, who perseveres and suffers and wins, then trickster is a non-heroic male. Nor is he that ascetic male, the one who develops the muscles of self-restraint, mastering himself instead of others. The lithe and small-bodied escape artist, he doesn't win the way the big guys do, but he doesn't suffer the way they do, either, and he enjoys pleasures they find too risky.

women will be a story with a male protagonist. That said, it isn't clear why the opposite is not the case as well: women may be the same sex as their mothers, but from all I've seen, mother-daughter relationships are just as fraught with ambiguity and with tensions over connecting and not-connecting. The fact that that tension has not found mythic elaboration in trickster tales probably brings us back to the earlier point that most of these stories belong to patriarchal religions.

APPENDIX III

MONKEY AND THE PEACHES
OF IMMORTALITY

MONKEY AND THE PEACHES
OF IMMORTALITY

In his meditations on non-violence, Mahatma Gandhi considers at various times the problem of killing agricultural pests. Is it right to destroy crop-eating insects? May the non-violent man shoot the deer that eat his corn? Monkeys are a particularly noisome problem in the orchards of India. It is almost impossible to keep a monkey from stealing fruit, and so Gandhi reluctantly makes an exception to his general principles and allows that in his opinion farmers may attack monkeys to protect their harvest.

The understanding that no monkey's hunger will ever respect the boundaries human beings erect around their groves undoubtedly lies behind the ancient Chinese trickster tale about the Monkey King who steals and eats the Peaches of Immortality, the sacred fruit that Taoist gods and goddesses must consume if they are to preserve their immortality. This story is told in its fullest detail in *The Journey to the West*, a huge—almost two thousand pages in English translation—sixteenth-century Chinese folk novel.* Loosely based on the actual seventh-century pil-

---

* Arthur Waley's translation, *Monkey*, is an abridged version of this classic. A full version

grimage of a monk who traveled from China to India (hence the journey "to the West") in search of Buddhist scriptures, the novel itself is a great mishmash of folktales, poems, and religious matter, mixing Buddhism, Confucianism, Taoism, and alchemical lore, without much consistent design. The main thing holding it together is the personality of the Monkey King, to whose story the early chapters are dedicated and who ends up accompanying the scripture pilgrim on his fourteen-year journey to India.

What interests me here is the theft-of-fruit episode. As background, one needs to know, first of all, that several hundred years after his birth the Monkey King "suddenly grew sad," having for some reason become conscious of his own mortality. "Though I am very happy at the moment, I am a little concerned about the future. . . . Old age and physical decay . . . will disclose the secret sovereignty of Yama, King of the Underworld." Thus begins his quest for immortality, in the course of which he gets into quite a bit of trouble, stealing weapons from dragons at the bottom of the ocean, and breaking into the underworld to erase his name from the Book of the Dead. Complaints about these disruptions eventually reach the ears of the Jade Emperor, who summons Monkey to heaven and, in hopes of getting him to settle down, gives him a series of jobs, the last of which is to guard the Garden of Immortal Peaches.

This sacred grove resembles the unmown meadows where Apollo's cattle grazed. There are no seasons in this orchard; the trees are always in blossom and always bearing fruit. When the peaches are half ripe their green skins seem encased in smoke, and when the sunlight strikes them they flash like cinnabar; when they are fully ripe they glow like faces reddened with wine. The best of these peaches ripen every nine thousand years, and whoever eats them will live as long as the Heaven and the Earth, the Sun and the Moon. Periodically the Lady Queen Mother who owns this peach orchard holds a Grand Festival of Immortal Peaches at the Palace of the Jasper Pool, and it is then that the immortals gather to consume the food that keeps old age and death at bay.

Now, it happened that one day as the Monkey King was inspecting the trees that were his charge, he noticed that over half of the best peaches had ripened. He longed to eat them, to know their secret taste. Dismissing his helpers in the orchard, he took off his cap, climbed into

---

has recently been translated by Anthony Yu. We do not know who wrote the original, but most likely it was Wu Ch'êng-ên, who died in 1582.

a tree, and feasted to his heart's—or, rather, his belly's—delight. This then became his habit; every few days he would feed in the grove, after which, making himself small, he would hide in the peach leaves and take a nap.

Soon thereafter the Lady Queen Mother decided to give one of her banquets. When her servants went to pick the peaches, they found the flowers sparse and the fruit scanty. Only a few peaches with hairy stems and green skins remained, for Monkey had eaten all the ripe ones. Unashamed, Monkey confronted the bewildered servants and thus discovered to his dismay that he had not even been invited to the banquet. In a fit of pique he headed for the Palace of the Jasper Pool, arriving early, as the meal was being prepared. Putting the attendants to sleep, he gorged himself on wine and delicacies (phoenix marrow, bear paws, that sort of thing).

Before long, he was quite drunk. Staggering home, he found himself standing in front of the Tushita Palace, the home of the immortal Lao Tzu. He broke in and found that great Taoist treasure, Lao Tzu's fabulous Elixir of Nine Turns, an alchemical distillation so powerful that those who eat it can become immortals in a weekend. Dumping the tablets from their gourds, Monkey ate them like fried beans.

When the Jade Emperor heard of all these transgressions, he ordered Monkey's arrest, the first of a long sequence of events in which the Taoist immortals tried to catch and confine the pest. They couldn't do it. They had to send for the Buddha himself, who pinned Monkey under a mountain and sealed the trap with a Buddhist prayer. Five hundred years later the Buddha released Monkey so that he (and three others—Pig, Horse, and a monk) might accompany the pilgrim Tripitaka on his journey to India in search of the Mahayana Buddhist scriptures.

A ll this action occupies only the first seven of the one hundred chapters that make up *The Journey to the West*. The remainder of the book is a picaresque road novel; the pilgrims suffer eighty ordeals before they get to India. In the last few pages they return to China with the scriptures, and the Buddha elevates them to Buddhahood. Monkey becomes "the Buddha Victorious in Strife." Only Pig remains in a lowly position. The Buddha makes him Janitor of the Altars, explaining that he's still talkative, lazy, and retains "an enormous appetite."

A word is in order about this Pig. After Monkey, he is the most fully developed of Tripitaka's helpers. He and Monkey usually operate together, a point worth noting because otherwise Monkey seems much less troubled by appetite than other tricksters. Monkey does eat the Immortal Peaches, drink the wine, gobble the Elixir, and so on, but once these appetite transgressions have set the plot in motion, and once the Buddha has suppressed him, he becomes a much more mental character. And yet that Pig is always with him, as if Belly and Mind had been differentiated but not detached. Moreover, to make the differentiation, whoever wrote this folk novel has participated in Monkey's suppression. As one critic puts it, the Monkey to be found in earlier Chinese narratives is "governed by carnal lusts which he transcended only under the fastidious hands of the sixteenth-century novelist." Even in *Journey*, Monkey is known as the Monkey of the Mind, a phrase that echoes an old Buddhist image for the restless mind (leaping from thought to thought like a monkey swinging from bough to bough) but also echoes the colloquial expression, "a mind like a monkey," which, at the time *Journey* was written, denoted someone possessed by sexual desire. In the novel we mostly find Pig carrying the problem of appetite, but he's never far from Monkey, and Monkey himself still bears traces of an older lusty beast whose hungers might lead Gandhi himself to buy a gun.

The story told in Chapter 4 about Loki and the Apples of Immortality clearly states that the Norse immortals "grow old and gray-haired" as a result of Loki's having lured Iddun and her apples from the garden. In the story at hand, this possible consequence is not as clearly announced, but if we look at the context of the telling, we will see the threat is there nonetheless. In China there is a tradition that Buddhism, Taoism, and Confucianism should live in harmony with one another, and sometimes *The Journey to the West* embodies that ecumenical spirit. Monkey himself says at one point: "Honor the unity of the Three Religions: revere the monks, revere also the Taoists, and take care to nurture the talented." But this remark comes right after Monkey has beaten to death two "perverse" Taoists and declared that "the true way is the gate of Zen," actions which more aptly reflect the theme of strife between Buddhism and Taoism that runs throughout the book.

Who, after all, does Monkey harass at the outset? He harasses Taoist immortals. The Peaches of Immortality belong to the Queen Mother of the West, and she turns out to be the highest goddess of popular Taoism. The other food that Monkey steals, the Elixir of Nine Turns, belongs to the Taoist patriarch Lao Tzu. The Taoist immortals, moreover, are powerless to control Monkey, and find they must call on the Buddha, who can not only bind the pest but who later releases him *in order to bring Buddhism to China.* Furthermore, once the pilgrimage to India begins, there are an inordinate number of anti-Taoist episodes.* Throughout the journey, Monkey's actions bear out his self-description early in the novel: "It's old Monkey who turned from wrong to right, who left the Taoist to follow the Buddhist."

The author of *Journey* draws on a long tradition of folklore about the Monkey King, and as he does so, he makes a few strategic changes in the content. I've already mentioned, for example, that the Monkey of *Journey* is not as lusty as his ancestors. More to the point here, *Journey* increases the Buddha's power. In earlier versions (particularly the Kō-zanji version from the thirteenth century), the divinity whose discipline can control Monkey is the Taoist Queen of the West. In replacing the Queen of the West with the Buddha, and in having the peach garden be so clearly a Taoist preserve, the author of *Journey* is like Snorri Sturluson undercutting the old Norse gods in favor of the Christian. Like the prose *Edda, Journey* reshapes an old story and in so doing enacts the disruptive theft that it describes. By the time the scripture pilgrims are beatified at the end of the book, the Taoist immortals *have* lost the Peaches of Immortality.

Such changes are not a matter of artistic whim; they reflect or embody shifting historical circumstances. What little plot there is in *Journey* records an actual cultural contingency, the coincidence of Chinese religions with a new dharma from the West. Once Monkey has traveled to India, the old Taoist truths seem a little less essential, a little more like local and contingent fictions. To put it in Buddhist terms, once Monkey has traveled, once he's eaten the peaches, what seemed substantial in the Taoist heaven suddenly appears to be marked by emptiness. Monkey's

---

* In Chapters 24–26, Monkey destroys a Taoist tree by stealing its fruit; in Chapter 33, the pilgrims defeat a demon who pretends to be a Taoist; in Chapter 37, they save a kingdom whose ruler has been murdered by a Taoist; in Chapters 44–46, they free a community of Buddhists who have been enslaved by evil Taoists; and so on and so on.

spiritual name in the novel is Wu-K'ung, which means Awake-to-Vacuity or Aware-of-Emptiness and refers to the Buddhist party line that all categories of thought will, if observed carefully, reveal themselves to be fictions, and dissolve. (Thus, the more "the self" is scrutinized in meditation, the less substantial it becomes: the self is empty.) When Awake-to-Vacuity invades the garden and eats the peaches, the forms of institutional Taoism lose their substance. Not that many institutions, cultures, or selves invite such an invasion. Most go to great lengths to preserve their boundaries from all contingency, whereupon, if there is to be a change, a hungry thief must sneak in from the shadows to get things going.

The theft of the peaches or the apples of immortality is a portable motif. It always speaks of change, but it speaks of a different change each time it is told. The evidence indicates that in sixteenth-century China it reflected some shifting of attention from Taoism to Buddhism, but it surely meant something different in the thirteenth century, and in more recent times, when it traveled to America, it signified something else again. For many years the Foreign Languages Press in Beijing exported to Chinese-American children a thirty-four-volume series of comic books based quite faithfully on *Journey*, and in 1989 one reader who knew that series well, Maxine Hong Kingston, published *Tripmaster Monkey*, a novel whose hero, Wittman Ah Sing, imagines himself to be "the present-day U.S.A. incarnation of the King of the Monkeys."

Kingston's hero is a bookish Berkeley graduate who wants to be a playwright and wants to fall in love. Wittman's story is, if anything, more episodic than *Journey*. He gets a job in a toy store, then loses it (having set up a monkey toy as if it were copulating with a Barbie Doll); he makes the obligatory sixties trip to the unemployment office; he attends an endless sixties party (music, drugs, strobe lights); he has a romance with a white girl named Taña; and toward the end, at the Benevolent Society in Chinatown, he stages the nearly endless play that he has written.

Wittman is obsessed with race. Or perhaps "obsessed" isn't the right word: American racism is all around him and he finds he is unable to not notice it. What, he wonders, do they call "Mongoloid" babies in Mongolia? What do they call "Siamese" twins in Siam? How can they market a Jade East aftershave bottle with a Buddha whose head screws off? How can someone as hip as Jack Kerouac write of "the twinkling little Chinese" without apparent self-consciousness? Why can a comedian always count on a laugh with a joke that ends "The Chinaman don't dig that shit either"? Kingston's book is larded with hundreds of such details, the subliminal background buzz by which Americans absorb and maintain the "truth" about race. Here let us remember Nietzsche's remark, that the truth is "a mobile army of metaphors, metonyms, [and] anthropomorphisms . . . which . . . after long use seem solid, canonical, and binding. . . . Truths are illusions about which it has been forgotten that they *are* illusions." There are those for whom the American thousand-knotted web of racial signifiers is more or less invisible, just part of the scenery, part of the way things are. These are the present-day U.S.A. party-givers, the American peach-eating immortals, and when they tell the joke that ends "The Chinaman don't dig that shit either," Wittman thinks to himself: "The King of the Monkeys hereby announces: I'm crashing parties wherever these jokes are told. . . ." After all, Monkey "is Aware of Emptiness. . . . He'll eat everything on the buffet. He'll overturn tables. He'll piss in the wine."

It isn't just the jokes at the party that the new Monkey King is after, either. The novel rings another change on the old motif: for Wittman, to sleep with Taña is to steal the American Peaches. One of the protocols of American racism is the injunction against miscegenation, for if the races can mix, how can they be essentially different? In fact, if the races mix, the whole idea of "race" may turn out to be empty. Therefore, around the garden where racism grows its sacred fruits the rule against cross-race love affairs has been erected. Wittman, at least, is hyperconscious of that prohibition where Taña is concerned. When he and Taña go to her apartment for the first time, they do not make love; she falls asleep and Wittman falls into one of his Monkey fantasies: "The curtain opens . . . the great killer ape in chains sees the audience. . . . The chains snap. . . . Swooping Fay Wray up in his mighty arm, he and she swing across the ceiling of the San Francisco Opera House. . . . The ape is loose upon America." The exaggerated bravado tells us how unsure of himself Wittman is. Attracted to Taña, he feels like the toy monkey with the Barbie Doll, and in his imagination the proud Chinese King Monkey becomes the hunted King Kong, American movie outlaw beast. We are in a modern novel, not an old Chinese legend; what Wittman wants comes to him slowly and imperfectly. Much as he would like to, he cannot quickly slip the illusions of race. (For one thing, they are not only all around him, they're *in* him: when first kissing Taña, he blurts out, "Are you a loose white girl?")

And yet, imperfect as their realization is, Wittman still preserves the ancient goals: to crash the party, to steal the peaches. Monkey's modern U.S.A. incarnation wants the ideal "America" to get a taste of what's going down in *his* time zone. If the movies cast a "pure American," Wittman wants a shot at the part. He doesn't want to be an excluded and resentful accidental. His goal is not to be American on America's terms, however, but to change the terms themselves. He wants to join the party and be himself, which means the party has to change, not the guest. He hopes, for example, to write a play unlike any previous American play. In traditional Chinese theater, a play did not begin and end in one evening. "I'm going to bring back to theater the long and continuous play that goes on for a week without repeating itself," Wittman declares, "because life is long and continuous. . . ." If Wittman has his way, a new and novel American drama will soon appear. In this Monkey's hands, American art will have a whole new sense of timing.

Wittman quotes James Baldwin at one point: "People are trapped in history and history is trapped in them . . . and hence all Black men have toward all white men an attitude which is designed, really, either to rob the white man of the jewel of his naïveté, or else to make it cost him dear." For Baldwin, the "white man" (or anyone unconscious of history and human artifice) takes the local and contingent to be universal and essential, "solid, canonical, and binding" (to recall Nietzsche's language from the end of Part I). Whosoever hopes to loosen that "binding" and reshape the essences will have to "steal the jewel of naïveté," which means to engage in transgressions sufficiently mind-boggling that illusion must resurface from the unconscious, where it lies forgotten. Thus does theft promise to change the mind, contingency to raise consciousness. If Monkey/Wittman could only get the peaches and be himself at the party, if he could love Taña and write an American play with Chinese roots, if the accidental could become part of the ideal, then America would "rise green again," a New World made new.

NOTES

Introduction

3:    "Every generation": Radin, p. 168.

3:    "We interpret": Kermode, p. 145.

3:    There are over a dozen versions of the eye-juggler story, ranging from the North Pacific to the Northeast Woodlands to South America. See Thompson, p. 299. I used the Cheyenne version to refresh my memory; see Kroeber, p. 168 (reprinted in Thompson, p. 63).

5:    "I am a Saturn who dreams": Italo Calvino, *Six Memos for the Next Millennium* (Cambridge, Mass.: Harvard University Press, 1988), p. 52.

6:    "he of the stone heap": See Jacqueline Chittenden, "The Master of Animals," *Hesperia* XVI (1947): 89–114, especially pp. 94ff.

7n: Trickster-Transformer-Culture Hero: Ricketts, "The Structure and Religious Significance. . . ."

7n: an invention of nineteenth-century anthropology: the nineteenth-century ethnologist Daniel Brinton is commonly given credit for introducing the term "trickster" in his book *The Myths of the New World*. Brinton's book went through three editions; in none of them have I found the word "trickster," though his description of the Algonquin Manabozho fits the pattern (Brinton, 1st ed., 1868, p. 162). I myself believe Franz Boas's 1898 introduction to James Teit's *Traditions of the Thompson River Indians* is where the term first appears in anthropology (Boas, "Introduction," p. 4).

7n: Hermes is called *mechaniôta*: *Hymn to Hermes*, line 436.

7n: Legba is called *Aflakete*: Pelton, pp. 80, 87.

7n: *Wakdjunkaga* means "the tricky one": Radin, p. 132.

7:    Trickster solving a problem he himself created: See Pelton, p. 78.

8:    female Coyote: See Ballinger. For more detail, see Appendix on Gender.

8:    For other essays defining "trickster," see Douglas Hill; Hynes, "Mapping the Characteristics of Mythic Tricksters"; Turner, "Myth and Symbol," pp. 580–81; and Sullivan et al.

9:    "The New People will not know anything": Lopez, p. 3. The story is an Okanagon creation myth.

9n: The list of figures who have been called trickster is vast. This book focuses on a small number of representative cases. From Europe, the Norse Loki and the Greek Hermes (with a bow to Prometheus, thief of fire, and several bows to

Odysseus); from Native American myth, Coyote, Raven, and the Winnebago trickster (Wakdjunkaga); from India, Krishna—or rather, the non-Sanskritic Krishna who as a baby and adolescent is a thief of butter and a thief of hearts; from West Africa, Eshu and Legba (both of whom come to the American continents in the slave trade); and finally, the Monkey King from China. African-American tricksters include Brer Rabbit and the Signifying Monkey. Others are touched on in passing—the Japanese Susa-nö-o, for example, and Mercury, the Roman descendant of Hermes, who later becomes Mercurius in alchemical lore.

A short list of Native American tricksters, would include: for the Northeast Algonquins, Glooscap; for the Iroquois, Flint and Sapling; for the Central Woodlands, Manabozho or Wiskajak; on the Plains, the Plateau, and in California, Coyote; in the North Pacific, Mink and Bluejay in addition to Raven. (See Thompson, p. 294.) The trickster Rabbit is found in the Southeast; his stories intermingle with the African-American Brer Rabbit stories, but the latter seem to have originated in Africa, not America (see Alan Dudes's essay, "African Tales Among the North American Indians"). Other well-known tricksters include Ananse in West Africa (see Pelton); Maui on the Pacific Islands (see Luomala); and Till Eulenspiegel in Europe (see Oppenheimer). For Irish tricksters, see Harrison and Doan. For South Africa, see Basso and Sullivan.

A full list of tricksters from around the world would be virtually endless. If trickster is the boundary-crossing figure, then there will be some sort of representative wherever humans invent boundaries, which is to say, everywhere. For those hoping for an even longer list, a good place to begin is the entry under "trickster" in *The Encyclopedia of Religion* (N.Y.: Macmillan, 1987). See also Ricketts's 1964 thesis on North American figures, and *Mythical Trickster Figures*, edited by Hynes and Doty.

My list should not close without my noting that I count Prometheus as a trickster, but with two reservations. First of all, he and his brother Epimetheus have been differentiated (they are opposites, Prometheus having "foresight" and Epimetheus "after-sight"). In the history of religion it is often the case that an early, ambivalent, and undifferentiated character splits over time into two figures, one good and one bad, one wise and one foolish, one high and one low. But trickster resists such distinctions. To separate the strands is to move away from this mythology.

We could treat Prometheus as a trickster if we always joined him with his brother, and in the central Promethean story that is what happens: *together* the two brothers are responsible for the good and the evil that follow the theft of fire. But, again, there *are* two of them, and that moment is really the only time we see them together. Prometheus is more commonly imagined working alone; his brother has no role, for example, in Aeschylus' play *Prometheus Bound*.

Which brings me to the second reason I call Prometheus a quasi-trickster:

he suffers too much! Zeus binds him to a rock and sets an eagle to work eating his liver for all eternity. The story ends with its hero in inexorable pain. Trickster, by contrast, is the consummate survivor, always slippery, always able to invert a situation and wiggle free, always willing to abandon a project or an ego position if the danger gets too high. Brer Rabbit appeals to us because he never gets caught. Tricksters sometimes suffer, but that is never the end of it; the end is levity and speed. Prometheus is too serious.

10n: Confusion of Eshu and the Devil: Herskovits, *Journal of American Folklore*, p. 455n; Frobenius I, p. 229; Ogundipe I, pp. 4, 177.

10n: Confusion of Legba and Satan: Herskovits and Herskovits, *Dahomean Narrative*, p. 151; Pelton, p. 87.

10n: Confusion of Winnebago trickster and the devil: Radin, p. 112.

10n: "We, the Winnebago, are the birds": Radin, p. 149; see also Radin, pp. 111–12, 147–51.

10: "Trickster is at one and the same time": Radin, p. xxiii.

10: On trickster and moral ambiguity, see Diamond.

11: "What is a god?": Ezra Pound, *Selected Prose 1909–1965* (N.Y.: New Directions, 1973), p. 47.

11: On the confidence man as a covert American hero, see Lindberg especially, but also Halttunen and Wadlington.

12: "White man was going along": Kroeber, p. 165.

12: On native people thinking of Europeans as tricksters: The Cheyenne calling Coyote "white man" is one example; there is another from West Africa, where a storyteller once remarked to Melville Herskovits that Eshu had shared his cunning more with the white man than with the black. See Herskovits, *Journal of American Folklore*, p. 455n.

12: On Navajo storytelling, healing, and witchcraft, see Toelken, "Life and Death in the Navajo Coyote Tales."

14: "Archetypes, like taxes": Ellison, *Shadow and Act*, pp. 46, 57.

1: Slipping the Trap of Appetite

17: "The whitebait": Basho in Blyth, *Haiku* I, p. 21.

The Bait Thief

17: "taught the rest of us": Aristotle, *Poetics* 1460.

17: Autolycus: *Odyssey* XIX:432.

18: Loki and the fish net: Young, pp. 84–85.

18: the first fish weir: Lopez, p. 73.

18: Raven made the first fishhook: Ricketts, "The Structure and Religious Significance . . . ," p. 139.

18:     he taught the spider: Ricketts, "The Structure and Religious Significance . . . ,"
        p. 142.

18:     *dólos:* See Norman O. Brown, *Hermes the Thief,* pp. 21–23, and Detienne, *Cunning*
        Intelligence, pp. 27–28. "The oldest known use" appears in one of Homer's offhand
        similes: "as a fisherman on a jutting rock . . . casts in his bait [*dólos*] as a snare
        to the little fishes, just so. . . ." (*Odyssey* XII:252).

18:     "Coyote was going along by a big river": Lopez, p. 73.

19:     Coyote traps two buffalo: Lopez, pp. 127–28.

19:     "Rabbit came to a field of watermelons": Lopez, p. 113.

20:     intelligence of meat-eaters and herbivores: Jerison, p. 313.

21:     "it is difficult to escape the conclusion": Leydet, p. 65; see also Leydet pp. 95,
        108ff, 126–27, 147; and Snyder, p. 68.

21:     "[Raven] came to a place": Swanton, p. 8; see also Thompson, p. 306.

21:     "cleverer than all others": Callaway, p. 3.

22:     A kind of jinx: Callaway, p. 4 and 4n.

22:     "I have important work for you": Lopez, p. 3.

Eating the Organs of Appetite

23:     "What god requires a sacrifice": Walker, *Nigerian Folk Tales,* p. 4.

23:     "Raven Becomes Voracious": Retold from the version in Boas, "Tsimshian My-
        thology," pp. 58–60.

26:     "the trickster with the scaly legs": Nelson, p. 279.

27:     entrails of the kill: Ricketts, "The Structure and Religious Significance . . . ,"
        p. 163.

28:     "Never kill this cow, Coyote": Lopez, p. 41.

29:     trickster's penis and intestines: Radin, p. 142.

29:     these bizarre organs are reduced: Radin, p. 59.

29:     "Now, you, my younger brother": Radin, p. 16.

29:     "Alas! Alas!": Radin, pp. 17–18.

30n: "forerunner of the savior": Jung in Radin, p. 203.

30:     trouble with it lifting his blanket: Radin, pp. 18–19.

30:     "So he took out his penis": Radin, pp. 38–39.

31n: the vagina-dentata motif: See, for example, Lopez, pp. 53ff.

31:     edible plants: for example, Lopez, p. 89.

32:     "His mind wandered": *Hymn to Hermes,* lines 62–64.

32:     "You're going to be a great nuisance": *Hymn to Hermes,* lines 286–88.

32:     "He cut up the richly marbled flesh": *Hymn to Hermes,* lines 120–41.

33:     an ordinary Greek sacrifice: In *Homo Necans,* Walter Burkert offers a descrip-
        tion of "an ordinary Greek sacrifice" (pp. 3–7, 12). He says, among other things,
        that the internal organs of the sacrificial animal "are quickly roasted in the fire
        from the altar and eaten at once. Thus the inner circle of active participants is

brought together in a communal meal. . . ." See also Camp, *The Athenian Agora*, p. 97.

33:    "I'm ready to do whatever I must": *Hymn to Hermes*, lines 166–72.

34:    *thymos*: Onians, pp. 13–14.

Meat Sacrifice

34n: "He establishes the first sacrifice": Vernant in Detienne, *Cuisine of Sacrifice*, p. 165.

34n: "ordained the ritual of sacrifice": Allen et al., *The Homeric Hymns*, p. 268.

34n: "regarded as the prototype": Otto, *The Homeric Gods*, p. 122.

34n: "He invents fire, fire-sticks, and sacrifice": Burkert, *Greek Religion*, p. 157.

34:    For my telling of the Prometheus story I use Hesiod's *Theogony*, lines 507–616, and *Works and Days*, lines 27–105, 112–15. Also Detienne, *Cuisine of Sacrifice*, pp. 24, 43, 253; Graves, pp. 144–45; Norman O. Brown, *Hermes the Thief*, p. 58; and Aeschylus' *Prometheus Bound*.

35:    Greeks did not eat the belly: Detienne, *Cunning Intelligence*, p. 58.

35:    "Zeus, whose wisdom is everlasting": Hesiod, *Theogony*, lines 550ff. (See *Hesiod, The Homeric Hymns and Homerica*, p. 19.)

35:    the bones stand for immortality: Detienne, *Cuisine of Sacrifice*, pp. 40–41.

36:    "Is there nothing more doglike": *Odyssey* VII:216–21.

36:    they become meat sacks: Detienne, *Cuisine of Sacrifice*, pp. 60–61.

36:    sacrifice is ritual apportionment: Detienne, *Cuisine of Sacrifice*, pp. 10, 13, 99, 102–5; see also Nagy, *Greek Mythology and Poetics*, pp. 269–75.

2: "That's My Way, Coyote . . ."

The Bungling Host

39:    "Today he toured the east": *Journey to the West* I, p. 134.

39:    "As he continued his aimless wandering": Radin, p. 21.

40:    "Coyote began to cry": Lopez, pp. 135–36. This is a Gros Ventre version of the story. The Gros Ventre tribes originated in the Eastern Woodlands; since the early nineteenth century, their homeland has been northern Montana.

40:    "As he did not . . . know": Radin, p. 11.

40:    "again he wandered aimlessly": Radin, p. 13.

40:    "He started to run": Radin, p. 27.

41:    "One time there was no food at Coyote's lodge": Lopez, pp. 30–32; see also Thompson, p. 72. The "Bungling Host" story is discussed in detail by Franz Boas in "Tsimshian Mythology," pp. 694–702. The story appears in several types, each of which—like the trees and the fish—has a definite area of distribution. Ricketts offers a variant reading that I discuss in Chapter 12.

43:    "stupider than the animals": Jung in Radin, p. 203.

43:    "a characteristic of all species": Cited in Bright, p. 55.

44:    "big gatherings of coyotes are seldom seen": Leydet, p. 71.
45:    The Maidu creation myth: Thompson, p. 27.

Hallmarks of Trickster's Mind
46:    "opportunity": Onians, pp. 343–48.
46:    Raven steals daylight: Boas, "Tsimshian Mythology," pp. 60–62; reprinted in Thompson, pp. 22–24.
48:    the Zulu trickster Thlókunyana: Callaway, pp. 24–27.
48:    Coyote lures his enemy into a tunnel: Radin, pp. 30–31; also Lopez, pp. 34–35.
48:    The Greeks thought the fox the epitome of animal cunning: Detienne, *Cunning Intelligence*, p. 35.
49:    Hermes resorts to several clever ruses to hide his theft: *Hymn to Hermes*, lines 73–86, 139–41, 348–60.
50:    "And when the Great Archer made out the footprints": *Hymn to Hermes*, lines 217–26.
51:    *Trypanosoma brucei: New York Times*, March 19, 1991.
52:    The wily octopus skin: Detienne, *Cunning Intelligence*, pp. 38ff.
52:    "Present a different aspect of yourself": Theognis cited in Detienne, *Cunning Intelligence*, p. 39.
52:    Hermes is the polytropic child: *Hymn to Hermes*, line 14.
52n: "Mercurius, following the tradition of Hermes": Jung, *Alchemical Studies*, p. 217.
52:    "Resorting to Tissaphernes": *Plutarch's Lives*, Bernadotte Perrin, trans., Loeb Classical Library (Cambridge, Mass.: Harvard University Press, 1914), pp. 67–69.
53:    "My skin did that": Nagy, *Greek Mythology and Poetics*, pp. 264–65.
53:    who is the real Odysseus?: *Odyssey* XII:256–86.
54:    "removes himself from his 'real' self": Pucci, p. 16.
54:    giving away gold pieces: Melville, p. 156.

3: The First Lie

A Sign of Youthful Theft
55:    "Trickster happened to look in the water": Radin, p. 28.
56:    "You cannot possibly miss the place": Radin, p. 29.
56:    "a red sky is the stereotype symbol for death": Radin, p. 57.
58:    "Then glorious Hermes longed to eat the sacrificial meat": *Hymn to Hermes*, lines 130–35.
58:    Apollo never does notice the token: We cannot actually be sure what happens in the scene in which Apollo might notice the meat, because lines from the *Hymn* are missing at that point. For debate over how to fill in the missing lines, see Allen, Halliday, and Sikes, pp. 332–33, and Norman O. Brown, pp. 145–46.

59: *Nóos* and *sêma* go together: Nagy, *Greek Mythology and Poetics*, pp. 202–22.

60: "Semiotics is concerned with": Eco, p. 7. Emphasis modified.

60: "takes these cows from the divine world": Detienne, *Cuisine of Sacrifice*, p. 165. Note that something similar can be said about the cattle in the Coyote story told earlier. Buffalo Bull has an immortal herd; Coyote creates the duality between those cows and cows who are butchered for meat.

61: "Why should we be the only gods": *Hymn to Hermes*, lines 167–72.

"Mere Bellies"

63: "The woman next to me": Tobias Wolff, *In the Garden of the North American Martyrs* (N.Y.: Ecco Press, 1981), p. 175.

64: Odysseus is given a task: *Odyssey* XI:126ff.

64: Odysseus and the oar: Nagy, *Greek Mythology*, pp. 212ff.

66: "Shepherds living in the fields": Hesiod, *Theogony*, lines 26–28; see also Nagy, *Greek Mythology*, p. 45.

66: Odysseus says that his belly makes him forget his story: *Odyssey* VII:215–21.

66: "If you want me to speak the truth": See Nagy, *Greek Mythology*, pp. 44–45.

66: "unwilling": *Odyssey* XIV:125; see Nagy, *Greek Mythology*, p. 45.

66: "Wandering men tell lies for a night's lodging": *Odyssey* XIV:251.

66: "Your lord is now at hand": *Odyssey* XIV:252.

67: "Why must you lie?": *Odyssey* XIV:119–359.

67: Cretans were understood to be "lazy bellies": See Detienne, *Cuisine of Sacrifice*, p. 59.

67: The history of archaic Greece: Nagy, *Greek Mythology*, pp. 43–46.

67: "surge of intercommunication": Nagy, *Greek Mythology*, p. 43.

67: the poet will be shifty, too: See Nagy, *Greek Mythology*, p. 43.

67: "to Hellenes at large": Nagy, *Greek Mythology*, pp. 42–43. Emphasis added.

68: He even lies to his wife: *Odyssey* XIX:203; see Nagy, *Greek Mythology*, p. 44.

68: Hesiod . . . a model of the later poet: Nagy, *Greek Mythology*, p. 42.

68: "can be taken as a manifesto of pan-Hellenic poetry": Nagy, *Greek Mythology*, p. 45.

68: "the many local theogonies": Nagy, *Greek Mythology*, p. 46.

68: The many North American names for trickster: Thompson, pp. xxi, 294.

68: Raven makes his parents-in-law young again: Ricketts, "The Structure and Religious Significance . . . ," p. 90.

68: In an Ingalik tale: Ricketts, "The Structure and Religious Significance . . . ," pp. 100–1.

68: upper Yukon reshaped coastal Raven stories: Ricketts, "The Structure and Religious Significance . . . ," p. 95.

69: Smart-Beaver: Ricketts, "The Structure and Religious Significance . . . ," p. 95.

69: "that bypasses the Promethean sacrifice": Detienne, *Cuisine of Sacrifice*, p. 61.

"Beautiful Untrue Things"

70:     "The truest poetry": Shakespeare, *As You Like It* II: iii, line 18.

70:     "Why are you yelling like a bully, Apollo?": *Hymn to Hermes*, lines 261–77.

71:     "Far-working Apollo laughed": *Hymn to Hermes*, line 282.

71:     Krishna's lies: See Hawley, especially *Parabola*, p. 10; *Krishna, the Butter Thief*, p. 9; and "Thief of Butter, Thief of Love," passim.

72:     "by means of a lie that is really a truth": Pelton, p. 79.

72:     "Far away in Crete": *Odyssey* XIII:256–86.

73:     "bright Apollo laugh[s] for joy": *Hymn to Hermes*, lines 416–23.

73:     "the story of the gods": *Hymn to Hermes*, lines 427–28.

73:     "placed his shining whip in Hermes' hand": *Hymn to Hermes*, lines 497–98.

73:     "tend . . . the ranging, twisted-horn cattle": *Hymn to Hermes*, line 567.

75:     language is not a medium: I am thinking here of Richard Rorty's discussion of Donald Davidson's philosophy of language. See Rorty, pp. 9–11, 13–20.

75:     "I should imagine that the name Hermes": Plato, *Cratylus* 407–8 (see, for example, Jowett, trans., *The Dialogues of Plato* I, p. 197).

76:     Sometimes he creates multiple languages: In medieval lore, Mercurius is said to have revealed the secret of hieroglyphics and to have invented the "inner writing" that is memory (see Jung, *Alchemical Studies*, p. 225; Frances Yates, *The Art of Memory* [Chicago: University of Chicago Press, 1966], p. 268). Legba is a master of the inner language of self-knowing (Pelton, p. 113). Manabozho, trickster of the American woodlands, is said to have invented writing with pictures (Hynes and Doty, p. 228). Both Coyote and Raven have been credited with creating the multiplicity of languages that replaced the original single speech (see Leydet, p. 78, and Ricketts, "The Structure," p. 140).

76:     "brought words over": Norman, p. 403.

76:     some shameless double-dealer is needed: Robert Pelton says, for example, that the West African trickster, Ananse, has "a duplicity that restarts the processes of speech" when they have for some reason failed (Pelton, p. 50).

77:     "a mobile army of metaphors": Nietzsche, p. 250.

78:     Hermes puts them into a stupor: See Hesiod, *The Homeric Hymns and Homerica*, pp. 264–65.

78:     "Homer more than any other": Aristotle, *Poetics* 1460a.

79:     "lie like the truth": Paul Zweig, *Walt Whitman: The Making of the Poet* (N.Y.: Basic Books, 1984), p. 255.

79:     "fiction is a dignified form of lies": Cited by the Chinese novelist Qin Mu in the PEN *Newsletter* #56, p. 3.

79:     truth is saved by a lie: Dostoevsky, *The Diary of a Writer II*, pp. 835–38 (but especially p. 838).

79:     "When we write novels": Mario Vargas Llosa, *Washington Post*, April 25, 1987, p. B5.

79: "Fiction here is likely": Virginia Woolf, *A Room of One's Own* (N.Y.: Harcourt, Brace & World, 1957), p. 4.

79: "take[s] advantage of the novel's capacity": Ralph Ellison, *Invisible Man*, pp. xxvi–xxvii.

79: "the right of the poet to invent": Milosz, p. 125.

79: "Art is a lie": Picasso, p. 21.

79: "The telling of beautiful untrue things": Wilde, p. 37.

79: "dominate us, and defy skepticism": Wilde, p. 11.

79: "simply to charm, to delight": Wilde, p. 19.

80: Burying the sailor's oar in a heap of earth: Nagy, *Greek Mythology*, p. 214.

80: "Rabbit jumped": A typical ending to a Coyote story. See, for example, Lopez, pp. 32, 126, 143.

Interlude: The Land of the Dead

Coyote's Impulse

83: Coyote and the Shadow People: Phinney, pp. 283–85. The story is reprinted in Ramsey, pp. 33–37.

An Old Story

87: "The Muses sing": *Homeric Hymn to Pythian Apollo*, lines 191–93. See, for example, *Hesiod, The Homeric Hymns and Homerica*, p. 339.

4: An Attack of Accidents

95: "The gods' carefree life": Govinda, in N. O. Brown, *Love's Body*, pp. 184–85.

96: On the *Edda*s, see Dronke, pp. xi–xiii; Young, p. 8; Faulkes, pp. xiv, 13.

96: Loki and the Apples of Immortality: Young, pp. 97–99. My source for the story of Idunn and the apples is Young's translation, but Young omits an important detail at the end (Loki's bawdy antics make the grieving daughter of the dead giant laugh), so see also Brodeur, pp. 91–92, or Faulkes, pp. 59–61. Another source is the skald Thiodolf's poem *Haustlöng* (see Page, p. 24). The poem "Skírnismál" also mentions the apples, calling them "apples of everlasting youth" (see Hollander, p. 69).

96: "At the time agreed on": Young, p. 98.

96: changing himself into a falcon: Young, pp. 97–99.

97: it is by a giantess that he fathers his children: Young, pp. 55–56.

97: In these and other ways: When giants threaten Asgard, it is the unsleeping Heimdall who watches lest they breach the Bifrost Bridge, and we know that Loki is in some sense Heimdall's opposite, for it is prophesied that at the end of time these two will kill each other. See Young, p. 88.

98: "George Mantor had an iris garden": Cage, *Silence*, p. 263.

99:    "When I was a little girl": Leslie Marmon Silko and James Wright, *The Delicacy and Strength of Lace* (St. Paul, Minn.: Graywolf Press, 1986), p. 76.

99:    "In 1978, at the U.S. Naval Observatory": Roberts, pp. 121–22.

101:   "so fair of face and bright": Young, p. 51.

101:   the death of Baldr: Young, pp. 80–81; also Faulkes, pp. 48–49. Walter Burkert thinks that the Greek story of Hermes killing Argus is a parallel to the Norse story of Loki killing Baldr. See *Homo Necans*, pp. 164–65.

102:   earthquakes: Hollander, p. 103.

102:   On the idea that Ragnarök always follows the binding of Loki (implying that the latter is the cause of the former), see, for example, the end of "Baldr's Dreams," which says that Baldr won't return "until Loki is loose from his bonds / and the day will come of the doom of the gods" (Hollander, p. 119). The same sequence is in the *Voluspá* (Hollander, pp. 6–9).

102n: *Ragnarök*: Page, pp. 56, 63.

102:   First will come three terrible winters: Young, pp. 87, 89.

102:   "I see the Earth rise from the deep": The lines from the *Voluspá* are my own version. For others, see Hollander, p. 12, or Vigfusson and Powell I, pp. 200–1. Snorri also cites the lines; see Young, p. 91.

103:   A learned and cosmopolitan man: Faulkes, p. xiii.

103:   the local name for Ulysses: Faulkes, p. 58.

104:   "makes it clear that": Faulkes, p. xiv.

104:   "father of lies": Young, p. 55.

104n: whoever wrote this poem does not believe: See Hollander, p. 90; see also Polomé and Schröder.

105:   "decided to seek protection for Baldr": Young, p. 80.

106:   "requires . . . the most delicate balance": Nussbaum, pp. 81, 89. Nussbaum takes the phrase "the razor's edge of luck" from Sophocles' *Antigone*, line 996.

107:   "it is a characteristic": Dumézil, *Gods*, p. 59; see Young, p. 51.

107:   Baldr embodies the will whose energy is spent: Dumézil, *Gods*, pp. 58ff.

5: The God of the Crossroads

108:   "Necessity knows no magic formulae": Kundera, p. 49.

The Palm-Nut Oracle

108:   "when an inner situation": Jung, in "Rachel V." (pseudonym), *Family Secrets* (N.Y.: Harper and Row, 1986), p. xiii.

109:   "the inner head": Abimbola, p. 216.

109:   The Yoruba believe: Bascom, pp. 115–16; Ogundipe I, p. 232.

109:   "a fixed day": Bascom, pp. 116, 62, and see pp. 115–16; Ogundipe I, pp. 232–34.

110:    Eshu: Eshu came to the New World in the slave trade and appears as Exú in
        Brazil, Echu-Elegua in Cuba, Papa Legba in Haiti, and Papa La Bas in the United
        States. See Frobenius I, p. 228; Wescott, p. 336n; and Gates, *The Signifying
        Monkey*, p. 5. For a fine account of some of Eshu's transformations, see Cosentino.
        Both Eshu and Ifa have other names. Ifa is also called Orunmila. Eshu is
        sometimes spelled Esu, Edshu, or Edju. He is more formally called Eshu-Elegba,
        and also Elégbara (Legba, from nearby Benin, is a related but distinct figure). I
        have unified the spelling and names throughout my account.

110:    "A tree on a mountain": *I Ching*, p. 204.

110:    Baldr is the essence of the Good: Young, p. 51.

111:    one of the gods is being chased by death: Ogundipe II, pp. 131–32.

111:    "Once upon a time the sixteen gods were very hungry": Frobenius I, pp. 229–
        32.
                There are two stories in Ogundipe's collection that give other versions of
        Eshu and the origins of sacrifice. In one of them (II, pp. 104ff), human beings
        turn greedy and cruel and the gods withdraw to heaven. This is a tale of a golden
        age ("there was no death") and its loss ("Then everything became worse"). Eshu
        then makes things worse again, until the people come to him for help, whereupon
        he institutes sacrifice: "In order to be at one with every living thing, [the people]
        must sacrifice. That is why men sacrifice today. Sacrificial food is placed at the
        crossroads where Eshu lived; birds and beasts partake of this food, in keeping
        with Eshu's dictum." Ogundipe II, p. 106; see also II, pp. 93ff.

112n: "extremely difficult to reconstruct": Gates, *Signifying Monkey*, p. 15.

113:    "the monkeys gave": Frobenius I, p. 230.

114:    "This has all happened before": Bascom, pp. 168–71.

115:    "the enforcer of sacrifice": Ogundipe I, p. 120.

116:    "Leather-Clothed Troublemaker": Ogundipe I, p. 138.

116:    "Through the use of divining seeds": Courlander, pp. 59–60.

116:    Ifa once staged his own mock funeral: Courlander, pp. 60–63.

116:    mothers nevertheless pray to Eshu: Ogundipe II, p. 18.

116:    "An individual cannot": Bascom, p. 118.

116:    "destiny is not fixed": Bascom, p. 115.

117:    "the Yoruba believe in destiny": Ogundipe I, pp. 232–33.

117n: "What is in store for a man": Herskovits, *Dahomey* II, p. 222.

117n: "Man is not a slave": Pelton, pp. 117–18.

117:    "the Yoruba have a singularly prescriptive culture": Wescott, p. 345.

118:    Tricksters are masters of reversal: Wescott, pp. 338, 346; Bascom, p. 159.

Pure Chance

118:    two kinds of chance: Monod, pp. 113–17.

119:    "in roulette the uncertainty": Monod, p. 113.

119:   "Chance is obviously the essential": Monod, p. 114.

119:   the coincidence of unrelated causes: Aristotle, *Physics* (II:iv–vi), pp. 138–39.

120:   "*absolute* newness": Monod, p. 116.

120:   it "*alone* is at the source": Monod, p. 112.

120n: "chance is a minor ingredient": Dawkins, p. 49.

120n: "Natural selection operates": Monod, pp. 118–19 (my emphasis); see also Dawkins, pp. 45, 288, 306.

       I recommend both Dawkins and Monod for a fuller account of the limits of chance in evolution. For a more complete list of the ways in which mutations are not random, for example, see Dawkins, pp. 306, 312, and Monod, p. 112. Both authors point out that a mutation must occur in a structure that can preserve it if it is to become part of creation. Evolution results, Monod writes, from "perturbations occurring in a structure *which already possesses the property of invariance*—hence is capable of preserving the effects of chance" (p. 23). See also Dawkins, pp. 170–72.

120:   "between the occurrences": Monod, p. 114 (emphasis deleted). See also Dawkins, pp. 307, 312.

120:   "the necessary information": Monod, p. 87.

121:   "arises from the essentially": Monod, p. 116.

121:   "All religions": Monod, p. 44.

121:   Eshu got one of the gods drunk: Ogundipe II, pp. 118–20.

121:   When geneticists breed fruit flies: Dawkins, p. 320.

122:   "look at any walls": Cited in McKenna, p. xi.

122:   Botticelli liked to throw a sponge: McKenna, p. xix.

122:   "The idea of 'chance' ": Cabanne, pp. 46–47.

122:   "Art is an outlet": Duchamp, *Salt Seller*, p. 137.

123:   "I like the cracks": Duchamp, *Salt Seller*, p. 127; see also Cabanne, pp. 75–76.

123:   Duchamp bought this neat bit of mercantile design: Cabanne, p. 47.

123:   "A kind of rendezvous": Duchamp, *Notes and Projects for the Large Glass*, p. 90; see also *Salt Seller*, p. 32.

125:   Humankind *must* sacrifice to the gods: Ogundipe I, pp. 120, 234–35; also Bascom, pp. 103, 105, 118.

125:   "enforcer of sacrifice": Ogundipe I, p. 234.

125:   "sacrificial food is placed at the crossroads": Ogundipe II, p. 106.

125:   "any sacrifices found outdoors": Ogundipe II, p. 95.

125n: "windfalls for hungry travelers": Kerényi, *Hermes*, p. 24.

125:   "as long as they sacrificed": Ogundipe II, p. 106.

126:   "For his part": Pelton, p. 139; Ogundipe II, p. 174; see also II, pp. 87, 90–91.

126:   "Your handling of sacrifice": Ogundipe II, pp. 9, 17, 18, 29; see also I, pp. 138–39, and II, pp. 22, 30, 38.

126:   "Everything existing": In Monod, p. v.

6: The Lucky Find

128: "Chance and chance alone": Kundera, p. 48.

A Gift of Hermes

128: "Chance itself pours in": Hacking, p. 200.

128: Antonio Stradivari: Nachmanovitch, p. 87.

129: Mozart heard a starling: Thanks to Eric Moe for the story about Mozart.

129: "Guess how I made that head of a bull": Picasso, p. 157. Telling the story of the *Tête de Taureau* another time, Picasso added an amusing fantasy: "Finally, I made this handlebar and seat a bull's head that everyone recognized as a bull's head. The metamorphosis was accomplished and I wish another metamorphosis would occur in the reverse sense. If my bull's head were thrown in a junk heap, perhaps one day some boy would say: 'Here's something which would make a good handlebar for my bicycle' " (Picasso, p. 156).

129: "pit of beads": Bascom, pp. 500–1, 157, 499, 173.

129: "Does Hermes wish to play?": Kerényi, *Hermes, Guide of Souls*, pp. iv–v.

129: "luck-bringing," etc.: Translations of the first descriptive name Hermes is given in the *Hymn to Hermes: erioúnion*. See line 3; see also line 551.

130: contingency can breed great tragedy: When I speak of contingency and tragedy, I am thinking of Martha Nussbaum's book, *The Fragility of Goodness*, on "luck and ethics in ancient Greece." For Nussbaum, the Greek tragedies arise out of inexorable contingencies, and Nussbaum judges the tragedians wiser than the idealist Plato for their recognition that contingency is inexorable. This world showers us with it; to rise above it would mean leaving this world, leaving the human as we know it. But sticking with this human world doesn't necessarily leave us with tragedy alone, for contingency and luck have a comic, even redemptive, side—about which Nussbaum is silent.

130: "When we were children": Wilson, *Nez Percé Stories* (audiotape).

130: "This was the greatest misfortune": Young, p. 81.

130: There is a Job-like story: Ogundipe II, pp. 136–42.

130: A newborn babe: *Hymn to Hermes*, lines 23–24.

130: "found a tortoise": *Hymn to Hermes*, line 24.

130: "generative" and "speculative": Turner, *Ritual Process*, pp. 127–28, 133.

130: "just as swift thought can fly": *Hymn to Hermes*, lines 43–46.

131: "the sense of sight enjoys being surprised": Picasso, p. 90.

131: "In my opinion to search means nothing": Picasso, pp. 71–72.

132: "gift of Fortune" examples: Foster, p. 307.

132: "If the soul is immortal": Plato, ed. Hamilton and Cairns, p. 89.

133: the fates . . . imagined as weavers: The best example is in Norse mythology, where the Norns are three female deities whose spinning and weaving determines the fates of human beings. On the idea that the fates express the demands of the collective, see (for the Greek case) Dodds, p. 8.

133:     *káiros*: Onians, pp. 343–48; also Hillman, pp. 152–53.

133n: "I touch on many issues": Hyde, *The Gift*, p. xvi.

134:     In Plato's *Gorgias*: Plato, ed. Hamilton and Cairns, p. 271 (*Gorgias* 489c).

134:     the Yoruba will often say: Bascom, p. 30; see also pp. 36, 68.

134:     "the drawing of lots": Flaceliere, p. 17.

135:     "Columbus did not find out America by chance": *Oxford English Dictionary*, s.v. "contingent" §4. Another example of a believer who thinks there are no accidents is Boethius. In Boethius' *The Consolation of Philosophy*, Lady Philosophy tells the Roman philosopher that if by "chance" he means events produced by "a confused motion, and without connection of causes," then no such thing exists, for "God disposeth all things in due order" (Boethius, p. 105).

135:     "perforated . . . like a sieve": Ogundipe I, p. 138.

135:     Pausanias described this oracle: Flaceliere, pp. 9–10.

135:     "Divination techniques": von Franz, p. 38.

135:     "the subjective . . . states of the observer": Jung, Foreword to *I Ching*, p. xxiv.

136:     "are not worth": Freud, p. 27.

136:     "masquerades as a lucky chance": Freud, p. 69.

136:     "are serious mental acts": Freud, p. 41.

136:     "as omens"; "courage and resolution": Freud, p. 53.

136:     no painting can be plotted out: See Ashton in Picasso, p. xxi.

136:     "I consider a work of art as the product of calculations": Picasso, p. 30.

136:     "what counts is what is spontaneous": Picasso, p. 21.

136:     "Art is not the application of a canon of beauty": Picasso, p. 11.

136:     One of Picasso's favorite assignments: Picasso, p. 47.

136:     "Try to make the circle as best you can": Picasso, p. 45.

136:     "from errors one gets to know the personality": Picasso, p. 45.

136:     "Accidents, try to change them": Picasso, p. 91; see also p. xxi.

137:     the god of thunder and lightning, Sango: Ogundipe II, p. 172.

137:     "Obatala had learned": Thompson, sect. V, p. 1; see also Cabrera, pp. 163–64.

137:     "Chance and accident": Kerényi, "Primordial Child," p. 57.

137:     "Opportunities are not plain, clean gifts": Hillman, *Puer Papers*, p. 154.

138:     "The real": Serres, p. xiii.

138n: "esemplastic powers": Hyde, *The Gift*, pp. 150–51.

138:     "Should a *stupid* fellow have good luck": Kerényi, *Hermes*, pp. 24–25. Emphasis added.

139:     "Apollo was seized with a longing": *Hymn to Hermes*, lines 436–38.

140n: "Dans les champs": J. H. Austin, p. 72.

140:     "Pasteur was studying chicken cholera": J. H. Austin, p. 202.

141:     "Moly is a nut to crack": Joyce, p. 272.

A Net to Catch Contingency

142:   "the ego can cut itself off": Kostelanetz, p. 52.

142:   "you go *in*"; "I decided to go *out*": Kostelanetz, p. 229.

142:   "I have used chance operations": Kostelanetz, pp. 52–53.

142:   "open the doors of the ego": Kostelanetz, p. 20.

142:   "we are made perfect": Cage, *Silence*, p. 64.

143:   often struggled to make clear: Kostelanetz, pp. 17, 42–43.

143:   "I'm not saying, 'Do whatever you like' ": Kostelanetz, p. 102.

143:   spend months tossing coins: Kostelanetz, p. 73.

143:   rode the New York subway: Kostelanetz, p. 67.

143:   One famous piece: Kostelanetz, p. 108.

143:   "The highest discipline": Kostelanetz, p. 219.

143:   "You could look at the part I had given him": Kostelanetz, pp. 68–69.

143:   Cage was not drawn to an art like that of Jackson Pollock: Kostelanetz, p. 177; see also Copeland.

144:   "Automatic art . . . has never interested me": Kostelanetz, p. 173.

144:   "The thing that is beautiful": Kostelanetz, p. 126.

144:   "I was standing at a corner of Madison Avenue": Kostelanetz, p. 175.

144:   "to open our eyes": Kostelanetz, p. 174.

144:   "Already it's a great deal": Copeland, p. 48.

145:   "I spent my life thinking": Kostelanetz, p. 97.

145:   "I think that music has to do with self-alteration": Kostelanetz, p. 99; see also p. 43.

145:   "Everyday life is more interesting than forms of celebration": Kostelanetz, p. 208.

146:   "and the change that has taken place": Kostelanetz, pp. 99–100.

146:   "As I was coming into the house": Cage, *For the Birds*, p. 22.

146:   "The accident *reveals* man": Picasso, p. 91. Emphasis added.

146:   earliest childhood drawings: John Richardson's biography reproduces two that Picasso drew when he was nine years old. See Richardson, p. 30.

147:   "The method actor . . . is reaching inside himself": Copeland, p. 47.

147:   "From errors one gets to know the personality": Picasso, p. 45.

147:   "Personality is a flimsy thing on which to build art": Cage, *Silence*, p. 90.

147:   "Composition is like writing a letter to a stranger": Kostelanetz, p. 74.

147:   "Not things, but minds": Cage, *Themes and Variations*, p. 11.

147n: Cage's father was an inventor: Kostelanetz, pp. 31, 237; *New York Times*, Aug. 13, 1992.

147:   "bring . . . new things into being": Kostelanetz, p. 207.

148:   In 1952, Cage and a group of friends: Revill, p. 161.

148:   "A Happening should be like a net": Kostelanetz, p. 113.

148:   Electric fish: Dawkins, pp. 97–99.

148:    "I placed objects on the strings": Kostelanetz, pp. 62–63.

149n: "I feel you should be able": Tomkins, p. 74.

149:    Alone in the room, Cage was surprised to hear two sounds: Revill, pp. 162–64; also Kostelanetz, pp. 228–29.

150:    "What they thought was silence": Kostelanetz, p. 65.

150:    "The same source of fortuitous perturbations": Monod, pp. 116–17.

7: Speechless Shame and Shameless Speech

The Immigrant Child

153:    " 'I will be the Sun-god' ": Mourning Dove, p. 181.

153:    "cloak of shamelessness": *Hymn to Hermes*, line 156. This epithet is used one other time in the Homeric literature; it is what Achilles calls Agamemnon after Agamemnon has insulted him in Book I of the *Iliad*. See Cairns, p. 159.

153:    It's the same with Old Monkey in China: *Journey* II, p. 23.

154:    "When he heard these words": *Journey* III, p. 57.

154:    No such paralysis ever strikes: *Journey* II, p. 28.

154:    In fact, his constant fluency: *Journey* III, pp. 57–62.

154:    "Master, please put away your compassion": *Journey* II, p. 235.

154:    Monkey's spirit: Moyers (videotaped interview).

154:    "When I went to kindergarten": Kingston, *Woman Warrior*, p. 165.

154:    " 'You must not tell anyone' ": Kingston, *Woman Warrior*, p. 3.

154:    " 'What happened to her' ": Kingston, *Woman Warrior*, p. 5.

155:    "The round moon cakes": Kingston, *Woman Warrior*, p. 13.

155n: the terms . . . by which E. R. Dodds: Dodds, Chap. 1.

155n: Douglas Cairns argues: Cairns, pp. 32–33.

155:    "The frightened villagers": Kingston, *Woman Warrior*, pp. 12–13.

156:    "the conduct of her rites": *Hymn to Demeter*, lines 475–79; see, for example, Hesiod, *The Homeric Hymns and Homerica*, p. 323.

156n: Paul Radin points out: Radin, pp. 111–12.

156n: "trickster tales of more sacred character": Hampton, p. 61.

156:    "I am set apart": Douglas, p. 8, referring to Leviticus 11:46.

156:    *temenos*: Lidell and Scott, p. 799.

157:    spheres of speech: In regard to spheres of speech and spheres of silence, it is worth noting that the Greek idea of "mystery" creates similar distinctions. The Greek root for "mystery" (*muo*) means "I have my mouth closed" when it is used in everyday situations, but it means "I speak in a special way" when it is used in ritual. Our word "myth" comes from this root, too, and myth is also therefore "special" as opposed to "everyday" speech. See Nagy's discussion of these terms in *Greek Mythology and Poetics*, p. viii. Nagy concludes: "From an anthropological point of view, 'myth' is indeed 'special speech' in that it is a means by which society affirms its own reality" (p. viii).

157: *Aidos*: The lumping together of shame, reverence, and awe is not confined to the Greek tradition. Exactly that complexity of feeling came over Adam and Eve when God met them in the garden, for example. The anthropologist Andrew Strathern reports that in Papua New Guinea's Western Highlands, the word for shame, *pipil*, has the same broad meaning: "In the presence of ghosts and other supernatural powers, people are expected to feel [a] kind of 'shame,' which we can perhaps translate best as 'awe' " (p. 100).

157: enter the grove of a god: See the description of Hippolytus' relationship to the sacred grove of Artemis in Euripides' play *Hippolytus*.

157: inhibitory shame: In the Buddhist tradition, shame is protective the way *aidos* is protective; it keeps men and women from acquiring karma.

158: "a confusion of amorous and excretory functions": Cleckley, p. 224. On the psychopath in general, see especially Chap. 6 of Cleckley.

158: "will commit thefts": Cleckley, p. 209.

158: "rudderless intelligence": The phrase comes from a news story on research on psychopaths, *New York Times*, July 7, 1987.

158: "at one and the same time": Radin, p. xxiii.

159: "The Chinese are always very frightened": Kingston, *Woman Warrior*, p. 16.

159: Immigrant parents and children: For the point about immigrant children and shame, I'm indebted to Helen Merrell Lynd (p. 55).

160: "like the night": Rodriguez, p. 15.

160: "A few minutes later": Rodriguez, p. 53.

160: "aristocratic reserve": Rodriguez, p. 183.

160: "Of those matters": Rodriguez, p. 185.

160: "I am writing about those very things": Rodriguez, p. 175.

161: "I am useless": Kingston, *Woman Warrior*, p. 52.

161: grandfather used to call her a "maggot": Kingston, *Woman Warrior*, p. 191.

161: "When I visit the family now": Kingston, *Woman Warrior*, 52.

Slayer of Argus

162: *aidos* is inborn: Euripides says *aidos* is known "without a teacher." When Dodds describes *aidos*, his language has the same import: against convention we sometimes have a "deeper claim," a "spiritual integrity," an "inward . . . morality," an "instinct [for] true *aidos*," and so on (p. 103). *Aidos* is a kind of prophetic shame, then, a feeling not just conventionally true but true at all times and in all places.

162: "The anus . . . had a special cover": Boelaars, p. 68.

162: debt to a stranger: Benedict, pp. 47–48, 104–6.

163: Beethoven: Wurmser, pp. 294–95.

163: Audubon: Adam Gopnik, "A Critic at Large: Audubon's Passion," *The New Yorker*, Feb. 25, 1991, pp. 96–97.

163: Ginsberg's family: See James Breslin in Hyde, *On the Poetry*, p. 418.

163: "The homosexual and the insane person": In Hyde, *On the Poetry*, p. 410.

163: "resign himself to pragmatic values": In Hyde, *On the Poetry*, p. 411.

164: an ethic of noble suicide: Benedict, pp. 116, 193–207.

164: "started to really get": In Hyde, *On the Poetry*, pp. 414–15.

164: "wandering in various": In Hyde, *On the Poetry*, p. 7.

164: "I went . . . to what my imagination believed": In Hyde, *On the Poetry*, p. 81.

164: "a plate of cold fish": Ginsberg, *Collected Poems*, p. 219.

164: "scars of operations": Ginsberg, p. 219.

165: "embarrassed him the most": The phrase paraphrases Ginsberg's own descriptions of how he wrote his early poems. See, for example, Allen Ginsberg, *Composed on the Tongue* (Bolinas, Calif.: Grey Fox Press, 1980), pp. 111–12.

165: strategies . . . to free his tongue: Some are not listed in the poem itself, but we know them from elsewhere. On amphetamines, for example, see Tytell in Hyde, p. 179.

165: "a head set round with a hundred eyes": Ovid, p. 49.

166: "With many a tale": Ovid, p. 51.

166: "Argus' eyelids were closed": Ovid, pp. 51–52.

166: "on the one hand shame": Ovid, p. 49.

168: "an attachment to ethics": Milosz, p. 111.

169: "The normal, extraordinary": Rodriguez, p. 126.

170: "As a boy, I'd stay in the kitchen": Rodriguez, p. 116.

171: "After that summer": Rodriguez, p. 136.

172: "My complexion . . . assumes": Rodriguez, p. 137.

8: Matter Out of Place

173: "Marcel Duchamp spoke to me": Dali in Cabanne, pp. 13–14.

Heaven's Privy

173: Once upon a time the gods were closer to this earth: Herskovits, *Dahomean Narrative*, pp. 149–50; see also Pelton, pp. 77–80. There are other stories in which a trickster uses dirt to effect the separation of heaven and earth. Ananse, for example, shames the high god Nyame into leaving the earth by making it look as if he has defecated indoors (Pelton, p. 47n).

175: "If you like that filth": Thwaites 44, p. 297; see also Greenblatt, p. 3. The complete passage deserves citation. A Catholic priest is writing in 1658 from Canada: "Politeness and propriety have taught us to carry handkerchiefs. In this manner the Savages charge us with filthiness—because, they say, we place what is unclean in a fine white piece of linen, and put it away in our pockets as something very precious, while they throw it upon the ground. Hence it happened that, when a Savage one day saw a Frenchman fold up his handkerchief after wiping his nose, he said to him laughingly, 'If thou likest that filth, give me thy handkerchief and I will soon fill it' " (Thwaites 44, p. 297).

175: "Cows are sometimes said to be gods": Douglas, p. 9.

176: "its proper kind of animal life": Douglas, p. 55.

176: Old Testament dietary laws: Douglas, pp. 54ff.

176n: Douglas removes questions of hygiene: Douglas, p. 35.

176: "dirt is the by-product": Douglas, p. 35.

177n: "Phoebus Apollo picked the child up": *Hymn to Hermes*, lines 293–98.

177: The stormy Susa-nö-o: *Kojiki* I, 16:3 (Philippi, p. 79). The ancient sources of Shinto mythology are the *Kojiki* and the *Nihon shoki*. I use Donald Philippi's translation of the *Kojiki*. The texts contradict each other and contradict themselves, and there is much debate over passages thought to be spurious. As a result, any reading of the story involves considerable speculation. I've based my own gloss on those offered by Philippi, Herbert, and Ellwood. See especially Philippi, pp. 68–87, 402–6; Herbert, pp. 284–300; and all of Ellwood.

178: In some versions of the story he defecates: Herbert, p. 299.

178: This sudden intrusion: *Kojiki* I, 16:8 (Philippi, p. 80); also Philippi, p. 80n.

178: "all manner of calamities": *Kojiki* I, 17:1–3 (Philippi, p. 81).

178: the harvest riches . . . are loosened: Herbert, p. 298.

180: "The sky was gloriously blue": Jung, *Memories*, p. 36.

180: "I gathered all my courage": Jung, *Memories*, p. 39.

180: "I felt an enormous, an indescribable relief": Jung, *Memories*, p. 40.

181: "a great many things": Jung, *Memories*, pp. 8, 40.

181: "Mercurius consists": Jung, *Alchemical Studies*, p. 237.

181: "*Sol Novus*": Jung, *Alchemical Studies*, p. 242.

181: "naturally involves cleansing": Jung, *Alchemical Studies*, pp. 242–43.

182: "In comparison with the purity": Jung, *Alchemical Studies*, p. 241.

182: "an aspect of the self which stands apart": Jung, *Alchemical Studies*, p. 241.

182: "The texts remind us": Jung, *Alchemical Studies*, p. 232.

183: "all those things": Jung, *Alchemical Studies*, p. 241.

183: "forced under the influence of Christianity": Jung, *Alchemical Studies*, p. 198.

183: "when the sons of God": Jung, *Alchemical Studies*, p. 242.

183: "hesitantly, as in a dream": Jung, *Alchemical Studies*, p. 245.

184: "throw a bridge across the abyss": Jung, *Alchemical Studies*, p. 245.

184: "it was the medical men": Jung, *Alchemical Studies*, p. 244.

184n: "is accustomed to divine secrets": Freud cited in Carlo Ginzburg, "Morelli, Freud and Sherlock Holmes: Clues and Scientific Method," *History Workshop Journal* 9 (Spring 1980), p. 10.

184: If Jung flirted with anti-Semitism: Jung's essay on the Spirit Mercurius is an exploration of what he would call "the Christian Shadow." Jung first presented the essay as two lectures in Ascona, Switzerland, in 1942. Though he ends with an oblique reference to Hitler and to the "twilight of the gods" that comes of trying to suppress one portion of the psyche, it is odd—especially given the time and place—that in speaking of the things that Christian purity excludes and demonizes he never mentions the Jews.

185: a pesky researcher: See *New York Times*, June 3, 1995. The scholar is Richard Noll, author of *The Jung Cult* (Princeton University Press, 1994). Noll is quoted as saying, "The whole Jungian belief system will collapse if the collective unconscious is a fallacy, if it is proved Jung knowingly lied." Franz Jung, Jung's son, called Noll's writings "pure nonsense" and then hung up the phone on the reporter who had called him. See also letters that followed, *Times*, June 10, 1995.

Democratic Carnival

185: "the existence of anomaly": Douglas, p. 39.

186: "the Winnebago tribal chief cannot": Radin, p. 54.

186: By the end of the first episode: Radin, pp. 4–7.

186: "an inconceivably sacrilegious": Radin, p. 54.

186: clowns enter the plaza backward: Masayevsa (videotape).

186: In Zuñi dirt rituals: Greenblatt, p. 1.

186: "In the very midst of divine service": Cited by Jung in Radin, p. 197.

187: From other descriptions we know: Greenblatt, p. 5; see also Jung in Radin, p. 198.

187: "carnival": For a key discussion of carnival, see Bakhtin, *Problem of Dostoevsky's Poetics*, pp. 122–32.

187: celebrations . . . are profoundly conservative: See especially the introduction to Stallybrass and White. At one point they write: "It actually makes little sense to fight out the issue of whether or not carnivals are *intrinsically* radical or conservative. . . . The most that can be said in the abstract is that for long periods carnival may be a stable and cyclical ritual with no noticeable politically transformative effects but that, given the presence of sharpened political antagonism, it may often act as *catalyst* and *site of actual and symbolic struggle*" (p. 14). For more examples of periodic change around carnival, see pp. 15ff.

187: a sort of psychic and social drainage system: The term "psychic drainage" comes from Bernard Wolfe's essay on Brer Rabbit, "Uncle Remus & the Malevolent Rabbit," in *Commentary* 8 (1949), pp. 31–41; reprinted in Dundes, *Mother Wit*, pp. 524–40.

188: carnival's ritual debasing of the Pope: On carnival and the Reformation in Germany, see Robert Scribner, "Reformation, carnival and the world turned upside-down," *Social History* III:3 (1978), pp. 303–29, cited in Stallybrass, p. 15.

188:    "*undermine* as well as reinforce": Davis, p. 131.

188:    "to sanction riot": Davis, p. 131.

188:    "promoted resistance": Davis, p. 143.

188:    "kept open an alternate way": Davis, p. 144.

188:    "a resource for feminist reflection": Davis, p. 151.

189:    Raven steals water from Petrel: Swanton, p. 4. For another trickster tale about dirt-work and the origins of things, see the Karok version of how Coyote stole fire, in Lopez, pp. 11–13.

193:    "Complex and unresolved feelings": Serrano, cited in Fox, p. 22.

193n: "During the Renaissance": Bakhtin, p. 130.

193n: "The Renaissance is the high point": Bakhtin, p. 130.

194:    "If it's in an art museum": *New York Times*, Oct. 18, 1990.

195:    "It's the tension": *New York Times*, Oct. 18, 1990; *Cincinnati Enquirer*, Oct. 2, 1990.

195:    "Led through . . . the photographs": *Cincinnati Enquirer*, Oct. 2, 1990.

195:    "All of them [the experts], to a person": *New York Times*, Oct. 10, 1990.

196:    "I sure didn't know this stuff existed": *New York Times*, Oct. 10, 1990.

196:    "I learned more about that type of lifestyle": *Cincinnati Enquirer*, Oct. 7, 1990.

196:    "Who *were* those people?": *Columbus Dispatch*, Oct. 6, 1990.

197:    "The contested, fleshy subject matter": *New York Times*, Oct. 18, 1990.

9: Hermes Slips the Trap

Hermes of the Light, Hermes of the Dark

203:    "I'm ready to do whatever I must": *Hymn to Hermes*, lines 166–75.

204:    Gift community: See Hyde, *The Gift*, Chap. 5, especially pp. 77–84.

206:    in Athens around 520 B.C.: N. O. Brown, *Hermes the Thief*, p. 126. On dating the *Hymn*: Richard Janko, in *Homer, Hesiod and the Hymns*, provides a concise summary of attempts to date the *Hymn*; he himself concludes that it should probably be dated between 535 and 515 B.C. (pp. 140–43).

206:    "Athenian industrial and commercial": N. O. Brown, *Hermes the Thief*, p. 110.

206:    "new ethics": N. O. Brown, *Hermes the Thief*, p. 60.

206:    "the archaic form": N. O. Brown, *Hermes the Thief*, p. 61n.

206:    In short, during the sixth century: N. O. Brown, *Hermes the Thief*, pp. 45, 47, 60, 61n, 85, 110.

207:    "regime of the landed aristocracy": N. O. Brown, *Hermes the Thief*, p. 47.

207:    "The theme of strife": N. O. Brown, *Hermes the Thief*, p. 85. There is at least one other social-political reading of the *Hymn* in addition to Brown's. A German scholar has suggested that the reconciliation of Hermes and Apollo at the end of the *Hymn* represents "the political relations between the democratic Themistocles and the aristocratic party of Cimon around 475 B.C." (see Clay, p. 100n).

207: "He didn't lie around": *Hymn to Hermes*, lines 21–24.

208: When Odysseus has slain the suitors: *Odyssey* XXIV:1–18.

208: Hermes who guides Persephone: *Hymn to Demeter*, in *Hesiod, The Homeric Hymns and Homerica*, pp. 334ff.

208: puts to sleep the watchmen: *Iliad* XXIV:334ff.

208: awakens Odysseus as he walks: *Odyssey* X:274ff.

209: "bewitches the eyes": *Iliad* XXIV:343–44.

210: "Colonel Lloyd kept": Douglass, *Narrative*, p. 59.

210: "All the education": Douglass cited in Gates, *Figures in Black*, p. 118.

211: " 'Robbery,' 'Shamelessness' ": N. O. Brown, *Hermes the Thief*, pp. 60–61.

212n: Karl Kerényi maintains: Kerényi, *Hermes*, pp. 28–29.

212n: illegitimate children: M. M. Austin, p. 95; Sealey, pp. 14–15.

212n: "the father retains": Clay, p. 136n.

212: "The whisper that my master": Douglass, *Narrative*, p. 49.

213: "The truth was": Douglass, *Narrative*, p. 151.

213: "the way teenagers sing": *Hymn to Hermes*, line 56.

214: "It is . . . plain": Douglass, *Narrative*, p. 50.

214: Archaic Greeks assumed: See line 356 of Hesiod, *Works and Days*; also N. O. Brown, *Hermes the Thief*, pp. 60–61n.

214: "happened on a turtle": *Hymn to Hermes*, line 24.

215: "My old master, Captain Anthony": Douglass, *Narrative*, pp. 89–91.

215: "Hermes . . . was the patron of lottery": N. O. Brown, *Hermes the Thief*, p. 101.

216n: women were citizens: Sealey, pp. 12–13.

216: "I was not about twelve": Douglass, *Narrative*, p. 83.

Change the Rap and Slip the Trap

216: change the rap and slip the trap: The phrase works a change on the title of an essay by Ralph Ellison, "Change the Joke and Slip the Yoke" (*Shadow and Act*, p. 45), a complaint about Stanley Edgar Hyman's attempt to read *Invisible Man* in terms of the trickster archetype.

218: "story of the gods": *Hymn to Hermes*, lines 426–33.

218n: "Such is clear": Lincoln, p. 169.

219: "And Apollo was seized": *Hymn to Hermes*, lines 434–38.

219: "By my dogwood staff": *Hymn to Hermes*, lines 460–62.

219: "ordain[s] him": *Hymn to Hermes*, line 498.

220: Misfortune or Lack: Propp, p. 39.

221: "Our raconteur": Radin, p. 139; see also pp. 153–54.

221: In an Alaskan story: Ricketts, "The Structure," p. 163.

223: "most of the time": *Hymn to Hermes*, lines 577–78.

223: "in the mind of Zeus": My remarks on Hermes' disruptions having taken place "in the mind of Zeus" were informed by the literary critic Sacvan Bercovitch's thinking about similar issues in American history. Bercovitch begins with the assumption that "fundamental protest" always involves taking a culture's claims to higher truth and showing that those truths are relative, that they depend on historical situations.

How does a culture or ideology respond to such historicizing? It scurries out of history and into eternity. It takes present protest and reframes it in terms of its own atemporal ideals. To do this, says Bercovitch, "ideology seeks to focus attention on the distance between vision and fact, theory and practice," so as to take failings in fact or practice and re-present them contained in the sacred language of vision or ideal. "To denounce a king through precepts derived from the divine right of kings," for example, "is to define government itself as monarchical; just as to denounce immoral Christians by contrast with the sacred example of Christ is to sacralize Christian morality. To define injustice through particular violations of free enterprise (or its constituent elements, such as social mobility, open opportunity, and self-fulfillment) is to consecrate free enterprise as *the* just society" (Bercovitch, p. 644).

223:   Zeus' "purpose": *Hymn to Hermes*, line 10.
223:   "Your father meant you": *Hymn to Hermes*, lines 160–61.
223:   "Zeus has given you the honor": *Hymn to Hermes*, lines 516–17.
223:   "Then [Zeus] nodded": *Hymn to Hermes*, lines 395–96; see Nagy, *Greek Mythology and Poetics*, p. 59.
223:   Brown surmises: N. O. Brown, *Hermes the Thief*, pp. 113–32.
224:   "those which practice cannibalism": Lévi-Strauss, cited in Bernstein, p. 14.

10: Frederick Douglass and Eshu's Hat

Answering Back

226:   "To all these complaints": Douglass, *Narrative*, pp. 60–61.
226:   "When Hate-to-be-contradicted": Pelton, p. 27.
227:   "bitter opposition": Douglass, *Narrative*, p. 79.
228:   "Just at this point": Douglass, *Narrative*, p. 78.
229:   Henry Louis Gates, Jr., offers a good summary: Gates, *Figures in Black*, pp. 5–6, 17–21, 104–5.
229:   "is no historical part of the world": Cited in Gates, *Figures in Black*, p. 20.
229:   "The absence and presence of writing": Gates, *Figures in Black*, p. 104.
230:   "She did not deem it impudent": Douglass, p. 77.
230:   "questions . . . concerning their ages": Douglass, *Life and Times*, p. 2.
230:   "guilty of impudence": Douglass, *Narrative*, p. 118.
230:   "He was one of those": Douglass, *Narrative*, p. 65.
230:   "a still tongue makes a wise head": Douglass, *Narrative*, p. 62.
230:   "I . . . never felt happier": Douglass, *Narrative*, p. 151.

231n: "an antithesis": Bingham, p. 28.

231n: "What [Auld] most dreaded": Douglass, *Narrative*, p. 79. On antithesis, see V. Smith, p. 24; Gates, pp. 286–87.

232:    "By far the larger part": Douglass, *Narrative*, p. 47.

232:    a series of oppositions: Gates, *Figures in Black*, pp. 88–92.

232:    "barriers of difference": Gates, *Figures in Black*, p. 89.

232:    "I indulge no animosity": Cited by Houston Baker in his introduction to Douglass's *Narrative*, p. 21.

232:    "is essentially true": From William Lloyd Garrison's introduction to Douglass's *Narrative*, p. 38.

233:    white women to sell . . . mulatto children: Douglass, *Narrative*, pp. 49–50.

233:    "as mediator and as trickster": Gates, *Figures in Black*, p. 92.

233:    "Colonel Lloyd could brook no contradiction": Douglass, *Narrative*, p. 61.

234:    "This time we regarded as our own": Douglass, *Narrative*, pp. 114–15.

234:    "From what I know": Douglass, *Narrative*, p. 115.

235:    Douglass's experiences with applejack: Preston, p. 132.

235:    "[The] object seems to be": Douglass, *Narrative*, pp. 115–16.

236:    corn mush in a pig trough: Douglass, *Narrative*, p. 72.

236:    Freeland fed his slaves well: Douglass, *Narrative*, pp. 119, 121.

236:    On the first of January 1836: Preston, p. 133.

236:    mark the calendar with such dates as: See Preston, pp. 160–61.

The Color Line

237:    "A protean Douglass": Walker, *Moral Choices*, p. 214.

237:    "As long as you think you're white": Baldwin in Thorsen (videotape).

238:    Eshu and the two friends: I reprint a version told in Nigeria by Baderinwa Esubunmi (Ogundipe II, pp. 133–35). There are many others: Ogundipe II, pp. 132–33; Frobenius I, pp. 240–42; Herskovits, "Tales in Pidgin English from Nigeria," p. 455; Bascom, p. 311. Bascom says there are four recorded versions (p. 132). Gates comments on the Ogundipe version, *Signifying Monkey*, pp. 32–35. Pelton comments on Frobenius's version, pp. 141–43.

240:    a Cuban version: Cabrera, pp. 93–94; English version in Thompson, part IV, p. 4.

240:    The Bailey family: Preston, Chap. 1.

240:    Aaron Anthony: Preston, Chap. 2 (on his books, p. 27).

241:    "When the duck-billed beaver": Melville, p. 59.

242:    "The basic characteristic": Walker, *Moral Choices*, p. 256.

242:    "to visit the home": In Preston, p. 201.

242:    "If I should meet you now": Walker, *Moral Choices*, p. 256.

242:    "there was a row": Walker, *Moral Choices*, p. 241.

243:    "Young, ardent, and hopeful": Douglass, cited in Walker, *Moral Choices*, p. 244; Douglass, *Life and Times*, p. 184.

243: "for the first time in his life": Walker, *Moral Choices*, p. 244.

243: "I found full soon": Walker, *Moral Choices*, p. 244; also Douglass, *Life and Times*, p. 185.

243: the passive voice: Walker, *Moral Choices*, p. 244.

243: "Give us the facts": Douglass, *Life and Times*, p. 185.

243: "It was impossible for me to repeat": Douglass, *Life and Times*, p. 185.

244: "It is not best": Douglass, *Life and Times*, p. 186.

244: "for a 'nigger' ": Cited in Walker, *Moral Choices*, p. 245.

244: "full blood black": Cited in Walker, *Moral Choices*, p. 258.

244: They cautioned him: Walker, *Moral Choices*, p. 366.

244: "language . . . possesse[d]": Cited in Preston, p. 191.

244: "a little of the plantation speech": Douglass, *Life and Times*, p. 186. Douglass's own account of some of these incidents is in Douglass, *My Bondage and My Freedom*, pp. 243–47.

244: Douglass revising his origins: See Douglass, *Narrative*, p. 48; *My Bondage and My Freedom*, p. 38; *Life and Times*, p. 3; and Walker, *Moral Choices*, pp. 249–50.

244: In the first autobiography, Douglass's mother: Douglass, *Narrative*, pp. 48–49.

245: "ineffaceably stamped upon my memory": Douglass, *Life and Times*, p. 10.

245: "I have . . . learned": Douglass, *Life and Times*, p. 10.

245: Douglass and Garrison argue: Douglass, *My Bondage and My Freedom*, pp. 240–42.

246: "The break was painful for both": Walker, *Moral Choices*, p. 258. For Garrison's account of their sicknesses, see Merrill, pp. 516–27; for Douglass's story of this fight, see *My Bondage and My Freedom*, pp. 240–42. Walker adds in a note that he has found "no instance of Douglass 'losing his voice' before the break with Garrison" (p. 366).

246: "It was with the utmost difficulty": Douglass, *Life and Times*, p. 183.

246: "a wet bandage": Merrill, p. 519.

247: "You will be surprised": Cited in Walker, *Moral Choices*, p. 246.

248: "I shall never get beyond Fredk Douglass": Cited in Walker, *Moral Choices*, p. 261.

248: "accommodated himself": Walker, *Moral Choices*, p. 259.

248: Old Man Eloquent: See Gates, *Figures in Black*, pp. 117–19, which first got me thinking along these lines.

248: Douglass had been converted: Preston, pp. 96–98.

248: pages from the Bible in the gutter: Preston, p. 97.

249: "I love the pure": Douglass, *Narrative*, p. 153.

249: the Constitution was a useful tool: Douglass, *My Bondage and My Freedom*, pp. 242–43.

249: his own set of organizing dualities: For example, see Douglass, *Narrative*, pp. 53, 67, 79, 82, 129.

249: "sable" mother's "native genius": Douglass, *Life and Times*, p. 101.

250: He did not go to the bank: Walker, *Moral Choices*, p. 231; Preston, p. 203.

250: "would at once become unmanageable": Douglass, *Narrative*, p. 78.

251: some modern mathematical topologist: See Gleick, p. 51, where the topologist is Stephen Smale.

251: "I have been known as a Negro": Preston, p. 9.

11: Trickster Arts and Works of *Artus*

252: "Humans . . . could not budge": Makarius in Hynes and Doty, p. 78.

252: "That science of apportionment": Barthes, p. 132.

252: "The word 'art' ": Duchamp in Cabanne, p. 16.

Go for the Joints

253: Syrdon kills Soslan: Dumézil, *Gods of the Ancient Norsemen*, p. 65; and Dumézil, *Loki*, pp. 166–72, especially 170, 172. The Ossetes of the Caucasus are descendants of the Iranian nomads variously known as the Scythians, Sarmatians, and Alans. The Narts are the folk heroes of the Ossetes, and the Nart legends are their stories. Not much is available in English from this tradition, but sources in other languages may be found in the bibliography of Dumézil's *Loki*, pp. 136–37.

253: mistletoe: For the symbolism of mistletoe, see Ad de Vries, s.v. "mistletoe." Sir James Frazer's classic *The Golden Bough* is all about the mistletoe; see especially pp. 229–35 of the edition listed in the bibliography.

253: the solstice is one of the nicks in time: In North America, southern Kwakiutl groups attribute the creation of alternating seasons to Raven (Ricketts, "The Structure," p. 143). There is a similar motif in Japan, where Susa-nö-o brings on the winter and the spring storms, as discussed in the chapter on dirt. Commonly, then, trickster reverses the weather, which may be one reason why his stories are told in winter in North America, and not in summer. To invoke trickster in the summer causes its end, and no one wants that; to invoke him in winter, however, hastens the spring.

254: The etymology of words deriving from the *-ar root is taken from *The Oxford English Dictionary; The Oxford Latin Dictionary;* Liddell and Scott's *Greek-English Lexicon*; and Barnhart, Klein, Mann, and Pokorny.

254: "The *árthron* connecting": Aristotle, *Historia Animalium* 494a.

254: "[The body's] most movable joints": *Oxford English Dictionary*, s.v. "articulate."

255: "The dolphin . . . makes a squeak": Aristotle, *Historia Animalium* 353b33ff. The citation comes from Peck's translation in the Loeb Classical Library, but I've changed the last phrase, "it has no articulation of the voice," to follow the Greek somewhat more literally.

256: "the one who cuts along the joints": Detienne, *Cuisine of Sacrifice*, p. 101.

256: In the ritual of sacrifice, the animal is first cut apart: Details of the social and spiritual apportionment of Greek sacrifice come from Detienne, *Cuisine of Sacrifice*, especially pp. 10, 13, 87–105.

256: the tongue went to Hermes: Farnell V, p. 30.

257n: "proceeds along": Detienne, *Cuisine of Sacrifice*, p. 101 (citing Plato, *Phaedrus* 265c). When describing thought in terms of carving, Socrates has been looking at kinds of madness and differentiating them one from another. He says the procedures of thought involve collecting and dividing. The latter is the procedure "whereby we are enabled to divide into forms, following the objective articulation; we are not to attempt to hack off parts like a clumsy butcher," but to divide where the parts are already divided each from each, "on the analogy of a single natural body" (Plato, *Collected Dialogues*, p. 511).

257n: "So goodbye": Aristotle, *Posterior Analytics* 83a32–34, cited in Nussbaum, p. 256. Nussbaum leaves "so much la-la-la" in the original, *teritismata*, explaining "*teritismata* are meaningless sounds you make when you are singing to yourself; we might render them as 'dum-de-dum-dums' " (Nussbaum, p. 256).

258: Hermes is the last one born: Clay, p. 98.

258: "Yet something essential": Clay, p. 98. Emphasis added.

259: "hear sixteen sayings": Frobenius I, pp. 229–32.

259: Legba is the cosmic linguist: Pelton, pp. 72–78; Herskovits, *Dahomean Narrative*, pp. 125–34 and 149–50.

260: "Papa Legba, remove the barrier": Cosentino, pp. 261–62. In a Haitian community in Brooklyn they say, "*Papa Legba, ouvri bàryè* [Papa Legba, open the gate]." See Cosentino, pp. 261–62; K. Brown, *Mama Lola*, p. 46.

260: "*within* the established order": Clay, pp. 101–2.

260: "power to open passages": Pelton, p. 88.

260: The cattle, once stolen, become domestic beasts: Detienne, *Cuisine of Sacrifice*, p. 165.

261: "in Apollo, the Greeks recognized": Clay, p. 101.

261: He separates earth and sky: Pelton, p. 75.

261: "To become a mediator": Pelton, p. 78.

262: a Danish forge stone: Pendlesonn, p. 24.

263: "the consumption of the meat": Detienne, *Cuisine of Sacrifice*, p. 7.

264: "to translate is to betray": The Walcott remark is in the preface to *O Babylon*, a play about Jamaicans and Rastafarians; I owe the citation, and the Italian word play, to an essay by Edward Chamberlin.

"The One They Call the Seventh Son"

265: "He sang the song of Zeus": *Hymn to Hermes*, lines 57–59.

265: "prelude-style": *Hymn to Hermes*, line 426; see Nagy, *Greek Mythology and*

Poetics, pp. 53–55. Nagy and others assume the *Homeric Hymns* were sung as preludes to longer performances, but I should add that Jenny Strauss Clay has a somewhat different sense of their place: she thinks the *Hymns* "were presented at the conclusion of a feast (*dais*), or what was later called a *symposion*" (p. 7). In her reading of the *Hymn to Hermes*, Clay also argues that the story of Hermes butchering the cattle is an origin myth of feasting rather than sacrifice (I find her argument persuasive, though I don't think it excludes the other reading) (pp. 119–26). These two points taken together add up to another way that the *Hymn* conflates the hymnist and Hermes; by Clay's line of argument, we see Hermes sing his theogony after a feast, just as the hymnist himself would have done.

265:   "I'm the one": Barlow, p. 49.

266:   "a cure for hopeless care": *Hymn to Hermes*, lines 447–49.

266:   psychoanalysts sometimes welcome: López-Pedraza, p. 85.

267:   Claude Lévi-Strauss commented directly: Lévi-Strauss I, p. 224.

268n: Coyotes are not: Marvin Harris, pp. 200–1; Carroll, pp. 302–4.

269:   the Roman festival: Frazer, p. 189.

269:   a reading of Barnum's autobiography: Especially the first edition; in later versions he becomes more proper.

A Corridor of Humor

271:   "He had drawn no blood from me": Douglass, *Narrative*, p. 113. On Douglass's sense of manhood in general, see David Leverenz, *Manhood and the American Renaissance* (Ithaca, N.Y.: Cornell University Press, 1989), pp. 108–34.

271:   "the blood-stained gate": Douglass, *Narrative*, p. 51. A remark of Valerie Smith's first set me thinking about Douglass inverting the terms of plantation culture but nonetheless working within them. See *Self-Discovery and Authority in Afro-American Narrative*, p. 22. Smith herself cites Houston Baker to the effect that Douglass is "entrapped in the very rhetorical and ideological structures he seeks to undermine."

272:   "He talked about yo' people": Dance, p. 198. There are many sources for Signifying Monkey stories. See especially Dance, Jackson, and Abrahams.

272:   "In the distance you could hear the monkey say": Abrahams, *Deep Down in the Jungle*, p. 155.

273:   "dozen": For the roots, see *Oxford English Dictionary*.

273:   "trope a dope": Kimberly Benston, cited by Gates, *Signifying Monkey*, p. 52.

274:   "humor": Barnhart, pp. 496–97.

274:   "While Dada was a movement of negation": Cited in Paz, p. 81.

275n: Duchamp maintained his style to the end: Naumann, p. 67.

275:   "America I'm putting my queer shoulder to the wheel": Ginsberg, *Collected Poems*, p. 148.

275: a rare collaboration of cold-war enemies: Hyde, *On the Poetry of Allen Ginsberg*, pp. 240–51; see especially pp. 244–45.
275: "Contradiction is a lever of transcendence": Simon Weil, cited in Robert Hass, *Twentieth Century Pleasures* (N.Y.: Ecco Press, 1984), p. 202.
276: "It is difficult to escape the conclusion": Leydet, p. 65.
276: "i am outside of history": Reed, p. 50.
277: "the brier-patch representative": Hemenway, p. 9.
277: "Old Massa and Old Miss": Hurston in Dundes, *Mother Wit*, p. 543.
278: Eugene Redmond: I heard Eugene Redmond speaking on the radio. His book about African-American poetry is *Drumvoices* (Garden City, N.Y.: Anchor Books, 1976).
279: "We live in an era of savage order": Hawley, *Parabola*, pp. 12–13.
280: "must soon become unscriptural": Douglass, *Narrative*, p. 50.

12: Prophecy

283: Prophecy: Several books informed the chapter on prophecy more fully than the notes would indicate. I'm indebted to Steiner's *After Babel*; Rorty's *Contingency, Irony, and Solidarity*; and Brown's *Love's Body*. E. M. Forster's *Aspects of the Novel* also has an illuminating chapter on the prophetic voice.
283: "I'm no prophet": Foucault made this remark to Hubert Dreyfus, Professor of Philosophy at the University of California, Berkeley. Dreyfus mentioned it in a talk at Kenyon College, March 27, 1995.
283: "A poeticized culture": Rorty, pp. 53–54.

Plenty

283: "There's someone here": *Journey* II, p. 238.
283: "I, old Monkey": *Journey* II, p. 242.
283: "the one who has perception": *Journey* II, p. 236.
283: "demonic miasma": *Journey* II, p. 199.
284: "His disciples said": J. Z. Smith, p. 1.
284: tricksters "steal the shame covers": For Krishna stealing clothes, see Hawley, *Parabola*, pp. 8–9, and Dimmitt, pp. 122–24. Both Eshu and Monkey engage in a similar play with the tension between local modesty and higher truths. Eshu steals a woman's clothing but as a result she learns the art of divination (Courlander, p. 67). For Monkey stealing shame covers, see *Journey* III, pp. 369–73.
285: "How could I steal it": Hawley, *Krishna, the Butter Thief*, p. 266.
285: "A flute, a tuneful bamboo flute": Hawley, *At Play with Krishna*, p. 115.
285: The night culminates in a circular dance: Dimmitt, pp. 124–27; Hawley, *Parabola*, pp. 6–7.
285: Only when she gives up and leaves: Hawley, "Thief of Butter, Thief of Love," passim.

286: Stolen butter . . . is unconditioned: See Hawley, *Krishna, the Butter Thief*, p. 299.

286: "should never be the basis of marriage": Hawley, *Krishna, the Butter Thief*, p. 275.

286: Krishna will steal the heart of anyone: Hawley, *Krishna, the Butter Thief*, p. 43.

286: Krishna disappears: Dimmitt, p. 103.

287: "God himself is the speaker": Plato, in Kugel, p. 16.

Gregory Nagy has interesting things to say on the origins of Greek prophecy. In Greek, the *prophetes* is the "declarer," as opposed to the *mantis*, the "seer." The seer is possessed, and a bit mad. The declarer has his wits about him. They work together: the seer sees what the oracle has to show, and utters it, but not— we gather—in a form that is really of use. "The *prophetes* declares, formalizes as a speech-act, the words of the inspired *mantis*" (in Kugel, p. 61).

So the "prophet" is the poet of the seer's words. Nagy says the seers "controlled the *content* of the mantic utterance. . . . The *prophetes* controlled the *form*. . . . The *prophetes* was involved in the poetic formalization of prophecy" (in Kugel, p. 61). *Prophetes* took the mantic gibberish and made it into dactylic hexameters.

287: "In preexilic Israel": Kugel, p. 14.

287: "the union of a divine Name": Corbin, cited in N. O. Brown, *Apocalypse*, p. 53. Emphasis deleted.

287: "I long ago lost a hound": Thoreau, *Walden*, Norton critical edition, 2nd ed. (N.Y.: W. W. Norton, 1992), p. 11.

287: meanings have proliferated: See Johnson, *A World of Difference*, pp. 49–56.

288: "A man comes and begs for admittance": Kermode, p. 27; Kafka, pp. 213–15.

288: "intermittent radiances": Kermode, p. 122.

288: "uninterpretable": Kermode, p. 128.

289: "We glimpse the secrecy": Kermode, pp. 144–45.

289: "The world is our beloved codex": Kermode, p. 145.

290: "There are certain sacred sisters": *Hymn to Hermes*, lines 552–63.

291: "Hermes cedes the lyre to Apollo": Nagy in Kugel, p. 58.

291: the honey that the Bee Maidens eat: Scheinberg, p. 5.

292n: Eshu . . . breaking calabashes: Wescott, p. 346.

292: "Any mother, they felt": Hawley, *Krishna, the Butter Thief*, p. 269.

293: Krishna eating dirt: Hawley, *Krishna, the Butter Thief*, p. 269.

293: The child eating dirt: Mary Douglas gives another example of how "eating dirt" makes the world plentiful. In Africa the Lele of the Kasai eat the pangolin, an animal that fits none of the local classifications and is therefore usually thought of as dangerous and unclean. But it can be eaten ritually. "Instead of being abhorred . . . the pangolin is eaten in solemn ceremony by its initiates, who are thereby enabled to minister fertility to their kind. . . . So the pangolin cult is capable of inspiring a profound meditation on the nature of purity and impurity and on the limitation on human contemplation of existence" (pp. 169–70). Again, the ritual presents the group with its dirt, which makes it clear that this world is always larger than human categories can contain. "Dirt eating" in the pangolin cult is prophetic in the sense I'm developing: it suspends the mundane in order to reveal how full the world is in fact. See Douglas, pp. 166–70.

293: the way of the trickster (and the humanists): Ricketts, "The Shaman and the Trickster," p. 88; see also Ricketts, "The North American Indian Trickster," p. 344.

293: "The trickster . . . embodies": Ricketts, "The Shaman," p. 87.

293: "the trickster is an outsider": Ricketts, "The Shaman," pp. 91–92.

294: "did not also obtain superhuman powers": Ricketts, "The Shaman," p. 92.

294: In shamanic initiation: Ricketts, "The Shaman," p. 89.

294: Likewise, dreams of flying: Ricketts, "The Shaman," pp. 89, 94.

294: "Humans were not made to fly": Ricketts, "The Shaman," pp. 94–95.

294: "may be viewed as mockery of shamans": Ricketts, "The Shaman," p. 95.

295: "Coyote functions in the oral literature": Toelken, "The 'Pretty Languages,'" p. 164.

295: unmediated prophecy is a special case: Cooper in Kugel, *Poetry and Prophecy*, pp. 37–40.

296: a confidence man is someone who is in the business of creating belief: See Lindberg, Introduction.

296: creating only rude awakenings: See Neil Harris on Barnum's museum.

297: motley: My remarks on motley were informed by Detienne and Vernant, *Cunning Intelligence*, especially the chapter on Fox and Octopus, and by parts of Mary Douglas, *Purity and Danger*, especially pp. 94, 160–61.

297: gillyflower: The gillyflower is one of the many pied things in *The Winter's Tale*. "The fairest flowers o' the season / Are our carnations, and streak'd gillyvors."

298: "many-coiled intelligence": Aristotle in Detienne, *Cunning Intelligence*, p. 39.

298: "I was the one with the tongue cut loose": Kingston, *Woman Warrior*, p. 197.

298: her mother did this deed: Kingston, *Woman Warrior*, p. 192.

298: so she could translate: Kingston, *Woman Warrior*, pp. 164.

299: "You just translate": Kingston, *Woman Warrior*, p. 170.

299: "My mouth went permanently crooked": Kingston, *Woman Warrior*, p. 171.

299: "the creator thought": Ricketts, "The Structure," p. 140.

299: "The common language was lost": Leydet, p. 78.

300: both translator and prophet: See Steiner, *After Babel*, Chap. 2.

300: Christian and Jewish hermeneuts: Steiner, p. 66.

Fragile Beauty

301: "The simplest term": Rexroth in Hyde, *On The Poetry of Allen Ginsberg*, p. 50.

301: "fucked in the ass": Ginsberg, p. 128.

301: "The tongue and cock and hand": Ginsberg, p. 134.

302: "The striving for the right": Tausk, cited in N. O. Brown, *Love's Body*, p. 149.

302:   Anatole Broyard: Gates, "White Like Me," pp. 74–75.

303:   "the highest duty of the artist": See Kostelanetz, p. 81.

303:   "In France before World War I": Seigel, p. 29.

304:   "When one undergoes": Seigel, pp. 29–30; see also Duchamp, *Salt Seller*, p. 74.

305:   There is a horizontal "horizon": Duchamp, *Salt Seller*, p. 20.

305:   "remain forever": Seigel, p. 97.

305:   "something from nature": Naumann, p. 73.

306:   "*bête comme un peintre*": Duchamp, *Salt Seller*, pp. 125–26.

306:   "Since Courbet": Cabanne, p. 43.

306:   "I wanted to put painting": Duchamp, *Salt Seller*, p. 125.

306:   "as if the two halves": Seigel, p. 105.

306:   "swung on its hinges": Seigel, p. 108.

306:   "I force myself to contradict myself": Duchamp, *Salt Seller*, p. 5.

307:   "Lord Lord Lord caw caw caw": Ginsberg, p. 227.

307:   "Culture is something that is done to us": Cited by Copeland, p. 38.

308:   "Without knowing it": Duchamp in Cabanne, p. 31.

308:   "I began to think": Duchamp in Cabanne, p. 37.

308:   "no one had thought of that": Duchamp in Cabanne, p. 99.

308:   "had the gift of total forgetting": Duchamp, *Salt Seller*, p. 167.

308:   "That is the only thing": Duchamp, *Salt Seller*, p. 126.

309:   "one who comes into a chaotic scene": Kingston in Moyers (videotape).

309:   "At the beginning of [*The Woman Warrior*], I write": Kingston in Moyers (videotape).

309:   "Master, please": *Journey* II, p. 235.

309:   "It is a joy to be hidden": Phillips, *Winnicott*, p. 167. Phillips takes Winnicott's remark about hiding and being found from the 1963 essay, "Communicating and Not Communicating."

310:   "making it part of America": Kingston in Moyers (videotape).

310:   "She brought her songs back from the savage lands": Kingston, *Woman Warrior*, p. 209.

311:   Odysseus is allowed to choose: When I speak of Odysseus choosing the mortal woman over the immortal, and the fragility of that beauty, I am working with ideas developed in the first chapter of Martha Nussbaum's *The Fragility of Goodness*.

312:   Odysseus's tomb: Nagy, *Greek Mythology and Poetics*, pp. 213–15.

Envoi

313:   "The fish trap exists": Chuang Tzu in Keys, p. 64.

313:   "In old times, it is said": Jetté, p. 304.

314:   the storyteller fell instantly silent: Jetté, pp. 298–99.

Appendix II: Trickster and Gender

335: "Most tricksters have an uncertain sexual status": Turner, "Myth and Symbol," p. 580.

335: The Winnebago trickster once disguises himself: Radin, pp. 21–24.

336: Loki once transformed himself: Young, pp. 66–68; Hollander, p. 62.

336: the half-cooked heart of a woman: Bellows, p. 231; Hollander, p. 139.

336: "Why am I doing all this?": Radin, p. 24.

336n: There is a similar motif in Japan: Chan, pp. 232–33; Stone II, p. 129.

336: Baubo: Lubell, passim.

337: "Careful Iambe": *Hymn to Demeter*, lines 200–41 (for example, Hesiod, *The Homeric Hymns and Homerica*, p. 303).

337: "the Orphic version": Allen, Halliday, and Sykes, pp. 150–51.

337: "[The] Athenians and the rest of Greece": *Clement of Alexandria*, G. W. Butterworth, trans., Loeb Classical Library (Cambridge, Mass.: Harvard University Press, 1919), p. 41.

338: "It is likely that the story": Spretnak in Judith Plaskow and Carol P. Christ, eds., *Weaving the Visions: New Patterns in Feminist Spirituality* (San Francisco, Calif.: Harper & Row, 1989), pp. 72–73.

338: Rachel tricks Laban: Genesis 29:31.

338: "the way of women is upon me": Genesis 31:35.

338: "She is a trickster who dupes": Steinberg in Exum, p. 7.

338: Aunt Nancy: Levine, p. 110.

339: Inanna: Fontaine in Exum.

339: Matlacihuatl: Sullivan, p. 51, citing Eva Hunt, *The Transformation of the Hummingbird: Cultural Roots of a Zinacantecan Mythical Poem* (Ithaca, N.Y.: Cornell University Press, 1977).

339: "Sometimes [the story] opens": Ballinger.

340: "The most obvious fact": Ballinger.

341: Matrilineal groups with male tricksters: See William C. Sturtevant, ed., *Handbook of North American Indians* 7 (Washington, D.C.: Smithsonian Institution, 1978), pp. 212, 274.

341: Hawley argues: Hawley, *Krishna, the Butter Thief*, Chap. 9.

341: "Her consistent desire": Hawley, *Krishna, the Butter Thief*, p. 128.

341: "Although his appetite is large": Hawley, *Krishna, the Butter Thief*, p. 295.

342: "Siva's method involves": Hawley, *Krishna, the Butter Thief*, p. 296.

Appendix III: Monkey and the Peaches

347: In his meditations on non-violence: Mohandas K. Gandhi, *All Men Are Brothers*, Krishna Kripalani, ed. (N.Y.: Continuum, 1982), pp. 33, 91.

347n: who wrote the original: See Anthony Yu's introduction to *Journey* I, p. 21.

348: "Though I am very happy": *Journey* I, pp. 72–73.

348: The story of the Peaches of Immortality: *Journey* I, pp. 131–49.

348: these peaches ripen: *Journey* I, pp. 135–36, 509; Nienhauser, p. 145.

349: Lao Tzu's fabulous Elixir: *Journey* I, p. 510.

349: Dumping the tablets: *Journey* I, p. 141.

349: "an enormous appetite": *Journey* IV, p. 425.

350: "governed by carnal lusts": Dudbridge, p. 126.

350: Even in *Journey*: Dudbridge, pp. 168, 170, 175.

350: "Honor the unity": *Journey* III, p. 354.

350: He harasses Taoist immortals: *Journey* I, p. 509; Nienhauser, p. 145.

351: "It's old Monkey": *Journey* I, p. 387; see also I, p. 56, and II, p. 3.

351: *Journey* increases the Buddha's power: Dudbridge, pp. 164, 112.

352: Monkey's spiritual name: *Journey* I, p. 82.

353: hundreds of such details: Kingston, *Tripmaster*, pp. 27, 69, 316; see especially pp. 310ff.

353: "a mobile army of metaphors": Nietzsche, p. 250.

353: "the present-day U.S.A.": Kingston, *Tripmaster Monkey*, p. 33.

353: "The King of the Monkeys hereby": Kingston, *Tripmaster*, p. 317.

353: "He'll eat everything": Kingston, *Tripmaster*, p. 137.

353: "The curtain opens": Kingston, *Tripmaster*, pp. 221–22.

354: "Are you a loose white girl?": Kingston, *Tripmaster*, p. 151.

354: "I'm going to bring back": Kingston, *Tripmaster*, p. 149; see also pp. 141, 250.

354: "People are trapped in history": Baldwin in Kingston, *Tripmaster*, p. 310.

BIBLIOGRAPHY

Abimbola, Wande, and Barry Hallen. "Secrecy and Objectivity in the Methodology and Literature of Ifa Divination." *Secrecy: African Art That Conceals and Reveals.* Mary H. Nooter, ed. N.Y.: Museum for African Art, 1993. 210–20.

Abrahams, Roger D. *Deep Down in the Jungle: Negro Narrative Folklore from the Streets of Philadelphia.* Chicago, Ill.: Aldine Publishing, 1970.

———. "Playing the Dozens," in Dundes, *Mother Wit,* 295–309.

Aeschylus. *Prometheus Bound.* Warren D. Anderson, trans. N.Y.: Bobbs-Merrill, 1963.

Allen, T. W., W. R. Halliday, and E. E. Sikes. *The Homeric Hymns,* 2nd ed. Oxford: Clarendon Press, 1936.

Aristotle. *The Physics.* 2 vols. Philip Wicksteed and Francis Cornford, trans. Loeb Classical Library. Cambridge, Mass.: Harvard University Press, 1929.

———. *Historia Animalium.* 2 vols. A. L. Peck, trans. Loeb Classical Library. Cambridge, Mass.: Harvard University Press, 1965.

Arnheim, Rudolf. "Accident and the Necessity of Art." *Toward a Psychology of Art.* Berkeley: University of California Press, 1966. 162–80.

Austin, M. M., and P. Vidal-Naquet. *Economic and Social History of Ancient Greece.* Berkeley: University of California Press, 1977.

Austin, James H. *Chase, Chance, and Creativity.* N.Y.: Columbia University Press, 1978.

Bakhtin, Mikhail. *Rabelais and His World.* Helene Iswolsky, trans. Cambridge, Mass.: MIT Press, 1968.

———. *The Problem of Dostoevsky's Poetics.* Minneapolis: University of Minnesota Press, 1984.

Ballinger, Franchot. "Coyote, She Was Going There: Prowling for Hypotheses about the Female Native American Trickster." Unpublished talk given at the Modern Languages Association meeting, December 1988.

Barlow, William. *"Looking Up and Down": The Emergence of Blues Culture in Philadelphia.* Philadelphia, Penn.: Temple University Press, 1989.

Barnhart, Robert K., ed. *The Barnhart Dictionary of Etymology.* N.Y.: H. W. Wilson Company, 1988.

Barthes, Roland. *The Grain of the Voice.* N.Y.: Hill and Wang, 1985.

Bascom, William. *Ifa Divination: Communication Between Gods and Men in West Africa.* Midland Book ed. Bloomington: Indiana University Press, 1991.

Basso, Ellen B. *In Favor of Deceit: A Study of Tricksters in an Amazonian Society.* Tucson: University of Arizona Press, 1987.

Beck, Mary L. "Raven." *The Indian Historian* 12.2 (Summer 1979): 50–53.

The Beginnings of Monkey. Adapted from the novel *Journey to the West* by Gao Mingyou. Beijing: Foreign Languages Press, 1985. [This is the first of the 34-volume "Monkey Series" from Foreign Languages Press.]

Bellows, Henry Adams, trans. *The Poetic Edda*. N.Y.: American-Scandinavian Foundation, 1923.

Benedict, Ruth. *The Chrysanthemum and the Sword: Patterns of Japanese Culture*. Boston, Mass.: Houghton Mifflin, 1946.

Bercovitch, Sacvan. "The Problem of Ideology in American Literary History." *Critical Inquiry* 12 (Summer 1986): 631–53.

Bernstein, Charles. *Artifice of Absorption*. Philadelphia, Penn.: Singing Horse Press, 1987.

Bingham, Caleb. *The Columbian Orator*. Boston, Mass.: J.H.A. Frost, Lincoln and Edmands, 1832.

Blyth, R. H. *Haiku*. 4 vols. Tokyo: Hokuseido, 1966.

Boas, Franz. Introduction to *Traditions of the Thompson River Indians* by James Teit. Memoirs of the American Folklore Society. Vol. 6. N.Y.: Houghton Mifflin, 1898. 1–18.

———. "Tsimshian Mythology." *Report of the Bureau of American Ethnology*. Vol. XXXI. Washington, D.C.: Government Printing Office, 1916. 30–1037.

Boelaars, J.H.M.C. *Headhunters about Themselves: An Ethnographic Report from Irian Jaya, Indonesia*. The Hague: Martinus Nijoff, 1981.

Boethius. *The Consolation of Philosophy*. Arundel, Eng.: Centaur Press, 1963.

Bright, William. *A Coyote Reader*. Berkeley: University of California Press, 1993.

Brinton, Daniel G. *The Myths of the New World: A Treatise on the Symbolism and Mythology of the Red Race of America*. 1st ed. N.Y.: Leypoldt & Holt, 1868.

Brodeur, Arthur Gilchrist, trans. *The Prose Edda*. N.Y.: The American-Scandinavian Foundation, 1929.

Brown, Karen McCarthy. *Mama Lola: A Vodou Priestess in Brooklyn*. Berkeley: University of California Press, 1991.

Brown, Norman O. *Hermes the Thief*. Madison: University of Wisconsin Press, 1947.

———. *Love's Body*. N.Y.: Vintage, 1966.

———. *Apocalypse and/or Metamorphosis*. Berkeley: University of California Press, 1991.

Burkert, Walter. *Homo Necans: The Anthropology of Ancient Greek Sacrificial Ritual and Myth*. Berkeley: University of California Press, 1983.

———. "Sacrificio-sacrilego: il trickster fondatore." *Studi Storici* 4 (1984): 835–45.

———. *Greek Religion*. John Raffan, trans. Cambridge, Mass.: Harvard University Press, 1985.

Cabanne, Pierre. *Dialogues with Marcel Duchamp*. Ron Padgett, trans. N.Y.: Da Capo Press, 1987.

Cabrera, Lydia. *El Monte*. Havana, Cuba: Ediciones CR, 1954.

Cage, John. *Silence*. Middletown, Conn.: Wesleyan University Press, 1961.

————. *For the Birds*. Boston, Mass.: Marion Boyars, 1981.

————. *Themes and Variations*. Barrytown, N.Y.: Station Hill Press, 1982.

Cairns, Douglas L. *Aidos: The Psychology and Ethics of Honour and Shame in Ancient Greek Literature*. Oxford: Clarendon Press, 1993.

Callaway, Canon. *Nursery Tales, Traditions, and Histories of the Zulus*. Vol. I. London: Trübner and Co., 1868.

Camp, John M. *The Athenian Agora*. N.Y.: Thames & Hudson, 1986.

Carroll, Michael P. "Lévi-Strauss, Freud, and the Trickster." *American Ethnologist* 8 (1981): 301–13.

Chamberlin, J. Edward. "Telling Tales." *Connotations* 1.1 (1993): 13–19.

Chan, Wing-Tsit, ed. *The Great Asian Religions: An Anthology*. N.Y.: Macmillan, 1969.

Clay, Jenny Strauss. *The Politics of Olympus*. Princeton, N.J.: Princeton University Press, 1989.

Cleckley, H. *The Mask of Sanity*, rev. ed. St. Louis, Mo.: Mosby, 1982.

Cooper, Alan. "Imagining Prophecy," in Kugel, *Poetry and Prophecy*, 26–44.

Copeland, Roger. "Against Instinct: The Denatured Dances of Merce Cunningham." *Working Papers* [London] (Fall 1990): 41–57.

Corbin, Henry. *Creative Imagination in the Sufism of Ibn Arabi*. Ralph Manheim, trans. Princeton, N.J.: Princeton University Press, 1969.

Cosentino, Donald. "Who Is That Fellow in the Many-colored Cap? Transformations of Eshu in Old and New World Mythologies." *Journal of American Folklore* 100 (1987): 261–75.

Courlander, Harold. *Tales of Yoruba Gods and Heroes*. N.Y.: Crown, 1973.

Cunliffe, Richard John. *A Lexicon of the Homeric Dialect*. Norman: University of Oklahoma Press, 1963.

Dance, Daryl Cumber. *Shuckin' and Jivin'*. Bloomington: University of Indiana Press, 1978.

Davis, Natalie Zemon. *Society and Culture in Early Modern France*. Stanford, Calif.: Stanford University Press, 1975.

Dawkins, Richard. *The Blind Watchmaker*. N.Y.: W. W. Norton, 1987.

Detienne, Marcel, and Jean-Pierre Vernant. *Cunning Intelligence in Greek Culture and Society*. Janet Lloyd, trans. Chicago: University of Chicago Press, 1991.

———— et al. *The Cuisine of Sacrifice Among the Greeks*. Paula Wissing, trans. Chicago: University of Chicago Press, 1989.

de Vries, Ad. *Dictionary of Symbols and Imagery*. N.Y.: Elsevier, 1984.

Diamond, Stanley. "Job and the Trickster," in Radin, *The Trickster*, xi–xxii.

Dimmitt, Cornelia, and J.A.B. van Buitenen, eds. *Classical Hindu Mythology*. Philadelphia, Penn.: Temple University Press, 1978.

Doan, James E. "Cearbhall Ó Dálaigh as Craftsman and Trickster." *Bealoideas: The Journal of the Folklore of Ireland Society* 50 (1982): 54–89.

Dodds, E. R. *The Greeks and the Irrational*. Berkeley: University of California Press, 1951.

Dollard, John. "The Dozens: Dialect of Insult," in Dundes, *Mother Wit*, 277–94.

Dostoevsky, F. M. *The Diary of a Writer*. 2 vols. Boris Brasol, trans. N.Y.: Octagon Books, 1973.

Douglas, Mary. *Purity and Danger*. London: Routledge & Kegan Paul, 1978.

Douglass, Frederick. *The Life and Times of Frederick Douglass, From 1817 to 1882, Written by Himself*. London: Christian Age Office, 1882.

——. *Narrative of the Life of Frederick Douglass, an American Slave, Written by Himself*. Houston A. Baker, Jr., ed. N.Y. and London: Penguin Books, 1982. [First ed.: Boston: Anti-Slavery Office, 1845.]

——. *My Bondage and My Freedom*. William L. Andrews, ed. Urbana and Chicago: University of Illinois Press, 1987. [First ed.: N.Y.: Miller, Orton and Mulligan, 1855.]

Dronke, Ursula. *The Heroic Poems*. Vol. 1 of *The Poetic Edda*. Oxford: Clarendon Press, 1969.

Duchamp, Marcel. *Notes and Projects for the Large Glass*. George H. Hamilton et al., trans. London: Thames and Hudson, 1969.

——. *Salt Seller: The Writings of Marcel Duchamp*. N.Y.: Oxford University Press, 1973.

——. *The Bride Stripped Bare by Her Bachelors, Even. A typographic version by Richard Hamilton of Marcel Duchamp's Green Box*. George Heard Hamilton, trans. Stuttgart: Edition Hansjörg Mayer, 1976.

Dudbridge, Glen. *The Hsi-yu chi: A Study of the Antecedents to the Sixteenth-Century Chinese Novel*. Cambridge, Eng.: Cambridge University Press, 1970.

Dumézil, Georges. *Gods of the Ancient Northmen*. Berkeley: University of California Press, 1973.

——. *Loki*. Paris: Flammarion, 1986.

Dundes, Alan. "African Tales Among the North American Indians." *Southern Folklore Quarterly* 29 (1965): 207–19.

——, ed. *Mother Wit from the Laughing Barrel*. Englewood Cliffs, N.J.: Prentice-Hall, 1973.

Eco, Umberto. *A Theory of Semiotics*. Bloomington: Indiana University Press, 1976.

Ellison, Ralph. "Change the Joke and Slip the Yoke." *Shadow and Act*. N.Y.: Random House, 1964. 45–59.

——. *Invisible Man*. N.Y.: Modern Library, 1992.

Ellwood, Robert S. "A Japanese Mythic Trickster Figure: Susa-nö-o," in Hynes and Doty, *Mythical Trickster Figures*, 141–58.

Exum, J. Cheryl, and Johanna W. H. Bos, eds. *Reasoning with the Foxes: Female Wit in a World of Male Power*. Atlanta, Ga.: Scholars Press, 1988.

Farnell, Lewis Richard. *The Cults of the Greek States*. 5 vols. Oxford: Clarendon Press, 1910.

Faulkes, Anthony. *Snorri Sturluson, Edda*. Anthony Faulkes, trans. and intro. London: Charles E. Tuttle Co., J. M. Dent & Sons, 1987.

Fischer, N.R.E. *Hybris: A Study in the Values of Honour and Shame in Ancient Greece*. Warminster, Eng.: Aris & Phillips, 1992.

Flaceliere, Robert. *Greek Oracles*. Douglas Garman, trans. N.Y.: W. W. Norton, 1965.

Fontaine, Carole. "The Deceptive Goddess in Ancient Near Eastern Myth: Inanna and Inaras," in Exum, *Reasoning with the Foxes*, 84–102.

Forster, E. M. *Aspects of the Novel*. N.Y.: Harcourt, Brace, 1927.

Foster, George. "Peasant Society and the Image of Limited Good." *American Anthropologist* 67 (1965): 293–315.

Fox, Nicols. "NEA Under Siege." *New Art Examiner* (Chicago) 16.11 (1989): 18–23.

Frazer, James George. *The Illustrated Golden Bough*. N.Y.: Doubleday, 1978.

Freud, Sigmund. *A General Introduction to Psychoanalysis*. Garden City: Garden City Publishing Company, 1943.

Frobenius, Leo. *The Voice of Africa*. 2 vols. Rudolf Blind, trans. N.Y.: Benjamin Blom, 1913.

Gates, Henry Louis, Jr. *Figures in Black: Words, Signs, and the "Racial" Self*. N.Y.: Oxford University Press, 1987.

———. *The Signifying Monkey*. N.Y.: Oxford University Press, 1988.

———. "White Like Me." *The New Yorker*, June 17, 1996: 66–81.

Ginsberg, Allen. *Collected Poems*. N.Y.: Harper & Row, 1984.

Glare, P.G.W., ed. *The Oxford Latin Dictionary*. Oxford: Clarendon Press, 1982.

Gleick, James. *Chaos: Making a New Science*. N.Y.: Penguin Books, 1988.

Graves, Robert. *The Greek Myths*. 2 vols. N.Y.: George Braziller, 1957.

Greenblatt, Stephen. "Filthy Rites." *Daedalus* 3.3 (Summer 1982): 1–16.

Hacking, Ian. *The Taming of Chance*. Cambridge: Cambridge University Press, 1990.

Halttunen, Karen. *Confidence Men and Painted Women*. New Haven, Conn.: Yale University Press, 1982.

Hampton, Bill R. "On Identification and Negro Tricksters." *Southern Folklore Quarterly* 31.1 (March 1967): 55–65.

Harris, Joel Chandler. *Uncle Remus, His Songs and His Sayings*. N.Y.: Penguin Books, 1982.

Harris, Neil. *Humbug: The Art of P. T. Barnum*. Boston, Mass.: Little, Brown, 1973.

Harris, Marvin. *Cultural Materialism*. N.Y.: Random House, 1979.

Harrison, Alan. *The Irish Trickster*. Sheffield, Eng.: Sheffield Academic Press, 1989.

Hawley, John Stratton. "Thief of Butter, Thief of Love." *History of Religions* XVIII.3 (1979): 203–20.

———. *Krishna, the Butter Thief*. Princeton, N.J.: Princeton University Press, 1983.

394 .... BIBLIOGRAPHY ....

————. *At Play with Krishna: Pilgrimage Dramas from Brindavan.* Princeton, N.J.: Princeton University Press, 1983.

————. "The Thief in Krishna." *Parabola* 9.2 (1984): 6–13.

Hemenway, Robert. Introduction to *Uncle Remus, His Songs and His Sayings* by Joel Chandler Harris. N.Y.: Penguin Books, 1982. 7–31.

Herbert, Jean. *Shinto; at the Fountain-head of Japan.* N.Y.: Stein and Day, 1967.

Herskovits, Melville J. *Dahomey: An Ancient West African Kingdom,* 2nd ed. 2 vols. Evanston, Ill.: Northwestern University Press, 1958.

————, and Frances S. Herskovits. "Tales in Pidgin English from Nigeria." *Journal of American Folklore* XLIV (1931): 448–66.

————. *Dahomean Narrative: A Cross-cultural Narrative.* Evanston, Ill.: Northwestern University Press, 1958.

Hesiod, The Homeric Hymns and Homerica. Hugh G. Evelyn-White, trans. Loeb Classical Library. Cambridge, Mass.: Harvard University Press, 1914.

Hill, Douglas. "Trickster." *Man, Mythic and Magic: An Illustrated Encyclopedia of the Supernatural.* Vol. 21. Richard Cavendish, ed. N.Y.: Marshall Cavendish, 1970. 2881–85.

Hillman, James. *Puer Papers.* Dallas, Tex.: Spring Publications, 1979.

Hollander, Lee M., trans. *The Poetic Edda.* 2nd, rev. ed. Austin: University of Texas Press, 1962.

Hurston, Zora Neale. "High John de Conquer," in Dundes, *Mother Wit,* 541–48.

Hyde, Lewis. *The Gift.* N.Y.: Random House, 1983.

————, ed. *On the Poetry of Allen Ginsberg.* Ann Arbor: University of Michigan Press, 1984.

Hymn to Demeter. See *Hesiod, The Homeric Hymns and Homerica.*

Hymn to Hermes. See Appendix I, and *Hesiod, The Homeric Hymns and Homerica.*

Hynes, William J., and William G. Doty, eds. *Mythical Trickster Figures.* Tuscaloosa: University of Alabama Press, 1993.

————. "Mapping the Characteristics of Mythic Tricksters: A Heuristic Guide," in Hynes and Doty, eds., *Mythical Trickster Figures,* 33–45.

The I Ching. 3rd ed. Princeton, N.J.: Princeton University Press, 1967.

Idewu, Olawale, and Omotayo Adu, eds. *Nigerian Folk Tales.* New Brunswick, N.J.: Rutgers University Press, 1961.

Jackson, Bruce. *Get Your Ass in the Water and Swim Like Me: Narrative Poetry from the Black Oral Tradition.* Cambridge, Mass.: Harvard University Press, 1974.

Janko, Richard. *Homer, Hesiod and the Hymns.* London: Cambridge University Press, 1982.

Jerison, Harry J. *Evolution of the Brain and Intelligence.* N.Y.: Academic Press, 1973.

Jetté, J. "On Ten'a Folk-Lore." *The Journal of the Royal Anthropological Institute of Great Britain and Ireland* 38 (1908): 298–367.

Johnson, Barbara. "A Hound, a Bay Horse, and a Turtle Dove: Obscurity in *Walden.*" *A World of Difference.* Baltimore, Md.: Johns Hopkins University Press, 1987. 49–56.

The Journey to the West. Anthony C. Yu, trans. and ed. 4 vols. Chicago: University of Chicago Press, 1977–83.

Joyce, James. *Selected Letters of James Joyce.* Richard Ellmann, ed. N.Y.: Viking Press, 1975.

Jung, Carl. *Alchemical Studies.* Vol. 13 of *The Collected Works.* Princeton, N.J.: Princeton University Press, 1966.

———. Foreword to *The I Ching,* 3rd ed. Richard Wilhelm and Cary F. Baynes, trans. Bollingen Series XIX. Princeton, N.J.: Princeton University Press, 1967. xxi–xxxix.

———. *Memories, Dreams and Reflections.* Aniela Jaffé, ed. N.Y.: Pantheon, 1973.

Kafka, Franz. *The Trial.* N.Y.: Schocken Books, 1995.

Kahn, Laurence. *Hermès Passe, ou les Ambiguïtés de la Communication.* Paris: François Maspero, 1978.

Kerényi, Carl. "The Primordial Child in Primordial Times," in *Essays on a Science of Mythology* by Carl Jung and Carl Kerényi. Princeton, N.J.: Princeton University Press, 1969. 25–69.

———. *Hermes, Guide of Souls.* Dallas, Tex.: Spring Publications, 1986.

Kermode, Frank. *The Genesis of Secrecy: On the Interpretation of Narrative.* Cambridge, Mass.: Harvard University Press, 1979.

Keys, Kerry Shawn. *Seams.* San Francisco, Calif.: Formant Press, 1985.

Kingston, Maxine Hong. *The Woman Warrior.* N.Y.: Vintage International, 1989.

———. *Tripmaster Monkey: His Fake Book.* N.Y.: Alfred A. Knopf, 1989.

Klein, Ernest. *A Comprehensive Etymological Dictionary of the English Language.* N.Y.: Elsevier, 1966.

Kojiki. Donald L. Philippi, trans. Princeton, N.J.: Princeton University Press, 1969.

Kostelanetz, Richard. *Conversing with Cage.* N.Y.: Limelight Editions, 1991.

Kroeber, A. L. "Cheyenne Tales." *Journal of American Folklore* XIII. 1 (July–September 1900): 161–90.

Kugel, James L., ed. *Poetry and Prophecy.* Ithaca, N.Y.: Cornell University Press, 1990.

Kundera, Milan. *The Unbearable Lightness of Being.* N.Y.: Harper and Row, 1984.

Levine, Lawrence. *Black Culture and Black Consciousness.* N.Y.: Oxford University Press, 1977.

Lévi-Strauss, Claude. *Structural Anthropology.* 2 vols. Claire Jacobson, trans. N.Y.: Basic Books, 1963.

Leydet, François. *The Coyote.* Rev. ed. Norman: University of Oklahoma Press, 1988.

Liddell, Henry George, and Robert Scott. *A Greek-English Lexicon,* 9th ed. Oxford: Clarendon Press, 1989.

Lincoln, Bruce. *Death, War, and Sacrifice.* Chicago: University of Chicago Press, 1991.

Lindberg, Gary. *The Confidence Man in American Literature.* N.Y.: Oxford University Press, 1982.

Lopez, Barry. *Giving Birth to Thunder, Sleeping with His Daughter: Coyote Builds North America*. N.Y.: Avon Books, 1990.

López-Pedraza, Rafael. *Hermes and His Children*. Einsiedeln, Switz.: Daimon Verlag, 1989.

Lubell, Winifred Milius. *The Metamorphosis of Baubo*. Nashville, Tenn.: Vanderbilt University Press, 1994.

Luckert, Karl W. *Coyoteway: A Navajo Holyway Healing Ceremonial*. Tucson: University of Arizona Press, 1979.

Luomala, Katharine. *Maui-of-a-Thousand-Tricks*. Bishop Museum Bulletin Series. Honolulu: Bernice P. Bishop Museum, 1949.

Lynd, Helen Merrell. *On Shame and the Search for Identity*. N.Y.: Harcourt, Brace, 1958.

McKenna, George L. *Art by Chance: Fortuitous Impressions*. Kansas City, Mo.: Nelson-Atkins Museum of Art, 1989.

Makarius, Laura. "The Myth of the Trickster: The Necessary Breaker of Taboos," in Hynes and Doty, *Mythical Trickster Figures*, 66–86.

Malotki, Ekkehart, and Michael Lomatuway'ma. *Hopi Coyote Tales: Istutuwutsi*. American Tribal Religion Series 9. Lincoln: University of Nebraska Press, 1984.

Mann, Stuart E. *An Indo-European Comparative Dictionary*. Hamburg, Ger.: H. Buske, 1984–87.

Masayevsa, Victor. *Ritual Clowns*. Videotape. Hotevilla, Ariz.: IS Productions, 1988.

Melville, Herman. *The Confidence-Man: His Masquerade*. Hershel Parker, ed. N.Y.: W. W. Norton, 1971.

Merrill, Walter M., ed. *No Union with Slave Holders, 1841–1849*. Vol. 3 of *The Letters of William Lloyd Garrison*. Cambridge, Mass.: Harvard University Press, 1973.

Milosz, Czeslaw. *Emperor of the Earth*. Berkeley: University of California Press, 1977.

Mingyou, Gao. See *The Beginnings of Monkey*.

Monod, Jacques. *Chance and Necessity*. Austryn Wainhouse, trans. N.Y.: Vintage, 1972.

Moure, Gloria. *Marcel Duchamp*. London: Thames and Hudson, 1988.

Mourning Dove. *Coyote Stories*. Lincoln: University of Nebraska Press, 1990.

Moyers, Bill. "An Interview with Maxine Hong Kingston. The Stories of Maxine Hong Kingston." Videotape. Public Affairs Television, Inc., Judith D. Moyers and Bill Moyers. *A World of Ideas* Series, 1990.

Nachmanovitch, Stephen. *Free Play: The Power of Improvisation in Life and the Arts*. Los Angeles, Calif.: Jeremy P. Tarcher, 1990.

Nagy, Gregory. "Ancient Greek Poetry, Prophecy, and Concepts of Theory," in Kugel, *Poetry and Prophecy*, 56–64.

———. *Greek Mythology and Poetics*. Ithaca, N.Y.: Cornell University Press, 1990.

Naumann, Francis. "The Bachelor's Quest." *Art in America*, September 1993: 73ff.

Nelson, Richard. *Make Prayers to the Raven: A Koyukon View of the Northern Forest*. Chicago: University of Chicago Press, 1983.

Nienhauser, William, ed. *The Indiana Companion to Traditional Chinese Literature*. Bloomington: Indiana University Press, 1986.

Nietzsche, Friedrich. "On Truth and Lying in an Extra-Moral Sense." *Friedrich Nietzsche on Rhetoric and Language*. N.Y.: Oxford University Press, 1989. 246–57.

Nihongi. See Herbert, Jean, *Shinto*.

Norman, Howard. "Wesucechak Becomes a Deer and Steals Language." *Recovering the Word: Essays on Native American Literature*. Brian Swann and Arnold Krupat, eds. Berkeley: University of California Press, 1987. 402–21.

Nussbaum, Martha. *The Fragility of Goodness*. N.Y.: Cambridge University Press, 1986.

Ogundipe, Ayodele. "Esu Elegbara, the Yoruba God of Chance and Uncertainty: A Study in Yoruba Mythology." 2 vols. Doctoral dissertation. Indiana University, 1978.

Onians, R. B. *The Origins of European Thought*. Cambridge and N.Y.: Cambridge University Press, 1951.

Oppenheimer, Paul, ed. *A Pleasant Vintage of Till Eulenspiegel*. Middletown, Conn.: Wesleyan University Press, 1972.

Otto, Walter F. *The Homeric Gods*. N.Y.: Pantheon, 1954.

Ouwehand, Cornelius. "Some Notes on the God Susa-nö-o." *Monumenta Nipponica* 14.3 (1958): 138–61.

Ovid. *Metamorphoses*. 2 vols. Frank Justus Miller, trans. Loeb Classical Library. Cambridge, Mass.: Harvard University Press, 1976–77.

Oxford English Dictionary. 20 vols. Oxford: Clarendon Press, 1989.

Page, R. I. *Norse Myths*. London: British Museum Press, 1990.

Parsons, Elsie Clews. *Tewa Tales*. N.Y.: American Folklore Society Memoirs, 1926.

Paz, Octavio. *Marcel Duchamp, Appearance Stripped Bare*. N.Y.: Arcade Publishing (Little, Brown), 1978.

Pelton, Robert. *The Trickster in West Africa*. Berkeley: University of California Press, 1980.

Pendlesonn, K.R.G. *The Vikings*. N.Y.: Windward Books, 1980.

Philippi. See *Kojiki*.

Phillips, Adam. *Winnicott*. Cambridge, Mass.: Harvard University Press, 1988.

Phinney, Archie. *Nez Percé Texts*. Vol. XXV. Columbia University Contributions to Anthropology. N.Y.: Columbia University Press, 1934.

Picasso, Pablo. *Picasso on Art*. Dore Ashton, ed. N.Y.: Da Capo Press, 1972.

Plato. *The Dialogues of Plato*. 2 vols. B. Jowett, trans. N.Y.: Random House, 1937.

———. *The Collected Dialogues*. Edith Hamilton and Huntington Cairns, eds. Princeton, N.J.: Princeton University Press, 1961.

The Poetic Edda. See Bellows, Henry Adams, and Hollander, Lee.

Pokorny, Julius. *Indogermanisches Etymologisches Wörterbuch*. Bern, Switz.: Francke, 1989.

Polomé, Edgar C. "Loki." *The Encyclopedia of Religion*. Mircea Eliade, ed. 16 vols. N.Y.: Macmillan, 1987.

Preston, Dickson J. *Young Frederick Douglass: The Maryland Years*. Baltimore, Md.: Johns Hopkins University Press, 1980.

Propp, Vladímir. *Morphology of the Folktale*. Austin: University of Texas Press, 1968.

The Prose Edda. See Young, Jean I., and Faulkes, Anthony.

Pucci, Pietro. *Odysseus Polutropos*. Ithaca, N.Y.: Cornell University Press, 1987.

Radin, Paul. *The Trickster: A Study in American Indian Mythology*. N.Y.: Schocken Books, 1972.

Ramsey, Jarold, ed. *Coyote Was Going There: Indian Literature of the Oregon Country*. Seattle: University of Washington Press, 1977.

Reed, Ishmael. *Conjure*. Amherst: University of Massachusetts Press, 1972.

Revill, David. *The Roaring Silence. John Cage: A Life*. N.Y.: Arcade Publishing, 1992.

Richardson, John. *A Life of Picasso 1881–1906*. N.Y.: Random House, 1991.

Ricketts, Mac Linscott. "The Structure and Religious Significance of the Trickster-Transformer-Culture Hero in the Mythology of the North American Indians." Doctoral dissertation. University of Chicago, 1964.

———. "The North American Indian Trickster." *History of Religions* 5.2 (1966): 327–50.

———. "The Shaman and the Trickster," in Hynes and Doty, *Mythical Trickster Figures*, 87–105.

Roberts, Royston M. *Serendipity: Accidental Discoveries in Science*. N.Y.: Wiley & Sons, 1989.

Rodriguez, Richard. *Hunger of Memory: The Education of Richard Rodriguez*. N.Y.: Bantam Books, 1983.

Rorty, Richard. *Contingency, Irony, and Solidarity*. N.Y.: Cambridge University Press, 1989.

Ryden, Hope. *God's Dog*. N.Y.: Penguin, 1975.

Scheinberg, Susan. "The Bee Maidens of the Homeric Hymn to Hermes." *Harvard Studies in Classical Philology* 83 (1979): 1–28.

Schröder, Franz Rolf. "Das Symposium der Lokasenna." *Arkiv for nordisk filologi* 67 (1952): 1–29.

Sealey, Raphael. *Women and Law in Classical Greece*. Chapel Hill: University of North Carolina Press, 1990.

Seigel, Jerrold. *The Private Worlds of Marcel Duchamp*. Berkeley: University of California Press, 1995.

Serres, Michel. *Hermes: Literature, Science, Philosophy*. Baltimore, Md.: Johns Hopkins University Press, 1983.

Smith, Jonathan Z. *Map Is Not Territory: Studies in the History of Religions*. Berkeley: University of California Press, 1993.

Smith, Valerie. *Self-Discovery and Authority in Afro-American Narrative*. Cambridge, Mass.: Harvard University Press, 1987.

Snyder, Gary. "The Incredible Survival of Coyote." *The Old Ways*. San Francisco, Calif.: City Lights Books, 1977. 67–93.

Stallybrass, Peter, and Allen White. *The Politics and Poetics of Transgression*. Ithaca, N.Y.: Cornell University Press, 1986.

Steinberg, Naomi. "Israelite Tricksters, Their Analogies and Cross-Cultural Study," in Exum et al., eds., *Reasoning with the Foxes*, 1–13.

Steiner, George. *After Babel*. London: Oxford University Press, 1975.

Stone, Merlin. *Ancient Mirrors of Womanhood*. 2 vols. N.Y.: New Sibylline Books, 1979.

Strathern, Andrew. "Why Is Shame on the Skin?" *The Anthropology of the Body*. John Blacking, ed. London: Academic Press, 1977. 99–110.

Sturluson, Snorri. *See* Young, Jean, *The Prose Edda*; Hollander, Lee, *The Poetic Edda*; Bellows, Henry Adams, *The Poetic Edda*; and Faulkes, Anthony, *Snorri Sturluson, Edda*.

Sullivan, Lawrence E., Robert D. Pelton, and Mac Linscott Ricketts. "Tricksters." *The Encyclopedia of Religion*. M. Eliade, ed. N.Y.: Macmillan, 1987. 45–53.

Swanton, John R. *Tlingit Myths and Texts*. Washington, D.C.: Smithsonian Institution Bureau of American Ethnology, 1909.

Thompson, Stith. *Tales of the North American Indians*. Bloomington: Indiana University Press, 1929.

Thorsen, Karen, and Douglas K. Dempsey. *James Baldwin: The Price of the Ticket*. Videotape. San Francisco: California Newsreel, 1989.

Thwaites, Reuben Gold. *The Jesuit Relations and Allied Documents*. 73 vols. Cleveland, Ohio: Burrows Brothers Company, 1896–1901.

Toelken, J. Barre. "The 'Pretty Languages' of Yellowman: Genre, Mode, and Texture in Navajo Coyote Narratives." *Folklore Genres*. Dan Ben-Amos, ed. Austin: University of Texas Press, 1976. 145–70.

———. "Life and Death in the Navajo Coyote Tales." *Recovering the Word: Essays on Native American Literature*. Brian Swann and Arnold Krupat, eds. Berkeley: University of California Press, 1987. 388–401.

Tomkins, Calvin. *The Bride & The Bachelors*. N.Y.: Viking Press, 1965.

Tompson, Robert Farris. *Black Gods and Kings: Yoruba Art at UCLA*. Bloomington: Indiana University Press, 1976.

Turner, Victor. "Myth and Symbol." *International Encyclopedia of the Social Sciences*. David Sills, ed. N.Y.: Macmillan & The Free Press, 1972. 580–81.

———. *The Ritual Process*. Ithaca, N.Y.: Cornell University Press, 1977.

Vigfusson, Gudbrand, and F. York Powell, trans. *Corpus Poeticum Boreale*. 2 vols. London: Oxford University Press, 1883.

Vizenor, Gerald. *Griever, An American Monkey King in China*. Normal: Illinois State University, 1987.

———. *The Trickster of Liberty: Tribal Heirs to a Wild Baronage*. Minneapolis: University of Minnesota Press, 1988.

von Franz, Marie-Louise. *On Divination and Synchronicity: The Psychology of Meaningful Chance*. Toronto, Canada: Inner City Books, 1980.

Wadlington, Warwick. *The Confidence Game in American Literature*. Princeton, N.J.: Princeton University Press, 1975.

Walker, Barbara K., and Warren S. Walker, eds. *Nigerian Folk Tales*. As told by Olawale Idewu and Omotayo Adu. New Brunswick, N.J.: Rutgers University Press, 1961.

Walker, Peter F. *Moral Choices: Memory, Desire, and Imagination in Nineteenth-Century American Abolition*. Baton Rouge: Louisiana State University Press, 1978.

Watts, Harriett Ann. *Chance: A Perspective on Dada*. Ann Arbor, Mich.: University Microfilms International Research Press, 1980.

Wescott, Joan. "The Sculpture and Myths of Eshu-Elegba, the Yoruba Trickster." *Africa* [Journal of the International African Institute, London] 32 (1962): 336–53.

Wilde, Oscar. "The Decay of Lying." *Selected Writings*. London: Oxford University Press, 1961.

Wilson, Elizabeth. *Nez Percé Stories*. Audiotape. San Francisco, Calif.: Wild Sanctuary Communications, 1991.

Wurmser, Leon. *The Mask of Shame*. Baltimore, Md.: Johns Hopkins University Press, 1981.

Young, Jean I. *The Prose Edda of Snorri Sturluson*. Berkeley: University of California Press, 1966.

Yu, Anthony C. See *The Journey to the West*.

ACKNOWLEDGMENTS

I'm grateful to the Kenyon College community for inviting me to teach and supporting me as the Henry Luce Professor of Art and Politics during most of the years it took to make this book. I'm grateful, also, to the Luce Foundation, which funds the Luce Professors Program. At Kenyon, members of the Kenyon Seminar responded to many chapters of the work in progress. Thanks go especially to Jennifer Clarvoe, Lori Lefkovitz, and Peter Rutkoff. Ron Sharp was always willing to mark up my pages and talk way past closing time. David Lynn helped me prepare several selections for publication in the *Kenyon Review*. I'm also grateful to Harry Brod, Wendy MacLeod, and Gregory Spaid. Several students helped with research over the years, among them Heather Clausen, Justin Richland, and Michael O'Leary. Jerry Kelly gave time and attention to the bibliography and the notes.

Before I moved to Kenyon, the Harvard English Department supported my translation of the *Homeric Hymn to Hermes*. The classicist Danielle Arnold took me slowly through the Greek text and introduced me to the secondary literature. Other colleagues at Harvard always stood ready to help, especially Michael Martone, Michael Blumenthal, Lucie Brock-Broido, Susan Dodd, Monroe Engel, and Sacvan Bercovitch.

A writing fellowship from the National Endowment for the Arts first gave me the time to stop teaching, gather my notes, and write a book proposal. After that, I was given some wonderfully hospitable places to work. The Centrum Foundation in Port Townsend, Washington, put me in House 255 for six weeks one summer. Another summer, the Headlands Center for the Arts in Marin County, California, loaned me a yellow room with a fourteen-foot ceiling in an old barracks. Several times the Mac-Dowell Colony fed and housed me. I wrote the initial draft of the first section of the book at the Rockefeller Foundation's Bellagio Study Center. I wrote the fourth section during a year at the Getty Research Institute in Santa Monica, California. (At the Getty I was lucky enough to have the research assistance of Melissa Schons.) Finally, I am grateful for a fellowship from the MacArthur Foundation.

A book like this is best written in conversation, and many friends deserve to be mentioned in that line. Norman Fischer and I took several long walks in the Marin headlands, during which my project's obscurities always seemed to lift as the coastal fog burned away. Taylor Stoehr took the book seriously over many a bluefish lunch. Max Gimblett responded as I read aloud in the painting studio. Steve Krugman listened skillfully and pointed out patterns I couldn't see. After looking over the entire book, Mona Simpson suggested several deft adjustments.

Thanks also to Linda Bamber, Robert Bly, Graeme Gibson, Tom Hart, Jack Hawley, Michael Ortiz Hill, Jane Hirshfield, Wes Jackson, Barry Lopez, Winnie Lubell, Tom Reese, Wendy Salinger, Marc Shell, Gary Snyder, Lee Swenson, and Gioia Timpanelli. In the final months, Kim Cooper went through the entire manuscript with astounding care. At Farrar, Straus and Giroux, I could always rely on Jonathan Galassi's patience and enthusiasm; Ethan Nosowsky guided the manuscript into print.

I owe my deepest gratitude to Patsy Vigderman.

ART CREDITS

iii   British Museum (E58). Detail of illustration after C. Lenormant. *Élite des Monuments Céramographiques* (Paris: Leleux, Libraire-Éditeur, 1858), plate 89.

15   Wheelright Museum of the American Indian, Santa Fe, New Mexico (P1A #10). *See also* David V. Villaseñor, *Tapestries in Sand*, rev. ed. (Happy Camp, California: Naturegraph Publishers, 1966), pp. 98–99.

81   Detail of photograph by Linda Connor. Used by permission of Linda Connor.

93   Reproduced from William Bascom, *Ifa Divination* (Bloomington: Indiana University Press, 1991), plate 12. Collection of William Bascom.

151   University of Pennsylvania Museum (neg. #S4-138106). Museum Expedition collection, Object NA 8502. See also Henry B. Collins et al., *The Far North: 2000 Years of American Eskimo and Indian Art* (Bloomington: Indiana University Press, 1977), plate 259.

201   Vatican Museums. Illustration after C. Lenormant, *Élite des Monuments Céramographiques* (Paris: Leleux, Libraire-Éditeur, 1858), plate 86.

262   Courtesy of the Moesgård Museum, Moesgård, Denmark

281   Reprinted from *Krishna The Divine Lover* by B. N. Goswamy, A. L. Dallapiccolla et al., by permission of David R. Godine, Publisher, Inc. Copyright © 1982 by Edita S. A., rue du Valentin 10, 1000 Lausanne 9, Switzerland.

315   Dallas Museum of Art, gift of the Junior League of Dallas.

333   © Bildarchiv Preussischer Kulurbesitz, Berlin. Reproduced from Francis Huxley, *The Way of the Sacred* (London: Aldus Books, 1974), p. 156.

345   Reproduced from *Ehon Saiyuki* [*Journey to the West*], translated by Nishida Korenori et al. (Osaka, 1806–33), Vol. XXI, plate 3. Courtesy of Harvard–Yenching Library.

INDEX